Competition Law in Small Economies

Unity of principles, diversity of approaches from competition authorities

Ernesto Kross, Yannick Lecornu,
Johanne Peyre, Vivien Terrien

Concurrences
2026
Paris – New York – Londres

106 West 32nd Street, Suite 144 New York, NY, 10001, USA
www.concurrences.com
book@concurrences.com

First Printing, May 2026
979-10-94201-44-2 (Paperback)
Library of Congress Control Number: 2026907333

Cover Design: Yves Buliard, www.yvesbuliard.fr
Book Design and Layout implementation: Nord Compo

CONCURRENCES BOOKS

The e-book version of these works is available on the website concurrences.com.

Tributes

Huang Yong – Leading and Riding the Tide of China's Competition Law, *Yong Bai (ed.), 2025*

Harry First – A Global Vision for Competition Law, *S. Waller, A. Gavil, D. Bush (eds.), 2025*

James F. Rill – A Life in Antitrust, *2024*

Eleanor M. Fox – Antitrust Ambassador to the World, *2021*

Herbert Hovenkamp – The Dean of American Antitrust Law, *2021*

Frédéric Jenny – Standing Up for Convergence and Relevance in Antitrust, (Vol. I & II), *2019 & 2021*

Albert Foer – A Consumer Voice in the Antitrust Arena, *2020*

Richard Whish – Taking Competition Law Outside the Box, *2020*

Douglas H. Ginsburg – An Antitrust Professor on the Bench (Vol. I & II), *2018 & 2020*

Wang Xiaoye – The Pioneer of Competition Law in China, *A. Emch, W. Ng (eds.), 2019*

Ian S. Forrester – A Scot without Borders (Vol. I & II), *A. Komninos (eds.), 2015*

William E. Kovacic – An Antitrust Tribute (Vol. I & II), *2013 & 2014*

Practical Books

Guide du droit polynésien de la concurrence, *W. Chaiehloudj, Y. Lecornu, J. Peyre, V. Terrien, (eds.), 2026*

Competition Law and the Challenges of Insular Economies – A Focus on French Polynesia and the Pacific Region, *J. Peyre, E. Silvestro, V. Terrien, T. Emen, Y. Lecornu (eds.), 2025*

Competition Inspections under EU Law, 2nd Edition, *N. Jalabert-Doury, 2025*

Navigating the DMA: Application Across National Jurisdictions, *G. Muscolo & A. Massolo (eds.), 2025*

Artificial Intelligence and Competition Policy, *A. Abbott, T. Schrepel (eds.), 2024*

State Aid & National Enforcement, *J. Derenne, D. Jouve, C. Lemaire, F. Martucci (eds.), 2024*

The 2023 U.S. Merger Guidelines: *A Review, Sean Sullivan (ed.), 2024*

Competition Inspections in 25 Jurisdictions 2nd Edition – A Practitioner's Guide, *N. Jalabert-Doury (ed.), 2024*

EU Antitrust Enforcement – Law, Economics, History, *Policy & Practice, Wouter P. J. Wils, 2024*

The EU Foreign Subsidies Regulation, *Andreas Reindl, Isabelle Van Damme, 2024*

Compendium of Antitrust Damages Actions – ICC – 2nd edition, *J.W.H. Denton AO, F. Brunet, S. Williams, C. Inthavisay (eds.), 2023*

Pharmaceutical Antitrust: An Analysis of US and EU Law, *M. Thill-Tayara, G. Gordon (eds.), 2023*

Innovation Paradox in Merger Control, *G. Gürkaynak, 2023*

Antitrust and the Digital Economy, *Y. Katsoulacos (ed.), 2023 (in collaboration with CRESSE)*

Judicial Review of Competition Cases, *D. Ginsburg, T. Eicke (eds.), 2023*

Competition Law Treatment of Joint Ventures, *B. Bleicher, N. Campbell, A. Hamilton, N. Hukkinen, A. Khan, A. Mordaunt (eds.), 2022 (in collaboration with the IBA)*

Information Exchange & Related Risks, *Z. Marosi, M. Soares (eds.), 2022 (in collaboration with the IBA)*

Rulemaking Authority of the US Federal Trade Commission, *D. Crane (ed.), 2022*

The International Competition Network at Twenty, *D. Anderson & P. Lugard (eds.), 2022*

Competition Case Law Digest – 5th Edition, *F. Jenny, N. Charbit (eds.), 2022*

Competition Inspections in 21 Jurisdictions – A Practitioner's Guide, *N. Jalabert-Doury (ed.), 2022*

Perspectives on Antitrust Compliance, *A. Riley, A. Stephan, A. Tubbs (eds.), 2022 (in collaboration with the ICC)*

Turkish Competition Law, *G. Gürkaynak, 2021*

Competition Law – Climate Change & Environmental Sustainability, *S. Holmes, D. Middelschulte, M. Snoep (eds.), 2021*

Merger Control in Latin America – A Jurisdictional Guide, *P. Burnier da Silveira, P. Sittenfeld (eds.), 2020*

Competition Inspections under EU Law – A Practitioner's Guide, *N. Jalabert-Doury, 2020*

Gun Jumping in Merger Control – A Jurisdictional Guide, *C. Hatton, Y. Comtois, A. Hamilton (eds.), 2019 (in collaboration with the IBA)*

Choice – A New Standard for Competition Analysis? *P. Nihoul (ed.), 2016*

PhD Theses

Intent in Competition Law, *M.S. Garnier, 2025*

Three Essays in Law and Economics: Digital Markets and Abuse of Dominance, *J. Mouton, 2025*

The Economics of Digital Markets – Essays in Theoretical and Empirical Industrial Organization, *E. Arnaud-Joufray, 2024*

Abuse of Platform Power, *F. Bostoen, 2023*

Reform of Chinese State-Owned Enterprises, *X. Bai, 2023*

Competition & Regulation in Network Industries – Essays in Industrial Organization, *J-M. Zogheib, 2021*

The Role of Media Pluralism in the Enforcement of EU Competition Law, *K. Bania, 2019*

Buyer Power, *I. Herrera Anchustegui, 2017*

General Interest

Why Competition? Voices from the Antitrust Community and Beyond, *D. Crane, D. Gerard, R. Tritell (eds.), 2024*

Competition Law Dictionary, *D. Healey, R. Whish, W. E. Kovacic, P. Trevisán (eds.), 2024*

The 5 Labours of Europe, *P.-E. Partsch, 2024*

Great Antitrust Enforcers, *W. E. Kovacic, 2023*

Competition – How to Speak Like an Expert, *E. Combe, 2023*

Women and Antitrust – Voices from the Field (Vol I & II), *E. Kurgonaite & K. Nordlander, 2020*

Competition Law in Small and Insular Economies

Unity of principles, diversity of approaches from competition authorities

Forewords by Gina Cass-Gottlieb, Caroline Inthavisay
Prologue by Jérôme Philippe

Edited by
Ernesto Kross
Yannick Lecornu
Johanne Peyre
Vivien Terrien

CONTRIBUTORS

Stewart Brittenden

Jean Dictus

Olga Droussioti Papachrysanthou

Christian Pierre Everts

Peter Hetherington

Charitee Henriquez

Steven Iraitogo Sugl

Nicolai Ödgaard Jensen

Kostas Karathymios

Alvin Koh

Ernesto Kross

Odeya de La Mure

Yannick Lecornu

Sarah Livestro

Krystle S. Maharaj

David Miller

Suyen Muñoz Rivera

Vipin Naugah

Bevan Narinesingh

Gwenaëlle Nouët

Páll Gunnar Pálsson

Johanne Peyre

Sarah Price

Chloé Racine

Sonia Ragoopath

Stéphane Retterer

Jérôme Schall

Vivien Terrien

María Elena Vásquez Taveras

Anne-Laure Vendrolini

SUMMARY OF CONTENTS

INSTITUTE FOR SMALL MARKETS IN LAW AND ECONOMICS

Advancing Competition Law in Island Economies and Small Markets

ISLE is a non-profit organization driven by a team of volunteers eager to contribute to a better understanding of competition mechanisms and regulation in small market economies and island territories.

Indeed, the application of the general principles of competition law must take into account the structural characteristics and specific economic functioning of each territory, particularly when they are small and/or isolated. This observation calls for the mobilization of diverse analytical capacities in order to formulate tailored rules capable of meeting the objectives of harmonious development for each territory.

Through research work, sectoral studies, impact analyses on competition policies, the development of training, awareness tools, and communication programs, ISLE members aim to contribute to a better understanding by stakeholders of the externalities of competition rules, while addressing the challenges of the cost of living and the sustainability of economic practices.

With a view to dynamically leading these initiatives, the ISLE project is based on a bicameral governance structure, namely an administration through a steering committee chaired by Johanne PEYRE and thought leadership under the presidency of Professor William E. KOVACIC.

For more information, visit our website: www.isle-research.org

FOREWORD

I am grateful for the opportunity to write this foreword for Competition Law in Small Economies. It is a timely resource to both understand the unique competition issues that arise in smaller economies and to assist small and developing agencies as they seek to harness the benefits of competition for their country.

The Australian Competition and Consumer Commission has been privileged to partner with competition agencies around the world, including new and developing agencies. We have greatly valued the opportunity to learn from each other. We know that what works in one jurisdiction may not be the right approach in another and sharing our experiences equips us to develop the right tools for the right situation.

Although there are well recognised international best practice standards for competition law, the design of competition policy and the specific application of the law needs to consider local issues. Working in partnership with smaller agencies in the Pacific region has reinforced for me the importance of determining how international best practice can be translated to fit each jurisdiction's own circumstances. This is where this book plays an important role. In explaining the laws, policies and institutions of countries in the Pacific, Europe and the Americas, it raises awareness of competition law and policy issues relevant to small economies.

Each country chapter highlights the geographic, demographic and economic factors of the country as well as country-specific challenges. While the challenges might be unique, the benefits of well-designed competition law and policies are similar. We each can learn from these country examples about how to apply a strong competition framework that supports local markets. Ensuring competition policy is reflected in all aspects of the market will lead to long term benefits, including better productivity, more consumer choice and greater innovation.

The book demonstrates that the design of, and resources given to, the institutional structures responsible for enforcement of competition law and policy are critical factors in understanding the relative capacity of each country. The study of different approaches to enforcement, including explanations of relevant cases, gives the reader an understanding of how different countries promote and protect competition. This will help citizens, governments and international counterpart agencies understand how competition law benefits local markets.

Competition law is, without doubt, vital to our economies. It drives productivity by incentivising investment, innovation and efficiency. Consumers benefit from a wider choice of high-quality goods and services at better prices. And competition law, and its rigorous enforcement, are important contributors to productivity growth. The role of competition authorities is no longer limited to traditional markets. Current challenges associated with digital transformation, the environment, the non-market sector, the cost of living crisis and declining productivity (among others) present us all with novel and difficult problems to solve.

Around the world, many governments have recognised that competition agencies have an important role to play in encouraging productivity and reducing regulatory burden. It is a time of rapid change and uncertainty in many markets. The demands on competition agencies to respond to disruption and complexity are high, particularly for small economies with constrained human and financial resources.

It is essential that we share our knowledge and experiences as competition agencies and advocate together for robust competition law and policy settings. Together, we can tell the story of why strong competition matters to market participants and to communities. Our actions lead to real and tangible benefits to consumers and more effective markets.

This book starts that conversation and will give readers much needed context about why competition matters for small and large economies. It will give its readers much to consider as these global challenges are debated.

Gina Cass-Gottlieb
Chair
Australian Competition and Consumer Commission
March 2026

PROLOGUE

Small but significant

Over the past several decades, competition law has become one of the most widely diffused fields of economic regulation in the world. More than 140 jurisdictions now operate competition regimes, reflecting a broad international consensus on the importance of open and competitive markets for economic development, innovation and consumer welfare.

Much of the intellectual architecture of modern competition law, however, has historically been shaped by the experience of large jurisdictions. The United States, the European Union and other major economies have provided the analytical frameworks, case law and enforcement models that have influenced competition policy across the globe.

Yet a significant number of jurisdictions operate under very different structural conditions. Small and insular economies face distinctive challenges: limited domestic market size, geographic isolation, high transport costs, concentrated market structures and a close interaction between economic policy and market dynamics. In such contexts, the application of competition law raises questions that differ in important respects from those encountered in larger markets.

How should competition rules operate where only a limited number of operators can realistically coexist?

How should authorities address structural concentration that results not from anticompetitive conduct but from the intrinsic characteristics of the market itself?

And how can competition policy promote contestability while remaining compatible with the economic realities of small and geographically fragmented economies?

These questions lie at the heart of the work carried out by many competition authorities across the world, yet they remain relatively underexplored in the global competition law literature.

It is precisely this gap that the Institute for Small Markets in Law and Economics (ISLE) seeks to address. Through its research and international initiatives, ISLE has contributed to the emergence of an analytical framework sometimes described as competition law for structurally constrained markets. This approach does not challenge the fundamental principles of competition policy. Rather, it seeks to understand how those principles can be applied effectively in economic environments where market size, geographic dispersion and logistical constraints significantly influence market structures.

In many respects, small economies function as laboratories for competition policy. Because structural constraints are more visible and market dynamics often more transparent, the effects of regulatory choices may appear more clearly and more quickly than in larger and more diversified economies. In this sense, the experience of small jurisdictions does not merely adapt competition law to specific constraints, it often helps reveal its underlying logic.

Competition law may have been designed in the context of large economies, but it is frequently tested most clearly in smaller ones.

The experience of small insular jurisdictions therefore offers highly valuable insights for the broader development of competition policy. By examining how authorities address concentrated markets, trade-off between scale efficiency and concentration, dependence on imports, policymakers and practitioners can gain a deeper understanding of the flexibility – and the limits – of existing competition frameworks.

This volume makes an important contribution to that discussion. By bringing together perspectives from competition authorities across the Caribbean, Europe, the Pacific, the Indian Ocean and Southeast Asia, it offers a rare comparative overview of how competition law is applied in small and structurally constrained economies.

For practitioners of competition law, these experiences are particularly instructive. They demonstrate how core principles – contestability, consumer welfare and the prevention of anticompetitive conduct – can be applied in economic environments that differ significantly from those of the largest jurisdictions. They also illustrate the importance of pragmatic and context-sensitive approaches to enforcement.

The development of effective competition regimes in smaller jurisdictions also depends on access to expertise and participation in international networks of knowledge and dialogue. Exchanges between authorities, academics, policymakers and practitioners therefore play a critical role in strengthening competition policy worldwide.

Law firms engaged in competition practice have a responsibility to contribute to this broader ecosystem. Beyond their advisory work in major markets, many firms are increasingly involved in initiatives aimed at strengthening regulatory capacity, supporting institutional dialogue and facilitating the exchange of legal expertise across jurisdictions.

At Freshfields, we have long been committed to supporting the development of sound competition policy and effective regulatory frameworks around the world. Alongside our client work, this commitment is reflected in academic collaborations, policy dialogue and pro bono initiatives relating to regulatory governance and the rule of law. On several occasions, these initiatives have involved working with institutions and stakeholders in smaller jurisdictions whose regulatory challenges are often underrepresented in global legal discussions.

In this context, we are particularly pleased to support the work carried out by ISLE. The Institute's efforts to develop analytical tools adapted to structurally constrained markets contribute meaningfully to the global debate on competition law and economic regulation.

Our support for this publication reflects that broader commitment. It also reflects the close engagement of members of our firm with the Institute's work. In particular, we have been actively involved in promoting dialogue between practitioners, scholars, competition authorities, policymakers and companies on the challenges faced by smaller, but so significant, jurisdictions.

We are therefore delighted to support both the publication of this volume and the wider initiatives developed by ISLE.

By bringing together the voices of numerous competition authorities operating in small and insular economies, this book contributes to a richer and more balanced understanding of how competition policy operates across the global economy.

Finally, this book will be an essential reference for practitioners and companies involved in M&A and commercial activity in smaller economies, where competition rules may be less familiar but can have a very significant impact on deal execution and operational success.

Jérôme Philippe
Vice-President of ISLE

INTRODUCTORY REMARKS

No Market is Truly Small: Competition Authorities and the Foundations of Global Trade

Small economies are often perceived as peripheral to global economic dynamics. In reality, they are at the heart of international trade.

For many businesses – particularly small and medium-sized enterprises – small and island markets are not marginal destinations but essential commercial partners. They are gateways between regions, testing grounds for innovation, and critical nodes in supply chains that connect larger economies. Yet these markets face structural constraints: geographic remoteness, limited domestic production capacity, dependence on imports, and concentrated distribution networks. These features can lead to high prices, fragile competition and vulnerability to disruptions.

In such contexts, competition authorities play a particularly demanding role. They must protect consumers and ensure fair market conditions while operating with limited resources, small administrations and legal frameworks often designed for larger jurisdictions. Their task is not simply to replicate models developed elsewhere but to interpret and apply competition principles in environments where markets are thin, entry barriers are structural and economic actors are few.

This publication is therefore timely and important. By bringing together contributions from competition authorities operating in small and insular economies, it provides rare and invaluable insight into how competition policy works in practice under structural constraints. More importantly, it shows that the implementation of competition law is not a uniform exercise but an adaptive process, requiring judgment, pragmatism and close engagement with economic realities.

For global business, these issues are critical. Predictable, transparent and well-functioning markets are essential to investment, trade and innovation. When competition frameworks are credible and adapted to local conditions, they strengthen investor confidence, facilitate market entry, and ultimately benefit consumers and entrepreneurs alike. Conversely, when markets are distorted by excessive concentration or regulatory capture, economic development and integration into global trade are hindered.

Small competition authorities therefore perform a function that extends beyond their jurisdictions. By promoting fair competition, they contribute to economic stability, trust in markets and sustainable development. They also provide valuable experience to the international community by demonstrating how fundamental economic principles can be applied in a flexible manner while preserving their core objectives.

The International Chamber of Commerce (ICC) has long promoted open markets, responsible business conduct and international cooperation across the globe. Dialogue between public authorities and the private sector is essential to achieving these goals. The ICC believes that initiatives such as the Small Economies Forum and the present publication can help foster a greater understanding between regulators and businesses and ensure that competition policy remains both effective and realistic.

This publication reminds us of an important lesson: competition policy is not only about large economies and major global mergers; it is also about ensuring that markets function fairly for communities, entrepreneurs and consumers everywhere in the world. In a globalized economy, no market is truly small, and the experience of small competition authorities enriches the collective understanding of how markets can remain open, fair and resilient.

Caroline Inthavisay
ICC Global Policy Lead for Competition

INTRODUCTION

Market Power Without Rivalry: Rethinking Competition Law in Small and Insular Economies

Yannick Lecornu, Johanne Peyre, Ernesto Kross, Vivien Terrien

Competition law is commonly presented as a legal framework intended to preserve competitive markets. Yet modern competition law was not designed for small economies.

Its intellectual foundations lie in the United States and Western Europe, where large domestic markets, diversified production structures and numerous undertakings create conditions in which rivalry between firms is expected to arise spontaneously. Antitrust rules were therefore constructed around a central presumption: markets are naturally competitive unless firms distort them.

The contributions gathered in this book collectively challenge that implicit assumption.

Across jurisdictions as diverse as Jamaica, Mauritius, Papua New Guinea, Curaçao, Trinidad and Tobago, the Dominican Republic, Honduras, Gibraltar, Jersey, New Caledonia, and the French overseas territories – Guadeloupe, Martinique, French Guiana, Réunion, Mayotte, Saint-Martin, Saint-Barthélemy, Saint-Pierre and Miquelon, and Wallis and Futuna – competition authorities operate in environments where rivalry does not emerge naturally. Instead, markets tend toward concentration even in the absence of unlawful conduct.

In these jurisdictions, the central policy question is not how to restore competition where it has been artificially restricted, but how to ensure fairness where structural competition may never fully exist.

This book proceeds from empirical observation but leads to theoretical implications.

The jurisdictions examined in this volume vary enormously in population size. Papua New Guinea has a population of several million inhabitants, while Saint-Barthélemy and Saint-Pierre and Miquelon have only a few thousand. Yet their competition authorities encounter remarkably similar issues.

This suggests that "small economy" cannot be defined demographically.

The relevant variable is not population, but effective market scale – the size of the economically contestable market relative to the minimum efficient scale of supply.

In island territories such as Wallis and Futuna or Saint-Martin, geographic isolation reduces the number of viable operators. In geographically larger jurisdictions such as French Guiana or Honduras, internal fragmentation and logistics constraints produce similar effects. Jersey and

Gibraltar illustrate another variant: proximity to major economic centers does not eliminate smallness when the domestic market remains narrow.

Smallness therefore arises from a combination of factors, including:

- limited domestic demand,
- transport costs,
- dependence on imports,
- and infrastructure indivisibility.

Across the Caribbean (the Dominican Republic, Jamaica, Trinidad and Tobago, and Curaçao), competition often occurs at the border rather than within the territory. Access to import channels can matter more than the number of domestic competitors. Similarly, in New Caledonia and the French overseas departments, supply chains themselves shape competition conditions.

Smallness is thus an economic structure, not a demographic condition.

This distinction explains why jurisdictions with very different populations may nonetheless face identical competition challenges. What matters is not the number of consumers but the relationship between demand and the minimum efficient scale of supply. When a single production unit, logistics chain or distribution network is sufficient to serve the entire market, entry becomes economically irrational rather than legally restricted.

Small economies therefore tend to operate as "single-facility markets." In such markets, competition takes place for access to the facility rather than through its duplication. The marginal cost of serving additional consumers is low once the infrastructure exists, but the fixed cost of duplicating it is prohibitive. Under such conditions, potential competitors do not stay away because of anticompetitive conduct; they do so because entry is not profitable. The competitive process is constrained before any firm acts.

This observation has an important implication: competition law in small economies cannot rely solely on entry as the corrective mechanism for market power. The possibility of entry, often central to antitrust analysis, may be more theoretical than credible.

In large markets, authorities often assume that if prices rise or conditions deteriorate, new competitors will enter and discipline the incumbent. In small economies, however, such entry may be economically unrealistic because the market cannot sustain additional operators. Authorities must therefore assess prices, access conditions and conduct directly, rather than assuming that potential entry will correct market outcomes.

A second recurring observation emerges from almost every contribution: concentration is persistent.

Telecommunications in New Caledonia, distribution systems in Guadeloupe and Martinique, fuel supply in island territories, and retail import markets in several Caribbean jurisdictions all display a common feature – a limited number of firms serving the entire population.

Traditional antitrust reasoning treats high concentration as a warning signal. In these economies, it appears as the normal market outcome.

The reason is straightforward. Where the market cannot sustain multiple infrastructures, duplication is inefficient. Ports, energy networks, shipping logistics, and wholesale importation frequently operate as natural monopolies or tight oligopolies. In such contexts, the number of firms reflects cost structure rather than market power strategy.

The experiences of Mauritius and Papua New Guinea particularly illustrate this phenomenon: geographic distance and logistics costs make entry difficult even when legal barriers are absent. Similarly, the cases reported in the Dominican Republic and Jamaica show that dominance often arises from control of distribution networks rather than from exclusionary conduct.

This does not mean that competition concerns are reduced or that rivalry cannot exist. The fact that a market can sustain only a limited number of actors does not imply the absence of competitive dynamics. Rather, it means that competition may take different forms and must be assessed in light of structural constraints.

In such settings, concentration is self-reinforcing. Once an operator has invested in infrastructure, logistics or brand networks, scale advantages increase over time. The largest firm can purchase at lower unit costs, maintain greater inventory, and absorb market fluctuations more easily than potential entrants. Competitive asymmetry grows not through exclusionary conduct but through cumulative efficiency.

This phenomenon explains why concentration often persists even after liberalization reforms. Removing legal barriers to entry does not necessarily generate new competitors if the underlying market size remains unchanged. The structure of the market is determined less by regulation than by the relationship between fixed costs and aggregate demand.

Competition authorities therefore face a structural dilemma. Intervening against concentration may weaken the only firms capable of ensuring continuous supply, while non-intervention may expose consumers to excessive prices.

Enforcement must consequently prioritize the control of conduct rather than the restructuring of market structures, although in certain configurations – particularly where vertical concentration entrenches foreclosure risks – structural remedies or injunctions may constitute the only effective means of restoring contestability.

This observation requires a clearer economic statement. In small economies, the limited number of firms is not primarily a policy choice but a structural constraint. Market size often allows only a few operators to reach the minimum efficient scale necessary to remain viable. Firms must therefore be sufficiently large to benefit from economies of scale and to ensure continuity of supply. However, the structural limitation in the number of undertakings does not eliminate the need for competition. On the contrary, precisely because only a few firms can operate sustainably, it becomes essential to ensure that competitive pressure remains sufficient to prevent monopolistic outcomes. The objective is not to increase the number of firms beyond what the market can sustain, but to preserve a level of rivalry and openness that constrains the exercise of market power within structurally concentrated markets.

Across the contributions, enforcement activity consistently targets behavior, e.g., exclusivity clauses, discriminatory access, collusion in procurement, and restrictive distribution practices.

The authorities in Martinique, Réunion and Mayotte, for instance, repeatedly confront exclusive import arrangements. Curaçao and Trinidad and Tobago report similar concerns relating to market access.

The practical objective of competition law in small economies is not to increase the number of competitors beyond what the market can viably sustain. In many cases, additional entry is economically unrealistic because the market size does not allow another operator to reach the minimum efficient scale. The central task is therefore to protect the contestability of the market and to preserve sufficient competitive pressure – so that existing firms retain incentives to lower prices, improve quality, expand choice and innovate – even within a structurally limited number of operators.

Competition policy thus becomes closer to a governance mechanism than a structural corrective tool.

Where behavior-based enforcement functions as a substitute for structural competition, competition policy takes on features of regulated competition. Rather than depending on the presence of multiple rivals, the authority seeks to replicate the disciplining effects of rivalry through obligations such as non-discrimination, fair access conditions, transparency, and the prohibition of exclusionary agreements. The authority does not supplant the market; it acts to maintain competitive pressure despite structural constraints. Sanctions deter abuses, while guidance and advocacy shape commercial practices. The aim is to approximate competitive outcomes in contexts where fully competitive market structures cannot realistically develop.

This transformation does not represent a departure from competition law principles. It reflects the core function of antitrust everywhere: preventing the harmful exercise of market power. The difference is not conceptual but contextual. In all economies, competition law addresses dominance and concentration where they arise. In small economies, however, structurally concentrated markets are more frequent and often unavoidable. As a result, situations involving significant market power are not exceptional but recurrent, and the authority's task is to ensure that such power – where it exists – is exercised under conditions consistent with contestability, fairness, and consumer welfare.

Another striking convergence appears: competition authorities perform functions extending far beyond litigation.

In many jurisdictions, advocacy occupies a central place. The authority advises governments, reviews legislation and participates in regulatory design. Mauritius explicitly integrates policy advice into the authority's mission. Jersey and Gibraltar emphasize cooperation with sector regulators. The French overseas authorities report frequent interactions with price regulation mechanisms.

This expansion of functions is not institutional drift. It is an adaptation to economic reality.

In markets where rivalry cannot alone discipline firms, the authority becomes a guardian of market functioning. Market studies, recommendations and public guidance may influence outcomes more effectively than sanctions.

The authority therefore evolves from an *ex post* enforcer into a permanent institution of market oversight.

This expanded role also affects institutional expectations. In large jurisdictions, competition authorities are primarily adjudicative bodies reacting to complaints or notifications. In small economies, they function as permanent market observers. Because the number of major economic actors is limited, authorities develop detailed knowledge of market functioning across sectors.

Their influence often derives less from coercive powers than from informational authority. Market studies, recommendations and public opinions may alter commercial behavior even in the absence of formal decisions. Businesses, regulators and governments rely on the authority's analysis as an economic reference point.

The authority thus acquires a hybrid character: partly enforcer, partly regulator, and partly economic advisor. This institutional flexibility reflects the absence of alternative specialized bodies capable of performing cross-sectoral market analysis in small economies.

The competition authority in a small economy thus fulfills a function closer to that of a market referee than that of a market architect. It does not attempt to design the market structure but to ensure that existing structures operate fairly. Its legitimacy derives less from its ability to create competition than from its capacity to prevent the harmful exercise of market power.

Small economies also present a distinctive political economy.

Economic actors are often major employers. Public authorities, regulators and firms operate in close social proximity. Decisions affecting a single undertaking may affect an entire territory's employment or supply.

Contributions from small island territories such as Saint-Barthélemy, Saint-Pierre and Miquelon and Wallis and Futuna implicitly illustrate this sensitivity. In such contexts, independence is not merely a legal status but a daily operational practice.

Transparency, procedure and justification become as important as sanctioning power. Judicial review and public communication are essential components of enforcement credibility.

Proximity also affects enforcement strategy. In closely interconnected communities, purely punitive approaches may produce economic and social effects disproportionate to the infringement. Authorities must therefore balance deterrence with market stability. Remedies, commitments and negotiated solutions may sometimes achieve better outcomes than extensive litigation.

The credibility of enforcement depends not only on sanctions but also on perceived fairness. Transparent reasoning, procedural guarantees and clear communication help maintain legitimacy in environments where economic actors and consumers directly observe the authority's actions. Independence becomes a matter of trust as much as institutional design.

The structural features described above reach their most visible form in remote oceanic economies, where geography itself becomes an economic variable and extreme logistical distance shapes competitive dynamics. Geography therefore becomes a structural determinant of market power.

In many small economies, import dependence already plays a significant role in shaping competitive dynamics. However, in certain oceanic territories, the issue is not only dependence on imports but the structure of the supply chain itself. The market is not simply open to international trade; it is organized around infrequent, costly and capacity-constrained transport links.

Where maritime shipping routes are long, irregular and concentrated in a limited number of carriers, logistics becomes a central determinant of competition. The cost of transport, storage capacity and shipping frequency influence retail prices as much as – and sometimes more than – the behavior of domestic firms. Entry barriers may therefore arise not from legal restrictions or strategic conduct but from the physical organization of supply.

In such environments, the wholesale importer often performs a structural function. Importers aggregate demand, finance inventories and secure shipping capacity. Their role cannot easily be replicated because entry requires not only capital but also access to logistics networks and shipping schedules. The competitive position of firms is therefore closely linked to their place within the supply chain.

This configuration produces a distinctive form of market power. Dominance may arise from logistical intermediation rather than production or retail market share. A firm controlling import channels, storage infrastructure or port access can influence downstream competition without engaging in traditional exclusionary practices.

Competition authorities in these contexts must therefore analyze markets along the supply chain. Vertical relationships, exclusive distribution and long-term supply agreements cannot be assessed solely through the lens of contractual restrictions; they may reflect risk allocation in uncertain logistical environments. Short shipping windows, stockout risks and high fixed storage costs can justify arrangements that, in larger economies, might appear restrictive.

The implication is significant. Competition law must distinguish between arrangements that secure supply continuity and those that foreclose entry. Excessively rigid application of standard antitrust tests risks discouraging investment in distribution infrastructure or reducing supply reliability, which may directly affect consumer welfare in remote territories.

Thus, in oceanic economies, the primary competitive variable may not be rivalry among retailers but supply resilience. Market functioning depends on the logistics chain's capacity to deliver goods regularly and predictably. Competition policy must therefore incorporate logistical analysis into its assessment of market power and competitive harm.

This "distance constraint" does not invalidate competition law principles. It requires their contextual application. Ensuring fair access to supply channels, non-discriminatory port and storage conditions, and transparency in import arrangements may be more effective than attempting to increase the number of firms operating downstream.

The experience of remote Pacific jurisdictions shows that, in certain environments, competition policy is inseparable from transport economics. The organization of shipping routes, port infrastructure and storage facilities becomes part of the competitive framework itself.

None of the contributions suggests departing from competition law principles. Cartels remain unlawful. Abuses remain prohibited. Consumers remain protected.

What differs is implementation. Authorities prioritize essential goods, procurement, and access conditions. They rely heavily on advocacy and cooperation. They accept that certain dominant positions are unavoidable but seek to prevent their misuse.

The unity of principles is preserved. The diversity lies in enforcement strategies.

Contextualization should not be confused with relativism. The core prohibitions of competition law remain unchanged. What differs is the assessment of competitive harm and the choice of enforcement instruments. The same legal rule may lead to different remedies depending on market structure.

In large economies, competition policy primarily promotes rivalry. In small economies, it preserves contestability – the possibility for firms to access markets and for consumers to benefit from fair conditions. Contestability becomes the operational equivalent of competition where structural rivalry is limited.

The experience of small economies therefore does not create an exception to competition law. It functions as a conceptual clarification. By observing markets in which rivalry cannot fully operate, the discipline is forced to identify what it ultimately seeks to protect. What emerges is not a different competition law, but a clearer understanding of the same one.

Taken individually, each chapter describes a jurisdiction. Taken together, they reveal a category. Across oceans, legal traditions and income levels, the same structural patterns appear:

- concentrated markets,
- dependence on imports,
- logistical constraints,
- expanded authority roles,
- and behavior-focused enforcement.

Small economies are therefore not isolated cases. They represent a recurring economic configuration within global competition policy.

Recognizing this category does not weaken competition law; it clarifies its application. The aim remains competitive fairness, but the path toward that aim varies with market structure.

Competition law was historically built on the expectation of rivalry. Small economies reveal what happens when that expectation cannot reliably be fulfilled. The experience of small and insular economies shows that its deeper purpose is different: not to guarantee the presence of many competitors, but to ensure that market power – inevitable in certain economic environments – is exercised under conditions consistent with fairness, access and consumer welfare.

Aruba

Ernesto Kross
Aruba Fair Trade Authority's Director

I. Overview

1. Aruba is a small island located in the southern Caribbean Sea, approximately 29 kilometers (18 miles) north of the Venezuelan coast. It lies in close proximity to the islands of Curaçao, situated about 120 kilometers (75 miles) to the southeast, and Bonaire, located approximately 195 kilometers (123 miles) to the east. The island is positioned outside the Atlantic hurricane belt, a geographical characteristic that has historically contributed to its stability as a tourism destination and commercial hub.

2. Aruba has a total surface area of approximately 180 square kilometers (69 square miles). The island is shaped like a narrow, slightly curved strip, extending roughly 32 kilometers (20 miles) from east to west. Its width from north to south reaches approximately 10 kilometers (6 miles) at its widest point. These geographic features contribute to the characteristics typically associated with small island economies, including spatial constraints and limited domestic market size.

3. Aruba is a constituent country within the Kingdom of the Netherlands and has enjoyed internal autonomy since 1986 under the constitutional arrangement known as the Status Aparte. Within this framework, Aruba maintains its own government, Prime Minister, parliament, central bank, and national currency. The country exercises responsibility for internal affairs, including education, healthcare, economic policy, and regulatory governance, while matters such as defense and foreign affairs remain within the competence of the Kingdom.

4. Dutch and Papiamento have been recognized as the official languages of Aruba since 2003. English and Spanish are also widely spoken and used in both commercial and administrative contexts. Papiamento is the native language for the majority of the population and constitutes a Creole language that developed in the Caribbean region, particularly on the islands of Aruba, Curaçao, and Bonaire. The language reflects a complex historical evolution shaped by trade, migration, and colonial influence, incorporating linguistic elements derived primarily from Portuguese and Spanish, as well as Dutch, African languages introduced during the period of enslavement, and certain English and indigenous influences.

II. Demographics and Economy

5. Aruba has a population of approximately 108,000 inhabitants as of 2024. The population density is estimated at around 600 inhabitants per square kilometer, reflecting the island's relatively compact geographic size and high level of urbanization. As in many small island economies, demographic concentration contributes to structural features such as limited labor market depth and a relatively small number of economic actors in key sectors.[1]

6. Aruba's nominal gross domestic product (GDP) is estimated at approximately USD 4.27 billion in 2024, according to data from the World Bank[2]. Projections by the International Monetary Fund (IMF) for 2025 indicate slightly higher figures[3], reflecting continued

---

[1] World Bank, *World Development Indicators*, 2024.

[2] World Bank, *GDP (Nominal) Data*, 2024.

[3] International Monetary Fund (IMF), *World Economic Outlook*, 2025.

economic recovery and growth following global disruptions in recent years. The country maintains a structural trade deficit in goods, primarily due to its strong dependence on imports for consumer products, intermediate goods, and capital equipment. This imbalance is partially offset at the current-account level by substantial revenues generated from tourism and related services.

7. Tourism constitutes the dominant sector of the Aruban economy and serves as the primary driver of employment, foreign exchange earnings, and overall economic activity. Additional important sectors include financial and business services, trade and logistics, and construction. These sectors collectively form the backbone of the domestic economy and play a central role in shaping market dynamics and regulatory priorities.

8. Publicly available information, including the work program of the Aruba Fair Trade Authority (AFTA), indicates relatively high levels of market concentration in several sectors of the economy. Notable examples include the markets for food products, container transport, telecommunications, and banking services. Such concentration is partly attributable to the structural characteristics of small island economies, including limited demand, economies of scale, and barriers to entry.

III. Legal Framework for Competition

9. The principal legal instrument governing competition in Aruba is the Competition Ordinance (*Mededingingsverordening*), which was formally adopted in 2020 (AB 2020 no. 103). Although the legislation established the legal foundation for competition regulation at that time, the substantive competition rules entered into force on 1 January 2024. The adoption of this framework marked a significant development in Aruba's economic governance, introducing a modern system of market oversight aligned with international competition law principles.

10. Following the entry into force of the Competition Ordinance, several implementing measures were adopted to operationalize the legal framework. In particular, a national decree dated 11 March 2024 established turnover thresholds for merger control and defined information requirements for notification procedures. Additional decrees addressed investigative powers and administrative enforcement mechanisms. In June 2025, a further national decree introduced provisions relating to administrative enforcement and consumer protection. Looking ahead, the AFTA is expected to initiate a regulatory project in 2026 aimed at establishing a framework for water and energy regulation.

11. The Competition Ordinance addresses the core categories of anticompetitive conduct, including anticompetitive agreements between undertakings, abuse of a dominant position, and concentrations such as mergers, acquisitions, and joint ventures. The legal framework is complemented by rules on consumer protection, which are likewise enforced by the AFTA. In addition to enforcement responsibilities, the Authority provides both solicited and unsolicited advice to government authorities on matters relating to market functioning, regulatory design, and competition policy.

12. The legal framework provides for exemptions in circumstances where cooperation between undertakings generates efficiencies or consumer benefits that outweigh potential restrictions on competition. These exemptions are subject to strict conditions and

require a case-by-case assessment. Importantly, the legislation does not provide for a general exemption for state-owned enterprises or specific markets, thereby ensuring that competition principles apply broadly throughout the economy.

IV. Institutional Structure

13. The Aruba Fair Trade Authority (AFTA) is the independent administrative authority responsible for enforcing competition law and consumer protection rules in Aruba. The AFTA was formally established when the Competition Ordinance partially entered into force in May 2023. Its operational enforcement role effectively commenced in January 2024, when the full legislative framework became applicable and the Authority recruited its first staff members. As of 15 March 2026, the AFTA's mandate has been expanded to include responsibility for collective consumer protection.

14. The AFTA operates as an autonomous administrative authority possessing legal personality and functioning as an independent supervisory body. In performing its statutory tasks, the Authority acts independently and without political instruction, thereby safeguarding institutional credibility and regulatory neutrality.

15. The Authority is governed by a Board composed of three members: a chairperson, a member, and a special member. The Board is supported by an executive structure, commonly referred to as the bureau, which is responsible for investigations, economic analysis, and day-to-day operations. The bureau is headed by a director and currently employs approximately ten full-time equivalents (FTEs), including seven researchers and two operations staff members.

16. In addition to its competition law responsibilities, the AFTA is entrusted with the enforcement of collective consumer protection rules. Following 2026, the Authority is expected to assume additional regulatory responsibilities in the sectors of water and energy, thereby further expanding its institutional mandate.

17. Since becoming operational in 2024, the AFTA's responsibilities have progressively expanded, resulting in a corresponding increase in its budget. The Authority's budget rose from approximately 1.0 million in 2024 to 1.5 million in 2026, primarily reflecting the expansion of staff from seven to ten full-time equivalents. A further increase of four additional positions is planned for 2027. At present, the AFTA is fully funded by the government and does not receive revenue from alternative sources. Any income generated through administrative sanctions is transferred to the government. The Authority publishes biannual reports on its activities, including information on budget expenditure. Its financial statements comply with international accounting standards and are subject to independent external audit.

18. The AFTA possesses a comprehensive set of investigative and enforcement powers. These include the authority to request information, conduct inspections, and collect data from undertakings. The Authority may impose administrative fines, binding instructions, and periodic penalty payments, and it may issue public warnings where appropriate. Decisions are published to ensure transparency and to promote compliance within the business community.

V. Enforcement and Sanctions

19. The AFTA is empowered to impose administrative sanctions, including monetary fines and periodic penalty payments. The level of sanctions is determined on the basis of factors such as the gravity and duration of the infringement, as well as the conduct and level of cooperation of the undertaking concerned. Under the applicable legislation, the maximum administrative fine amounts to Afl. 1,000,000. Where the turnover of the relevant undertaking in the financial year preceding the decision exceeds Afl. 10,000,000, the fine may reach a maximum of 10 percent of the company's turnover.

20. Enforcement activity in Aruba remains in a developmental phase, reflecting the relatively recent introduction of the competition law framework. During its first operational year in 2024, the AFTA organized sixteen information sessions, conducted a market study on food products, intervened in matters relating to brokerage fees in the real estate sector, and provided policy advice concerning mobile telecommunications. In 2025, the Authority completed investigations into three markets: real estate agents, distribution agreements for food products, and payment card fees. In addition, the Minister responsible for Economic Affairs received advice on draft legislation affecting the banking sector. During this period, the AFTA also prepared for the implementation of consumer protection enforcement and provided guidance and information to various organizations and members of the public.

21. Although no case law has yet emerged in this area, private enforcement of competition rules is legally possible under general principles of civil law. In practice, however, private litigation in competition matters has not yet developed significantly, a situation commonly observed in jurisdictions where competition law is relatively new and awareness among market participants is still evolving.

VI. Noteworthy Cases

A. *Market study on Food Products*

22. In September, a report was published presenting the results of a market study on prices and the market structure in the food sector in Aruba. The general perception is that food products are expensive in Aruba. The primary objective of the study was to determine to what extent this perception of high food prices is supported by factual evidence. Secondly, the study aimed to map the food sector and examine the factors influencing food prices. The report provides insight into price developments in recent years and includes a concise price comparison with Curaçao, the Netherlands, and the United States. In addition, the report offers insight into the structure of the food market in Aruba.

a) Key findings

23. The findings show that food prices in Aruba are significantly higher than in the Netherlands and the United States, although they are currently comparable to those in Curaçao. Aruban households at the subsistence level spend approximately 40% of their monthly income on food products, a significantly higher percentage than in the Netherlands and the United States.

b) *Market Structure*

24. The market structure in Aruba, characterized by multiple links in the supply chain and partly due to heavy reliance on imports, contributes to higher costs. Although part of the price differences with the Netherlands and the United States can be attributed to transport costs – since a large portion of food products must be imported – the impact of these transport costs on final prices appears relatively stable over time. Other factors, therefore, also account for the price differences.

25. For example, the tax burden on food products in Aruba is higher than in the Netherlands and the United States, primarily due to the cumulative tax system of the Turnover Tax (BBO).

26. The market structure may also explain part of the price differences. The analysis of the food market structure leads to the following findings:
    - Competition in container transport is limited, which may lead to higher costs.
    - The prevalence of exclusive distribution agreements with importers and wholesalers may drive up prices, partly due to limited competition and active obstruction of parallel trade.
    - Competition between supermarkets in Aruba appears to be sufficient.

27. Given the importance of affordable food products for Aruban society, two follow-up studies were initiated based on these findings: one on exclusive distribution agreements and one on competition in container transport to Aruba. These studies began in December 2024. The study on exclusive distribution agreements was completed in 2025. The results of the study on container transport are expected to be published before July 2026.

B. *Market study on exclusive distribution agreements*

28. AFTA's 2024 study on prices and market structure in the food sector in Aruba led to an investigation of distribution agreements in 2025. During the 2024 study, indications emerged that exclusive distribution agreements may affect pricing and competition within this sector. The results of the investigation into exclusive distribution agreements were published in October 2025. The study focused on the nature, extent, and effects of exclusive distribution agreements, with particular attention to their impact on market access, pricing, parallel imports, and competition in Aruba.

29. For this investigation, the AFTA employed various research methods, including document analysis and semi-structured interviews. In addition, information requests were sent to companies to obtain relevant documents and data, such as distribution agreements.

30. During the investigation, the AFTA encountered the operation of the *Canasta Basico*. Although this subject fell outside the original scope of the study, the AFTA decided to examine it further and, based on its findings, make concrete recommendations.

31. Exclusive distribution refers to a supplier granting one or a limited number of distributors the exclusive right to sell certain products in a specific territory or to a specific group of customers. Such arrangements are permitted as long as they do not significantly restrict

competition and do not include prohibited practices, such as price fixing or restrictions on parallel imports.

a) Key findings

32. De facto exclusive distribution relationships: Although this investigation focused on formal exclusive distribution agreements, such agreements are relatively rare. In practice, de facto exclusive distribution relationships are common, where a single distributor effectively and structurally acts as the sole supplier of a brand or branded product in Aruba, without this being formally documented. Whether such exclusivity can be legally enforced by the distributor against the supplier depends on the circumstances of each case. In any event, this factual exclusivity generally affects market access and competition in ways comparable to formal exclusive distribution agreements.

b) Market Structure

33. The import side of the Aruban market is dominated by a limited number of distributors with de facto exclusive brand rights, resulting in an oligopolistic market structure for many products. Established relationships between distributors and brand owners, coupled with the limited incentive for suppliers to appoint additional distributors given the small size of the Aruban market, create high barriers to entry for new importers and distributors.

c) Competition

34. There is interbrand competition (between brands), but intrabrand competition (within the same brand) is largely absent because brand owners typically work exclusively with one distributor, usually without legally binding, formally documented exclusivity agreements. At the retail level, however, there is significant competition between supermarkets, neighborhood stores, and minimarkets.

d) Parallel imports

35. Parallel imports can strengthen intrabrand competition by making the same brand products available through alternative channels outside the official distribution network. In practice, parallel imports are mainly accessible to larger supermarkets with sufficient purchasing power and logistical capacity. There are indications that some neighborhood stores and minimarkets also engage in joint parallel importing, but the frequency and scale could not be established with certainty within this study. Based on available data, the impact of parallel imports on overall market functioning appears limited.

e) Vertical integration

36. Many distributors also operate at the retail level. This vertical integration may create competition risks, as integrated distributors have incentives to favor their own outlets through better pricing, improved availability, or exclusive promotions. In addition, they have access to commercial information from competing customers, which may provide a strategic advantage and further increase barriers to entry.

f) Price structure and perception

37. Data from the Central Bureau of Statistics (CBS) show that large supermarkets consistently charge lower prices than neighborhood stores and minimarkets for most product categories, despite the public perception that large supermarkets are more expensive.

g) Competition law assessment

38. The distribution agreements examined generally do not contain restrictions on competition, such as vertical price fixing, exclusive purchasing obligations, or restrictions on parallel imports, and are therefore not in conflict with the Competition Ordinance. Since the entry into force of the Competition Ordinance on 1 January 2024, there have been no indications of (threats of) boycotts, refusals to supply, or other sanctions in response to observed or suspected parallel imports. However, there are signals that such practices occurred prior to that date.

h) Basic necessities basket 'Canasta Basico'

39. The Canasta Basico, in its current form, provides insufficient protection against international price fluctuations and is partially circumvented in practice. As a result, it fails to achieve its objective of offering consumers a set of basic food products at low prices. The instrument is therefore not effective and may even be market-distorting. The AFTA recommends reconsidering this instrument so that supply and demand, supported by healthy competition, play the main role in ensuring the affordability of food products in Aruba.

i) Conclusion

40. Although exclusive distribution agreements are not unlawful in themselves, this study shows that the combination of de facto exclusivity, limited intrabrand competition, high barriers to entry, and vertical integration creates structural risks for healthy competition. Parallel imports can strengthen intrabrand competition, but in practice they remain mainly accessible to larger supermarkets due to logistical and scale advantages.

41. Based on this study, it cannot be concluded that exclusive distribution agreements alone explain the relatively high prices of food products in Aruba. However, there are indications that the widespread de facto exclusive distribution relationships, combined with limited parallel import activity, contribute to these prices without necessarily constituting a breach of the rules.

42. The AFTA therefore calls on market participants to report suspected exclusive agreements in the distribution of food products in Aruba, as well as any supplier- or distributor-imposed restrictions on parallel imports, particularly in markets with limited intrabrand competition. Based on such reports, the AFTA can conduct further investigations and, where necessary, take enforcement action.

C. *Payment card fees of commercial banks*

43. Following signals from the market, the AFTA conducted an investigation into payment card transaction fees in Aruba. This concerns the fees charged by banks in Aruba to retailers, restaurants, and other points of sale (hereinafter: merchants) when customers

pay with a debit or credit card. These fees are charged for processing debit and credit card payments. AFTA's investigation shows that these fees in Aruba are higher than in other countries, such as the European Union, the United States, and New Zealand.

44. The main cost component for processing a debit or credit card payment for banks consists of fees set by Mastercard and Visa for executing and settling transactions between the cardholder's bank and the merchant's bank. For Aruban banks, this fee is higher than what is common in many other countries. Because the fee that banks in Aruba must pay to cardholder banks is high, the fees charged by Aruban banks to merchants for debit and credit card payments are also high.

45. The transaction fees set by Mastercard and Visa for Aruba are currently not subject to legal regulation, whereas in many other countries, including the European Union, they are capped at a lower level than the fees charged by cardholder banks to merchant banks in Aruba. AFTA therefore makes several recommendations to lower these fees and, in turn, reduce the fees charged by banks in Aruba to merchants. The main recommendation is that Aruba, like many other countries, introduces a statutory cap on the fees between the cardholder's bank and the merchant's bank.

a) Background information

46. Paying with a payment card is very common in Aruba. Aruban commercial banks issue different types of payment cards, and merchants accept various global card brands. When an Aruban or foreign consumer uses a payment card to pay for goods or services, the Aruban merchant providing the goods or services does not receive the full amount paid by the consumer.

47. A portion of the amount paid by the consumer is retained by the merchant's bank (the « acquirer ») as the *Merchant Discount Rate* (MDR). This is the fee charged by the merchant's bank for processing the payment. However, the largest part of the MDR consists of the fee set by the card schemes, the so-called *Interchange Fee* (IF). The IF is paid by the merchant's bank to the bank that issued the payment card to the consumer (the issuer) (see Figure S1).

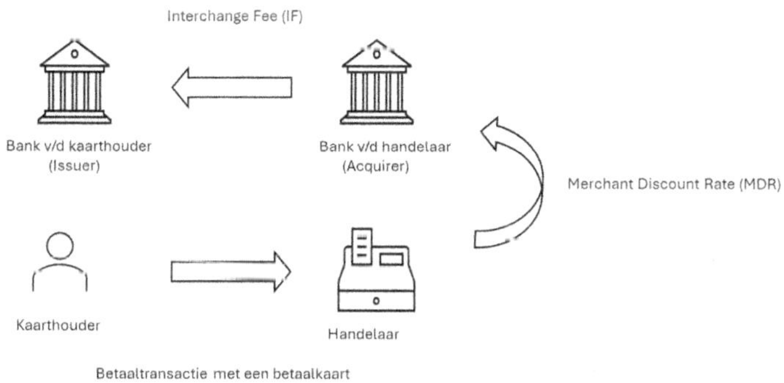

Figure S1. Direct costs related to payment card transactions.[4]

4 Source: AFTA based on European Commission (2016).

48. A key development in Aruba's payment system was the replacement of Maestro by Mastercard Debit as of 1 July 2023. As a result, commercial banks in Aruba have switched to issuing Mastercard Debit or Visa Debit cards. Following this change, the AFTA received signals that the transition was accompanied by an increase in the average MDR charged by banks in Aruba to merchants. Mastercard approximately doubled the IF during the transition from Maestro to Mastercard Debit. This resulted in a 52% increase in the average MDR charged for transactions made with a payment card issued by an Aruban bank.

49. AFTA emphasizes the seriousness of high IFs in the Aruban context. Most payment cards are used by tourists, whose cards are issued by foreign, mainly US-based banks. Aruban merchant banks must pay the high IF per transaction to these often foreign issuers. These costs are passed on by Aruban banks to merchants through the MDR, which merchants in turn incorporate into the prices of their goods and services. Ultimately, all consumers in Aruba bear the cost of fees that are largely transferred to mostly foreign banks.

50. The IFs set by card schemes, which apply uniformly across participating banks (*Multilateral Interchange Fees*, MIFs), also have a competition-restricting effect among banks in Aruba. The collective application of MIFs effectively establishes a price floor for MDRs; merchants cannot negotiate the level of the IF with their bank.

51. The IF often constitutes the main component of the MDR. Annual IF costs for the Aruban banking sector (acquiring banks) are estimated at USD 28 million, or Afl. 50 million. A portion of these costs relates to domestic transactions between Aruban banks (acquirers and issuers). However, the majority (approximately 88%) involves transfers from Aruban acquirers to foreign issuers. This reflects the size of the tourism sector in Aruba but means that significant payments flow to banks outside Aruba.

52. The IF in Aruba is significantly higher than in countries where IF levels are regulated. International examples (the United States, the European Union, and New Zealand) show that regulation leads to substantially lower IFs.

53. In addition to the level of IFs and MDRs, there are other concerns regarding payment card services. There is a lack of transparency regarding the structure of transaction fees. Various restrictions also apply, including the *"Honor All Cards Rule"* and the *"Non-Discrimination Rule"* imposed by card schemes on merchants. These restrictions prevent merchants from taking measures to reduce payment costs.

54. In Aruba, consumers can use various alternative payment methods, each with its own costs. In addition to card payments, consumers can pay in cash or use services such as Pay.aw and Sentoo. The I-Pago infrastructure managed by the Central Bank of Aruba (CBA) also provides technology for modernization of the payment system, enabling new payment services. However, these alternatives are currently limited in scale and exert little competitive pressure on card payment fees charged by Mastercard and Visa.

b) Recommendations

55. Following this investigation, the AFTA makes the following recommendations to the legislator:

- Introduce regulation establishing a maximum cap on IFs in Aruba. Mastercard and Visa's terms and conditions allow for such regulation. Several countries, including the United States, the European Union, and New Zealand, have implemented legislation capping IFs, resulting in significantly lower fees.
- Introduce regulation limiting the *Honor All Cards Rule* (HACR). Prohibiting merchants from being required to accept all cards of a brand, regardless of higher costs, would strengthen merchants' bargaining position and enhance their ability to control costs. It would also increase competition between card issuers.
- Introduce regulation requiring banks in Aruba to provide transparency regarding the fees charged to merchants. This would strengthen merchants' position and promote competition with alternative payment methods. The AFTA calls on banks to jointly develop a periodic, standardized reporting system on cost structures for merchants and offers to facilitate this process.
- Encourage the development and expansion of alternative payment methods. This is important for competition in the payment services market. Banks can play an important role by cooperating with each other and with providers of new payment services. If barriers to market entry are identified, the AFTA will investigate further.

D. *Medlab v. UOAZV and SZA* (Decision of 20 January 2025)

56. *Facts.* Medlab filed a request for enforcement concerning agreements between healthcare institutions and laboratories within Aruba's social health system.

57. *Legal Issue.* Whether the public healthcare body UOAZV qualifies as an "undertaking" under competition law.

58. *Outcome.* The AFTA rejected the request, finding that UOAZV was not acting as an undertaking when performing its statutory public healthcare function.

59. *Impact.* The decision clarifies the boundary between public functions and economic activity under Aruba's competition law framework.

VII. Merger Control

60. Applicability: Merger control is provided for under the Competition Ordinance and covers a notification duty for mergers, acquisitions, and joint ventures. The legal authority to assess concentrations has not yet been fully incorporated into the legislation. The AFTA intends to submit a proposal to this effect in 2027.

61. Notification Thresholds: Notification is required based on turnover and/or market share criteria defined by implementing decrees. Concentrations must be reported to the AFTA if they meet specific thresholds, including: a combined annual turnover exceeding AWG 125 million, individual turnover of at least AWG 15 million for at least two parties or a combined market share of 30% or more.

62. Review Process: The framework provides for notification and review by the AFTA.

63. Practice: Notified transactions to date include Boogaard / Seguros Geerman and the acquisition of Nagico Road & Claims Services N.V. by 2 Fast 4 U Company VBA.

VIII. Advocacy and Policy Initiatives

64. When the AFTA began operations in 2024, competition law was new in Aruba. As a result, considerable time and attention were devoted to advocacy and awareness-building. The approach to providing information about the new competition rules and the role of the AFTA followed three main tracks: information was made available digitally, information sessions were organized, and one-on-one interactions took place with various companies and institutions.

65. Outreach: The AFTA organized multiple information sessions for businesses, professionals, and consumers, and operates a dedicated consumer information platform.

66. Policy Work: The AFTA has adopted policy rules on enforcement priorities and communication and has issued advisory opinions, notably in the telecommunications sector.

67. Market Studies: The Authority has conducted several sectoral studies, including on the food sector (2024), exclusive distribution agreements (2025), and payment card fees (2026).

68. Capacity Building: Advocacy and education constitute central pillars of the AFTA's work, aimed at fostering a competition culture in a newly regulated environment.

IX. Regional and International Cooperation

69. Institutional Context: Aruba is not a member of CARICOM.

70. Cooperation: The AFTA cooperates with national and international supervisory authorities and may enter into formal cooperation arrangements.

71. **ACM**: The Netherlands Authority for Consumers and Markets (ACM) has been involved with the AFTA since the implementation project supporting the launch of the authority, including the provision of an experienced "quartermaster" expert. In addition, Martijn Snoep holds a dual role as a board member of the AFTA and as Chair of the ACM.

72. Since 18 July 2024, a formal cooperation agreement has been in place between the ACM and the AFTA. This agreement provides, among other things, that the ACM and AFTA strengthen each other through the rapid and careful exchange of advice and knowledge. To implement the agreement, the ACM has appointed a contact person responsible for directing the AFTA's questions to the relevant ACM specialists. Regular sessions are organized to transfer knowledge and share information, typically concerning topics where the AFTA seeks expert insights related to ongoing investigations or completed ACM investigations of interest.

73. **FTAC**: The Fair Trade Authority Curaçao (FTAC) is the competition authority of Curaçao, established in 2017. Prior to the establishment of the AFTA, there was already

a relationship between the FTAC and the AFTA. Two AFTA employees involved in the implementation project completed internships at the FTAC in 2022. The same experienced ACM expert who acted as quartermaster for the FTAC became quartermaster for the AFTA in 2021.

74. Shortly after the AFTA's establishment, the FTAC provided basic competition law training to the authority. On 13 March 2024, the FTAC and the AFTA signed a cooperation protocol. Following the recruitment of new staff, the FTAC provided further assistance, including additional basic competition law training. New employees who joined the AFTA in early 2025 received this training in February. In April 2025, the two authorities jointly attended training on interview techniques and hearings, provided by the law firm Lindenbaum. There is regular contact between the directors of the FTAC and the AFTA.

75. **ICPEN**: The International Consumer Protection and Enforcement Network (ICPEN) is a global network of government authorities responsible for enforcing consumer protection laws. It supports regulators from different countries in cooperating to combat fraud, scams, and unfair commercial practices, especially cross-border activities. ICPEN exists primarily because consumer fraud and misleading practices often occur internationally, usually online.

76. The AFTA participated in the ICPEN High-Level Meeting & Conference in Santo Domingo, Dominican Republic, from 30 September to 3 October 2025. At the time, the AFTA was not yet a member of ICPEN and participated as a guest through the introduction of the ACM. The AFTA was presented as a prospective member.

77. **ICN**: The International Competition Network (ICN) is a global network of competition authorities. The network promotes cooperation and knowledge exchange to improve the effective enforcement of competition law. Through ICN cooperation, authorities can exchange information more quickly, develop similar rules and procedures, and more effectively address cross-border competition issues.

78. The AFTA participated in the annual ICN conferences in 2024 and 2025. During the ICN conference in Edinburgh from 7 to 9 May 2025, the AFTA chaired a breakout session titled "Island and Small Economies," which focused on the specific challenges faced by islands and small economies in supervising and enforcing competition rules.

79. **CARICOM**: The Caribbean Community (CARICOM) is a regional organization of Caribbean countries that cooperate in economic, political, and social areas. Its objective is to promote economic integration, trade, and development in the Caribbean region.

80. The AFTA was invited to contribute to the first regional consultation on competition policy aimed at supporting the implementation of competition rules under Chapter Eight of the Revised Treaty of Chaguaramas. On 7 November 2025, the AFTA participated as a panel member, sharing its experience on the implementation of competition policy within the Caribbean Community.

81. **ISLE**: ISLE ("island" in historical French) is a non-profit research institute dedicated to contributing to competition policy that is optimal for the development of island economies. ISLE promotes a deep understanding of competition law and economics,

tailored to the unique challenges faced by small markets and island economies. It also facilitates international cooperation to support the development of effective and sustainable competition policy that promotes fair markets and addresses cost-of-living issues for consumers.

82. In June 2025, the AFTA became a member of ISLE and, in March 2026, joined its scientific committee. The AFTA participates in the ISLE workgroup that organized the first Small Economies Forum on the eve of the ICN conference in Manila on 5 May 2026.

X. Challenges and Country-Specific Features

83. Aruba exhibits several structural characteristics typical of small island economies: a small domestic market, high levels of concentration in key sectors, strong dependence on imports, exposure to logistical constraints and transport costs.

84. AFTA's own work highlights specific concerns related to exclusive distribution arrangements, logistics and container transport, and pricing in essential goods markets.

85. The AFTA is a relatively young and small authority. Since its operational launch in 2024, enforcement practice has been progressively emerging, with an initial focus on advocacy, market studies, and targeted interventions.

XI. Author's Perspective

86. Aruba is in the midst of a transition – from the absence of a competition framework to the establishment of both a legal regime and a fully operational authority beginning in 2024. For the AFTA, it is essential to develop a deep and comprehensive understanding of the Aruban economy. This foundation enables the authority to carry out meaningful interventions and implement targeted, effective enforcement.

87. The AFTA continues to evolve, not only by gaining experience but also by assuming increasing responsibilities. In this process, learning from the experiences of other authorities in small economies facing similar challenges remains a key factor in ensuring the AFTA's success.

XII. References and Resources

- Aruba Fair Trade Authority (AFTA)
- World Bank – Aruba country data
- Government of the Netherlands – governance of Caribbean parts of the Kingdom
- Central Bank of Aruba – macroeconomic and trade reports

88. To learn more about the Aruba Fair Trade Authority (AFTA):
Website: https://afta.aw/pages/en/home-en/
Contact: info@afta.aw

Cyprus

Olga Droussioti Papachrysanthou
Director of the Service of the Commission for the Protection of Competition of the Republic of Cyprus

Kostas Karathymios
Officer at the Service of the Commission for the Protection of Competition of the Republic of Cyprus

I. Overview

1. Cyprus is a sovereign state in the Eastern Mediterranean Sea. It is situated south of Turkey, west of Syria and Lebanon, northwest of Israel, north of Egypt, and southeast of Greece. Its geographic position places it at the crossroads of Europe, the Middle East, and North Africa, a factor that has historically shaped both its geopolitical significance and its economic structure. The surface area of Cyprus is approximately 9,251 square kilometers.[1]

2. Cyprus became an independent republic in 1960, and its official languages are Greek and Turkish. Since 1974, following the Turkish military invasion, part of its territory has been under Turkish military occupation. As a result of this, the Government of the Republic of Cyprus which is the sole legal and internationally recognized government on the island, is not in a position to exercise effective control over the occupied areas of its territory.

3. The entire territory of the Republic of Cyprus acceded to the European Union in 2004. However, pursuant to Protocol No. 10 of the Act of Accession, the application of the EU *acquis* is suspended in those areas of the Republic in which the government does not exercise effective control.

II. Demographics and Economy

4. According to official records, the population in the government-controlled areas amounted to approximately 983,000 inhabitants at the end of 2024, corresponding to a population density of roughly 106 inhabitants per square kilometer.

5. Cyprus's nominal GDP reached EUR 34.77 billion at current prices in 2024. Preliminary quarterly estimates for 2025 indicate continued growth, but a final official annual nominal GDP figure for 2025 has not yet been published.

6. The Republic of Cyprus constitutes a paradigmatic example of a small, open and island-based economy within the European Union. The Cypriot economy is service-dominated, with services accounting for more than 75% of GDP. Sectors like tourism, finance, professional services and real estate are driving growth. Industry and construction represent a significantly smaller share, while agriculture contributes only a minor percentage of total output. The total imports of goods in January–December 2025 amounted to EUR 13,551.8 million as compared to EUR 12,582.0 million in January–December 2024, recording an increase of 7.7%. Moreover, the total exports of goods between January and December 2025 were EUR 5,550.4 million compared to EUR 5,186.7 million in 2024, registering an increase of 7.0%. The trade deficit was EUR 8,001.4 million in January–December 2025, compared to EUR 7,395.3 million in the corresponding period of 2024.[2]

7. Structural business statistics show that while the economy is characterized overall by a high number of micro and small enterprises, certain sectors operate with a limited

---

[1] Cyprus Deputy Ministry of Tourism, https://www.visitcyprus.com/.

[2] Press Release, CYSTAT, Foreign Trade Statistics: November 2025 (Final Data) and December 2025 (Provisional Data) (Feb. 9, 2026) https://www.cystat.gov.cy/en/PressRelease?id=73031.

number of active firms. In small markets with limited demand and economies of scale, this structural feature can naturally result in higher concentration levels in specific industries. As a result, although no official concentration index is published, the structural characteristics of the economy suggest that concentration issues may arise more frequently than in larger jurisdictions, a factor that is relevant for competition law enforcement in small economies.

III. Legal Framework for Competition

8. Cyprus' competition law framework was developed progressively, largely in anticipation of and following its accession to the European Union. The first comprehensive competition legislation in Cyprus was adopted in 1989, marking the beginning of a structured national competition regime. This initial framework was designed to introduce rules against anticompetitive agreements and abuse of dominance, laying the foundation for alignment with EU competition principles. Subsequent legislative amendments sought to ensure formal alignment with articles 101 and 102 of the Treaty on the Functioning of the European Union (TFEU).

9. Competition law in Cyprus is currently governed by the Protection of Competition Law of 2022 (Law 13(I)/2022), which repealed and replaced the Protection of Competition Law of 2008, which had previously repealed and replaced the Law of 1989. The 2022 reform represents a watershed moment in the development of Cypriot competition law, as it transposed Directive (EU) 2019/1 (the ECN+ Directive) into national law and substantially upgraded the institutional and procedural framework for enforcement.

10. Law 13(I)/2022 applies horizontally across all sectors of the economy and to all undertakings, irrespective of their legal form or ownership structure. It prohibits anticompetitive agreements, decisions by associations of undertakings and concerted practices, as well as the abuse of a dominant position, in terms that closely mirror articles 101 and 102 TFEU. Furthermore, the scope of application of Law 13(I)/2022 extends to undertakings entrusted with services of general economic interest, in accordance with section 7. Such undertakings remain subject to competition rules unless their application would obstruct the performance of the tasks assigned to them. This mirrors article 106(2) TFEU and confirms that any derogation from competition law must be strictly justified.

11. Moreover, Law 13(I)/2022 expressly provides for the parallel application of national and EU competition law where trade between Member States may be affected, thereby ensuring the effective decentralized enforcement of EU competition rules and the full integration of Cyprus within the European Competition Network (ECN). In parallel, certain national block exemptions have historically been implemented through ministerial orders, allowing specific categories of agreements to benefit from exemption where they satisfy predefined conditions consistent with EU block exemption regulations.

12. The national legislative framework is further complemented by the Exemption from and Reduction of Administrative Fines in Cases of Cartels in Breach of Section 3 of the Protection of Competition Law and/or Article 101 TFEU (Leniency Program)

Regulations of 2022 (P.I. 442/2022). These Regulations establish the framework for the leniency treatment of undertakings that choose to cooperate with the Commission in uncovering secret cartels prohibited under section 3 of Law 13(I)/2022 and article 101 TFEU.

13. It should be noted that the Commission for the Protection of Competition (CPC or the "Commission") is currently in the process of amending the competition legislation, with a view to further refining procedural mechanisms, enhancing investigative effectiveness and ensuring continued alignment with evolving EU competition law standards.[3]

14. Concurrently, the CPC, together with the Central Bank of Cyprus and the Consumer Protection Service of the Ministry of Energy, Commerce and Industry, has been designated as a competent authority for the enforcement of the Interchange Fees for Card-Based Payment Transactions Law of 2018 (Law 77(I)/2018). Accordingly, the CPC is entrusted with ensuring the application of specific provisions of Regulation (EU) 2015/751 on Interchange Fees for Card-Based Payment Transactions. In this context, the CPC is empowered to investigate relevant infringements and to exercise investigative powers, including the collection of information and evidence, the conduct of on-site inspections, and the imposition of administrative fines and sanctions.

IV. Institutional Structure of the Commission for the Protection of Competition

15. The CPC is an independent administrative authority that was originally established under Law 207/1989 and continues to operate under the Protection of Competition Law of 2022. The CPC has as its mission to safeguard effective competition in the market and to foster a culture of competition so that the Cypriot economy operates efficiently for the benefit of consumers, businesses and society at large. This mandate extends to ensuring the proper functioning of competition in the card payment systems sector, in the interests of merchants, consumers and payment service providers. The CPC's strategic objectives include:

- Safeguarding and restoring conditions of fair and open competition so that undertakings compete on equal terms;
- Ensuring effective market structures through rigorous merger control;
- Enhancing consumer welfare by promoting wider choice, lower prices, improved quality and better services; and
- Maintaining effective competitive conditions in card payment systems.

16. Pursuant to Law 13(I)/2022, the CPC is composed of a chairperson and four members, appointed by the Council of Ministers, following a proposal by the Minister of Energy, Commerce, and Industry, for a period of five years, which is renewable once. The CPC acts as the decision-making body.

---

3 *See* News, CPC, Extension of the Deadline for the Submission of Views and Suggestions regarding the Public Consultation: Draft Bill Titled "The Protection of Competition (Amending) Law of 2024" (Apr. 30, 2024) (in Greek), https://www.competition.gov.cy/competition/Competition.nsf/All/0D6724E3A2E961DEC2258B0F0018E09E?.

17. A Service supports the CPC with investigative and administrative functions and is headed by a director who oversees the authority's daily operations and coordinates investigative and analytical work. The Service is staffed by a small team of competition officers (lawyers and economists) and administrative personnel. These permanent public officers possess expertise in competition law and are responsible for the technical preparation of cases before the Commission.

18. The CPC's budget is allocated annually through the State budget and is intended to cover staffing costs, operational expenses, investigative activities, training, and participation in international cooperation networks. The total annual budget for 2025 was EUR 2,548,174, and for 2026 is EUR 2,723,966.

V. Competition Enforcement Powers and Sanctions

19. To enable the effective exercise of its competences, the legislative framework vests the CPC with broad investigative and enforcement powers. More specifically, pursuant to Law 22(I)/2022, the CPC is empowered to (i) conduct sector inquiries, investigations *ex officio* or following complaints; (ii) request the supply of information, data and documents from undertakings and third parties; and (iii) conduct interviews. It may conduct unannounced inspections at business premises and, subject to judicial authorization, at other premises, including private residences, where there is reasonable suspicion that relevant evidence may be found. During inspections, the CPC may examine books and records, take copies (including digital data), seal premises or files, and request explanations on facts or documents relating to the subject matter of the investigation. Failure to comply with investigative measures may result in administrative fines or periodic penalty payments.

20. The CPC has the power to order the termination of infringements, adopt interim measures where necessary, accept binding commitments offered by undertakings, adopt behavioral or structural remedies as required to address the circumstances to restore effective competition and impose administrative fines and periodic penalty payments.

21. In particular, the legislative framework also provides for a comprehensive system of sanctions designed to ensure effective compliance with competition rules. More concretely, pursuant to Law 13(I)/2022, the CPC may impose administrative fines of up to 10% of the total worldwide turnover of the undertaking or the association of undertakings concerned in the preceding financial year. The CPC may also impose periodic penalty payments to compel compliance with its decisions or with investigative measures, including requests for information and cooperation during inspections. Fines are determined based on the gravity and duration of the infringement, taking into account aggravating and mitigating circumstances.

22. It is noteworthy that infringement decisions of the CPC constitute irrebuttable presumptions before national courts in follow-on actions as regards the existence of the infringement. Although the legal framework fully enables damage actions, and Cyprus implemented Directive 2014/104/EU on Antitrust Damages Actions through the Actions for Damages for Infringements of Competition Law of 2017 (Law 113(I)/2017), private enforcement in Cyprus appears to be limited in practice when compared to administrative enforcement.

VI. Noteworthy Cases

A. *Vassiliko Cement Works (2023)*

23. One of the most significant antitrust decisions issued by the CPC in recent years concerns Vassiliko Cement Works Public Company Ltd., the dominant supplier of gray cement in Cyprus. In Decision No. 3/2023, the CPC found that the undertaking had engaged in excessive pricing of cement in the local market over a prolonged period, in breach of national competition law and article 102 TFEU.

24. The Commission conducted a detailed assessment of pricing behavior, cost structures and profitability indicators, concluding that the prices charged bore no reasonable relation to the product's economic value. According to the economic analysis conducted by the CPC, pricing for domestic sales during the period 2013–2018 in relation to gray cement was found to be excessively high, resulting in an abnormally large profit margin for Vassiliko Cement Works. Furthermore, a comparison between the prices charged to domestic customers and those applied in export markets revealed significant differentiation, reinforcing the finding that domestic pricing levels were not competitively justified. The decision demonstrates the CPC's willingness to intervene decisively in structurally concentrated markets where dominance is reinforced by high barriers to entry and limited import substitutability. The CPC imposed an administrative fine of EUR 5,070,950, emphasizing the detrimental effects of the infringement on downstream construction markets and ultimately on consumers.

B. *Ready concrete (2024)*

25. The CPC, by Decision No. 73/2024 of December 17, 2024, concluded an *ex officio* investigation into the market for the production, marketing, supply and/or placement of ready-mix concrete covering the period 2010–2014. The Commission found that several undertakings infringed section 3(1) of Law 13(I)/2022 by participating in secret collusive practices, including price fixing, restriction and control of production and supply, market (customer) allocation, and the exchange of sensitive business information. One infringement concerned the exchange of information relating to financial offers submitted for the construction of the new passenger terminal at the Port of Limassol. The Commission also found collusion in the market for aggregates involving price fixing and restriction/control of production and supply.

26. The Commission ordered all companies involved to cease the infringements and avoid any repetition. It imposed total administrative fines of EUR 1,947,140.71, taking into account the seriousness and duration of each infringement, mitigating circumstances where applicable, and the turnover of each company.

VII. Merger Control

27. A significant development following the implementation of the first competition legislation was the enactment of the Control of Concentrations between Undertakings Law of 1999 (Law 22(I)/1999), which entrusted the national competition authority with exclusive competence to review concentrations that met the relevant jurisdictional thresholds.

The national merger regime has evolved since its first introduction to the national legal system. Currently, the Control of Concentrations between Undertakings Law of 2014 (Law 83(I)/2014) is in force and has replaced Law 22(I)/1999. The 2014 reform modernized the merger control regime by aligning substantive assessment more closely with EU standards, refining jurisdictional thresholds, clarifying the concept of concentration, introducing a more structured two-phase review process, and strengthening investigative and sanctioning powers.

28. Only concentrations meeting the statutory thresholds are subject to mandatory notification and prior approval. In exceptional circumstances, however, the competent minister retains the power to request the CPC to examine a transaction that does not meet the statutory turnover thresholds where it is considered that the concentration may nevertheless be of major importance for the Cypriot economy or affect competition conditions, thereby extending the preventive reach of merger control beyond strictly notifiable cases.

29. Pursuant to Law 83(I)/2014, the CPC has jurisdiction to review mergers, issue clearance decisions, impose structural or behavioral remedies or prohibit a concentration where the statutory criteria are not satisfied. Moreover, it should be noted that the CPC has the power to impose administrative fines, including for implementing a concentration prior to clearance, with these fines potentially reaching up to 10% of the total turnover of the undertaking concerned, depending on the specific infringement.

30. Notably, the CPC is presently in the process of amending the merger legislation, with a view, inter alia, to further refining procedural mechanisms and revising the national thresholds described below, so as to reduce the number of notifiable concentrations.[4] In practice, a significant proportion of notified concentrations did not give rise to any substantive competition concerns, as many had no appreciable impact on the competitive structure of the market, while several did not meet the affected market thresholds despite formally triggering the turnover-based notification criteria.

A. *Notification Thresholds*

31. Currently, a concentration is notifiable if it qualifies as a "concentration of major importance" under Law 83(I)/2014. This requires that:

- the aggregate worldwide turnover of at least two undertakings concerned exceeds EUR 3.5 million;
- at least two of the undertakings concerned each achieve turnover in Cyprus; and
- at least EUR 3.5 million of the aggregate turnover of all undertakings concerned is achieved within the Republic of Cyprus.

B. *Review Timeframes*

32. The merger control regime is characterized by strictly defined statutory timeframes for the assessment of concentrations, aimed at ensuring both expeditious review and legal

---

4 Press Release, CPC, Public Consultation on the Draft Bill Titled "The Control of Concentrations between Undertakings (Amending) Law of 2025" (Sept. 15, 2025) (in Greek), https://www.competition.gov.cy/competition/competition.nsf/All/5FFA1669A87040E2C2258D06003CBA65?OpenDocument.

certainty for the undertakings concerned. Upon submission of a complete notification, the Service of the CPC conducts a Phase I (preliminary investigation), which must be completed within one month of receipt of the notification or the submission of all the necessary information provided for in Annex III of the Law.

33. If the CPC, following the completion of the preliminary investigation, determines that the concentration raises serious doubts as to its compatibility with the competitive market, it initiates a Phase II (full investigation). The Phase II investigation must be completed by the Service of the CPC within three months of receipt of the notification or the submission of all the necessary information provided for in Annex III of the Law. During Phase II, and within the prescribed time limits, the parties may submit commitments or propose modifications to the concentration, and negotiations may take place. Following the completion of the full investigation, the CPC has one month to issue a decision, either clearing the merger (with or without remedies) or prohibiting it.

C. *Examples of Notified Mergers*

1. Eurobank/Hellenic Bank – Banking Sector Consolidation

34. In the banking sector, the CPC's approval of the acquisition of a significant shareholding in Hellenic Bank Public Company Ltd. by Eurobank S.A. (Decision No. 14/2024) constitutes a landmark merger control case. The Commission examined the transaction's effects on the retail and corporate banking markets, in the context of already high concentration, as well as the parties' activities in the insurance sector.

35. Following an in-depth assessment, the CPC cleared the transaction, concluding that it would not significantly impede effective competition. The decision illustrates a context-sensitive approach to merger control in a small economy, considering not only market shares but also the ability of the remaining banking institutions to compete, financial stability considerations, regulatory oversight and potential competitive constraints.

2. Petrolina/Esso – Conditional Clearance in the Petroleum Products Sector

36. Another emblematic decision concerns the acquisition of ExxonMobil Cyprus Ltd. (Esso) by Petrolina (Holdings) Public Ltd. through Med Energywise Ltd. (Decision No. 10/2022). The CPC identified serious horizontal and vertical concerns in the markets for the importation, wholesale supply and retail distribution of petroleum products. Following a Phase II investigation, the CPC entered into discussions with Petrolina (Holdings) Public Ltd. with a view to addressing the serious doubts identified in relation to the compatibility of the concentration with effective competition. After assessing the final package of commitments and the findings of the full investigation, the CPC concluded that the proposed remedies were sufficient to eliminate the competition concerns and unanimously declared the concentration compatible with the market subject to binding conditions.

37. The commitments included:

- the divestment, sale or termination of operation of 21 fuel stations;
- long-term non-reacquisition and non-substitution obligations in relation to divested stations (up to 10 years), including geographic restrictions;
- the temporary provision (for at least two years, extendable) of access to storage capacity at the Vasiliko terminal on market terms;
- strict information-firewall obligations preventing the exchange of commercially sensitive information between wholesale/import and retail levels;
- maintenance and, where applicable, renewal or open tendering of service contracts previously held by Esso;
- the prohibition of exclusivity obligations on service providers;
- a 10-year prohibition on imposing exclusive supply obligations for lubricants at acquired stations; and
- the appointment of an independent monitoring trustee to oversee compliance and the divestment process.

38. These structural and behavioral commitments collectively aimed to prevent horizontal concentration effects, vertical foreclosure risks, and information spillovers within the fuel supply chain.

VIII. Advocacy and Policy Initiatives

39. A key aspect of the CPC's advocacy function is the submission of reasoned opinions to the House of Representatives. These opinions are issued in relation to draft legislation that may affect competition conditions, as well as on other matters examined *ex officio* by Parliament. Through this advisory role, the CPC contributes to the legislative process by identifying potential anticompetitive effects, proposing alternative regulatory approaches and promoting competition-friendly solutions at an early stage, in line with EU principles and international best practices.

40. In parallel, the CPC undertakes policy initiatives and sector-specific interventions aimed at raising awareness of competition law obligations among businesses, professional associations and public authorities. These initiatives seek to reduce compliance risks, discourage anticompetitive practices and foster a culture of competition, particularly in markets characterized by repeated interactions and structural concentration.

A. *Sectoral Studies or Market Inquiries*

41. An important dimension of the CPC's enforcement activity is reflected in the sector inquiries it has undertaken:

- On December 17, 2024, a sector inquiry was initiated into the motor fuel industry for the period 2023–2024. More specifically, the CPC decided on the initiation of the sector inquiry, taking into account the structure of the petroleum products market, information provided by the Ministry of Energy, Commerce and Industry concerning the Retail Fuel Price Observatory, as well as various press reports and official statements, and the broader perception that fuel prices in this market vary by district and by specific location or area.[5]

- On September 1, 2023, a sector inquiry was initiated into the goat, sheep and cow milk industry, specifically at the stage between production and the supply/marketing of milk by producers and/or associations to cheese producers and dairy processors regarding the period July 2022–July 2023.[6]
- On December 17, 2014, a sector inquiry was initiated into the fuel industry for the period 2008–2014. Although there were no indications of anticompetitive concerns, CPC submitted proposals to several ministries in order to introduce policies and/or amend legislative acts that would enhance competition in the market.

B. *Education and Capacity Building*

42. The CPC also places emphasis on capacity building. It actively participates in and organizes conferences, workshops and training seminars directed at a broad range of stakeholders, including public officials involved in procurement, legal and economic practitioners, and representatives of the business community.

43. In this context, the CPC took part in a multi-country project, "Fighting Bid Rigging in Public Procurement," in collaboration with the Organisation for Economic Co-operation and Development (OECD), Austria, Bulgaria, Croatia, Greece and Romania. The project was funded by the European Commission. This cooperation, focused on raising awareness of cartel prevention and detection in public procurement markets, is particularly relevant in small markets where public procurement represents a significant share of economic activity. The project combines technical analysis, policy and practice recommendations, and capacity building.

IX. Regional and International Cooperation

44. Regional and international cooperation plays an important role in enhancing the effectiveness of competition enforcement in Cyprus, particularly in light of the structural constraints faced by a small jurisdiction. Cooperation mechanisms contribute to the exchange of expertise, the development of common approaches and the strengthening of institutional capacity.

45. At the EU level, the CPC participates actively in the ECN, which provides a structured framework for cooperation, coordination and information exchange among national competition authorities and the European Commission. Through the ECN, the CPC engages in discussions on case handling, policy developments and best practices, benefiting from peer support and contributing to the consistent application of EU competition law.

---

5 Press Release, CPC, Decision to Conduct a Sector Inquiry into the Motor Fuel Market (Dec. 18, 2024) (in Greek), https://www.competition.gov.cy/competition/competition.nsf/All/1D1981E7CC92B9F1C2258BF7003B08D2?.

6 Press Release, CPC, Decision to Conduct a Sector Inquiry into the Production and Distribution of Goat, Sheep, and Cow Milk (Sept. 1, 2023) (in Greek), https://www.competition.gov.cy/competition/competition.nsf/All/FC7F33588A4ACFFCC2258A1D002B0C2C?.

46. Beyond EU-level cooperation, the CPC has entered into bilateral cooperation arrangements with competition authorities in neighboring jurisdictions. In particular, the CPC has signed a memorandum of understanding (MoU) with the Hellenic Competition Commission and with the Egyptian Competition Authority. These MoUs provide a framework for cooperation, including the exchange of non-confidential information, technical assistance and the sharing of experience on enforcement and advocacy matters of common interest.

47. At the international level, the CPC participates in the International Competition Network (ICN), which offers a global platform for dialogue and cooperation among competition authorities. Participation in ICN activities facilitates exposure to comparative perspectives, soft law instruments and practical guidance, which are especially valuable for small authorities seeking to align their practice with international standards.

X. Challenges and Country-Specific Features

48. Cyprus is a small island economy with a limited population and a geographically isolated market. The small size of its domestic demand naturally limits the number of viable competitors in certain sectors, particularly those characterized by economies of scale or network effects. As a result, several markets may structurally sustain only a small number of operators. While this does not itself imply anticompetitive conduct, it increases the likelihood of high market shares and oligopolistic structures in certain industries, thereby requiring careful application of antitrust rules and merger control principles.

49. Historically, certain sectors in Cyprus have involved significant state participation, particularly in utilities and infrastructure-related activities, i.e., telecom and energy sectors. Although liberalization and EU accession have progressively opened markets to competition, the presence of public or semi-public entities in specific sectors remains a structural feature of the economy. Under EU and national competition law, public undertakings are subject to competition rules when engaged in economic activity, but their institutional role may influence market dynamics in smaller jurisdictions.

50. In addition, as an island economy with limited natural resources and industrial production capacity, Cyprus is structurally dependent on imports for energy, manufactured goods, and intermediate inputs. At the same time, the economy is highly open and relies significantly on foreign direct investment and cross-border services. These characteristics affect competitive conditions, particularly in sectors linked to trade, shipping, tourism, and financial services, and increase the relevance of EU internal market rules.

51. Institutionally, the competition authority operates within a comparatively limited administrative and human resource framework. Although the Protection of Competition Law of 2022 strengthens independence and investigative powers, overall institutional capacity remains proportionate to the scale of the jurisdiction and may require further reinforcement to ensure effective enforcement in increasingly complex market environments, particularly given that the CPC is responsible for overseeing all sectors of the economy.

XI. Author's Perspective

52. In a small and highly open economy such as Cyprus, competition law plays a structurally stabilizing role rather than merely a corrective one. Market size constraints and limited economies of scale mean that high concentration levels may arise naturally in certain sectors. The evolution of competition law in Cyprus should therefore continue to focus not only on finding and sanctioning infringements but also on ensuring market contestability, transparency, and predictable enforcement.

53. Looking forward, further strengthening the capacity of the CPC and deepening cooperation within the ECN will be essential, especially in complex cross-border cases. At the same time, advocacy efforts can play a significant role in embedding a culture of competition compliance among businesses. In small economies, where commercial relationships are often close-knit, proactive guidance and clarity may prevent infringements more effectively than purely reactive enforcement. Competition policy in Cyprus is likely to evolve towards a more integrated model, combining robust enforcement with strategic advocacy to safeguard both market efficiency and long-term economic resilience.

XII. References and Resources

A. *Laws and Regulations*

- P.I. 43/2025 – The Block Exemption (Certain Categories of Vertical Agreements and Concerted Practices in the Motor Vehicle Sector) (Amendment) Order of 2025.
- P.I. 42/2025 – The Block Exemption (Agreements, Decisions and Concerted Practices in the Insurance Sector) (Repeal) Order of 2025
- P.I. 41/2025 – The Block Exemption (Vertical Agreements and Concerted Practices) Order of 2025
  Full text available in Greek
  https://www.competition.gov.cy/competition/competition.nsf/page15_gr/page15_gr?OpenDocument
- The Protection of Competition Law 2022 (in English https://www.competition.gov.cy/competition/competition.nsf/All/21705DCE5C2FDBD5C22589E300449AB3?OpenDocument)
- The Protection of Competition Law 2008–2014
- The Protection of Competition Law 1989, as amended
- The Control of Concentrations Between Undertakings Law 83(I)/2014 (in English https://www.competition.gov.cy/competition/competition.nsf/All/5937AB49B8B38080C2257FB2003A442B?OpenDocument)
- The Control of Concentration between Undertakings Law 1999 to 2000 (in English https://www.competition.gov.cy/competition/competition.nsf/page16_arch_en/page16_arch_en?OpenDocument&Start=1&Count=1000&Expand=1)
- The Interchange Fees for Card-Passed Payment Law 2018 (in English https://www.competition.gov.cy/competition/competition.nsf/page40_en/page40_en?OpenDocument)

B. *Case Law*

- CPC, Decision No. 72/2025 – Notification of a concentration concerning the acquisition of share capital of ExxonMobil Cyprus Limited by Petrolina (Holdings) Public Limited through its wholly owned subsidiary, Med Energywise Ltd. (in Greek), https://www.competition.gov.cy/competition/Competition.nsf/All/DEB80FB30F90D182C2258D64003FCBBE?OpenDocument&highlight=Petrolina
- CPC, Decision No. 74/2024 – *Ex officio* investigation into the market for the production, trading, supply and/or installation of concrete (in Greek), https://www.competition.gov.cy/competition/Competition.nsf/All/418BEC5A020C6837C2258D38002BA1FB?OpenDocument
- CPC, Decision No. 10/2024 – Notification of a concentration concerning the acquisition of share capital in Hellenic Bank Public Company Limited by Eurobank S.A. (in Greek), https://www.competition.gov.cy/competition/Competition.nsf/All/B6093F9B49A86D6BC2258B9A002C18D8?OpenDocument&highlight=Eurobank
- CPC, Decision No. 3/2023 – *Ex officio* investigation against Vassiliko Cement Works Public Company Ltd. for alleged infringements of articles 3(1) and 6(1) of Law 13(I)/2008, as amended, and articles 101 and 102 TFEU, in the cement supply sector (in Greek), https://www.competition.gov.cy/competition/Competition.nsf/All/10AE023CC36D1235C225899B002FEB04?OpenDocument

C. *Public Reports*

- CPC, Sector Inquiry in the Petroleum Market, https://www.competition.gov.cy/competition/competition.nsf/All/1D1981E7CC92B9F1C2258BF7003B08D2?

54. To learn more about the Commission for the Protection of Competition (CPC):
- Website: www.competition.gov.cy
- Contact[7]: chairman@competition.gov.cy

[7] The CPC provides a dedicated webpage containing its contact details: https://www.competition.gov.cy/competition/competition.nsf/contact_en/contact_en?OpenDocument

Curaçao

Jean Dictus
Fair Trade Authority Curaçao's Chairman of the Board

Christian Pierre Everts
Fair Trade Authority Curaçao's Board member

Charitee Henriquez
Fair Trade Authority Curaçao's Board Director

I. Overview

A. *Geographical Location*

1. Curaçao is an island located in the southern Caribbean Sea, approximately 65 kilometers north of the Venezuelan coast, and forms part of the Leeward Antilles. Its geographical position has historically made the island a strategic hub for maritime trade, transshipment, and regional services. Its closeness to South America, along with strong historical ties to Europe and North America, has created an economy that depends heavily on international trade. Hence, Curaçao has an open economy. This openness has direct implications for competition dynamics. Many markets are influenced by import conditions, transport costs, and regional competitive pressures rather than purely domestic factors.

B. *Surface Area*

2. The island's size is approximately 444 square kilometers. Hence, Curaçao is a small island economy and is categorized as a Caribbean SIDS (Small Island Developing State).

C. *Political Status*

3. Curaçao is an autonomous country within the Kingdom of the Netherlands. While it enjoys a high degree of internal self-government, it shares a constitutional and legal system with the Netherlands. This constitutional structure has influenced the design of Curaçao's competition regime, including the establishment of an independent administrative authority to enforce competition law. The legal system is rooted in civil law traditions, with a strong emphasis on administrative law principles, legal certainty, proportionality, and judicial review.

D. *Official Languages*

4. The official languages of Curaçao are Dutch, Papiamentu, and English. This multilingual environment reflects the island's cultural diversity and international orientation. From a competition law perspective, it necessitates that legislation, decisions, guidance, and advocacy materials are accessible to a broad audience. The use of multiple languages also facilitates cooperation with international and regional competition authorities.

II. Demographics and Economy

A. *Population*

5. Curaçao has a population of approximately 155,000 inhabitants as of 2024. The population density of Curaçao is approximately 418 inhabitants per square kilometer. The population is highly urbanized, with a significant concentration in and around the capital, Willemstad.

6. Labor markets are relatively small and specialized, which can result in skill shortages in certain sectors and increase dependency on a limited number of providers. These

structural labor market characteristics reinforce entry barriers and contribute to persistent concentration in several key markets.

B. *Density and Economic Structure*

7. The demographics mentioned above contribute to the prevalence of oligopolistic market structures and increase the risk of coordination or dominance. Economic activities in Curaçao are predominantly service-oriented. Manufacturing is limited, mostly due to geographic constraints, scale limitations, and high input costs. The government sector was restructured and reduced from 19% of GDP to 10% in 2012.

C. *GDP and Trade Balance*

8. Curaçao's nominal gross domestic product is estimated at approximately USD 3.6 billion in 2024. The economy is import-dependent, with a persistent trade deficit. Most consumer goods, intermediate inputs, and capital goods are imported. This dependence exposes domestic markets to external price fluctuations and supply chain disruptions, while simultaneously limiting the scope for domestic upstream competition

D. *Main Economic Sectors*

9. The main economic sectors include tourism, port and logistics services, financial services, construction, and retail trade. Tourism is a key driver of employment and foreign exchange earnings, while the port plays an important role in regional logistics. Several of these sectors are characterized by high fixed costs, network effects, or regulatory constraints, which, as a result, limit the number of viable market participants.

E. *Level of Market Concentration*

10. Many markets are highly concentrated due to scale effects and entry barriers, which are a result of the small size of the economy. In some cases, markets are dominated by one or two undertakings with substantial market power. While such concentration may be economically efficient in certain contexts, it also increases the risk of anticompetitive conduct, making effective competition law enforcement particularly important.

III. Legal Framework for Competition

A. *Name and Date of First Competition Law*

11. The National Ordinance on Competition (*Landsverordening inzake concurrentie*) was adopted in March 2016 and became effective on September 1, 2017. This legislation introduced a comprehensive competition law framework for the first time in Curaçao, marking a shift in economic regulation and market oversight.

B. *Subsequent Revisions or Updates*

12. Since its entry into force, the Ordinance has been subject to limited technical amendments, most notably in 2024. These amendments primarily addressed procedural clarifications

and technical improvements rather than substantive changes to the core competition law prohibitions. The relative stability of the legal framework has contributed to legal certainty and predictability for market participants.

C. *Scope of the Legal Framework*

13. The National Ordinance on Competition includes a cartel prohibition, which prohibits anticompetitive agreements and concerted practices between undertakings. Decisions by associations of undertakings may constitute a breach of the cartel prohibition. The Ordinance also prohibits abuse of a dominant position and establishes a mandatory merger notification regime. In addition, it provides the legal basis for competition advocacy, market studies, and advisory opinions to authorities on measures that may affect competition.

D. *Applicable Sectors*

14. The competition rules apply economy-wide, including to public and regulated sectors, unless explicitly exempted. This broad applicability reflects the legislator's intention to address competition distortions across all parts of the economy, including sectors where state involvement or regulation is significant. In practice, enforcement in regulated sectors often requires close coordination with sector-specific regulatory frameworks.

E. *Exemptions and Limitations*

15. The National Ordinance on Competition contains limited *de minimis* exceptions and allows for efficiency-based justifications under strict conditions. There is no general exemption for state-owned enterprises, although the application of competition law may take into account public interest considerations and statutory obligations. The informal sector remains difficult to address in practice, due to enforcement limitations rather than legal exclusions.

F. *Influence of European Union Competition Law*

16. The Curaçao competition regime draws heavily on concepts, terminology, and analytical frameworks derived from European Union competition law. This alignment enhances legal certainty and allows the Fair Trade Authority Curaçao to draw on extensive EU jurisprudence and international best practices. At the same time, enforcement is adapted to the specific economic and institutional realities of a small island economy.

IV. Institutional Structure

A. *Competition Authority*

17. The Fair Trade Authority Curaçao (FTAC) is the independent administrative authority responsible for the enforcement of the National Ordinance on Competition. The FTAC became operational in 2017, coinciding with the entry into force of the substantive competition law provisions. Its establishment marked the introduction of a dedicated

competition authority in Curaçao, designed specifically to address competition issues in a small island economy with structurally concentrated markets.

B. *Supervising Body and Legal Status*

18. The FTAC is established as an autonomous administrative authority (*zelfstandig bestuursorgaan*) operating at arm's length from the executive branch. Although the FTAC formally falls within the public administration, it performs its statutory tasks independently and without political instructions. This institutional design reflects the importance attached to independence, impartiality, and credibility in competition law enforcement, particularly in a small jurisdiction where economic and political interests may be closely intertwined.

C. *Organizational Structure*

19. The FTAC consists of a board composed of three members, including a chair and a vice-chair. Board members are appointed for a fixed term of four years and are selected based on their expertise in competition law, economics, or public administration. Board members can be reappointed once. The board is supported by a professional bureau staffed with legal and economic experts who are responsible for investigations, case preparation, advocacy activities, and advisory work. The bureau operates under the strategic direction of the board but enjoys operational autonomy in day-to-day enforcement activities.

D. *Budget and Resources*

20. The FTAC operates with a modest yearly budget (approx. USD 0.9 million) and a relatively small staff (7 full-time equivalents), reflecting the jurisdiction's limited scale. While this resource constraint poses challenges for extensive investigations and litigation, it has also shaped a pragmatic enforcement approach focused on prioritization, procedural efficiency, and the strategic use of guidance and advocacy. Resource limitations are a persistent feature of competition authorities in small economies and play a significant role in shaping enforcement choices.

E. *Enforcement Powers*

21. Under the National Ordinance on Competition, the FTAC is endowed with a range of investigative and enforcement powers. These include the authority to request information, conduct hearings, issue binding instructions, impose administrative fines, and levy periodic penalty payments. While the FTAC does not routinely conduct dawn raids, its formal powers are sufficient to ensure effective investigation, particularly when combined with strong procedural obligations imposed on undertakings.

F. *Additional Regulatory Mandates*

22. At present, the FTAC's mandate is limited to competition law enforcement and advocacy. However, policy discussions have long considered expanding the FTAC's responsibilities to include consumer protection. Such an expansion could create institutional synergies,

but it would also require careful consideration of resource implications and the potential impact on the authority's core competition enforcement function.

V. Enforcement and Sanctions

A. *Fines and Sanctions*

23. The National Ordinance on Competition empowers the FTAC to impose administrative fines of up to 10% of an undertaking's worldwide turnover. In addition to fines, the FTAC may issue binding instructions requiring undertakings to cease unlawful conduct or take corrective measures. Periodic penalty payments may be imposed to ensure compliance with FTAC decisions. This toolkit provides flexibility, allowing the authority to tailor sanctions to the nature and seriousness of the infringement.

B. *Enforcement Strategy and Practice*

24. In the initial years following its establishment, the FTAC adopted a cautious and guidance-oriented enforcement strategy. Given the novelty of competition law in Curaçao, the authority placed strong emphasis on awareness-raising, compliance, and voluntary adjustment of market behavior. Over time, as familiarity with the competition rules increased, enforcement gradually became more assertive, particularly in cases involving procedural non-compliance or repeated infringements.

C. *Procedural Enforcement and Compliance*

25. Procedural enforcement has played a particularly important role in Curaçao's competition regime. The FTAC has actively enforced obligations relating to cooperation, information provision, and merger notification. Sanctions for failure to cooperate or to comply with information requests have been instrumental in establishing the Authority's credibility and ensuring the effectiveness of investigations. In a small economy with limited investigative resources, procedural compliance is essential to substantive enforcement.

D. *Judicial Review and Legal Certainty*

26. Decisions of the FTAC are subject to judicial review by the administrative courts. Several enforcement decisions, including those imposing fines for non-cooperation, have been upheld on appeal. Judicial confirmation of the FTAC's powers has strengthened legal certainty and reinforced the legitimacy of the competition enforcement framework. The availability of judicial review also ensures that enforcement remains subject to proportionality and due process safeguards.

E. *Private Enforcement*

27. Although private enforcement through civil damages actions is legally possible under general civil law principles, it has not yet played a significant role in practice. The limited size of claims, combined with litigation costs and a relatively low level of awareness, may explain the absence of private competition litigation. As the competition regime

matures, private enforcement could potentially complement public enforcement, but this remains a long-term prospect.

VI. Noteworthy Cases

28. The following cases illustrate how competition law in Curaçao evolved from guidance-based intervention to firm procedural and substantive enforcement in a small economy.

A. *Guidance-Based Enforcement in the Early Phase of FTAC: Professional Associations in Healthcare and Construction*

29. In the initial years following the entry into force of the National Ordinance on Competition, the FTAC deliberately adopted a phased enforcement strategy in which guidance and voluntary compliance by undertakings and professional associations played a central role.

1. Facts

30. In the initial years following the entry into force of the National Ordinance on Competition in 2017, the FTAC dealt with several cases involving professional associations in the healthcare and construction sectors. These sectors had long operated under regimes of price regulation or strong self-regulation, where collective tariff setting and standardized commercial conditions were common practice.

31. The FTAC identified infringements of the cartel prohibition by professional associations of architects and engineers, general practitioners, and medical specialists, all of which had engaged in collective price setting or coordination of commercial conditions. Rather than immediately imposing sanctions, the FTAC opted to address these practices through guidance and dialogue.

2. Legal Issue

32. The central legal issue was not whether collective tariff setting and standardized conditions imposed by professional associations constituted prohibited decisions of associations of undertakings under the cartel prohibition. The main issue was how to enforce the recently introduced competition law, particularly in sectors where infringements resulted from legacy practices, sometimes condoned or encouraged by the government, rather than deliberate anticompetitive intent.

3. Outcome

33. In all cases, the FTAC formally established infringements of the cartel prohibition. However, instead of imposing administrative fines, it engaged in guidance-based enforcement. Through meetings, written guidance, and follow-up communication, the professional associations withdrew collective tariff decisions, amended statutes and professional conditions, and explicitly confirmed that pricing decisions would henceforth be taken independently by individual members. The FTAC closed the cases without fines, citing the novelty of the legal framework, the transitional regulatory context, and the effectiveness of voluntary compliance.

4. Impact or Precedent Set

34. These cases illustrate the FTAC's initial enforcement philosophy, in which guidance and voluntary compliance were used as primary tools to achieve rapid behavioral change in a small economy. At the same time, the formal decisions left no ambiguity as to the illegality of collective price setting by professional associations, while safeguarding those associations' legal remedies of the professional associations. The cases set an important precedent for a phased approach to enforcement, demonstrating how competition authorities can combine legal clarity with proportionality during the early implementation of a new competition regime.

B. *Failure to Notify a Notifiable Concentration: The EY–KDC Case*

35. One of the most consequential enforcement actions taken by the Fair Trade Authority Curaçao concerns the failure to notify a notifiable concentration in the professional services sector, arising from the transition of audit and assurance activities from KPMG Dutch Caribbean (operating under the name KDC Interim) to Ernst & Young Dutch Caribbean. This case represents the first fully litigated merger notification infringement in Curaçao and has had a significant impact on merger control enforcement.

1. Facts

36. Following extensive media reporting in late 2018 regarding a possible "merger" between KPMG Dutch Caribbean and Ernst & Young, the FTAC reminded the parties of the merger notification obligation and subsequently initiated supervisory inquiries by sending a request for information. Despite these warnings, no notification was submitted. After reviewing the documents received, the FTAC concluded that Ernst & Young had acquired control over a substantial part of KDC's economic activity – specifically its client portfolio and the employees servicing those clients – through a series of contractual arrangements and factual measures implemented before the formal termination of the underlying conditional agreements.

2. Legal Issue

37. In its decision of 15 June 2021, the FTAC held that these arrangements constituted a concentration within the meaning of the National Ordinance on Competition, even though the conditional agreements were later dissolved. The FTAC emphasized that, in line with EU competition law concepts, a concentration is deemed to be "brought about" once transactions are undertaken that contribute to a durable change in control, regardless of whether formal completion is ultimately achieved. Because the combined market share of Ernst & Young and the acquired KDC activities exceeded the statutory 30% threshold in the relevant market for audit and assurance services in Curaçao, the concentration was subject to mandatory prior notification. The FTAC therefore imposed an administrative fine of XCG 400,000 for failure to notify the concentration before its implementation.

3. Outcome

38. The decision was challenged before the Court of First Instance of Curaçao, which delivered its judgment on 25 August 2023. The court upheld the FTAC's decision in full. The Court of Appeal subsequently affirmed the judgment of the Court of First Instance, thereby definitively confirming the FTAC's approach. The appellate court endorsed the lower court's reliance on EU merger control jurisprudence and reiterated that the merger notification obligation is triggered at the moment parties begin implementing measures that contribute to a lasting change in control.

4. Significance and Precedent Value

39. This case has had a profound impact on merger control enforcement by the FTAC. It clarified that the notification obligation is not a mere formality, but a substantive procedural safeguard designed to allow the competition authority to monitor structural changes in a small and highly concentrated economy. The judgments firmly establish that "gun-jumping" concepts, as developed in EU law, are fully applicable in Curaçao, and that early integration steps – particularly in service-based industries – can constitute implementation of a concentration.

40. From an institutional perspective, the case significantly strengthened the FTAC's authority and credibility. It demonstrated that merger notification rules are enforceable in practice. After this case, the FTAC noticed a structural increase in merger notifications and requests for pre-notification meetings.

C. *Failure to Cooperate with Information Requests: The DCTA and Supermarket Cases*

41. This line of cases concerns the failures by undertakings and individuals to comply with information requests issued by the FTAC in the exercise of its supervisory powers.

1. Facts

42. The first fully litigated case arose in the taxi sector, where the Dutch Caribbean Taxi Association (DCTA) refused to provide organizational and decision-making information requested in the context of an investigation into possible collective price coordination. Despite reminders and a formal demand, DCTA declined to cooperate.

43. Building on this case, the FTAC later encountered similar non-cooperation in the food retail sector during an investigation into potential price coordination for specific coffee products. Five supermarkets failed to respond adequately to information requests, reminder letters, and formal demands. In subsequent cases, the FTAC also addressed deliberate obstruction by individual directors and managers who were in a position to provide information but failed to do so.

2. Legal Issue

44. The central legal issue was whether the statutory duty to cooperate with FTAC investigations constitutes an autonomous and enforceable obligation, independent of

any finding of a substantive competition law infringement. The cases also addressed the personal scope of this obligation, including whether it applies not only to undertakings and associations but also to a natural person.

45. More broadly, these cases tested the effectiveness of the FTAC's investigative powers as described in the National Ordinance on Competition and their role within the overall enforcement system.

3. Outcome

46. In the *DCTA* case, the FTAC found a breach of the duty to cooperate and imposed an administrative fine, emphasizing that effective supervision depends on timely and complete access to information. The decision was upheld on appeal.

47. The FTAC subsequently imposed fines on five supermarkets for similar failures to cooperate. All supermarkets lodged objections with the FTAC; in four cases, the FTAC reduced the fines during administrative reconsideration based on mitigating factors such as later procedural conduct and proportionality of the fine given the size of the company, while maintaining the infringement finding. In the remaining case, the fine was upheld in full due to the continued refusal to supply information. Two supermarkets filed an appeal with the court. The court corroborated the reasoning and the decision of the FTAC

48. In addition, the FTAC imposed personal administrative fines on individual directors and managers who deliberately obstructed investigations, making clear that the cooperation obligation extends beyond corporate entities. In these two cases, the imposed fine and underlying reasoning were also upheld on appeal.

4. Impact or Precedent Set

49. Together, these cases established the duty to cooperate as a central and enforceable pillar of Curaçao's competition enforcement regime. They clarified that non-cooperation constitutes a serious procedural infringement and that investigative powers apply broadly to undertakings, associations, and individuals. The cases demonstrate how procedural enforcement can compensate for limited resources in a small and highly concentrated economy, ensuring the effectiveness, credibility, and authority of competition law enforcement in Curaçao.

D. *Abuse of Dominance in the Healthcare Sector*

50. This case arose from complaints by general practitioners concerning access to the centrally organized out-of-hours general practitioner service. The out-of-hours general practitioner services are provided by Huisartsenpost Curaçao (HAP), which is managed by Stichting Primary Care Curaçao (SPCC). This centrally organized out-of-hours general practitioner service is for urgent health complaints that cannot wait until the next working day, but are not life-threatening situations. Participation in this general practitioner service is practically indispensable for general practitioners, as it ensures continuity of care during evenings, nights and weekends.

1. Facts

51. SPCC imposed a contractual condition requiring general practitioners wishing to participate in the HAP to use a specific general practitioner information system supplied by

a single software provider. General practitioners using alternative systems could only participate if they switched systems, which involved significant costs and operational consequences.

2. Legal Issue

52. The central legal issue was whether SPCC qualified as an undertaking holding a dominant position and, if so, whether the imposition of an exclusive software requirement constituted an abuse of dominance. The case examined the extent to which a dominant entity operating in a publicly funded and regulated healthcare context bears a special responsibility to avoid conduct that restricts competition, particularly where such conduct affects adjacent markets such as healthcare IT.

3. Outcome

53. The FTAC found that SPCC engaged in economic activity and held a dominant position, given the essential nature of access to the HAP and the high level of participation by general practitioners. While the use of a digital information system was considered objectively justified, the FTAC concluded that mandating the exclusive use of a single system went beyond what was necessary.

54. By imposing exclusivity, SPCC applied an unfair contractual condition and foreclosed competition in the healthcare IT market. The FTAC therefore found an abuse of dominance and issued a binding instruction requiring SPCC to enable interoperability and ensure freedom of choice of information systems, without imposing a fine.

4. Impact or Precedent Set

55. This case marks the first abuse of dominance decision in Curaçao. The decision established that public funding or regulatory objectives do not shield dominant entities from competition law. Due to media coverage of this case, the FTAC also saw an increased awareness of potentially abusive behavior by large companies. This resulted in new complaints and tip-offs that sparked new investigations.

E. *Impact and Precedent Value*

56. Together, these cases have played a crucial role in shaping Curaçao's competition enforcement culture. They have clarified legal standards, strengthened procedural discipline, and demonstrated that competition law is a practical and enforceable tool, even in a small economy. The focus on strategically selected cases has allowed the FTAC to achieve meaningful impact despite limited resources.

VII. Merger Control

A. *Is Merger Control Applicable?*

57. Curaçao operates a mandatory merger notification regime under the National Ordinance on Competition. Undertakings that intend to implement a concentration meeting the statutory thresholds are required to notify the transaction to the Fair Trade Authority Curaçao prior to completion. The introduction of merger notification obligations was

intended to provide oversight of structural changes in a small economy where even a single transaction can have a significant impact on market structure.

B. *Notification Thresholds*

58. Under the National Ordinance on Competition, a concentration is subject to mandatory prior notification to the Fair Trade Authority Curaçao if either of the following thresholds is met:

- Turnover threshold: The combined net turnover of the undertakings concerned exceeds XCG 125 million (approximately USD 70 million) in the calendar year preceding the concentration, and at least two of the undertakings concerned each achieved a net turnover of at least XCG 15 million (approximately USD 8.4 million) in Curaçao in that year.
- Market share threshold: The undertakings concerned together hold a combined market share of 30% or more in any relevant market in Curaçao, or a substantial part thereof.

59. These thresholds are set out as alternative notification criteria, meaning that meeting either the turnover-based threshold or the market share-based threshold is sufficient to trigger the notification obligation.

C. *Practical Application and Structural Challenges*

60. In practice, the turnover thresholds play a limited role in Curaçao's merger control regime. Given the small size of the economy and the prevalence of relatively low domestic turnover levels – even for structurally significant undertakings – many transactions with potentially substantial competitive impact do not meet the statutory turnover thresholds. As a result, the market share threshold has become the primary gateway for merger notification, rather than a supplementary safeguard.

61. This has important practical implications for enforcement. Because market share information is rarely readily available or uncontested in Curaçao, the FTAC is required to conduct market research in almost every notified merger in order to assess whether the 30% threshold is met. This entails defining the relevant product and geographic markets, identifying competitors, and estimating market shares – often on the basis of limited or fragmented data. For a competition authority operating with modest resources, this significantly increases the administrative burden of merger control.

62. From a comparative perspective, this situation contrasts with the design logic of merger control systems in larger jurisdictions, where turnover thresholds typically function as the primary notification trigger, ensuring legal certainty and predictability for undertakings, while market share thresholds serve as a back-up mechanism to capture atypical transactions. Examples include acquisitions of nascent competitors or so-called killer acquisitions, where turnover may be low but competitive significance is high.

D. *Review Timeframes and Procedure*

63. The National Ordinance on Competition provides for defined review periods within which the FTAC assesses merger notifications. The review is primarily formal in nature

and focuses on verifying whether the notification thresholds are met and whether the transaction has been properly notified. The procedure also allows the FTAC to request additional information from the notifying parties, which can contribute to a better understanding of market dynamics.

E. *Substantive Assessment and Powers*

64. At present, the FTAC does not have the power to prohibit mergers or impose remedies based on a substantive competitive effects assessment. As a result, merger control in Curaçao functions primarily as a monitoring and transparency mechanism rather than a full-fledged substantive control regime. While this limitation reflects legislative choices and resource considerations, it also raises questions about the adequacy of merger control in the context of increasing concentration.

F. *Practical Experience and Policy Debate*

65. In practice, merger notifications have proven valuable in providing the FTAC with insights into structural developments across various sectors, including professional services, telecommunications, and tourism-related markets. These insights inform both advocacy and enforcement priorities. There is ongoing policy debate as to whether Curaçao's merger control regime should evolve toward a system with substantive assessment powers, particularly in light of the structural characteristics of small markets.

VIII. Advocacy and Policy Initiatives

A. *Outreach to Businesses and Consumers*

66. Advocacy is a central pillar of the FTAC's mandate and is particularly important in a small economy where competition law is a relatively recent development. The FTAC actively engages in outreach activities aimed at businesses, sector associations, public institutions, and consumers. These activities include presentations, workshops, and direct engagement with stakeholders to explain competition law principles and compliance obligations.

B. *Policy Papers and Guidelines*

67. The FTAC has issued various guidance documents and policy statements, including guidance on cooperation between competitors. These documents provide practical directions for undertakings on how to assess their conduct in light of competition law and help reduce legal uncertainty. Soft law instruments play a significant role in shaping market behavior, especially in an environment where formal enforcement resources are limited.

C. *Sectoral Studies and Market Inquiries*

68. Sectoral studies and market inquiries are important tools for identifying structural competition problems that may not be addressed effectively through individual enforcement cases. The FTAC has conducted market studies in sectors such as food retail and

financial services. These studies aim to identify barriers to entry, regulatory constraints, and market practices that may hinder effective competition.

D. *Education and Capacity Building*

69. The FTAC places strong emphasis on education and capacity building, both internally and externally. Internally, staff members participate in international training programs and workshops to enhance expertise in competition law and economics. Externally, the FTAC contributes to broader capacity building by sharing knowledge with stakeholders and promoting a culture of competition compliance within the business community.

IX. Regional and International Cooperation

A. *Regional Cooperation*

70. Given the openness of Curaçao's economy and the regional scope of many markets, regional cooperation is essential. The FTAC maintains cooperative relationships with regional organizations, including the CARICOM Competition Commission. Such cooperation facilitates the exchange of information and best practices and helps address competition issues with cross-border dimensions.

B. *Bilateral Cooperation*

71. Bilateral cooperation plays an important role in strengthening institutional capacity. In particular, formal cooperation with the Dutch Authority for Consumers and Markets has been valuable in terms of training, technical assistance, and comparative analysis. This relationship allows the FTAC to draw on the experience of more established authorities while adapting lessons to local circumstances. There is also frequent bilateral cooperation with the more recently established Aruba Fair Trade Authority.

C. *Participation in Global Networks*

72. The FTAC is a member of the International Competition Network (ICN). Participation in ICN working groups and conferences enables the FTAC to engage with competition authorities from around the world, contribute to discussions on best practices, and stay informed about developments in competition policy and enforcement. The FTAC is associated with Grupo de Agencias de Competencia de América. For a small authority, such participation is an important means of maintaining expertise and legitimacy. The FTAC also participates in activities of the Organisation for Economic Co-operation and Development (OECD) Regional Centre for Competition, hosted by the Peruvian Authority INDECOPI.

D. *Importance of International Engagement*

73. International cooperation is not merely complementary but essential for effective competition enforcement in a small economy. Through regional and global engagement, the FTAC mitigates resource constraints, enhances analytical capacity, and ensures that its enforcement approach remains aligned with internationally accepted standards.

X. Challenges and Country-Specific Features

A. *Small Market Size and High Concentration*

74. One of the defining characteristics of Curaçao's economy is its very small market size. The limited scale of demand means that many markets can sustain only a small number of efficient operators. As a result, high levels of concentration are not an exception but rather a structural feature of the economy. In some sectors, monopoly or duopoly structures may be economically rational from an efficiency perspective, yet they simultaneously increase the risk of abuse of market power or coordinated behavior. Competition law enforcement in this context must, therefore, distinguish carefully between unavoidable concentration and anticompetitive conduct.

B. *Dominance of Public Enterprises and Regulation*

75. Public sector involvement remains significant in several key sectors of Curaçao's economy, either through state ownership, exclusive rights, or extensive regulation. This creates complex interactions between competition law and sector-specific regulation. In some cases, regulatory frameworks may unintentionally restrict entry or shield incumbents from competitive pressure. The FTAC must navigate these overlaps carefully, ensuring respect for statutory mandates while advocating for regulatory reforms that promote competition where feasible.

C. *Dependence on Imports and Foreign Investment*

76. Curaçao's economy is highly dependent on imports and foreign investment. While import competition can discipline domestic market power, transport costs, scale effects, and logistical constraints may limit the effectiveness of this discipline in practice. Foreign investment is often essential to economic development, but it can also lead to further concentration if acquisitions reduce the number of independent market players. These dynamics require competition enforcement that is sensitive to development goals while remaining vigilant against anticompetitive outcomes.

D. *Limited Resources and Enforcement Capacity*

77. As is common in small economies, the FTAC operates with limited financial and human resources. These constraints affect the scope and depth of investigations and necessitate careful prioritization. Rather than pursuing a large number of complex cases, the FTAC focuses on strategically selected matters with the greatest potential impact. Procedural enforcement, advocacy, and sector studies are used to complement formal enforcement and extend the authority's influence beyond individual cases.

E. *Balancing Competition and Broader Public Interests*

78. Competition law enforcement in Curaçao must take into account broader public interests, such as continuity of supply, employment, and economic resilience. In small economies, the failure or exit of a single undertaking can have significant social and economic consequences. The challenge lies in enforcing competition rules rigorously while

remaining proportionate and attentive to these broader considerations. This balancing exercise is a recurring theme in both enforcement practice and policy debates.

XI. Author's Perspective

79. From the perspective of Curaçao as a small island economy, the experience with competition law demonstrates that effective enforcement does not require weaker rules, but rather appropriately adapted instruments and expectations. The core prohibitions against cartels and abuse of dominance are as relevant in small markets as they are in larger economies. However, enforcement strategies must be tailored to local realities, including high concentration, limited resources, and close-knit business communities.

80. Procedural enforcement has proven to be a particularly powerful tool. By strictly enforcing cooperation obligations, information requests, and notification requirements, the FTAC has been able to establish credibility and ensure compliance even where substantive investigations are resource-intensive. Advocacy and guidance play an equally important role, fostering a culture of compliance and helping undertakings understand their responsibilities under competition law.

81. The Curaçao experience also highlights the importance of institutional independence and international cooperation. Alignment with European Union competition law concepts has enhanced legal certainty and facilitated knowledge transfer, while participation in regional and global networks has helped mitigate resource constraints. Overall, Curaçao illustrates that competition law can function effectively in small economies when institutional design, enforcement priorities, and policy objectives are carefully aligned.

XII. References and Resources

A. *Laws and Regulations*

- National Ordinance on Competition [*Landsverordening inzake concurrentie*] (Mar. 29, 2016), as amended, https://ftac.cw/en/regulations/national-ordinance-on-competition/.

B. *Case Law and Decisions*

- Published decisions and binding instructions of the Fair Trade Authority Curaçao are available on the FTAC website.

C. *Public Reports and Policy Documents*

- Annual Reports of the Fair Trade Authority Curaçao (2017–2025) (in Dutch), available on the FTAC website.
- FTAC guidelines and policy papers on cooperation between competitors and enforcement priorities (in Dutch), available on the FTAC website.

D. *International and Academic Sources*

- ICN, Recommended Practices and Reports, https://www.internationalcompetitionnetwork.org/document-library/.
- UNCTAD publications on competition law and policy in small and developing economies, https://unctad.org/publications.

82. To learn more about Fair Trade Authority Curaçao (FTAC):
    - Website: https://ftac.cw/
    - Contact: info@ftac.cw

Dominican Republic

María Elena Vásquez Taveras
President of the board of directors of ProCompetencia

I. Overview

1. The Dominican Republic is a sovereign state located in the Caribbean, characterized by a civilian, republican, democratic, and representative form of government.[1] The country occupies the eastern two-thirds of the island of Hispaniola and is the second-largest nation in the Greater Antilles archipelago, after Cuba.

2. The Dominican Republic is bordered by the Atlantic Ocean to the north and the Caribbean Sea to the south. It shares its western border with Haiti, while the Mona Passage separates it from Puerto Rico to the east. The country is located in the Northern Hemisphere, south of the Tropic of Cancer, between latitudes 17° 36′ and 19° 58′ N and longitudes 68° 19′ and 72° 01′ W.

3. With an area of 48,442 square kilometers, the Dominican Republic enjoys a strategic geographic location that has historically facilitated both the development of international trade and tourism. According to the 2022 National Population and Housing Census, the country has a population of 10,773,983 inhabitants, representing a population density of approximately 225 inhabitants per square kilometer.[2] The population is concentrated mainly in the cities of Santo Domingo, the National District (seat of the national authorities), and Santiago de los Caballeros. Spanish is the official language of the country.

II. Demographics and Economy

4. The Dominican Republic ranks as the seventh-largest economy in Latin America, with a nominal gross domestic product (GDP) of USD 124.3 billion in 2024, according to the International Monetary Fund (IMF).[3] Sustained economic growth of around 5%, largely driven by foreign direct investment (FDI), has enabled the country to attract capital and maintain macroeconomic stability. This economic environment underscores the importance of competition law in regulating key sectors and ensuring equitable market participation.

5. The Dominican Republic's economic structure, dominated by services (59.8% of GDP), followed by industry (28.7%) and agriculture (4.5%),[4] shapes the application of competition law across sectors. Continued macroeconomic stability and market reforms have attracted investors, underlining the significance of fair competition in promoting sustainable development and consumer welfare.

6. The tourism sector plays a fundamental economic role, accounting for approximately 7% of GDP in 2023.[5] In 2024, record revenue and tourist arrivals generated significant

---

1 Constitution of the Dominican Republic, art. 4.

2 National Statistics Office (ONE), General Report X National Population and Housing Census (2022) (in Spanish), https://www.one.gob.do/media/ahziolzm/informe-general-xcnpv-2022-digital.pdf.

3 Press Release, Int'l Monetary Fund, IMF Executive Board Concludes 2025 Article IV Consultation with the Dominican Republic (Nov. 18, 2025), https://www.imf.org/es/news/articles/2025/11/18/pr-25378-dominican-republic-imf-executive-board-concludes-2025-article-iv-consultation.

4 CIA, The World Factbook: Dominican Republic (2026), https://www.cia.gov/the-world-factbook/countries/dominican-republic/.

5 *Real Sector Statistics*, Central Bank of the Dominican Republic (in Spanish), https://www.bancentral.gov.do/a/d/2533-sector-real.

resources (USD 10,972.4 million and 11.2 million tourists),[6] reinforcing the need for effective competition law to ensure fair practices and prevent dominance in this vital sector.

7. Meanwhile, the Dominican Republic's free trade zones continue their transformation toward higher value added and more diversified activities, with notable growth in high-tech and specialized sectors, particularly medical and surgical equipment. In 2024, the free trade zones generated exports of USD 8,417.2 million,[7] consolidating this sector as a key driver of the country's productive transformation and competitive integration into international markets. Additionally, remittances reached USD 10,756.0 million in 2024, reinforcing their role as a pillar of stability for foreign exchange earnings and Dominican household consumption.

8. The external sector underpins the Dominican Republic's economic growth as tourism, free trade zones, and remittances generate foreign exchange and drive domestic consumption. Participation in global value chains, aided by trade agreements, increases the significance of robust competition policy to maintain competitiveness and prevent anticompetitive behavior as the economy becomes more interconnected.

9. However, structural challenges remain that require attention. Several international studies have identified market concentration levels above the regional average in strategic sectors such as food processing, fuel production, telecommunications, and financial services, which can limit consumer choice, reduce competitive pricing, and hinder overall economic growth. According to the Organisation for Economic Co-operation and Development (OECD) analysis, these concentration levels may be linked to the need to strengthen institutional capacity for the effective implementation of competition policy, as well as to regulatory barriers that limit the entry of new competitors into the market.[8]

III. Legal Framework for Competition

10. The first traces of Dominican initiatives in the area of competition emerged in 1997 with the presentation of the first draft of the Market Regulation Code, which was later revised in a second version in 2001. This initial effort marked the start of the country's first institutional development initiatives to defend competition.

11. The signing of the Dominican Republic–Central America–United States Free Trade Agreement (DR-CAFTA) in 2004 significantly increased the importance of robust economic competition regulations, as the Treaty obligated signatory countries to adopt competition law frameworks. As a result of this international commitment and the need to modernize the national regulatory framework, Law No. 42-08, the General Law for the Defense of Competition, was enacted on January 16, 2008, and published in Official Gazette No. 10458. This legislation represented a historic

---

6 Central Bank of the Dominican Republic, Report on the Dominican Economy (Jan. Dec. 2024) (in Spanish), https://www.bancentral.gov.do/Publicaciones/Consulta.

7 *Id.*

8 OECD, Multi-dimensional Review of the Dominican Republic: Towards Greater Well-Being for All 89, OECD Development Pathways (2022), https://doi.org/10.1787/560c12bf-en.

milestone, becoming the first comprehensive legal instrument for the defense of competition in the Dominican Republic and marking a turning point in the country's competition law.[9]

12. Article 1 of Law No. 42-08 clearly establishes the purpose of the Dominican competition regime by stipulating that the law aims, as a matter of public order, "to promote and defend effective competition in order to increase economic efficiency in the markets for goods and services, thereby generating benefits and value for consumers and users of these goods and services within the national territory."[10] This normative formulation is particularly important because it defines not only the law's instrumental purpose – the promotion and defense of effective competition – but also its ultimate objective – the generation of benefits and value for consumers and users.

13. The wording of article 1 demonstrates that the Dominican legislator adopted a conception of competition law that aligns fundamentally with the consumer welfare standard, a doctrinal approach that has shaped the interpretation and application of competition rules in developed jurisdictions, particularly in the United States since the 1970s and in the European Union progressively since the 1990s. This conceptual approach maintains that the central purpose of antitrust legislation should be the maximization of consumer welfare, understood primarily in terms of economic efficiency that translates into lower prices, higher-quality products and services, greater variety of available options, and the promotion of innovation.

14. The explicit emphasis on economic efficiency as a means to benefit consumers distinguishes Law No. 42-08 from alternative conceptions of competition law that prioritize different or complementary objectives. In particular, it distances itself from structuralist approaches that consider the decentralization of economic power and the protection of the opportunity to compete as values in themselves, independent of their effects on consumer welfare. Likewise, it differs from models that incorporate multiple objectives, such as protecting employment, promoting domestic industry, correcting regional inequalities, or fostering national champions, thereby subordinating all these potential objectives to the guiding principle of consumer benefit.

15. This focus on consumer welfare as the central criterion for evaluating business conduct has fundamental practical implications for the application of the law. It means that the competition authority (ProCompetencia) must assess reported practices not only on their effects on specific competitors or on market structure, but fundamentally by considering whether these practices harm consumers through higher prices than those that would prevail under competitive conditions, reduced quality, limited options, or stifled innovation. It also implies that certain practices that could harm individual competitors may not be sanctionable if they simultaneously generate efficiencies that benefit consumers, a principle that finds concrete expression in article 7 of the law, which authorizes the evaluation of pro-competitive effects and economic efficiency in cases of abuse of dominant position.

---

9 National Commission for the Defense of Competition (ProCompetencia), *Cronológico Pro-Competencia* [*Chronological ProCompetencia*], Anuario de Competencia 2023, 14–15 (2023).

10 Our translation.

16. Notwithstanding the foregoing, Law No. 42-08 also incorporates elements that qualify this predominant focus on consumer welfare with broader considerations. Article 5 establishes per se prohibitions for certain categories of horizontal agreements between competitors, particularly those related to price fixing and manipulation of public tenders, without requiring proof of concrete anticompetitive effects on consumers. This approach reflects the recognition that certain conduct is so inherently harmful to the competitive process that it justifies an absolute presumption of illegality, an approach that aligns with the tradition of North American competition law regarding hardcore cartels. Likewise, the inclusion in the law of an entire chapter dedicated to unfair competition (arts. 10 to 12) incorporates considerations of fairness in commercial practices that transcend the purely economic analysis of consumer welfare, venturing into areas more characteristic of continental European conceptions of competition law that emphasize the protection of fair trade as an autonomous value.

17. Taken together, these provisions demonstrate that the Dominican legislature designed a competition regime with a predominant focus on consumer welfare, although complemented by rules on illegality by object and regulatory categories that address market fairness concerns. However, despite its enactment in 2008, Law No. 42 08 did not enter into force until 2017, when the first executive directorate of ProCompetencia was appointed. This delay was due to the law itself stipulating the formal appointment of the members of the board of directors and the executive directorate of the institution as a condition for its entry into force, thereby formally initiating the operation of the Dominican competition authority.

18. Law No. 42-08 applies to all natural and legal persons, public or private, that conduct economic or commercial activities within the territory of the Dominican Republic, as well as to conduct that, even if carried out outside the country, produces or may produce effects on the national market, as established in article 3 of said law. The regulations establish three main categories of prohibited conduct that constitute violations of the Dominican competition law.

19. First, article 5 of the law prohibits concerted practices and anticompetitive agreements between competing economic agents, specifically:

- agreeing on prices, discounts, extraordinary charges or other sales conditions, as well as the exchange of information with these same effects;
- arranging or coordinating bids or refusals to bid in tenders, competitions and public auctions;
- dividing, distributing or allocating market segments by specifying time, space, suppliers or clientele;
- limiting the production, distribution or marketing of goods or the provision of services; and
- eliminating competitors from the market or limiting their access to it, whether as buyers or sellers.

20. Secondly, article 6 of the law prohibits conduct that constitutes an abuse of a dominant position in a relevant market and is likely to create unjustified barriers to third parties. Such conduct includes:

- making a sale conditional on the buyer refraining from purchasing or distributing products from competing companies;
- unjustifiably imposing prices and sales conditions on resellers;
- conditioning sales on the purchase of an additional good or service other than the main one;
- subjecting sales to not contracting with third parties;
- unjustifiably imposing to sell or provide available goods and services when no alternative suppliers exist in the relevant market; and
- applying unequal conditions for equivalent services that place competitors at a disadvantage without commercial justification.

21. Third, articles 10 and 11 of the law regulate acts of unfair competition, defined as any behavior contrary to good faith and commercial ethics that aims to illegitimately divert demand. The regulations specifically list:
    - acts of deception through false indications or misleading advertising;
    - acts of confusion that may be associated with the activity or products of third parties;
    - improper public comparison that is not objectively verifiable or contains false statements;
    - systematic imitation of a competitor's commercial practices;
    - unauthorized appropriation or disclosure of trade secrets;
    - non-compliance with regulations that generates significant competitive advantages;
    - denigration through the dissemination of news that undermines the reputation of third parties; and
    - intentional inducement to breach of contract for anticompetitive purposes.

22. In matters of unfair competition, article 12 of the law establishes a specific regime that allows those affected to resort directly to the courts, and, if the administrative procedure before the competition authority is chosen, the authority is limited to ordering the cessation of the unfair conduct, without the power to impose pecuniary sanctions.

23. Subsequently, in the 2010 constitutional reform, following the enactment of the Competition Law, the new Constitution of the Dominican Republic established a solid legal framework for the protection of free competition through three fundamental dimensions. First, article 50 enshrines free competition as an inherent guarantee of free enterprise, placing it within the catalog of economic and social rights. This provision recognizes that effective competition constitutes a fundamental right in the national economic order. Second, article 217 defines the Dominican economic model as a social-market economy, establishing free competition as one of its guiding principles. This constitutional characterization determines the State's approach to regulating markets and promoting competitive conditions.

24. Third, the Constitution imposes on the State the obligation to adopt the necessary measures to protect free competition against anticompetitive practices. This protective dimension makes the protection of competition a constitutional duty of the State, providing the legal basis for the creation of specialized institutions and regulations in

this area. Together, these three dimensions form the constitutional pillar upon which the entire competition protection system in the Dominican Republic is structured.[11]

25. More than a decade after the enactment of the competition law, the Regulations for the Application of Law No. 42-08, General Law for the Defense of Competition, were approved by Decree No. 252-20, which represented an important advance in the institutional development of the country's competition protection system by providing clarity on fundamental procedural aspects.

26. In 2025, the Dominican Republic approved its national competition policy through Decree No. 196-25, dated April 10, 2025,[12] becoming the first country in Latin America to adopt such an instrument. This policy establishes a comprehensive strategic framework aimed at promoting sustainable economic growth, strengthening a level playing field in markets, and consolidating a culture of competition as a cross-cutting principle of public action.

27. The policy involves 34 state institutions and is structured around three fundamental strategic pillars, each with specific action guidelines to ensure effective, measurable implementation. Its implementation covers priority sectors such as agriculture, industry, services, and energy, guaranteeing a cross-cutting impact across the entire national economy.

28. In the field of competition law, the Dominican Republic presents a significant institutional peculiarity: it coexists with specialized sectoral regulators that exercise authority over specific markets. This dual configuration of the regulatory system means that, in addition to ProCompetencia as the general competition authority, there are specialized agencies with regulatory and supervisory powers in specific sectors of the national economy, as provided for in article 16 of the Implementing Regulations, and to comply with the provisions of article 69 of Law No. 42-08.

29. Building on this institutional foundation, the evolution of the Dominican Republic's competition law framework has been characterized by progressive advancements that have strengthened the system's institutional and regulatory base. However, the effectiveness of any competition regime depends not only on the existence of formal regulatory frameworks but also on its capacity to adapt to international standards and respond to the increasingly complex dynamics of contemporary markets. Aware of this reality and the potential for improvement presented by Law No. 42-08, ProCompetencia made the strategic decision to subject the country's legal framework and competition policies to a rigorous external evaluation process through a peer review conducted by specialized international organizations.

A. *Peer Review of the Dominican Republic*

30. During the 21st Latin American and Caribbean Competition Forum, held on September 28, 2023, in Quito, Ecuador, the Dominican Republic formally presented its regulatory

---

[11] María Elena Vásquez Taveras, *La dimensión social del derecho de la competencia en la República Dominicana* [*The Social Dimension of Competition Law in the Dominican Republic*], ANUARIO DE COMPETENCIA 2023, 83 (2023).

[12] Decree No. 196-25, dated Apr. 10, 2025, National Competition Policy of the Dominican Republic.

and institutional framework for competition to be evaluated through a peer review mechanism. This strategic initiative by ProCompetencia stemmed from the recognition that, while Law No. 42-08 represented a fundamental step forward for the country, there are opportunities to strengthen it that require a rigorous external technical evaluation and specialized recommendations for modernization and alignment with contemporary international standards.

31. Peer review is an institutional evaluation mechanism based on a state's sovereign right to submit its legal frameworks and public policies to substantive technical scrutiny by other members of the international community specializing in economic competition. This peer review process identifies regulatory gaps, institutional weaknesses, and areas for improvement by comparing them with international standards and best practices observed in other jurisdictions. As a result of this evaluation, the reviewing international organizations issued a series of technical recommendations to strengthen the competition system of the country being evaluated.

32. In 2024, the OECD and the Inter-American Development Bank (IDB) jointly published the findings of their peer review of the Dominican Republic's competition law and policy. This document constitutes a comprehensive technical diagnosis of the Dominican competition system and formulates recommendations to modernize legislation and strengthen the institutional capacity of the Dominican Republic's competition authority. The main recommendations included in the report are as follows:

- Adopt a common competition framework, including substantive and procedural rules, and apply it uniformly across all sectors;
- Strengthen the budgetary and human resources dedicated to the application of competition in the Dominican Republic;
- Allow ProCompetencia to prioritize enforcement and protection actions based on transparent criteria, including the power not to take enforcement actions or to close investigations based on its priorities and resource availability;
- Adopt a general regime of *ex ante* control of mergers in line with OECD standards and international best practices;
- Develop effective cartel detection tools, such as proactive methods and anonymous reporting;
- Ensure that the applicable sanctions have a deterrent effect, which implies modifying the current system of fines based on minimum wages and replacing it with one based on flexible elements that take into account the specific circumstances of each case and the markets affected;
- Extend the statute of limitations and increase the time limit;
- Introduce deterrent fines for lack of response, late responses, and the use of incomplete or misleading information regarding information requests required by ProCompetencia; and
- Ensure that the coordination mechanisms between ProCompetencia and sectoral regulators with enforcement powers are effectively implemented.

33. The set of these recommendations constitutes a comprehensive agenda of legislative and institutional reforms that, if properly implemented, would substantially transform

the Dominican competition protection system, aligning it with international standards and significantly strengthening its capacity to promote competitive, efficient markets that benefit consumers and the country's sustainable economic development.

34. In addition to legislation that regulates and protects free competition, the State may also establish a government agency with a degree of autonomy to serve as the governing body for free competition. In the Dominican Republic, this agency is the National Commission for the Defense of Competition (ProCompetencia).

IV. Institutional Structure

A. *National Commission for the Defense of Competition (ProCompetencia): National Competition Authority*

35. Article 16 of Law No. 42-08 establishes the National Commission for the Defense of Competition (ProCompetencia) as the national authority for competition matters. ProCompetencia is a decentralized agency with its own legal personality, assets, and legal and administrative autonomy. It enjoys administrative, technical, and financial independence and is attached to the Ministry of Industry, Commerce, and MSMEs (MICM). This autonomous status is also recognized in article 7(7) of Law No. 37-17, which reorganizes the Ministry of Industry and Commerce.

36. Pursuant to article 17 of Law No. 42-08, ProCompetencia has the fundamental mandate to "promote and guarantee the existence of effective competition in the markets for products and services, through the execution and application of competition policies and legislation, and the exercise of investigative, reporting, regulatory, adjudicative, decision-making, and sanctioning powers."[13]

37. In this context, the fundamental objective of ProCompetencia is to ensure the efficient functioning of markets through free competition. This is achieved by generating a culture of good practices across the various sectors of national economic activity, as well as promoting public policies that encourage competition by eliminating undue restrictions on the responsible exercise of the right to free enterprise.

B. *Institutional Structure*

38. ProCompetencia is a state institution that exercises a diverse range of powers and responsibilities in matters of competition law. Just as free competition itself has several dimensions within the Dominican legal system, ProCompetencia performs varied and complementary functions in its role as guarantor of free and effective competition in national markets.

39. The organizational structure is based on two distinct bodies that perform specific functions within the institutional framework. The executive directorate is responsible for investigating and processing complaints of anticompetitive practices, with the aim of submitting duly substantiated cases to the appropriate administrative sanctioning

---

13 Our translation.

authority. The board of directors, composed of five members (a president and four advisors), is the collegiate body responsible for exercising sanctioning powers by imposing fines, as well as for directing institutional functions related to advocacy and the promotion of competition.

40. The members of the board of directors enjoy irremovability during their five-year term and may only be removed if the board of directors itself determines that a serious offense has occurred in the performance of their duties, as established in paragraph II of article 26 and article 29 of Law No. 42-08. This guarantee of irremovability constitutes a fundamental mechanism to ensure the independence and autonomy of the competition authority in the face of external pressures.

41. ProCompetencia is not limited to the typical sanctioning functions that characterize other regulatory bodies of Dominican law. In addition to these traditional powers, the institution exercises authority to promote and develop competition policies, enabling it to carry out activities aimed at strengthening the culture of free competition in the country. Furthermore, it performs expert and technical review functions, given that public institutions and regulatory bodies of sectoral markets must submit draft regulations or resolutions that could affect free competition to ProCompetencia, pursuant to article 20 of Law No. 42-08, for the authority's review and opinion.

42. Similarly, ProCompetencia exercises advisory and specialized legal powers under article 31, subparagraphs n) and o), of Law No. 42-08. These powers allow it to issue technical reports and recommendations on the management of state institutions that could affect competition, actively participate during the processes of forming laws and other legal norms whose object could affect free competition, suggest national policies to the executive branch for the promotion and protection of competition, as well as participate in the negotiation of international agreements, conventions and treaties on the subject.

C. *Budget and Resources*

43. The authority has budgetary and spending autonomy; however, it faces significant limitations in financial and human resources. Its funding comes primarily from the general state budget. These funds are supplemented by additional income from international technical cooperation and fines imposed on economic actors.

44. Despite this legal framework, ProCompetencia's financial capacity remains limited. The budget allocated for 2026 was approximately USD 3 million (DOP 195.4 million), a figure that has not increased since 2018. Notably, the budget was frozen in 2022 due to post-pandemic fiscal constraints, underscoring the persistent challenges in securing adequate funding for effective law enforcement. These limitations continue to hinder the agency's operational expansion and institutional strengthening.

D. *Human Resources*

45. ProCompetencia operates with a relatively small workforce compared to competition authorities in similar jurisdictions. The agency has 90 full-time employees, of whom only about 31% are dedicated to competition enforcement functions, while the remaining 69% perform administrative support tasks.

46. The technical staff is primarily composed of lawyers specializing in competition law, complemented by economists who support economic analysis of cases, as well as a limited number of specialists in market research and sector analysis. Despite institutional efforts to progressively transform administrative positions into technical roles, the total number of employees per million inhabitants in the Dominican Republic remains significantly lower than the average observed in OECD member countries, other Latin American and Caribbean nations, countries with comparable GDP per capita, and countries with similar population sizes.[14]

47. This limitation in human resource capacity represents a structural challenge to the effective application of competition law and to the development of institutional advocacy work, thereby reducing the possibility that the authority will achieve international standards in the implementation and execution of competition policies. Strengthening the staff of specialized technical personnel is therefore a strategic priority for the institutional development of ProCompetencia and for the effective fulfillment of its legal mandate.

V. Enforcement and Sanctions

48. Pursuant to article 61 of Law No. 42-08, economic agents who engage in anti-competitive conduct are subject to administrative sanctions, without prejudice to any applicable criminal and civil liabilities. The board of directors of ProCompetencia is authorized to impose the following sanctions, depending on the severity of the violations:

- fines ranging from 30 to 3,000 minimum wages for the practices outlined in article 5, subparagraphs a), c), d), and e) of the law, concerning anticompetitive agreements;
- fines ranging from 200 to 3,000 minimum wages for engaging in the practice established in article 5, subparagraph b), concerning manipulation of public tenders;
- fines ranging from 30 to 3,000 minimum wages for the practices listed in article 6, concerning abuse of a dominant position;
- fines ranging from 50 to 200 minimum wages for providing false information to ProCompetencia.

49. In matters of unfair competition, the legal framework has particular characteristics, derived from article 12 of the law, which grants affected parties the option to directly pursue legal action before the courts of first instance in their civil and commercial jurisdictions, without having to exhaust administrative remedies. When affected parties opt for the administrative procedure before the competition authority, the authority is limited to ordering the cessation of the unfair conduct and lacks the power to impose monetary penalties in these specific cases.

50. Article 62 of the law establishes the criteria that the competition authority must consider to determine the severity of an infraction and impose the corresponding sanctions. These parameters include the type and scope of the restriction on free competition, the size of the affected market, the effect on competitors and consumers, the premeditation

---

[14] *Id.*

and intent of the conduct, the economic agent's market share and financial capacity, the duration of the prohibited practice, as well as any prior offenses or record of the offender. The regulations allow for additional fines up to twice the amount in cases of recidivism and provide for monthly increases of 3% when sanctions are not paid within the established timeframe.

51. Finally, it is important to note that the sanctions system based on multiples of the minimum wage has significant limitations in its deterrent effect, particularly for large companies or economic groups, because the maximum fines may be insufficient relative to the economic benefits derived from anticompetitive conduct. This situation has been identified in the recommendations of the OECD-IDB peer review as a priority area for reform, suggesting the adoption of a more flexible system of fines based on a percentage of revenue or on factors that take into account the specific circumstances of each case and the affected markets.

VI. Noteworthy Cases

52. The history of ProCompetencia's application of Law No. 42-08 has generated significant legal precedents that have helped shape the contours of competition law in the Dominican Republic. The cases presented below illustrate both the institutional advances and the structural challenges faced by the competition authority in carrying out its mandate.

A. *Abuse of Dominant Position in the Market for the Production, Marketing and Distribution of Beer*[15]

53. *Facts.* In January 2017, the executive directorate of ProCompetencia initiated an investigation into the beer market following the publication of a study, conducted with IDB support, that analyzed competitive conditions after the 2012 merger between Cervecería Nacional Dominicana and AmBev Brasil Bebidas.

54. The investigation, which extended until December 2017, included 825 consumer and commercial establishment surveys, 39 interviews with market participants, and information requests to public and private institutions. During this process, various business practices implemented by Cervecería Nacional Dominicana were documented, including contractual clauses that made the sale of its products contingent upon buyers refraining from acquiring or distributing products from competing companies, imposition of prices and sales conditions without commercial justification, restrictions on visibility and shelf space for competing brands, exclusive promotional contracts, and limitations related to the placement of refrigeration equipment that hindered competitors' access to essential distribution channels.

55. *Legal problem.* The case required determining whether Cervecería Nacional Dominicana's business practices constituted abuses of its dominant position under subparagraphs a), b), and d) of article 6 of Law No. 42-08. The central issue was to assess whether the company,

[15] Resolution No. 018-2018, dated Dec. 10 [See Fecha Publicación], 2018, issued by the board of directors of the National Commission for the Defense of Competition (ProCompetencia) (in Spanish), https://procompetencia.gob.do/resoluciones-procompetencia/resolucion-num-018-2018/.

in exercising its dominant position in the relevant market, had implemented business strategies whose object or effect was to create unjustified barriers to competitors' entry or expansion, or whether these practices could be explained as reasonable responses to competitive market conditions. The analysis required establishing criteria to distinguish between legitimate business practices and exclusionary conduct that exceed the scope of competition on the merits.

56. *Decision.* By Resolution No. 018-2018, dated December 10, 2018, the board of directors of ProCompetencia declared Cervecería Nacional Dominicana responsible for violating subparagraphs a), b), and d) of article 6 of Law No. 42-08. The Board first determined the relevant market and found that the company held a dominant position in it. Subsequently, it concluded that the investigated practices constituted abuses of a dominant position by making sales contingent upon the exclusion of competitors, imposing prices and conditions without commercial justification, and conditioning transactions on not contracting with third-party competitors.

57. As a sanction, the Council imposed the most severe fine allowed by law, equivalent to 3,000 minimum wages, totaling DOP 46,342,800. Additionally, it ordered the immediate cessation of the anticompetitive practices and declared the agreements signed in violation of the law null and void.

58. *Impact.* This case established the first precedent regarding abuse of a dominant position in the Dominican Republic, confirming ProCompetencia's authority to investigate and sanction exclusionary practices implemented by economic agents with a dominant position. The ruling established jurisprudential criteria for determining the relevant market, evaluating dominant position, and analyzing anticompetitive effects, in addition to establishing the principle that dominant agents have a special responsibility in matters of competition.

59. The case demonstrated ProCompetencia's institutional capacity to conduct complex investigations in concentrated markets, but it also highlighted the limitations of the existing sanctions regime. While the maximum legal fine was imposed, it was modest compared to the sanctioned company's revenue, calling into question its deterrent effect and underscoring the need for reforms that would allow sanctions based on a percentage of revenue. This precedent has served as a reference for subsequent investigations and has raised awareness among economic actors about the need to implement competition compliance programs.

B. *Concerted Practices and anticompetitive Agreements in the Drug Market*[16]

60. *Facts.* In 2019, ProCompetencia initiated administrative sanctions proceedings after identifying reasonable grounds to suspect collusion among distributors of GlaxoSmithKline-brand medications in the Dominican Republic. The investigation

[16] Resolution No. 010-2021, dated June 25, 2021, issued by the board of directors of the National Commission for the Defense of Competition (ProCompetencia) (in Spanish), https://procompetencia.gob.do/resoluciones-procompetencia/resolucion-num-010-2021/.

focused on four economic agents: Profarma Internacional, SRL; Sued & Fargesa, SRL; J. Gassó Gassó, SAS; and Mercantil Farmacéutica, SA.

61. During the investigation, the executive directorate gathered evidence suggesting coordination among these distributors to establish uniform commercial terms, limit competition among them, and create artificial barriers that hindered other distributors' access to the market. The practices under investigation included possible agreements on prices, sales conditions, and customer allocation, resulting in detrimental effects on competitors and end consumers. The seriousness of the case was heightened by the fact that it involved the pharmaceutical market, where restrictions on competition directly impact the population's access to essential health products.

62. *Legal problem.* The case required determining whether the conduct of the investigated distributors constituted concerted practices and anticompetitive agreements prohibited by article 5 of Law No. 42-08, specifically subparagraph a), which penalizes agreeing on prices, discounts, surcharges, and other sales conditions among competitors. The central issue was to assess whether distributors effectively coordinated to limit competition in the pharmaceutical market and whether that coordination had generated anticompetitive effects. The analysis had to consider the particularly sensitive nature of the pharmaceutical market and establish the applicable evidentiary standard regarding concerted practices.

63. *Decision.* By Resolution No. 010-2021, dated June 25, 2021, the board of directors declared the four investigated economic agents responsible for violating subparagraph a) of article 5 of Law No. 42-08. The Board applied the per se rule established by the law, under which certain agreements between competitors are considered absolute prohibitions due to their inherently anticompetitive nature, without the need to demonstrate concrete market effects.

64. As a sanction, differentiated fines were imposed according to the degree of participation of each economic agent:

- J. Gassó Gassó received a fine of 38 minimum wages, equivalent to DOP 609,202;
- Mercantil Farmacéutica was sanctioned with 167 minimum wages, equivalent to DOP 940,970;
- Profarma Internacional received a fine of 315 minimum wages, equivalent to DOP 547,339; and
- Sued & Fargesa was sanctioned with 281 minimum wages, equivalent to DOP 948,578.

65. *Impact.* This case set an important precedent regarding cartels in the Dominican pharmaceutical market, confirming the per se applicability of the standard to horizontal price and sales conditions between competitors. The ruling emphasized the particular seriousness of anticompetitive practices in sensitive markets where artificial restrictions impact the population's access to essential health goods.

66. The decision demonstrated ProCompetencia's capacity to investigate collusive conduct in complex markets and established a precedent for proportionate sanctions by recognizing varying levels of responsibility among cartel participants. The case laid the groundwork for future investigations in the pharmaceutical sector and other

essential goods markets, strengthening the competition authority's role in protecting access to healthcare.

C. *Administrative Offense for Providing False Information in an Investigation Procedure*[17]

67. *Facts.* In January 2020, the executive directorate of ProCompetencia initiated an investigation through Resolution No. DE-020-2021 within the framework of the SODETRANSP case against Johnny Zabala Alcántara. During the course of this investigation, the executive directorate requested information from SODETRANSP as part of the evidentiary proceedings necessary for the case file.

68. During the course of the proceedings, the executive directorate discovered that SODETRANSP had submitted false information in response to requests from the competition authority. This conduct constituted a serious administrative offense that hindered the proper conduct of the investigation and compromised the authority's ability to determine the facts and make informed decisions. The submission of false information not only represented a breach of the cooperation obligations of economic agents in administrative proceedings, but also constituted conduct expressly defined as an infraction under Law No. 42-08.

69. *Legal problem.* The case concerned whether SODETRANSP's conduct in providing false information to the executive directorate constituted a violation of subparagraph d) of article 61 of Law No. 42-08, which establishes specific penalties for those who provide false information to ProCompetencia during administrative proceedings. The legal question was whether the information provided by the investigated economic agent was indeed false and whether the conduct was intentional or at least negligent.

70. The problem also involved establishing the scope of the obligation of cooperation that economic agents have in ProCompetencia's investigation procedures, as well as determining the legal consequences of failing to comply with this fundamental obligation for the proper functioning of the competition defense system. Additionally, the case required clarification of the procedural treatment of this independent infringement in relation to the ongoing main investigation.

71. *Decision.* By Resolution No. 001-2022, dated November 15, 2022, the board of directors of ProCompetencia declared SODETRANSP responsible for having provided false information to the executive directorate during the investigation procedure initiated by Resolution No. DE-020-2021, constituting a violation of subparagraph d) of article 61 of Law No. 42 08.

72. The board of directors determined that the information provided by SODETRANSP was indeed false and that this conduct had hindered the proper conduct of the investigation. The resolution emphasized that the obligation to provide truthful and complete information is a fundamental duty of economic agents in their dealings with the competition authority,

---

17 Resolution No. 001-2022, dated Jan. 17, 2022, issued by the board of directors of the National Commission for the Defense of Competition (ProCompetencia) (in Spanish), https://procompetencia.gob.do/resoluciones-procompetencia/resolucion-numero-001-2022/.

and that failure to comply with this obligation warrants sanctions regardless of the outcome of the main investigation.

73. As a sanction, the board of directors imposed a fine of 200 minimum wages on SODETRANSP, in accordance with the range established in subparagraph d) of article 61 of Law No. 42-08, which stipulates fines between 50 and 200 minimum wages for those who provide false information to ProCompetencia. The authority considered that the seriousness of the conduct justified the imposition of a significant sanction within the legally available range, given that the deliberate provision of false information seriously compromises the institution's investigative capacity.

74. *Impact.* This case established an important precedent regarding the cooperation obligations of economic agents in ProCompetencia administrative proceedings and the consequences of failing to comply with these obligations. The ruling confirmed that providing false information constitutes an independent offense punishable regardless of the outcome of the main investigation, strengthening the authority's ability to demand effective cooperation in its investigations.

75. The case sent a clear signal to the market about the importance of the truthfulness and completeness of the information provided to ProCompetencia during administrative proceedings. The decision established that the authority will not tolerate conduct that obstructs its investigations by providing false, misleading, or incomplete information, and that it will exercise its sanctioning powers to ensure the integrity of its investigative processes. This precedent is fundamental to ensuring that economic agents comply with their cooperation obligations, enabling the authority to conduct effective investigations based on reliable, verifiable information.

D. *First Sanctioning Precedent for Collusion in Public Procurement*[18]

76. *Facts.* In September 2022, the Dominican State Economic Dining Halls (Comedores Económicos del Estado Dominicano – CEED) referred to ProCompetencia a complaint filed by Condelca, SRL against Proviluz, SRL and Grupo Maccabi, SRL, for alleged collusion in the public procurement process Comedores Económicos CCC-LPN-2022-0009.

77. The ProCompetencia executive directorate formally initiated an investigation after identifying reasonable indications of collusion, carrying out evidentiary procedures such as interviews, information requests, and address verifications. Following an extension of the investigation period, it was concluded that both companies coordinated technical and economic bids, exhibiting overlapping patterns that could not be explained independently.

78. *Legal problem.* To determine whether the conduct of Proviluz and Grupo Maccabi constituted a collusive practice in the field of public procurement, typified in article 5, subparagraph b), of Law No. 42-08, and whether the executive directorate had legal power to extend the maximum investigation period provided for in said law.

---

18 Resolution No. 009-2024, dated Sept. 25, 2024, issued by the board of directors of the National Commission for the Defense of Competition (ProCompetencia) (in Spanish), https://procompetencia.gob.do/resoluciones-procompetencia/resolucion-num-009-2024/.

79. *Decision.* The board of directors of ProCompetencia, through Resolution No. 009-2024, dated September 25, 2024, declared the existence of bid rigging through concerted practices proven. The Board validated the extension of the investigation period based on the supplementary application of Law No. 107-13 and adopted a standard of proof based on consistent evidence. As a sanction, it imposed a fine equivalent to 294 minimum monthly wages on each company and recommended to the General Directorate of Public Procurement the disqualification of the sanctioned economic agents as suppliers to the State.

80. *Impact.* This case establishes the first precedent for sanctions against public collusion in the Dominican Republic, thereby strengthening ProCompetencia's role as the sole authority to investigate and penalize such practices. Furthermore, it established important criteria for the use of circumstantial evidence in cartel cases, highlighted the limitations of the existing sanctions regime, and underscored the need for legal reforms to extend investigation periods, strengthen the deterrent effect of fines, and incorporate measures such as leniency programs.

VII. Merger Control

81. The Dominican Republic currently lacks a comprehensive system for merger control and acquisitions. Law No. 42-08 does not include a mandatory notification system or *ex ante* review of economic concentrations, placing the country among the few jurisdictions that still lack this fundamental competition policy instrument. This absence represents a significant structural limitation to the effectiveness of the competition system, as it prevents the creation or strengthening of dominant positions before they become established in the market.

82. However, scattered sectoral provisions establish fragmented control mechanisms in specific markets. In the telecommunications sector, article 4.4 of the Regulations for Free and Fair Competition in the Telecommunications Sector establishes that mergers and concentrations in this market are subject to prior authorization from the Dominican Telecommunications Institute. However, these regulations lack clearly defined mandatory notification thresholds and do not provide for the competition authority's formal participation in the evaluation process, although the authority may be consulted and may issue non-binding technical reports.

83. Similarly, in the financial sector, Monetary and Financial Law No. 183-02 grants the Monetary Board, in article 9, subparagraph g), the power to authorize mergers, acquisitions, spin-offs, and similar transactions between financial intermediation entities, upon the proposal of the Superintendency of Banks. As in the case of telecommunications, these provisions lack specific thresholds and systematic procedures for assessing whether a transaction could generate problematic levels of economic concentration or market power from a competitive perspective.

84. This regulatory framework leads to significant institutional fragmentation of the merger control system. Only a limited number of sectoral regulators can review transactions in their respective markets, preventing ProCompetencia from directly intervening in matters related to competition, even though its specialized technical expertise would be essential

to ensuring a rigorous analysis of the competitive impact of such transactions. This situation contrasts sharply with international best practices, where competition authorities constitute the specialized technical body responsible for centralized preventive merger control across economic sectors, thereby enabling a coherent, technically sound, and uniform assessment of potential anticompetitive effects.

85. The absence of a comprehensive merger control regime is particularly relevant in the Dominican economy, which is characterized by high levels of concentration in strategic sectors and increasing integration into international investment flows. Cross-border mergers have increased significantly since the 1990s, and the Dominican Republic, as an emerging middle-income economy, faces significant challenges in establishing an effective system to control these transactions. The lack of preventive mechanisms means that the competition authority can only act *ex post* by prosecuting abuses of dominant position, once the market structure has been irreversibly altered, which is considerably less effective than proactively preventing problematic mergers.

VIII. Advocacy and Policy Initiatives

86. Effective competition protection goes beyond mere coercive enforcement and also requires the capacity to influence regulatory frameworks, eliminate barriers to market access, and foster a culture of competition in society. Law No. 42-08 expressly recognizes this preventive and promotional dimension, establishing a regulatory framework that empowers ProCompetencia to carry out advocacy activities to improve the structural conditions of competition in the Dominican economy.

87. Chapter IV of Title I of Law No. 42-08 establishes the legal basis for this advocacy function. Article 14 empowers the institution to submit public reports to the authorities suggesting corrective measures regarding anticompetitive effects arising from laws, regulations, and other state legal acts that unjustifiably restrict free enterprise. Article 15 complements this power by establishing the mandate to examine the competitive effects of subsidies, state aid, or incentives granted with public funds, allowing ProCompetencia to request, through reasoned reports, the elimination or modification of such measures when they generate disproportionate competitive distortions.

88. Furthermore, article 20 of Law No. 42-08 establishes a coordination mechanism with other regulators, stipulating that administrative acts related to competition must be submitted to ProCompetencia for review. The board of directors must respond with a reasoned opinion, which is public but non-binding and may include specific recommendations. Similarly, article 31 of the aforementioned law outlines the broader powers of ProCompetencia in the area of advocacy, authorizing the board of directors to engage in advocacy activities in government management, promote competition during legislative processes, propose national competition policies to the executive branch, represent the country in international competition negotiations, and promote cooperation at the national, regional, and international levels. In exercising these legal powers, ProCompetencia has developed a robust advocacy program that complements its law enforcement work.

A. *Economic Studies and Methodological Guides*

89. ProCompetencia has developed a strategic line of economic research to diagnose competitive conditions in key sectors of the Dominican economy. These studies provide essential technical input for both law enforcement and the formulation of public policy recommendations. Among the studies conducted, the analysis of competitive conditions in the Health Risk Administrators market for the Family Health Insurance system during the period 2010–2024 stands out. This analysis[19] revealed moderate concentration in this essential market and identified significant barriers to entry for new companies, including complex regulatory requirements and high operating costs.

90. Additionally, ProCompetencia has developed the Market Conditions Observatory,[20] a strategic analytical tool designed to systematically monitor and evaluate the level and dynamics of competition across markets, using specific criteria to identify risks that could lead to anticompetitive practices. This observatory represents a significant advance in the institution's capacity to adopt a preventive, proactive approach to competition law, anticipating potential issues before they become violations.

91. The institution has also developed specialized analyses on the interaction between public policy and competition, such as the study on the impact of state aid from a competition perspective, focusing on Law No. 28-01 on Border Development. This work estimated the impact of this legislation on competitive conditions in the markets and provinces benefiting from this special regime, concluding that while the legal framework does not contravene the Constitution or the principle of equal participation, since the economic and social development of the border region is a constitutional mandate, its effectiveness requires being complemented by greater public investment in infrastructure to ensure the success of the public policy.

92. Of particular relevance is the *Study of Competitive Conditions in Public Procurement and Contracting Processes in the Dominican Republic*,[21] published in 2022, which formulates recommendations to strengthen competition, improve transparency, and align public procurement processes with the principle of free and fair competition. Furthermore, the study provides a solid technical basis for designing regulatory reforms, adopting pro-competitive measures, and strengthening the role of the competition authority in protecting the public interest and social welfare.

93. Similarly, the *Guide for the Prevention and Detection of Collusion in Public Procurement*, launched in 2020 and subsequently updated in 2025,[22] is a fundamental

---

19 ProCompetencia, Study of Competition Conditions in Health Risk Administrators (ARS) in the Dominican Republic (2025) (in Spanish), https://procompetencia.gob.do/wpfd_file/estudio-de-condiciones-de-competencia-en-la-administradoras-de-riesgos-de-salud-ars-en-la-republica-dominicana/.

20 Market Conditions Observatory, ProCompetencia (in Spanish), https://procompetencia.gob.do/observatorio-de-condiciones-de-mercado/.

21 ProCompetencia, Study of Competitive Conditions in Public Procurement and Contracting Processes in the Dominican Republic (2022) (in Spanish), https://procompetencia.gob.do/wpfd_file/estudio-de-condiciones-de-competencia-en-los-procesos-de-compras-y-contrataciones-publicas-en-la-republica-dominicana/.

22 ProCompetencia, Guide for the Prevention and Detection of Collusion in Public Procurement 2025 (2025) (in Spanish), https://procompetencia.gob.do/wpfd_file/guia-para-la-prevencion-y-deteccion-de-colusion-en-la-contratacion-publica-2025/.

instrument for promoting competition among public-sector entities in the procurement and contracting processes for goods, works, services, and state concessions. This guide includes the innovative Collusive Traffic Light, a risk assessment tool that enables procurement officials to identify warning signs of potential collusive practices in bidding processes.

94. Another important input is the *Methodological Guide for Determining the Relevant Market and Dominant Position*,[23] which provides clear, consistent, and verifiable criteria for establishing the boundaries of the relevant market and determining whether an economic agent holds a dominant position – fundamental concepts for the application of competition law. This tool has contributed to greater predictability and transparency in the competition authority's actions, facilitating voluntary compliance by economic agents.

95. Furthermore, the *Methodological Guide for the Evaluation of State Aid from a Competition Perspective* establishes a conceptual and procedural framework for analyzing government interventions, such as subsidies, incentives, or transfers of public resources, that may affect competition in markets. This guide is particularly relevant in a context where the Dominican State implements various support programs for specific sectors, requiring assurance that these interventions do not unnecessarily distort competitive conditions.

96. Furthermore, in 2024, the *Methodological Guide for Screening Techniques in Cartel Detection* was published.[24] This guide is an essential tool for competition policy, providing competition authorities with objective economic and statistical tools to identify collusion early and transparently. Its importance lies in strengthening the legal certainty of economic actors, improving the quality and effectiveness of investigations, and providing technical input for public policy design and academic analysis, thus contributing to the consolidation of a culture of free competition oriented toward consumer welfare.

B. *Creating a Culture of Competition and Disseminating Knowledge*

97. Consolidating an effective competition system goes beyond simply enacting regulations and creating specialized institutions. It fundamentally requires developing a culture of free and fair competition deeply rooted in all sectors of society, particularly among economic actors, legal professionals, public officials, and the general public. Recognizing this strategic need, ProCompetencia has, since its inception, implemented a systematic policy of training, outreach, and awareness-raising to promote knowledge and understanding of competition principles and regulations in the Dominican Republic.

98. In this regard, the *Competition Law Yearbook* (*Anuario de Competencia*) is an academic publication that compiles essays on competition law by national and international authors. This initiative, which to date has three editions corresponding to the years 2023, 2024, and 2025, has been recognized by The City College of New York as an international

---

[23] ProCompetencia, Methodological Guide for Determining the Relevant Market and Dominant Position (2024) (in Spanish), https://procompetencia.gob.do/wpfd_file/guia-metodologica-para-la-determinacion-de-mercado-relevante-y-posicion-dominante/.

[24] ProCompetencia, Methodological Guide for Screening Techniques in Cartel Detection (2024) (in Spanish), https://procompetencia.gob.do/wpfd_file/guia-metodologica-tecnicas-de-screening-en-la-deteccion-de-carteles/.

academic reference, contributing to the doctrinal development of competition law in Latin America and to the positioning of the Dominican Republic within the academic community specializing in this field.

99. Furthermore, this strategy to promote a culture of competition has been implemented through a comprehensive program that includes specialized workshops, technical training courses, informational talks, industry meetings, and the organization of national and international forums. These activities have been aimed at diverse target audiences, including businesspeople, lawyers, economists, judges, prosecutors, industry regulators, academics, and public officials, recognizing that each stakeholder plays a crucial role in building a robust, competitive environment.

100. The organization of national and international forums has been a particularly valuable dimension of this strategy to promote a culture of competition. These events have facilitated exchanges with competition authorities from other jurisdictions, enabling Dominican stakeholders to learn about international best practices, emerging trends in the application of competition law, and innovative approaches to addressing common challenges. Additionally, these forums have positioned the Dominican Republic within the international competition community, strengthening its ties with regional and international networks specializing in this area.

101. Of particular note is the organization of Competition Weeks, annual events that bring together national and international experts to address current issues in competition law. The third Competition Week, which hosted the first International Congress on Competition Law, held in October 2025, focused on the theme of "digital markets and free competition," bringing together representatives from the OECD, competition authorities from Latin America, and academic experts to discuss the challenges that the digital economy poses for the application of competition rules.

102. Within the framework of competition advocacy and promotion activities, the essay contest "Writing for Competition" has become a key strategy for fostering critical study and research in competition law, starting within the university setting and, in 2025, adding a new category for professionals. Through its three editions, this initiative has sparked academic interest, strengthened analytical skills, and introduced students and professionals to the principles governing competitive markets, thereby contributing to the development of a sustainable culture of competition and reaching a total of 928 participants.

103. In addition, ProCompetencia has developed specialized training programs for judges in competition law, recognizing their crucial role in reviewing and overseeing administrative decisions. These programs, taught by national and international experts, are essential for ensuring consistent interpretation and application of competition law, thereby strengthening legal certainty, improving the quality of case law, and consolidating judicial criteria aligned with the principles of free and fair competition.

104. In addition, two awareness-raising workshops have been conducted for communicators and journalists. These workshops play a strategic role in promoting more rigorous, technical, and responsible media coverage, as these professionals are primarily responsible for communicating coherent and truthful information to the public. This effort broadens the social reach of competition policy, clarifies the public understanding of its objectives

and impacts, and reinforces the perception of free competition as an essential instrument for protecting the public interest and consumer welfare.

105. Within the framework of an inter-institutional collaboration agreement with the Directorate General of Ethics and Governmental Integrity, a comprehensive training program has been implemented to strengthen transparency and prevent collusive practices in public procurement. This initiative represents a strategic investment in protecting public assets by directly strengthening institutional mechanisms for controlling and overseeing government spending.

106. As a result of this agreement, more than 800 public officials, members of the Ethics and Integrity Commissions and Procurement Committees of 196 Dominican state institutions, have been trained in the identification, detection, and prevention of collusive conduct. This effort has significantly expanded the technical capabilities of the administrative apparatus to recognize and mitigate risks associated with anticompetitive practices in public procurement.

107. The impact of this initiative transcends quantitative indicators, as each trained official acts as a multiplier of competition oversight within their respective institutional sphere – a true watchdog of competition. In this way, the decentralized supervision of public procurement processes is strengthened, increasing the likelihood of early detection of collusive agreements and other irregularities. This translates into a greater guarantee that the acquisition of essential goods and services, such as medicines, educational infrastructure, supplies for social programs, and public services, is carried out under conditions of effective competition, economic efficiency, and respect for the public interest.

108. In terms of training and awareness-raising, the efforts undertaken over the past four years have had a significant impact. Specifically, in 2025, 43 training activities were conducted, benefiting approximately 15,000 people. This marks the highest number of training sessions conducted by ProCompetencia in a single year since its inception. Cumulatively, these actions have enabled the training of nearly 28,000 people over the last four years, demonstrating a sustained commitment to disseminating knowledge and consolidating a culture of competition in the Dominican Republic.

109. This sustained policy of training and outreach is essential for strengthening the Dominican Republic's competition system. The success of any regulatory framework ultimately depends on its understanding and acceptance by the economic and social actors it seeks to address. Building a robust competition culture requires time, resources, and a persistent institutional commitment to education and awareness-raising – elements that ProCompetencia has systematically sought to develop as an indispensable complement to its regulatory and enforcement functions.

C. *National Competition Policy*

110. On April 10, 2025, through Decree No. 196-25, the Dominican Republic formally approved its national competition policy, becoming the first country in Latin America to adopt such a strategic instrument. This historic achievement represents the culmination of a rigorous technical process that involved extensive consultations with public, private, and academic stakeholders and establishes a comprehensive framework for the

promotion and protection of competition as a fundamental instrument for sustainable and inclusive economic development.

111. The policy strategically addresses the sectors prioritized by the Dominican government in the 2025–2028 Multi-Year Public Investment Plan, including decent and formal employment, agricultural development, institutional strengthening, tourism, domestic and international trade, and industrial development. Furthermore, the policy directly contributes to achieving the objectives set forth in the Dominican Republic's 2036 goal of doubling the GDP within ten years by promoting more efficient, transparent, and equitable markets that drive productivity and sustainable growth.

112. The development of this policy also responds to the recommendations made in the peer review on competition law and policy carried out by the OECD and the IDB, which showed that the regulatory framework for competition in the Dominican Republic faces challenges that limit its effectiveness, including the absence of a merger control regime, the lack of leniency programs, insufficiently dissuasive sanctions and the need to strengthen coordination between ProCompetencia and sectoral regulators, challenges that are accentuated by the high levels of concentration in strategic sectors with possible negative impacts on economic efficiency, innovation and consumer welfare.

113. The national competition policy is structured around three fundamental strategic pillars that coherently articulate its objectives, principles, and action guidelines.

- The first pillar (Strengthening Competition Enforcement) aims to enhance the institutional mechanisms and technical capacities needed to detect, investigate, and sanction anticompetitive conduct.
- The second pillar (Consolidating the Regulatory Framework for Competition) focuses on promoting a regulatory and normative environment that facilitates the entry of new competitors, reduces unjustified barriers, and strengthens market transparency.
- The third pillar (Strengthening Technical Coordination with Regulators and Developing a Common Framework for Competition) aims to build an integrated, coordinated institutional framework that enables the evaluation, harmonization, and strengthening of public policies and regulations promoting free competition.

114. Decree No. 196-25 designates ProCompetencia as the main implementing entity of the national competition policy, responsible for coordinating, implementing, and monitoring the actions established in collaboration with the other institutions involved. As the implementing entity, ProCompetencia must coordinate the development of operational plans for policy implementation, assist participating institutions in aligning actions with their strategic and operational plans, provide technical assistance to the institutions involved, prepare periodic progress reports, propose adjustments and improvements when necessary, and develop management and evaluation indicators.

115. To ensure the effective implementation of the policy, the decree establishes an inter-institutional governance structure comprised of three main bodies. The National Competition Policy Steering Committee is the highest-level body responsible for overseeing, monitoring, and evaluating the policy's implementation. This committee is composed of the Minister of the Presidency, who chairs it; the Minister of Industry, Commerce, and SMEs; the Minister of Finance; the president of the board of directors

of ProCompetencia; and the executive director of the National Competitiveness Council. The Steering Committee's functions include overseeing policy implementation, periodically evaluating progress, identifying obstacles and opportunities, proposing corrective measures, ensuring inter-institutional coordination, reviewing and approving management reports, and submitting periodic reports to the President of the Republic on implementation progress.

116. ProCompetencia serves as the Technical Secretariat of the Steering Committee, providing technical, administrative, and logistical support for its operations. Additionally, the decree establishes three Technical Working Groups, one for each of the strategic pillars of the national competition policy: the Technical Working Group on Competition Defense, the Technical Working Group on the Regulatory Framework for Competition, and the Technical Working Group on Interinstitutional Coordination. Each Technical Working Group is coordinated by a representative appointed by the Steering Committee and is responsible for developing and proposing action plans for the implementation of the strategic pillars, executing and monitoring the actions corresponding to its strategic pillar, preparing periodic progress reports, proposing improvements and adjustments, coordinating joint actions with other institutions, and recommending measures to the Steering Committee to strengthen the implementation of the policy.

117. The implementation of the national competition policy requires the collaboration of all public sector institutions, which must provide the necessary information and support upon request from the Steering Committee, the competition authority, or the Technical Working Groups. Additionally, the decree promotes the active participation of the private sector, academia, and civil society organizations in the implementation and monitoring of the policy through consultation, dialogue, and collaboration mechanisms, recognizing that the effectiveness of a competition policy depends on the involvement of all relevant actors in the economic and social ecosystem.

118. The adoption of the national competition policy represents a fundamental qualitative leap forward in the maturation of the Dominican Republic's competition system. It provides a long-term strategic framework that transcends political cycles and establishes verifiable institutional commitments to promoting competitive markets. The policy sends a clear signal to the international community and investors regarding the Dominican Republic's commitment to establishing a level playing field, respecting the rule of law in economic matters, and promoting market efficiency as an engine of sustainable development. Furthermore, it positions the country as a regional leader in competition policy, establishing a model that can serve as a reference for other Latin American jurisdictions seeking to strengthen their own competition systems.

IX. Regional and International Cooperation

119. The Dominican Republic actively participates in regional and international trade agreements that strengthen economic integration and competition. It is a member of the DR-CAFTA and the Economic Partnership Agreement (EPA) with the European Union. It is also part of the Central American Integration System (SICA), which is the main institutional framework for regional integration. These agreements aim to promote market liberalization, reduce trade barriers, and foster a more competitive environment,

aligning the country with international standards and facilitating cross-border economic cooperation.

120. ProCompetencia complements these efforts through institutional collaboration and participation in global networks. The authority has signed international cooperation agreements with competition agencies such as the Commission for the Promotion of Competition (COPROCOM) of Costa Rica, the National Commission for Competition Defense (CNDC) of Argentina, the Superintendency for the Control of Market Power (SCPM) of Ecuador, the Federal Economic Competition Commission (COFECE) of Mexico, and the National Commission for Markets and Competition (CNMC) of Spain. These agreements facilitate the exchange of experiences for capacity building, study visits, and internships in other countries.[25]

121. ProCompetencia is also an active member of international forums such as the International Competition Network (ICN), the United Nations Conference on Trade and Development (UNCTAD), the Central American Network of National Competition Authorities (RECAC), and the OECD. These partnerships strengthen technical capacity, facilitate knowledge exchange, and improve the application of competition policy in accordance with international best practices.

X. Challenges and Country-Specific Features

122. The effective implementation of competition policy in the Dominican Republic faces structural and contextual challenges that affect both the application of Law No. 42-08 and ProCompetencia's ability to fully fulfill its institutional mandate. These challenges are not unique to the Dominican case but rather reflect characteristics common to small, open economies, though they manifest in ways that require responses tailored to the national context.

123. The analysis of these challenges can be organized around three fundamental dimensions that are intertwined and mutually reinforcing. First, the structural characteristics of the Dominican economy, including the small size of its domestic markets, high levels of sectoral concentration, and significant dependence on imports and foreign investment, create a unique competitive environment that poses specific challenges for the application of competition rules. Second, the institutional limitations of the competition system, ranging from budgetary and human resource constraints to the fragmentation of the regulatory framework resulting from the coexistence of multiple authorities with competition jurisdiction, weaken the State's capacity to guarantee competitive markets. Third, factors of political economy and institutional culture, including the incipient development of a culture of competition in Dominican society and the inherent tensions between competition-promotion objectives and other public policy priorities, constrain the political space for reforms aimed at strengthening the competition regime.

124. A thorough understanding of these three dimensions and their interactions is fundamental to identifying reform priorities and designing strategies that strengthen competition

---

25 *Id.* at 82.

policy as an instrument for sustainable economic development. The challenges presented below are not insurmountable obstacles, but rather priority areas where well-designed interventions can substantially improve the effectiveness of the national competition system.

A. *Small Market Size and High Structural Concentration*

125. The Dominican Republic, with a population of approximately 11 million and a nominal GDP that places it among the medium-sized economies of Latin America, faces the challenges characteristic of small domestic markets. The small size of the domestic market generates particular competitive dynamics that translate into high levels of concentration in strategic sectors of the national economy. Dominican domestic markets are perceived as less competitive than those of comparable countries, as they are dominated by a small number of companies that control significant portions of sales, production, and employment in their respective sectors.

126. This structural concentration does not necessarily reflect anticompetitive practices, but rather frequently stems from economies of scale and scope that, in small markets, enable the efficient operation of a few competitors. However, it raises legitimate concerns about the market power of dominant players and their ability to exert pressure on suppliers, distributors, and end consumers. High concentration hinders the entry of new competitors due to natural barriers such as economies of scale, incumbents' control over distribution channels, and the costs of establishing a foothold in markets where margins can be tight. It also increases the risk of tacit or explicit collusion among the few competitors present, particularly in markets characterized by relatively homogeneous products and price transparency.

B. *Dominance of Public Companies in Strategic Sectors*

127. The Dominican State acts as a direct economic actor in several strategic sectors through state-owned enterprises operating in productive and service activities. This state participation generates complex competitive dynamics in which business profitability objectives coexist with public policy mandates, such as universal service provision, regional development, or price stabilization. Public enterprises frequently enjoy structural competitive advantages derived from their preferential access to public financing, tax exemptions, government guarantees, or favorable regulatory positions, which can distort competitive conditions in the markets where they operate.

128. The presence of public enterprises does not in itself constitute a violation of competition rules, but it requires clear regulatory frameworks that ensure equitable conditions of competition between public and private operators. Article 15 of Law No. 42-08 stipulates that the State must not adopt or maintain measures regarding public enterprises that could unjustifiably create market barriers or generate opportunities for unfair competition. However, the effective application of this principle faces practical challenges related to defining what constitutes an unjustified advantage over legitimate instruments of public policy, evaluating the competitive effects of state aid, and the institutional capacity of the competition authority to influence economic policy decisions that transcend the purely competitive sphere.

C. *Dependence on Imports and Foreign Direct Investment*

129. The Dominican Republic exhibits significant import dependence across its economy, ranging from essential consumer goods to capital equipment and intermediate inputs indispensable to local production. This structural characteristic of the Dominican economy reflects both the country's comparative advantages in certain sectors and the limitations of the national production base in meeting the total domestic demand for goods and services. Import dependence has important implications for competition policy, as competitive discipline in many domestic markets stems primarily from international competition rather than from rivalry among local producers.

130. In this context, tariff and non-tariff barriers to imports are particularly relevant from a competition perspective, as their elimination or reduction can be the most effective mechanism for increasing competitive pressure in concentrated domestic markets. However, the interaction between trade and competition policies creates tensions between the objectives of protecting emerging domestic industries, promoting local employment, and fostering effective competition for the benefit of consumers. The competition authority faces the challenge of influencing trade regulatory frameworks that have traditionally been designed without adequate consideration of their effects on competitive conditions in domestic markets.

131. Furthermore, the country's economic growth over the past two decades has been strongly supported by FDI, which averages around 4% of GDP. FDI has boosted key sectors such as tourism, real estate, manufacturing, and mining, with tourism alone accounting for 28% of FDI in 2024. This reliance on external capital flows shapes economic policy priorities, creating incentives to maintain regulatory frameworks perceived as investment-friendly. This can conflict with competition-strengthening objectives when the latter require regulatory reforms affecting sectors with significant foreign capital participation. The challenge lies in developing a competition policy that is compatible with attracting foreign investment, recognizing that competitive markets are themselves an attractive factor for high-quality investors who compete based on efficiency and innovation.

D. *Limitations of Institutional Capacity and Resources*

132. ProCompetencia faces significant budgetary and human resource constraints that limit its ability to fully fulfill its legal mandate. As documented in peer reviews by the OECD and the IDB, the institution's staffing levels are significantly lower than those of competition authorities in countries with similar levels of economic development or population size. This shortage of human resources directly affects the institution's capacity to conduct complex investigations simultaneously, develop in-depth sectoral economic studies, implement ambitious competition advocacy programs, and actively participate in international cooperation networks.

133. Budgetary constraints also limit ProCompetencia's ability to recruit and retain specialized technical talent, particularly in advanced economic analysis, econometrics applied to competition, digital forensics, and merger control. Competition from the private sector and international organizations offering more attractive salaries presents a constant

challenge to building strong technical teams. Additionally, resource constraints limit investments in technological systems that could enhance the institution's operational efficiency, including case management platforms, data analysis tools, market monitoring systems, and specialized databases.

134. Strengthening ProCompetencia's institutional capacity is a strategic priority for the effectiveness of the national competition system. This requires not only sustained budget increases to expand staffing and improve salaries, but also investments in continuing education, the development of specialized skills, and the modernization of technological infrastructure. The national competition policy explicitly recognizes these limitations and establishes strengthening ProCompetencia's technical capabilities and resources as one of its fundamental guidelines.

E. *Fragmentation of the Application of Competition Rules in Regulated Sectors*

135. The Dominican Republic has a complex institutional framework for competition policy, characterized by the coexistence of ProCompetencia, the general competition authority, with specialized sectoral regulators that have the power to promote competition within their respective areas of operation. This institutional fragmentation stems from sectoral laws enacted prior to Law No. 42-08, which established specific competition powers for regulators in sectors such as telecommunications, electricity, banking and insurance, securities, ports, and airports.

136. Article 69 of Law No. 42-08 recognized this pre-existing institutional reality by stipulating that ProCompetencia should convene the sectoral regulators to jointly review, propose, and enact the competition regulations governing the operation of these markets. It further established that these regulations should be based on the specific legislation governing their operation, Law No. 42-08, the Constitution, and international treaties. However, more than a decade after the law came into effect, this regulatory harmonization process remains incomplete, generating legal uncertainty regarding the division of powers between ProCompetencia and the sectoral regulators in the investigation and sanctioning of anticompetitive practices.

137. This institutional fragmentation generates several practical problems. It leads to overlapping mandates between the competition authority and sectoral regulators, with the potential for duplicate investigations, contradictory decisions, or enforcement gaps when no authority considers itself to have clear jurisdiction over a given matter. The weak application of competition rules by some sectoral regulators, who prioritize other regulatory objectives such as universal service, technical quality, or the sector's financial stability over competitive considerations, creates spaces of impunity for anticompetitive practices in regulated sectors. Coordination challenges among multiple authorities with related competencies hinder the adoption of coherent and predictable approaches to applying competition principles. Finally, legal uncertainty regarding which authority has jurisdiction over specific cases discourages complaints and weakens the effectiveness of the sanctions regime.

F. *Need for a Legal Harmonization and Strengthening of Governance*

138. The challenges described above converge on the urgent need to undertake a comprehensive modernization of the legal framework for competition and to strengthen the institutional governance of the system. This need has been recognized in both the OECD-IDB peer review and the national competition policy, which establishes the consolidation of the regulatory framework on competition as one of its strategic pillars.

139. The legal reform agenda must prioritize the incorporation of a comprehensive *ex ante* control regime for economic concentrations, the introduction of leniency programs that incentivize the detection of cartels, the modification of the sanctions system to ensure an effective deterrent effect through the adoption of fines based on percentages of turnover, the clarification of the distribution of powers between ProCompetencia and sectoral regulators through the harmonization of applicable legislation, and the strengthening of the investigative powers of the competition authority, including the extension of deadlines for complex investigations.

140. Strengthening institutional governance requires:

- ensuring ProCompetencia's operational independence through robust guarantees of budgetary, technical, and administrative autonomy;
- developing institutionalized coordination mechanisms between ProCompetencia and sectoral regulators that go beyond the current scheme of non-binding opinions;
- establishing clear protocols for information exchange between authorities that respect confidentiality duties while facilitating effective investigations; and
- promoting the professionalization of the regulatory function in competition matters through specialized training programs for ProCompetencia officials and sectoral regulators.

G. *Low Level of Competitive Culture*

141. The Dominican Republic exhibits an incipient development of a competition culture compared to jurisdictions with a longer history of implementing such policies. The very concept of competition as a public good deserving of legal protection remains unfamiliar to large sectors of Dominican society, including economic actors, legal professionals, public officials, and the general public. This limited competition culture manifests itself in various ways that affect the effectiveness of the competition enforcement system.

142. Among business owners and business associations, attitudes favoring restrictions on competition persist when these benefit their own sectors, without full recognition of the social costs of such restrictions. Within the judicial system, specialized knowledge of competition law and economics remains limited, generating uncertainty about how the courts will review ProCompetencia decisions and whether they will apply appropriate technical standards in competition matters. Public officials involved in designing economic policies and sectoral regulations do not always incorporate competition considerations into their decisions, thereby perpetuating unnecessary regulatory barriers. Finally, consumers and society in general show little understanding of how anticompetitive practices directly affect them through higher prices, lower quality, or reduced innovation.

143. Building a strong culture of competition is a long-term process that requires sustained education and awareness-raising efforts targeting multiple audiences. ProCompetencia has developed significant initiatives in this area, including training programs for public officials, outreach activities for the business sector, participation in academic forums, and the organization of international events. However, the magnitude of the challenge requires significantly expanding the scale and scope of these activities, incorporating competition education into academic programs in law, economics, and business administration, developing communication campaigns aimed at the general public that explain the importance of competition for everyday well-being in an accessible way, and strengthening ties with the media to achieve greater coverage of competition-related issues.

144. These challenges, while significant, do not constitute insurmountable obstacles to strengthening the Dominican Republic's competition system. The national competition policy, approved in 2025, provides a strategic framework for systematically addressing these limitations through coordinated actions by multiple state institutions. The political commitment demonstrated in approving this policy, coupled with the institutional progress achieved by ProCompetencia since its effective implementation in 2017, lays a solid foundation for progressively consolidating an effective competition regime that contributes to the sustainable and inclusive economic development of the Dominican Republic.

XI. Author's Perspective: A Necessary Structural Reform in the Competition Policy of the Dominican Republic

145. The Dominican Republic is currently at a turning point in its competition policy. Seventeen years after the enactment of Law No. 42-08, the accumulated experience, along with evaluations by the OECD and the IDB Peer Review, has revealed structural limitations that now prevent an effective response to increasingly concentrated, dynamic, and digitized markets.

146. Although Law No. 42-08 was enacted in 2008, it did not come into effect until 2017. This marked a significant advance in the institutionalization of economic public law in the Dominican Republic; however, recent market evolution and comparisons with international best practices reveal regulatory gaps that limit the effectiveness of the current regulatory framework.

147. Among these limitations are the lack of clear and systematic provisions regarding economic concentrations, the incomplete regulation of vertical agreements and abuses of dominant position, and an insufficiently dissuasive sanctions regime. These deficiencies reduce ProCompetencia's capacity to prevent and sanction conduct that harms economic efficiency and consumer welfare, particularly in structurally concentrated markets.

148. In this context, a comprehensive reform is essential to address these shortcomings and provide the country with a regulatory framework that meets the challenges of the contemporary economy. Comparative experience demonstrates that states adopt competition policies not only to correct market failures, but also to increase productivity, prevent anticompetitive practices such as collusion, abuse of dominant position,

and unfair competition, and mitigate distortions that generate economic inefficiency and increase social inequality.[26]

149. From this perspective, the draft reform does not merely introduce marginal adjustments, but rather proposes paradigm shifts in how competition law is conceived and applied in the Dominican Republic. Its central objective is to equip the Dominican Republic's competition authority with modern and effective tools, aligned with international standards but adapted to the Dominican economic and institutional reality. Empirical evidence supports this approach: various studies show that countries with robust competition frameworks experience GDP growth between 2% and 3% higher than jurisdictions lacking effective legislation in this area.[27]

150. The most significant innovation of the draft bill is the introduction of a comprehensive system for controlling economic concentrations, which has been nonexistent until now. This omission has allowed transactions with potential anticompetitive impacts to be executed for years without prior assessment. The absence of a merger and acquisition control regime is, in effect, the most significant deficiency in the current regulatory framework, placing the Dominican Republic at a disadvantage compared to the vast majority of modern competition jurisdictions. This structural deficiency is corrected by introducing an *ex ante* system for controlling concentrations, which will substantially transform how corporate transactions are structured and executed in the country.

151. The new regime establishes a mandatory notification system based on objective, precise thresholds that combine market share and business volume criteria. This allows for the detection of both transactions in highly concentrated markets and large-scale economic transactions that could affect the competitive structure. The procedure is structured in two clearly differentiated phases that balance administrative efficiency with the necessary analytical rigor. The first phase, with a maximum term of 30 business days, allows for a preliminary analysis that may result in direct authorization, conditional authorization, or the initiation of a second phase if competitive concerns requiring in-depth scrutiny are identified. The second phase, reserved for complex or problematic transactions, involves a detailed analysis that culminates within a maximum of 60 days with a final decision that may authorize, condition, or prohibit the merger.

152. A second fundamental pillar of the reform is the creation of a leniency program, which introduces for the first time in the Dominican legal system a structured incentive scheme for detecting cartels. The system provides full immunity to the first informant and tiered reductions to subsequent informants, aligning with international best practices and substantially strengthening the actual capacity to prosecute the most harmful practices for the market and consumers.

153. The requirements for obtaining full immunity reflect a careful balance between incentivizing cooperation and ensuring its effectiveness. The applicant must cooperate fully, continuously, and diligently throughout the administrative proceedings, providing all available information and evidence. It must immediately cease its participation in the

---

26 Pablo Martín Urbano & Juan Ignacio Sánchez Gutiérrez, *La política de competencia, crecimiento y globalización* [*The Policy of Competition, Growth and Globalization*], 9 Contabilidad y Negocios 83 (2014).

27 OECD, Factsheet on Competition and Macro-Economic Outcomes 23 (2014), https://doi.org/10.1787/660b93ab-en.

cartel and must not have destroyed evidence or disclosed its intention to seek leniency to third parties. Crucially, it must not have taken steps to compel or coerce other firms to participate in the infringement, thereby excluding the cartel's leaders or instigators. The program incorporates sophisticated procedural mechanisms such as the placeholder system, which allows a firm to reserve its position in the leniency queue by submitting a preliminary application while gathering the evidence necessary for a full application.

154. A third structural transformation responds to the accelerated advance of the digital economy. The draft bill explicitly incorporates digital markets into competitive analysis, recognizing phenomena such as network effects, data power, multilateral markets, interoperability, and new forms of abuse. To this end, it introduces specific definitions such as "digital economy" and "digital market," and adapts the criteria for determining the relevant market to realities that transcend the traditional analysis of substitutability based on price and physical characteristics.

155. The reform also more precisely defines collusion in public procurement, a practice that causes significant losses to the State and has, until now, been addressed in a generic way. It also introduces the concept of aggravated unfair competition, enabling the competition authority to intervene when such conduct transcends private disputes and affects the public economic interest.

156. From an institutional standpoint, the draft bill proposes a real functional separation between the investigating and decision-making bodies, since it strengthens the Directorate of Investigations, creates the position of the investigating advisor, and establishes a proportional sanctioning regime based on gross income, thus overcoming a system of fines that is merely symbolic in the face of large economic agents.

157. This reform represents a qualitative and structural leap forward in the Dominican Republic's competition system. It is not merely a cosmetic modernization, but a direct response to identified weaknesses, aimed at building more competitive and transparent markets aligned with the challenges of a 21st-century digital, globalized economy. The proposed innovations – merger control, leniency programs, regulation of digital markets, and proportionate sanctions – will allow the country to align itself with international standards and more effectively achieve its constitutional objectives of free competition, equity, and sustainable development, thereby consolidating a genuine social and democratic state governed by the rule of law in the economic sphere and boosting productivity and innovation.

XII. References and Resources

A. *Regulations*

- Decree No. 196-25, dated Apr. 10, 2025, National Competition Policy of the Dominican Republic, published in Official Gazette No. 11193 of Apr. 15, 2025 (in Spanish)
- Constitution of the Dominican Republic (2024), voted and proclaimed on Oct. 27, 2024, published in the Official Gazette No. 11170, dated Oct. 31, 2024 (in Spanish)
- Decree No. 252-20, which establishes the Regulations for the Application of Law No. 42-08, General Law for the Defense of Competition, published in the Official Gazette No. 10979 of July 16, 2020 (in Spanish)

- Law No. 42-08, General Law for the Defense of Competition, dated Jan. 16, 2008, published in the Official Gazette No. 10458 (in Spanish)

B. *ProCompetencia's Resolutions*

- Resolution No. 009-2024, dated Aug. 14, 2024, issued by the board of directors of the National Commission for the Defense of Competition (ProCompetencia) (in Spanish), https://procompetencia.gob.do/resoluciones-procompetencia/resolucion-num-009-2024/
- Resolution No. 001-2022, dated Jan. 4, 2022, issued by the board of directors of the National Commission for the Defense of Competition (ProCompetencia) (in Spanish), https://procompetencia.gob.do/resoluciones-procompetencia/resolucion-numero-001-2022/
- Resolution No. 010-2021, dated June 14, 2021, issued by the board of directors of the National Commission for the Defense of Competition (ProCompetencia), (in Spanish), https://procompetencia.gob.do/resoluciones-procompetencia/resolucion-num-010-2021/
- Resolution No. 018-2018, dated Dec. 4, 2018, issued by the board of directors of the National Commission for the Defense of Competition (ProCompetencia) (in Spanish), https://procompetencia.gob.do/resoluciones-procompetencia/resolucion-num-018-2018/

C. *Doctrine*

- Central Bank of the Dominican Republic, *Real Sector Statistics* (in Spanish), https://www.bancentral.gov.do/a/d/2533-sector-real
- Central Bank of the Dominican Republic, Report on the Dominican Economy (Jan.-Dec. 2024) (in Spanish), https://www.bancentral.gov.do/Publicaciones/Consulta CIA, The World Factbook: Dominican Republic (2026), https://www.cia.gov/the-world-factbook/countries/dominican-republic/
- IMF, Press Release, IMF Executive Board Concludes 2025 Article IV Consultation with the Dominican Republic (Nov. 18, 2025), https://www.imf.org/es/news/articles/2025/11/18/pr-25378-dominican-republic-imf-executive-board-concludes-2025-article-iv-consultation
- Martín, Pablo, Urbano & Juan Ignacio Sánchez Gutiérrez, *La política de competencia, crecimiento y globalización* [*The Policy of Competition, Growth and Globalization*], 9 Contabilidad y Negocios 83 (2014)
- National Statistics Office (ONE), General Report X National Population and Housing Census (2022) (in Spanish), https://www.one.gob.do/media/ahziolzm/informe-general-xcnpv-2022-digital.pdf
- OECD/IDB, Peer Reviews of Competition Law and Policy: Dominican Republic (2024) https://doi.org/10.1787/18f04007-en
- OECD, Multi-dimensional Review of the Dominican Republic: Towards Greater Well-Being for All, OECD Development Pathways (2022), https://doi.org/10.1787/560c12bf-en

- OECD, Fact sheet on competition and macro-economic outcomes 23 (2014), https://doi.org/10.1787/660b93ab-en
- ProCompetencia, Guide for the Prevention and Detection of Collusion in Public Procurement 2025 (2025) (in Spanish), https://procompetencia.gob.do/wpfd_file/guia-para-la-prevencion-y-deteccion-de-colusion-en-la-contratacion-publica-2025/
- ProCompetencia, Study of Competition Conditions in Health Risk Administrators (ARS) in the Dominican Republic (2025) (in Spanish), https://procompetencia.gob.do/wpfd_file/estudio-de-condiciones-de-competencia-en-la-administradoras-de-riesgos-de-salud-ars-en-la-republica-dominicana/
- ProCompetencia, Methodological Guide for Determining the Relevant Market and Dominant Position (2024) (in Spanish), https://procompetencia.gob.do/wpfd_file/guia-metodologica-para-la-determinacion-de-mercado-relevante-y-posicion-dominante/
- ProCompetencia, *Cronológico Pro-Competencia* [*Chronological ProCompetencia*], Anuario de Competencia 2023, 14–15 (2023)
- ProCompetencia, Study of Competitive Conditions in Public Procurement and Contracting Processes in the Dominican Republic (2022) (in Spanish), https://procompetencia.gob.do/wpfd_file/estudio-de-condiciones-de-competencia-en-los-procesos-de-compras-y-contrataciones-publicas-en-la-republica-dominicana
- ProCompetencia, Market Conditions Observatory (in Spanish), https://procompetencia.gob.do/observatorio-de-condiciones-de-mercado/
- Vásquez Taveras, María Elena, *La dimensión social del derecho de la competencia en la República Dominicana* [*The Social Dimension of Competition Law in the Dominican Republic*], Anuario de Competencia 2023, 83 (2023)

158. To learn more about ProCompetencia:
   - Website: www.procompetencia.gob.do

French Guiana

Odeya de La Mure, Jérôme Schall and Anne-Laure Vendrolini
French Competition Authority's Case Handlers

Supervised by Gwenaëlle Nouët
General Rapporteur at the French Competition Authority

I. Overview

1. French Guiana is located on the northern coast of South America and is bordered by Suriname to the west and Brazil to the east and south. It has a total surface area of approximately 83,846 square kilometers. French Guiana is an overseas department and region of France governed by Article 73 of the French Constitution[1], under which it operates with a single assembly exercising the powers devolved to overseas departments and regions. It is also classified as an outermost region of the European Union[2]. The official language of French Guiana is French.

II. Demographics and Economy

2. French Guiana had a population of approximately 292,354 inhabitants in 2024, corresponding to an overall population density of about 3.5 inhabitants per square kilometer. The population is primarily concentrated along the coastal zone and the major border rivers, where economic activity and infrastructure are more developed; in these coastal areas, population density reaches approximately 6.3 inhabitants per square kilometer. The nominal gross domestic product (GDP) of French Guiana is estimated at EUR 5.037 billion.

3. The territory maintains a structural trade deficit, amounting to approximately EUR 2,074 million in 2024, reflecting a high dependence on imports. In that year, imports totaled approximately EUR 2,245 million, while exports amounted to about EUR 172 million, resulting in a trade deficit that increased by 9.3 percent between 2023 and 2024. The economy of French Guiana is predominantly service-oriented, with services generating nearly three-quarters of total value added; within this sector, market services account for approximately 37 percent of value added, including 4.8 percent from transport and 1.3 percent from accommodation and food services, while non-market services represent approximately 35.9 percent of total value added.

III. Legal Framework for Competition

4. Article 73 of the French Constitution establishes the principle of legislative identity. French competition law therefore applies automatically to overseas territories.

(For further details, please refer to the "Guadeloupe" chapter.)

IV. Institutional Structure

5. The Autorité de la concurrence (hereafter, the "French Competition Authority" or "FCA") was established in 2008 as a successor to the Conseil de la concurrence (French Competition Council).

---

1 Subject to the principle of legislative identity (French laws and regulations apply under the same conditions as in mainland France, unless otherwise specified by law or regulation).

2 These regions are an integral part of the EU. Therefore, EU law and all the rights and duties associated with EU membership apply to the outermost regions. In accordance with article 349 of the Treaty on the Functioning of the European Union, specific measures and provisions in EU legislation may be taken.

(For details regarding the supervising body, organizational structure, additional regulatory mandates, budget, resources, and enforcement powers, please refer to the "Guadeloupe" chapter.)

V. Enforcement and Sanctions

6. Since 2018, the FCA has issued approximately six decisions involving French Guiana. These mainly concern abuse of a dominant position (one) and exclusive import rights (five). For instance:

  - Decision 23-D-02 of March 8, 2023, concerning practices implemented in the marketing of Canard-Duchêne champagne in the French West Indies and French Guiana (see below);
  - Decision 19-D-20 of October 8, 2019, concerning practices implemented in the distribution of perfumery and cosmetic products in the French West Indies, French Guiana, and Réunion: In this decision, the FCA fined several suppliers, importers and their parent companies for granting or benefiting from exclusive import rights for perfume and cosmetic products in the French overseas territories, in breach of article L. 420-2-1 of the French Commercial Code ("Lurel Law"). The infringements concerned products marketed by Procter & Gamble, Coty and Bourjois in Guadeloupe, Martinique, French Guiana and Réunion after March 22, 2013. The FCA imposed fines on both the suppliers that granted the exclusivities and the distributors that benefited from them, in accordance with the transaction procedure accepted by the parties;
  - Decision 19-D-11 of May 29, 2019, regarding practices implemented in the marketing of reagents and consumables for hospital laboratories in French Guiana (see below);
  - Decision 18-D-03 of February 20, 2018, regarding practices implemented in the marketing of biocidal termite traps in Réunion, the French West Indies, and French Guiana (see below).

7. Regarding French Guiana, Outremer Télécom brought an action for damages against Decision 09-D-36 of December 9, 2009, relating to practices implemented by Orange Caraïbe and France Télécom in various electronic communications service markets in the departments of Martinique, Guadeloupe and French Guiana. The Paris Court of Appeal, in a ruling issued on June 17, 2020, No. 17/23041, ordered Orange Caraïbe SA and Orange SA jointly to pay Digicel Antilles Françaises Guyane SA EUR 173.64 million in compensation for lost profits. Orange Caraïbe SA is ordered to pay Digicel Antilles SA EUR 7.12 million in compensation for the additional costs incurred as a result of the exclusivity agreements it imposed on distributors, as well as compensation for its financial loss. Orange Caraïbe SA is ordered to pay Digicel Antilles SA EUR 737,500 in compensation for the additional costs incurred as a result of the exclusive repair agreement it entered into, as well as compensation for its financial loss.

(For information on fines, sanctions, and private enforcement, please refer to the "Guadeloupe" chapter.)

VI. Noteworthy Cases

A. *Decision 23-D-02 of March 8, 2023, concerning practices implemented in the marketing of Canard-Duchêne champagne in the French West Indies and French Guiana*

8. *Facts.* The FCA sanctioned several companies in the Arvitis Group and two wholesale importers for maintaining exclusive import rights in French Guiana and Guadeloupe after the Lurel Law.

9. The sanctioned companies maintained contracts containing exclusive distribution clauses until December 31, 2013. Furthermore, it was established that these exclusive practices continued outside the contractual framework until December 31, 2016. The FCA found, for example, that Arvitis refused to sell its Canard-Duchêne products directly to potential buyers in French Guiana and redirected them to its exclusive local importer. Arvitis also implemented a promotion mechanism in favor of the sole exclusive importer, intended to encourage local buyers to acquire its products via the latter.

10. *Legal issue.* Breach of article L. 420-2-1 of the Commercial Code prohibiting exclusive import rights/financial penalties.

11. The total amount of the fines is EUR 283,000:
    - TCD (jointly with Champagne Canard-Duchêne and Arvitis as parent companies): EUR 29,000 (French Guiana) and EUR 10,000 (Guadeloupe);
    - TCD, Champagne Canard-Duchêne, C&C Export and Arvitis (jointly with Champagne Canard-Duchêne, Dourthe, Arvitis Bordeaux and Arvitis as parent companies): EUR 59,000 (French Guiana) and EUR 19,000 (Guadeloupe);
    - Sodis Chrismay (jointly with Tallandier Frères as parent company): EUR 119,000 (French Guiana);Sodipa (jointly with SGPM as parent company): EUR 47,000 (Guadeloupe).

12. *Outcome.* No appeal was filed within the legal time limits.

13. *Impact or precedent set.* This is the tenth decision issued by the FCA concerning exclusive import practices in overseas territories.

B. *Decision 19-D-11 of May 29, 2019, regarding practices implemented in the marketing of reagents and consumables for hospital laboratories in French Guiana*

14. *Facts.* The FCA has fined the companies bioMérieux SA and Guyane Service Médical for having, from March 22, 2013, to August 25, 2016, in the case of the former, granted exclusive import rights on its medical biology products and, in the case of the latter, benefited from these rights.

15. These rights, which stemmed from an exclusive distribution agreement concluded in 1995, continued to be contractually stipulated after March 22, 2013, in violation of article L. 420-2-1 of the French Commercial Code, inserted by Law No. 2012-1270 of November 20, 2012, concerning economic regulation overseas, known as the “Lurel

Law," which prohibits agreements or concerted practices whose object or effect is to grant exclusive import rights to a company or group of companies in the overseas territories.

16. *Legal issue.* Breach of article L. 420-2-1 of the Commercial Code/financial penalties.

17. The company bioMérieux SA was fined EUR 75,000, and Guyane Service Médical, which directly benefited from the existence of exclusive rights in its favor, was fined EUR 150,000.

18. *Outcome.* No appeal was filed within the legal time limits.

19. *Impact or precedent set.* This is the sixth decision issued by the FCA concerning exclusive import practices in overseas territories.

C. *Decision 18-D-03 of February 20, 2018, regarding practices implemented in the marketing of biocidal termite traps in Réunion, the French West Indies, and French Guiana*

20. *Facts.* Located in the intertropical zone, France's overseas territories provide particularly favorable conditions for termite infestations. To address this issue, the legal and regulatory framework mandates strict building-protection measures. To this end, buyers and owners can utilize various preventative or curative eradication methods, such as biocide-impregnated bait traps. The Dow Agrosciences group markets, under the brand name Sentri Tech™, the only biocide-based bait trap whose effectiveness was certified in the French overseas territories.

21. The FCA found that Dow Agrosciences had maintained exclusive import clauses in its marketing contracts for traps several years after the ban came into effect in March 2013, with Emeraude Environnement in Réunion and CTC in the French West Indies and French Guiana.

22. These agreements could not benefit from the exemption provided for in paragraph III of article L. 420-4 of the French Commercial Code because the companies involved failed to demonstrate the existence of objective reasons based on economic efficiency that could justify granting unlimited import exclusivity, and to provide proof, or at least an estimate, of the qualitative or financial benefit that the consumer could derive from such import exclusivity.

23. Furthermore, Emeraude Environnement, the sole importer-wholesaler for Dow Agrosciences in Réunion until December 31, 2016, refused to supply Sentri Tech products to a company specialized in termite control.

24. *Legal issue.* Breach of articles L. 420-2-1 and L. 420-2 of the Commercial Code/financial penalties.

25. The Dow Agrosciences group companies were fined EUR 60,000. Emeraude Environnement and Carib Termite Control were each fined EUR 5,000.

26. Furthermore, the Dow Agrosciences group companies were ordered, within two months, to remove any provision establishing import exclusivity or any clause having an equivalent effect, and to inform all companies using the Sentri Tech process overseas of this removal in writing. These companies must also refrain from including any

provision establishing import exclusivity or any clause having an equivalent effect in their overseas distribution contracts for a period of two years.

27. *Outcome.* No appeal was filed within the legal time limits.

28. *Impact or precedent set.* This is the fourth decision issued by the FCA concerning exclusive import practices in overseas territories.

VII. Merger Control

29. As with antitrust law, French merger control applies in French Guiana. However, the French Commercial Code lays down specific rules for mergers concerning overseas territories in article L. 430-2, III.

30. Examples of notified mergers:

- Decision 24-DCC-154 of July 24, 2024, concerning the acquisition of sole control of Nouveau Comptoir Caraïbe d'Importation et d'Exportation by Citadelle: Thresholds of article L. 430-2, III / Automotive distribution sector / Clearance decision;
- Decision 21-DCC-172 of October 1, 2021, concerning the creation of a joint venture by AGI, EDF PEI, Genak, and SAFO: Thresholds of article L. 430-2, I / Electricity sector / Clearance decision;
- Decision 19-DCC-180 of September 27, 2019, concerning the acquisition of sole control of NDIS by SAFO: Thresholds of article L. 430-2, III / Food distribution sector / Clearance decision subject to remedies;
- Decision 14-DCC-15 of February 10, 2014, concerning the acquisition of sole control of Mediaserv, Martinique Numérique, Guyane Numérique, and La Réunion Numérique by Canal Plus Overseas: Thresholds of article L. 430-2, I / Telecommunications sector / Clearance decision subject to remedies.

(For information on notification thresholds and review timeframes, please refer to the "Guadeloupe" chapter.)

VIII. Advocacy and Policy Initiatives

(See the "Guadeloupe" chapter)

IX. Regional and International Cooperation

(See the "Guadeloupe" chapter)

X. Challenges and Country-Specific Features

A. *Dependence on Imports/Foreign Investment*

31. In its Opinion 19-A-12 of July 4, 2019, regarding the functioning of competition in the French overseas territories, the FCA indicated:

> Overseas departments are characterized by a structurally negative trade balance. The trade deficit is caused by the fact that these regions have a high level of

> imports relative to their exports. . . . The small size of local markets often prevents local businesses from reaching optimal production levels and achieving economies of scale, which affects their competitiveness and the prices of consumer goods.[3]

32. According to IEDOM's annual report for 2024:

> Imports of goods and services are estimated at EUR 3,001 million in 2023 in value. ...At the same time, exports contracted in value by 24.5%, amounting to EUR 866.3 million... As in the other French overseas departments and regions (DROM) and in most island economies, French Guiana's trade balance is structurally in deficit. In 2024, this deficit in trade in goods worsened (+ 9.2% to – EUR 2,032 million). The sharp increase in imports, combined with a less pronounced growth in exports in value, explains this further deterioration. This deficit has increased by 60.7% in ten years. The weakness of the local production sector, which can only absorb a small share of the growing demand, is one of the main causes. Although the trade deficit affects all product categories, investment goods and non-durable consumer goods constitute the majority.[4]

33. In its Opinion 19-A-12 of July 4, 2019, the FCA indicated:

> Martinique, Guadeloupe, French Guiana, and Réunion continue to suffer from a significant trade imbalance... For French Guiana, the negative trade balance is due to the volume of imports rather than exports, which are comparable to the national level... Finally, despite the distance, the bulk of the French overseas departments' trade – both imports and exports – is conducted with mainland France, and this despite the geographical proximity of major markets with which France maintains strong trade relations (such as Brazil and the United States for the French West Indies/French Guiana region).[5]

34. Concerning foreign investment, metropolitan France is the main investor according to IEDOM's annual report for 2024:

> In order to accelerate the economic, social, and environmental development of the French overseas departments and regions (DROM) and to reduce quality-of-life disparities at the EU level, significant financial resources are being allocated within the framework of the two main multiannual programming instruments: the Convergence and Transformation Contract (CCT) and European programs. EU support is intended to bolster the investments planned under the CCT, which constitute a large share of the national contributions to European programs.[6]

B. *Lack of Resources or Expertise*

35. According to the French Development Agency, French Guiana faces a shortage of infrastructure, equipment and qualified personnel, particularly in the health sector.

---

3 Opinion 19-A-12 of July 4, 2019, paras. 339 and following (in French) (our translation).

4 IEDOM, Annual Economic Report of French Guiana 2024, p. 48, 52 (June 2005) (in French) (our translation), https://www.iedom.fr/Rapport-annuel-economique-de-la-Guyane-2024.

5 FCA, Opinion 19-A-12 of July 4, 2019, paras. 21–22 (in French) (our translation).

6 IEDOM, *supra* note 5, at 53 (our translation).

(Small market size, high concentration, and the balancing of competition with development goals are addressed in the "Guadeloupe" chapter.)

XI. References and Resources

A. *Laws and Regulations*

- Book IV of the legislative part of the French Commercial Code: On Freedom of Prices and Competition (arts. L. 410-1 to L. 490-14) (in French)
- Book IV of the regulatory part of the French Commercial Code: On Freedom of Prices and Competition (arts. R. 410-1 to R. 490-10) (in French)

B. *Case Law*

- FCA, Decision 24-DCC-154 of July 24, 2024, concerning the acquisition of sole control of Nouveau Comptoir Caraïbe d'Importation et d'Exportation by Citadelle (in French)
- FCA, Decision 23-D-02 of Mar. 8, 2023, concerning practices implemented in the marketing of Canard-Duchêne champagne in the French West Indies and French Guiana (in French)
- FCA, Decision 21-DCC-172 of Oct. 1, 2021, concerning the creation of a joint venture by AGI, EDF PEI, Genak, and SAFO (in French)
- FCA, Decision 19-D-20 of Oct. 8, 2019, concerning practices implemented in the distribution of perfumery and cosmetic products in the French West Indies, French Guiana, and Réunion (in French)
- FCA, Decision 19-DCC-180 of Sept. 27, 2019, concerning the acquisition of sole control of NDIS by SAFO (in French)
- FCA, Decision 19-D-11 of May 29, 2019, regarding practices implemented in the marketing of reagents and consumables for hospital laboratories in French Guiana (in French)
- FCA, Decision 18-D-03 of Feb. 20, 2018, regarding practices implemented in the marketing of biocidal termite traps in Réunion, the French West Indies, and French Guiana (in French)
- FCA, Decision 14-DCC-15 of Feb. 10, 2014, concerning the acquisition of sole control of Mediaserv, Martinique Numérique, Guyane Numérique, and La Réunion Numérique by Canal Plus Overseas (in French)
- FCA, Decision 09-D-36 of Dec. 9, 2009, relating to practices implemented by Orange Caraïbe and France Télécom in various electronic communications service markets in the departments of Martinique, Guadeloupe and French Guiana (in French)
- CA Paris [Paris Court of Appeal], June 17, 2020, No. 17/23041

C. *Public Reports*

- IEDOM, Annual Economic Report of French Guiana 2024 (June 2005) (in French), https://www.iedom.fr/Rapport-annuel-economique-de-la-Guyane-2024
- INSEE, Economic Review 2024 – French Guiana (June 2005) (in French), https://www.insee.fr/fr/statistiques/8569859?sommaire=8354904#figure
- FCA, Opinion 26-A-01 of Feb. 10, 2026, concerning the margins of wholesale importers and distributors of essential food products in Martinique (in French)
- FCA, Opinion 19-A-12 of July 4, 2019, regarding the functioning of competition in the French overseas territories (in French)
- FCA, Opinion 09-A-45 of Sept. 8, 2009, concerning the mechanisms for importing and distributing consumer goods in overseas departments (in French)

36. To learn more about the French Competition Authority (FCA):

Website: https://www.autoritedelaconcurrence.fr/

Contact: communication@autoritedelaconcurrence.fr

French Polynesia

Johanne Peyre
Chair of the ISLE's Executive Committee

I. Overview

1. French Polynesia is an overseas collectivity of the French Republic located in the South Pacific Ocean. It is composed of five archipelagos – namely, the Society Islands, Tuamotu, Gambier, Marquesas, and Austral – spread across an extensive maritime area. Although its landmass remains relatively limited in comparative terms, its geographical dispersion and insularity significantly shape the structure and functioning of its domestic economy.

2. The territory benefits from a high degree of institutional autonomy within the French constitutional framework. In this context, the Autorité polynésienne de la concurrence (Polynesian Competition Authority – hereafter, "APC" or the "Authority") was established as an independent administrative authority under the Loi du pays No. 2015-2 of February 23, 2015. In French Polynesia, a *loi du pays* is a normative act with the force of law, adopted by the deliberative assembly of French Polynesia.

3. French is the official language of administration and legislation, while several Polynesian languages, including Tahitian, are widely spoken and recognized in social and institutional practice.

II. Demographics and Economy

4. French Polynesia's demographic and economic characteristics are typical of small island economies marked by geographic remoteness and structural dependence on imports. Its population amounts to approximately 280,000 inhabitants.[1]

5. The territory's gross domestic product (GDP) reflects a service-oriented economy in which tourism constitutes a central pillar. Financial support from the French government also contributes to growth (these represent approximately one third of GDP). Economic activity is also supported by retail distribution, fisheries, pearl farming and a significant public sector presence (approximately 30% of employees). Owing to the limited size of the domestic market and high logistical costs associated with maritime transport, several sectors display relatively high levels of concentration.

6. French Polynesia traditionally records a structural trade deficit, with imports substantially exceeding exports. This imbalance reflects both the limited diversification of local production and the territory's reliance on imported consumer goods, intermediate inputs and capital equipment.

III. Legal Framework for Competition

7. The modern competition law regime in French Polynesia was introduced by the Loi du pays No. 2015-2 of February 23, 2015, which established a comprehensive Code de la concurrence (hereafter, the "Competition Code") and created the APC. The merger control regime has been implemented since February 1, 2016.

8. Subsequent legislative developments, including Ordonnance No. 2017-157 and Loi du pays No. 2018-31, have modified the APC's investigative and decision-making

---

1 Source: Institut de la statistique de la Polynésie française (ISPF), demographic estimates based on the 2022 census update.

powers, including by removing certain regulatory tools initially available under the 2015 framework, such as the ability to address import exclusivity arrangements and to impose structural injunctions in specific circumstances.

9. The Polynesian competition framework addresses the principal pillars of contemporary competition law, including the prohibition of anticompetitive agreements and abuse of dominant positions and the *ex ante* control of concentrations. In addition, the APC exercises specific regulatory authority over large-scale retail developments exceeding locally defined thresholds, reflecting a policy objective of preserving competitive dynamics in structurally constrained markets.

10. The regime applies across the economy as a whole, subject to any statutory exemptions that may be provided for under the Competition Code.

IV. Institutional Structure

11. The APC operates as an independent administrative authority. Its institutional architecture is composed of a decision-making body (the "Collège") and an investigation service placed under the authority of a general rapporteur (*rapporteur général*). This dual structure mirrors the separation between investigative and adjudicative functions commonly found in modern competition authorities.

12. In addition to its traditional enforcement mandate in relation to anticompetitive practices and merger control, the APC is entrusted with decision-making powers concerning retail commercial development projects. This additional competence constitutes a distinctive feature of the Polynesian institutional framework. The Authority also exercises an advisory (consultative) function, providing opinions to the government and the Assembly of French Polynesia on draft legislation, regulatory measures, and sectoral public policies likely to affect competitive conditions in local markets.

13. As of 2024, the APC operates with an annual budget of approximately XPF 50 million and a total headcount of 11 staff members. Two positions were eliminated in 2024, further constraining the Authority's operational capacity. These resource limitations are broadly reflective of the structural challenges faced by competition authorities operating in small market jurisdictions.

14. In addition, since 2021,[2] responsibility for managing the Authority's recruitment budgets and validating staff profiles and pay grades has been transferred from the APC to the government of French Polynesia (the "Pays"). This reallocation has reduced the Authority's discretion over workforce planning and recruitment timelines.

V. Enforcement and Sanctions

15. The APC is empowered to investigate potential infringements of competition law and, where appropriate, to impose corrective measures and sanctions within the limits defined by the Competition Code.

---

2 Loi du pays No. 2021-40 of Sept. 7, 2021, amending the legislative provisions of the Competition Code (*Loi du pays n° 2021-40 du 7 septembre 2021 portant modification de la partie législative du code de la concurrence*).

16. Its enforcement practice encompasses merger review decisions, authorizations or refusals relating to commercial development projects, as well as antitrust proceedings. In urgent circumstances, the APC may also adopt interim measures (*mesures conservatoires*) designed to prevent serious and immediate harm to competition pending the outcome of a full investigation.

17. Pursuant to article LP. 641-2 of the Competition Code, the APC may impose financial penalties of up to 5% of the highest turnover (excluding taxes) achieved in French Polynesia by the undertaking concerned during any of the three financial years preceding the decision. In addition to administrative fines, infringements may give rise to civil liability, allowing affected parties to seek damages before the competent courts. Criminal sanctions are also provided for individuals under the Competition Code.

VI. Noteworthy Cases

18. A number of recent decisions illustrate the APC's approach to preserving competitive market structures in a small and geographically fragmented economy.

19. In Opinion 2019-AO-02 on import and distribution mechanisms, the Authority conducted a comprehensive assessment of the regulatory and contractual arrangements governing the importation and distribution of consumer goods in French Polynesia. The analysis focused in particular on the prevalence of exclusive import agreements and their interaction with downstream distribution networks in a structurally concentrated and import-dependent economy. The APC identified that, in small island markets characterized by high transport costs and limited scale, exclusive import rights may operate as significant barriers to entry by restricting parallel sourcing opportunities for competing distributors and retailers. The Opinion further examined the competitive effects of vertically integrated supply chains, including the risk that exclusive arrangements – combined with selective distribution or pricing practices – could limit contestability and facilitate the transmission of upstream market power into downstream retail markets. In this context, the Authority emphasized that import exclusivities, while not per se unlawful, may produce foreclosure effects where they result in the de facto elimination of alternative sources of supply for independent operators. The APC therefore recommended a series of policy measures aimed at enhancing competitive neutrality in import channels, including increased transparency in supply conditions, the facilitation of multi-sourcing by distributors, and the careful scrutiny of regulatory frameworks likely to reinforce territorial exclusivities. The Opinion has since informed subsequent advocacy work by the Authority in relation to the cost of living and the structure of retail distribution chains in French Polynesia.

20. In Decision 2022-SC-09, the Authority refused authorization for the proposed establishment of a Carrefour retail outlet in Paopao (Moorea), on the grounds that the project was liable to result in the foreclosure of existing competitors and to alter local market dynamics in a manner detrimental to effective competition.

21. In Decision 2023-PAC-01, concerning mobile roaming services in certain remote archipelagos, the APC adopted interim measures following allegations by a new entrant that the incumbent operator had proposed excessive or discriminatory access conditions. The decision constitutes a notable precedent regarding the use of interim relief to safeguard market entry.

22. In Decision 2024-CC-01 concerning the proposed acquisition of Bolloré Logistics by CMA CGM, the APC conducted an in-depth assessment of the competitive effects of the transaction in the freight forwarding and logistics services markets in French Polynesia. The Authority identified risks of vertical foreclosure and the strengthening of market power arising from the integration of maritime transport and downstream logistics activities. The transaction was ultimately cleared subject to structural commitments, notably the divestiture of Bolloré Logistics' activities in French Polynesia.

VII. Merger Control

23. Merger control (*contrôle des opérations de concentration*) is applicable in French Polynesia pursuant to the Competition Code, in particular articles LP. 310-1 *et seq.*

24. Pursuant to articles LP. 310-2 and LP. 310-3 of the Competition Code, a concentration must be notified to the APC where the following jurisdictional thresholds are met. For the purposes of this regime, "statutory thresholds" refer to the turnover thresholds expressly set by articles LP. 310-2 and LP. 310-3:

- the *combined global turnover* of all undertakings or groups of undertakings concerned exceeds *XPF 1,000,000,000; and*
- at least *two undertakings concerned each achieve a turnover exceeding XPF 200,000,000 in French Polynesia* (local nexus requirement).

25. Alternatively, pursuant to article LP. 310-3, notification is also required where the undertakings concerned hold a *combined market share of 25% or more* on a relevant market in French Polynesia and the transaction involves the acquisition of control over an undertaking carrying out economic activity within the territory.

26. Transactions meeting these thresholds are subject to prior review by the APC. Following notification, the Authority assesses whether the proposed concentration is likely to harm effective competition, notably by creating or strengthening a dominant position within the meaning of article LP. 310-6 of the Competition Code.

27. Pursuant to articles LP. 310-5 to LP. 310-7, the APC may (i) clear the transaction unconditionally, (ii) clear it subject to commitments proposed by the notifying parties, or (iii) prohibit it where the competitive harm identified cannot be remedied. Commitments may be behavioral or structural in nature and are designed to prevent anticompetitive effects arising from the transaction.

28. In addition, under article LP. 310-7, the president of French Polynesia may exercise a power of evocation to take a final decision on a concentration previously assessed by the APC where considerations of general interest – such as economic development or the maintenance of employment – so require. This mechanism allows for a distinction between the competition assessment conducted by the Authority and broader public interest considerations.

VIII. Advocacy and Policy Initiatives

29. Beyond its enforcement activities, the APC engages in advocacy initiatives aimed at promoting a competition culture among public institutions, businesses, and consumers.

These initiatives include the publication of guidelines, outreach activities and the conduct of sectoral inquiries where appropriate.

30. The Authority is also actively involved in academic and policy-oriented research relating to the application of competition law and economics in small and insular economies. In this regard, the APC supports and contributes to the Institute for Small Markets in Law and Economics (ISLE) initiative, which seeks to develop analytical frameworks, policy tools and enforcement methodologies adapted to structurally constrained markets. Through this involvement, the APC participates in capacity-building programs and collaborative research aimed at improving the effectiveness of competition policy in island jurisdictions.

IX. Regional and International Cooperation

31. The APC maintains cooperative relations with France's Autorité de la concurrence and participates in regional networks of competition authorities within the Pacific area. In particular, it is a founding member of the Pacific Island Network of Competition Consumer and Economic Regulators (PINCCER).

32. The Authority also maintains close institutional cooperation with the New Caledonia Competition Authority (ACNC), including through the participation of the president of the APC as a board member of the ACNC. Such cooperation supports the exchange of expertise and contributes to the progressive alignment of enforcement practices with international standards.

X. Challenges and Country-Specific Features

33. The enforcement of competition law in French Polynesia must take into account a number of structural constraints, including the small size of domestic markets, geographic dispersion, high transport costs and dependence on imports. These characteristics often result in concentrated market structures and may increase the risk of exclusionary practices.

34. Accordingly, the Authority's intervention seeks to balance the promotion of competitive market outcomes with broader economic development objectives in a context marked by logistical and structural limitations.

XI. Author's Perspective

35. In small and insular economies, competition enforcement frequently requires a forward-looking approach, as individual transactions or contractual arrangements may exert a disproportionate and lasting impact on market structure. The Polynesian framework's combination of traditional antitrust instruments, interim measures and *ex ante* control of commercial development provides a tailored mechanism for preserving contestability in such environments.

XII. References and Resources

A. *Laws and Regulations*

- Loi du pays No. 2015-2 (Feb. 23, 2015)

B. *Case Law*

- APC, Decision 2024-CC-01 of Jan. 31, 2024 (CMA CGM / Bolloré Logistics)
- APC, Decision 2023-PAC-01 of Mar. 31, 2023 (Viti / Onati)
- APC, Decision 2022-SC-09 of June 23, 2022 (Carrefour Moorea) (in French)
- APC, Opinion 2019-AO-02 of Sept. 19, 2019 (Import and distribution mechanisms)

C. *Public Reports*

- APC Annual Reports
- IEOM Annual Reports

D. *Academic Articles or Books*

- Competition Law and the Challenges of Insular Economies: A Focus on French Polynesia and the Pacific Region (Johanne Peyre, Enzo Silvestro, Vivien Terrien, Teuraterai Emen & Yannick Lecornu eds., 2025)
- OECD, From Globalisation to Regionalisation – Contribution from French Polynesia (OECD Global Forum on Competition, DAF/COMP/GF/WD(2023)4, Dec. 4, 2023)
- Peyre, Johanne, William E. Kovacic & Alejandro Ibarra, *An Overview of the Competition Law and Policy Challenges in the Pacific Islands: The Case of French Polynesia*, 30 CLJP/JDCP 199 (2024)

Gibraltar

Stewart Brittenden
Head of Competition
Gibraltar Competition and Markets Authority

I. Overview

1. Gibraltar is located at the southern tip of the Iberian Peninsula, bordering Spain to the north and facing the Mediterranean Sea to the east and the Atlantic Ocean to the west. It overlooks the Strait of Gibraltar, a strategic waterway separating Europe from Africa. This has made Gibraltar one of the most important maritime and military locations in the world, historically serving as a key naval base and gateway between continents.

2. Gibraltar is a British Overseas Territory under the sovereignty of the United Kingdom (UK) but with a high degree of internal self-government. It has its own parliament, chief minister and constitution, which give it authority over domestic affairs, while the UK retains responsibility for defence and foreign relations. Although Spain claims sovereignty over Gibraltar, its people have consistently rejected this in referendums, choosing to remain British. Gibraltar is not part of the UK itself, but it is part of the British family of territories, enjoying a distinct constitutional relationship with the UK based on self-determination and democratic governance.

3. English is the official language of Gibraltar, although Spanish is widely spoken. There is also an unofficial local dialect unique to Gibraltar called Yanito, which is a mixture of English, Spanish, and some Italian. Its most prominent feature is the Rock of Gibraltar, a towering limestone monolith rising over 400 meters above sea level. The territory has a total surface area of 6.8 km^2, making it one of the smallest territories in the world.

4. Gibraltar's relationship with the European Union (EU) has been shaped by its status as a British Overseas Territory. When the UK joined the EU in 1973, Gibraltar was included as a European territory for whose external relations the UK was responsible, giving it partial membership. However, it was excluded from certain EU arrangements, such as the Customs Union, Common Agricultural Policy, and VAT area. Following Brexit in 2020, Gibraltar left the EU along with the UK, despite its residents voting overwhelmingly (96%) to remain. Since then, the UK, EU, and Spain have been negotiating a post-Brexit agreement to manage Gibraltar's border, customs, and travel arrangements, with the aim of maintaining fluid movement across the Gibraltar–Spain frontier while respecting its British sovereignty.

5. Gibraltar's legal system is based on English common law, supplemented by local statutes enacted by its Parliament, meaning its courts follow much of the same legal tradition as the UK but with laws tailored to local needs. The territory's currency is the Gibraltar pound (GIP), which is pegged at parity with the British pound sterling (GBP); both currencies are accepted locally, though Gibraltar-issued notes and coins are not used outside the territory. Gibraltar operates in the Central European Time (CET) zone (UTC+1), the same as neighboring Spain, and observes Central European Summer Time (CEST) (UTC+2) during daylight saving months.

6. Gibraltar's hybrid identity, distinctly British yet Mediterranean, defines its unique culture and lifestyle. The combination of legal stability, cultural vibrancy and favorable climate makes it an attractive place to live and work. The international airport connects to UK cities, including London, Manchester and Bristol, and offers seasonal or charter flights.

II. Demographics and Economy

7. Gibraltar has a population of approximately 38,000 residents (2025 estimate). Given its small area of 6.8 km², this results in a very high population density of roughly 4,000–5,000 persons per square kilometer, making it one of the most densely populated territories in the world. The population is ethnically and culturally diverse. Gibraltarians are primarily descendants of settlers who arrived after the British took control in 1704, including British, Genoese (Italian), Portuguese, and Maltese families. Over time, other groups have contributed to the population, including Spanish, Moroccan, and smaller communities from India and other Mediterranean countries. Many residents today have mixed ancestry, reflecting this historical layering of communities. Additionally, Gibraltar's workforce includes frontier workers, mainly Spaniards who commute daily from nearby Spanish towns, adding to the broader demographic and cultural interaction of the territory.

8. Gibraltar's economy is service-based, with virtually all economic output coming from a few key sectors:

   - Financial services: banking, insurance, investment management;
   - Online gaming and gambling: a major international hub;
   - Tourism: including day visitors from Spain and cruise ships;
   - Shipping and port services: bunkering, transshipment, and marine services.

9. Together, these sectors account for around 70–80% of GDP, making the economy highly concentrated and specialised. Gibraltar's nominal GDP is approximately GBP 3.1 billion, reflecting its small population but high-value service economy.

10. The territory is highly open economically, with total trade in goods and services amounting to several times its GDP. Gibraltar generally runs a trade deficit in goods – for example, imports from the UK exceed exports – but this is offset by service exports, especially in finance and online gaming, making the overall balance more positive.

11. Gibraltar's economy is highly concentrated, dominated by a few sectors and major firms within each sector. This small-scale concentration means the economy is vulnerable to regulatory or market changes in key areas like online gaming, finance, or cross-border trade, but it also allows Gibraltar to specialize efficiently in high-value services.

12. Gibraltar maintains robust telecommunications infrastructure, including three independent full-fibre broadband networks and 4G/5G mobile coverage. Gibraltar is connected internationally through submarine fibre-optic cables linking it to Spain, the UK, and other parts of Europe, ensuring reliable global communications. The government and private sector have invested heavily in digital infrastructure, supporting data centres and secure online services, making Gibraltar one of the most digitally connected territories in the region despite its limited size.

III. Legal Framework for Competition

A. *The Gibraltar Regulatory Authority*

13. The Gibraltar Regulatory Authority (the "Authority") is designated as the competent authority for the promotion and enforcement of competition law in Gibraltar. Pursuant to such designation, the Authority must discharge all the functions, duties and obligations in accordance with the Competition Act 2020, acting in its capacity as the Gibraltar Competition and Markets Authority (GCMA).

14. The Authority was established in 2000 under the Gibraltar Regulatory Authority Act and is a converged regulator responsible for overseeing the electronic communications, broadcasting, postal, cybersecurity, higher education, online accessibility, spectrum management, data protection, and competition law fields.

15. The Authority is independent of government. It has a board consisting of three members appointed by the chief minister, and currently employs 25 staff members.

B. *The Competition Act 2020*

16. The Competition Act 2020 (the "Act") came into force on January 1st, 2021, and provides a comprehensive legal framework for regulating competition across Gibraltar's economy, aiming to ensure fair market practices and protect consumer interests. The Act addresses several key areas, including agreements between undertakings, abuse of dominance, mergers, cartels, super complaints, market studies and market investigations. Under the provisions relating to agreements, any arrangement, decision, or concerted practice between businesses that has the object or effect of restricting, preventing, or distorting competition in Gibraltar may be prohibited. This includes price-fixing agreements, market-sharing arrangements, and other forms of anti-competitive coordination.

17. The Act also targets the abuse of a dominant position by firms that hold significant market power. Such abuse can take multiple forms, including imposing unfair terms on customers, limiting production or supply, or engaging in practices that exclude competitors from the market. By addressing abuse of dominance, the Act seeks to prevent large or powerful businesses from exploiting their position in a way that harms consumers or reduces market efficiency.

18. Another key element of the Act is its regulation of mergers and acquisitions. Businesses planning mergers that may substantially lessen competition in Gibraltar are recommended to notify the GCMA, which has the authority to review the merger, impose remedies, or, in extreme cases, block it. This provision ensures that market consolidation does not lead to monopolistic structures that could stifle competition.

19. The Act also contains specific provisions targeting cartels, which are considered among the most serious violations of competition law. Cartels, including price-fixing, bid rigging, and output restrictions, are strictly prohibited, with severe penalties for infringements. In addition, the Act introduces the concept of super complaints, allowing consumer bodies or designated organizations to raise concerns about market practices that may harm consumers on a systemic level, ensuring that the regulatory authority can investigate widespread market problems proactively.

20. Furthermore, the Act empowers the GCMA to conduct market studies and market investigations. These tools allow the authority to examine the functioning of specific sectors, assess competition levels, and identify potential areas for regulatory intervention. Such investigations provide the foundation for evidence-based policy and help maintain a competitive and efficient economic environment across Gibraltar.

21. The Act applies to all sectors of the economy, from finance and online gaming to retail, shipping, and professional services. However, the Act recognizes that smaller businesses may not have the same market impact as larger firms and allows for certain exemptions or simplified requirements in specific areas. This approach ensures that the regulatory framework remains proportionate, targeting businesses whose activities have significant implications for competition while minimizing burdens on smaller enterprises.

22. Overall, the Act establishes a modern, robust legal framework for promoting competition in Gibraltar, aligning the territory's approach with international standards while addressing its unique economic and geographic context. By covering agreements, dominance, mergers, cartels, and market investigations, the Act provides the GCMA with a wide range of tools to monitor, investigate, and enforce competition law effectively, helping maintain fair markets and protect consumers.

23. The GCMA can carry out investigations into markets, agreements, dominance, mergers and cartels. Enforcement includes entry into business and domestic premises, the imposition of fines (on firms and individuals), and imprisonment (for individuals).

IV. Enforcement and Sanctions

A. *Agreements between Undertakings (Chapter 1 Prohibition)*

24. The Act prohibits any agreements, decisions, or concerted practices between undertakings that have the *object or effect* of restricting, preventing, or distorting competition in Gibraltar. Examples include price-fixing, bid rigging, output limitation, and market sharing. The GCMA has the authority to initiate investigations, request information, and enter business and domestic premises to collect evidence. If a breach is established, the GCMA may declare the agreement void and impose financial penalties. Fines can reach up to 10% of an undertaking's worldwide turnover.

B. *Abuse of a Dominant Position (Chapter 2 Prohibition)*

25. The GCMA can investigate undertakings suspected of abusing a dominant position in a market, for example by imposing unfair trading conditions, refusing to supply essential inputs, predatory pricing, or restricting market access. Where dominance is abused, the GCMA can order the company to cease the abusive conduct, implement behavioural or structural remedies and impose monetary penalties similar to those for anti-competitive agreements.

C. *Mergers*

26. The Act grants the GCMA the power to review mergers or acquisitions that may substantially lessen competition in Gibraltar. Mergers can be voluntarily pre-notified

to the authority, or the GCMA can call in a merger for investigation if concerns arise. Following an inquiry, the GCMA may approve, approve with conditions, or prohibit the merger. Where parties proceed in breach of a prohibition, the GCMA can impose substantial financial penalties, require divestiture of assets, or unwind the merger to restore competitive conditions.

D. *Market Studies and Investigations*

27. The Act empowers the GCMA to conduct market studies to assess the overall level of competition within a sector and, where necessary, escalate to a market investigation if it believes structural or behavioural features are harming competition. During these investigations, the GCMA has powers to compel information, summon witnesses, and enter premises under warrant. Following an investigation, the authority may recommend legislative or regulatory changes, impose binding remedies, or refer the matter to the government if broader intervention is required.

E. *Cartels and Criminal Enforcement*

28. Cartels are treated as the most serious form of anti-competitive conduct under the Competition Act 2020. The GCMA has dedicated powers to investigate cartel activity, including leniency provisions allowing participants to disclose information in exchange for reduced penalties. Proven cartel behavior can result in corporate fines of up to 10% of turnover and criminal prosecution of individuals, carrying penalties of imprisonment of up to five years and/or unlimited fines. The GCMA may also seize materials, freeze assets, and cooperate with foreign authorities in cross-border cases.

29. The Act also allows private parties (such as consumers, competitors, or businesses) who have suffered loss or damage as a result of a breach of the competition rules to bring a civil claim for damages before the Supreme Court of Gibraltar. This right arises primarily from infringements of either:

   - the Chapter 1 Prohibition (anti-competitive agreements or cartels), or
   - the Chapter 2 Prohibition (abuse of a dominant position).

30. In such cases, the claimant must prove that:

   - an infringement of the Competition Act has occurred (for example, price-fixing or abuse of dominance);
   - they suffered identifiable loss or damage as a result of that infringement; and
   - there is a direct causal link between the infringement and the harm suffered.

31. The GCMA's findings can be used as strong (often decisive) evidence in these civil proceedings. Once an infringement decision becomes final, claimants can rely on it to pursue compensation without needing to demonstrate the underlying breach.

32. Remedies can include compensatory damages for actual financial loss, interest, and in some cases, injunctive relief to prevent ongoing harm. Collective or representative actions (where a group of affected parties brings a single claim) may also be possible under Gibraltar's procedural law.

V. Merger Control

33. The GCMA can investigate voluntary notifications of anticipated and completed mergers and also conduct its own initiative investigations into mergers that have not been notified. There is no requirement to notify mergers to the GCMA; therefore, notification is voluntary. However, the GCMA has the power to determine whether any unnotified merger may give rise to competition concerns.

34. Mergers are usually assessed in three stages: Pre-notification, Phase 1 and Phase 2.

35. Pre-notification involves preliminary meetings with parties to help clarify the information and evidence that the GCMA will require, discuss the approach to the assessment of potential competition concerns and, in some cases, potential remedy options if the probability of the merger lessening competition is high.

36. Where merger parties wish to formally notify a merger to the GCMA for investigation, they must submit a Merger Notice. The submission of a Merger Notice enables the GCMA to allocate a case team to lead the GCMA's Phase 1 investigation. The case team is the principal point of contact within the GCMA for the merger parties and their representatives.

37. The GCMA has a statutory deadline of 40 working days to complete this initial stage of the merger review process, although the deadline can be suspended in certain circumstances, such as when specific information requested by the GCMA remains outstanding.

38. During Phase 1, the GCMA must consider whether to refer the merger for a Phase 2 investigation. This will be the case where the GCMA believes that a relevant merger situation has been or will be created and the creation of that situation has resulted, or may be expected to result, in a substantial lessening of competition within any market or markets in Gibraltar for goods or services. A Phase 2 investigation involves a more substantial analysis and will determine whether the GCMA will need to take any action to remedy, mitigate or prevent any anti-competitive effects.

39. For a merger to be investigated, the Gibraltar turnover of the enterprise being acquired must exceed GBP 25 million, or the enterprises merging must together supply or acquire at least two-thirds of all the goods of a particular description that are supplied in Gibraltar after the merger.

VI. Advocacy and Policy Initiatives

40. The GCMA has recently published the following guidelines:
   - CP01/24 – Prioritisation Principles
   - CP03/24 – The Chapter 1 Prohibition
   - CP04/24 – The Chapter 2 Prohibition
   - CP05/24 – Market Investigation References
   - CP06/24 – Merger Assessment Guidelines
   - CP07/24 – Merger and Market Remedies – Reporting, Investigation, and Enforcement of potential breaches

- CP08/24 – Merger and Market Remedies – Variation and termination of merger and market final undertakings and orders
- CP03/25 – Administrative Penalties
- CP04/25 – Applications for leniency in Cartel Cases.

41. The guidelines can be found on the Gibraltar Regulatory Authority's website.

VII. Challenges and Country-Specific Features

42. Administering competition law in Gibraltar presents significant challenges for a small regulator with limited resources, primarily due to the scale of the jurisdiction and the complexity of the markets it oversees. Despite its small population and limited market size, Gibraltar's economy is highly open and globally integrated, involving cross-border transactions, multinational firms, and complex digital industries such as online gambling and fintech. This creates a disproportionate regulatory burden for an authority that must monitor sophisticated market behaviors with only a small number of staff and a constrained budget.

43. A key challenge lies in technical capacity. Competition investigations require advanced economic and legal analysis, market definition studies, and access to data resources that are often scarce in a small jurisdiction. The GCMA struggles to attract and retain experienced economists, lawyers, and data analysts capable of handling complex cases involving multi-jurisdictional conduct or digital markets. Furthermore, as Gibraltar's markets are closely linked with the UK and EU, the regulator must often interpret and apply competition principles consistent with larger jurisdictions and keep pace with evolving international best practices and case law.

44. Another challenge is limited enforcement power in practice. While the Act gives the GCMA strong statutory powers, including the ability to impose fines and order remedies, effective enforcement depends on the regulator's capacity to investigate, collect evidence, and pursue lengthy legal proceedings. Large companies operating in Gibraltar may have substantial legal resources, creating an imbalance that may deter smaller regulators from engaging in protracted litigation. Additionally, the GCMA must balance competition enforcement with its other responsibilities, such as telecommunications and data protection, which stretch its resources further.

45. Public awareness and compliance culture also pose difficulties. In small markets, there may be limited understanding among businesses, particularly small to medium-sized enterprises, of competition rules, leading to inadvertent infringements. The GCMA must invest in advocacy, training, and outreach to build a culture of compliance, which can divert resources from enforcement. Moreover, Gibraltar's small size can lead to overlapping business interests, making it challenging to maintain confidentiality, avoid conflicts of interest, and ensure independence in decision-making.

46. The GCMA faces a demanding task. It must apply a sophisticated competition regime within a small, resource-constrained environment while maintaining credibility, independence, and effectiveness. Balancing enforcement, education, and international alignment remains its central challenge in ensuring that Gibraltar's markets remain fair, open and competitive.

VIII. References and Resources

47. All competition legislation can be found on the Gibraltar Regulatory Authority's website. To learn more about the Gibraltar Regulatory Authority:
    - Website: www.gra.gi
    - Email: info@gra.gi

Greenland

Nicolai Odgaard Jensen
Senior Consultant at the Greenland Consumer and Competition Authority

I. Overview

1. Greenland is a vast Arctic territory within the Kingdom of Denmark, characterized by a very small and geographically dispersed population and a correspondingly small, open economy. These structural conditions shape both market outcomes and the practice of competition law. Many markets are local by necessity, and several sectors display high levels of concentration, reflecting scale constraints, significant fixed costs, and logistics driven by distance, weather, and limited transport capacity.

2. Against this backdrop, Greenland's competition regime has gradually evolved from a transparency- and control-based system into a modern, prohibition-based framework inspired by European competition principles. The current framework combines *ex post* enforcement against anticompetitive agreements and abuse of dominance with a mandatory and suspensory merger control regime and, in selected sectors, *ex ante* market regulation (notably in telecommunications). The competition authority's toolkit also includes market studies and advocacy aimed at addressing competition problems rooted in sectoral regulation or structural barriers rather than private conduct alone.

3. In a small economy, competition enforcement often requires balancing a principled application of the law with a pragmatic understanding of how markets function when there are few undertakings, limited entry prospects, and frequent public sector involvement. The Greenlandic experience therefore illustrates how competition policy may serve both as an enforcement framework and as a governance instrument supporting pro-competitive regulation, transparency, and efficient market organization in circumstances where "workable competition" may be a more realistic benchmark than atomistic rivalry.

II. Demographics and Economy

Population ≈ 56,500
Population Density ≈ 0.03 inhabitants per km^2
Highly concentrated in coastal towns; limited and declining settlement population
Nominal GDP ≈ USD 3.4 billion
GDP per capita ≈ USD 59,970
Trade Balance (Goods)
Deficit ≈ USD 75.8 million
Exports ≈ **USD 653 million**
Imports exceed exports, reflecting high import dependency
Main Economic Sectors

- Fisheries and fish processing (dominant export sector)
- Wholesale and retail trade
- Transport and logistics
- Public sector services
- Tourism (growing, but still limited in scale)

Market Structure
High degree of market concentration
Several key sectors characterized by few large players, often publicly owned or state-influenced

4. Greenland is a vast Arctic territory of 2.2 million square kilometers within the Kingdom of Denmark. Yet it is home to a relatively small population. As of January 2025, Greenland's population was 56,542, making it one of the least densely populated places in the world (roughly 0.03 people per km^2).

5. The majority of residents live in the capital, Nuuk (35%), and regional towns (30%) – Sisimiut, Ilulissat, Aasiaat, and Qaqortoq – while many smaller settlements have seen declining populations in recent years.

6. Greenland's towns and settlements are not connected by roads, and transport is therefore primarily by air or sea. These constraints often imply that competitive conditions need to be assessed locally, meaning that relevant geographic markets will frequently be delineated at the level of the individual town or settlement.

7. In economic terms, Greenland's nominal gross domestic product (GDP) was DKK 22.9 billion (USD 3.39 billion) in 2023, reflecting the scale of its small, open economy. GDP per capita was DKK 405,200 (USD 59,970), illustrating relatively high output per resident compared with global averages.

8. Foreign trade plays a significant role in Greenland's economy. In 2025, total exports of goods amounted to about DKK 4.4 billion (USD 653 million), with fish and fish products forming the core of export revenues at DKK 3.4 billion (USD 508 million). Imports were also substantial, at DKK 4.9 billion (USD 729 million), resulting in a trade deficit in goods terms.

9. Greenland's economic structure is shaped by its natural environment and small internal market. Fisheries and fish processing dominate the export sector and are central to economic activity. Other important sectors include wholesale and retail trade, transport and logistics, and a sizeable public sector that provides essential services and employment.

10. Market concentration is a characteristic of Greenland's economy. The limited number of large enterprises, often in publicly owned or closely held sectors such as fishing, shipping and key services, means that competition dynamics differ from larger economies, with relatively few major players in core markets.

III. Legal Framework for Competition

11. Greenland's first competition law was adopted in 1992. The Competition Council (Konkurrencenævnet), which is responsible for enforcement, was established only in the late 1990s. In its early years, the Council was supported by the Danish Competition Authority, before the secretariat function was transferred to Greenland in 2002.

12. The 1992 Act was based on two core principles: control and transparency.

13. Under the control principle, a restrictive agreement or conduct became prohibited only once the competition authority had intervened.

14. Transparency referred to ensuring the simplest and least costly access for producers, traders and consumers to obtain relevant information on prices, trading conditions and other parameters of competition. The underlying assumption was that the need for regulatory intervention would diminish as market transparency increased. The 1992 Act applied only to private commercial activity (Competition Act, 1992).

15. A new competition law was adopted in 2007. This reform replaced the control-and-transparency approach with a prohibition-based regime, under which anticompetitive agreements and abuse of a dominant position are unlawful per se.

16. The 2007 Act introduced a *de minimis* exemption for restrictive agreements: the prohibition does not apply where undertakings hold market shares below 10%, or where their combined turnover is below DKK 5 million (USD 740,000), unless the conduct constitutes a hardcore restriction.

17. Hardcore restrictions include agreements on or coordination of prices and margins, as well as bid coordination.

18. The 2007 Act drew inspiration from European competition rules, but did not include merger control. Instead, it introduced a notification obligation for undertakings entering into merger agreements, enabling the competition authority to monitor developments in market concentration.

19. The reform also placed public and private commercial activity on an equal footing. In the Greenlandic context, where large publicly owned commercial undertakings operate, this more than doubled the practical scope of the law.

20. The 2007 Act further established the Competition Authority (Konkurrencetilsynet), which, together with the Competition Council, is responsible for enforcement. Infringements of the prohibition provisions are sanctioned by criminal fines (Competition Act, 2007).

21. In 2014, the competition law was updated to introduce merger control (Competition Act, 2014).

22. In 2017, the law was amended to assign the competition authority responsibility for sector-specific competition regulation in telecommunications. The objective was to implement an open and transparent regulatory framework and to streamline administrative procedures relating to interconnection and network access. This constitutes *ex ante* regulation, intended to support the development of competition in Greenland's telecommunications sector.

23. The 2017 amendment also substantially increased the level of fines for infringements of competition law. In addition, the law introduces the possibility of imprisonment for individuals who enter into cartel arrangements, where the infringement is intentional and of a serious (aggravated) nature (Competition Act, 2017).

24. In 2020, the turnover thresholds for merger control were revised. At the same time, a whistleblowing scheme was introduced to facilitate the reporting of potential infringements to the competition authority. The amendments also expanded the enforcement toolbox by introducing the possibility of civil administrative fines (Competition Act, 2020).

IV. Institutional Structure

25. Greenland's competition enforcement is carried out by an independent competition authority consisting of the Competition Council and the Consumer and Competition Authority.

26. Together, the two bodies are responsible for enforcing the competition rules in Greenland and ensuring fair and effective competition for the benefit of businesses and consumers.

27. The competition authority operates independently of Naalakkersuisut (the government of Greenland). The Consumer and Competition Authority handles day-to-day casework, including guidance, investigations and the processing of competition cases. Depending on the nature of the case, it either adopts a decision itself or submits the case to the Competition Council for a decision.

28. The Competition Council has overall responsibility for the administration of the Competition Act and related regulations. It decides cases of particular importance or cases that raise issues of principle. In addition, the Council sets the strategic direction for competition enforcement in Greenland and approves sector inquiries, market investigations and analytical work carried out by the Authority.

29. The Competition Council consists of seven members, including a chair and a vice-chair. All members are appointed by Naalakkersuisut, but both the Council and the Authority act independently when handling competition cases. The Council is composed to ensure broad expertise across public and private sectors, covering legal, economic, financial and consumer matters. Three of the seven members are appointed following nominations from business and consumer non-governmental organizations (NGOs) and the Greenlandic municipalities.

30. Most enforcement cases involving interventions against undertakings are reviewed and decided by the Competition Council. The director of the Consumer and Competition Authority determines whether a case should be referred to the prosecuting authority for potential criminal proceedings, including recommendations on fines or other sanctions.

31. In addition to general competition law enforcement, the competition remit also includes sector-specific market regulation in the telecommunications sector. In this role, the Authority adopts market decisions imposing obligations on providers with a dominant position. These obligations may include network access, non-discrimination, transparency, accounting separation and price control. Where necessary, the Authority may also impose functional separation.

32. The Consumer and Competition Authority employs around 20 staff, comprising both case officers and administrative personnel. The Authority has a broad mandate: in addition to handling competition and consumer protection matters, it also provides secretariat support and case handling appeals in other areas of public administration, including the social, housing, and environmental fields. Competition enforcement is carried out by a dedicated team of three case officers.

V. Enforcement and Sanctions

33. Undertakings that intentionally or negligently infringe the Competition Act may be subject to civil administrative fines and/or criminal fines. Individuals who intentionally or with gross negligence contribute to an undertaking's infringement may be subject to criminal fines and, in certain cases, imprisonment.

A. *Fines*

34. When setting fines for undertakings for infringements of sections 6 (prohibits cartels and anticompetitive agreements) and 11 (prohibits abuse of a dominant position) of the Competition Act, the authorities take into account the gravity and duration of the infringement, as well as the undertaking's turnover. The assessment is based on a structured approach, whereby infringements are categorized as minor, serious or very serious, with a corresponding base amount reflecting the gravity of the conduct.

35. In determining the specific fine, greater weight is placed on the undertaking's turnover, particularly in cases involving serious and very serious infringements. The objective is to ensure that fines represent a meaningful economic cost relative to the size of the undertaking, so that sanctions for comparable infringements have a broadly equivalent deterrent effect for both small and large undertakings.

36. The duration of the infringement is also taken into account. Infringements are assessed as being of short duration (less than one year), medium duration (one to five years), or long duration (more than five years). The base amount reflecting the gravity of the infringement is increased by supplements corresponding to its duration.

37. In practice, the prosecuting authority is expected to seek fines of up to DKK 4 million (USD 0.6 million) for minor infringements of the Competition Act. For serious infringements, fines are expected to range between DKK 4 million and DKK 20 million (USD 0.6–3.0 million), while fines for very serious infringements are expected to start from DKK 20 million (USD 3.0 million) and upwards. In all cases, the fine may not exceed 10% of the worldwide turnover of the corporate group to which the undertaking belongs.

B. *Imprisonment*

38. Where an individual has contributed to an undertaking's participation in a cartel, sanctions may be increased from a fine to imprisonment for up to one year and six months. This requires that the infringement be committed intentionally and be of a serious nature, in particular due to its scope or the harm it is capable of causing. In particularly aggravating circumstances, the penalty may be increased to imprisonment for up to six years.

C. *Private Enforcement*

39. Businesses and consumers may seek damages from undertakings that infringe the Competition Act. In practice, however, private enforcement is rare. The level of fines is therefore designed to reflect, among other things, the deprivation of unlawful gains when an undertaking is fined for an infringement.

40. Only a limited number of civil damages actions have been brought in relation to competition law infringements in Greenland, and these cases have often been settled out of court. As a result, there is limited publicly available case law to draw on.

VI. Noteworthy Cases

A. *Konkurrencenævnet v. KNI A/S – Scope of the Greenlandic Competition Act vis-à-vis Public Regulation*

41. These two cases concerned the boundary between the Greenlandic Competition Act and other forms of public regulation, focusing on the statutory exception whereby the Act's intervention powers do not apply to the extent a given conduct is exercised pursuant to a special legal basis and is, accordingly, subject to public regulation.

42. In the first case, the Competition Council sought a declaration that KNI Pilersuisoq A/S's activities under an agreement with Nuuk Imeq A/S on the purchase and distribution of beer and carbonated soft drinks were not covered by the exception. KNI argued that the arrangements were embedded in political decisions and legislative measures concerning the public sector's role in establishing and reorganizing relevant entities.

43. In the second case, the Competition Council challenged restraints in KNI's "oil dealer" framework (including terms on transfer restrictions, margin/fee setting, reporting obligations, and a duty to apply prices/discounts determined by KNI), arguing that these contractual provisions likewise remained subject to competition law. KNI maintained that the arrangements should be viewed against the background of public supply objectives and the broader public framework surrounding nationwide fuel provision.

44. *Central holding (common to both judgments).* Østre Landsret (Eastern High Court) took a restrictive approach to the public-regulation carve-out. The Court held that general public ownership, political establishment decisions, and organizational or restructuring legislation do not, as such, constitute a sufficiently specific "special legal basis" capable of displacing the Competition Act for particular commercial conduct. Instead, the exception presupposes a concrete and legally defined regulatory framework that specifically governs the conduct at issue (here, the challenged distribution arrangements and dealer-related contractual restraints). Where such specific public regulation is not demonstrated, competition law remains applicable.

45. On that basis, the Court upheld the Competition Council's claims in both matters, amended the prior judgments, and directed that the substantive assessment under the Competition Act proceed before the court of first instance (see Konkurrencenævnet mod KNI A/S, B-1900-07 and B-1820-07, 2008).

B. *Greenland Venture A/S v. the Competition Authority (Konkurrencetilsynet), Greenland High Court (Landsret), judgment of November 24, 2009 (Case No. A 605/08)*

46. In October 2008, the Greenlandic Competition Authority requested information from Greenland Venture A/S pursuant to section 21 of the Greenlandic Competition Act. The request covered, inter alia, the undertakings in which Greenland Venture had invested, to

which it had provided subordinated loan capital, or for which it had granted guarantees. The Authority stated that the information was needed to ensure that Greenland Venture did not infringe the Competition Act, in particular section 12 on distorting subsidies.

47. Greenland Venture refused to provide the information. It argued that it operated on commercial terms as an independent limited company and that its investment decisions were taken by its board, not by the government of Greenland. Greenland Venture therefore considered itself outside the scope of section 12 and objected to the disclosure of what it regarded as confidential business information concerning portfolio companies and partners. Following the refusal, the Authority maintained its request and announced the imposition of periodic coercive fines under section 28 if the information was not provided within seven days. The Authority subsequently imposed weekly coercive fines of DKK 10,000, although the High Court granted the action suspensive effect pending final judgment.

48. The claimant sought (i) a declaration that the Authority's information request and the coercive fines were invalid; (ii) in the alternative, a declaration that the Authority lacked a legal basis to issue orders against Greenland Venture under section 12; and (iii) in a further alternative, a declaration that the section 21 request was not justified. The Authority sought dismissal (and, in part, rejection), arguing that it acted on behalf of the Competition Council under the relevant executive order, and that section 21 provides a broad power to obtain information necessary to assess whether conduct may fall within the Competition Act.

49. The High Court held, first, that the Authority had competence to request information under section 21 on the Council's behalf. The fact that the secretariat, rather than the Council itself, decided to seek the information did not render the request invalid. Secondly, on the merits, the Court emphasized that Greenland Venture was wholly owned by the government of Greenland and had received substantial capital injections in 2005–2007. Given Greenland Venture's purpose of providing "risk-willing" and "patient" capital, the Court found it could not be excluded that its activities might, depending on the circumstances, give rise to an order under section 12. Accordingly, the information request could not be set aside on the basis that section 12 was inapplicable as a matter of principle.

50. The Court further held that whether Greenland Venture's activities could ultimately be subject to section 12 required a concrete assessment on a case-by-case basis, and that no final decision under section 12 had been taken, only an investigative information request. The Court also rejected challenges based on proportionality and the procedural rule cited by the claimant, finding no basis to set aside the Authority's assessment of necessity. An incorrect appeal instruction, if any, was not considered to entail invalidity.

51. The Authority was therefore fully acquitted. The judgment confirms a broad interpretation of the competition authority's investigative powers and underscores that publicly owned entities operating commercially may still fall within provisions addressing advantages conferred through publicly controlled resources, subject to a fact-specific assessment (see Greenland Venture A/S mod Styrelsen for Råd og Nævn, Konkurrencetilsynet, 2009).

C. *Public Prosecutor v. B.J. Entreprise A/S, Kang-Total-Byg ApS and Permagreen Grønland A/S – Bid Rigging in Public Tenders and the Relationship between Procurement Rules and Competition Law (Retten i Grønland, April 4, 2012)*

52. This set of cases comprises three parallel criminal judgments delivered on April 4, 2012, against construction undertakings active in Greenland. The proceedings concerned alleged bid coordination in several public tenders in 2008 (and related conduct), prosecuted as infringements of the prohibition on anticompetitive agreements under section 6(1) of the Greenlandic Competition Act, with corporate fines sought under section 29 and personal fines under the Act's individual-liability provisions (inter alia, sections 30–31, as applied in the indictments).

53. *Facts and conduct.* Across the three judgments, the Court addressed a pattern of coordination between competitors in connection with public procurement procedures. The evidence base (common to all cases) included tender documents and bid calculation material, as well as two recorded conversations obtained during the investigation and discussed at trial. In essence, the prosecution alleged that the undertakings exchanged sensitive price information and/or coordinated bids to ensure that a designated bidder would submit the lowest (winning) bid, while other participants would submit higher "cover" bids or abstain. The file material also referenced subcontracting arrangements linked to the tender outcome (e.g., arrangements concerning concrete works).

54. A central episode concerned a tender issued by Grønlands Lufthavnsvæsen (the airport authority) relating to works at Kangerlussuaq (a transit hall extension), where the Court found coordination between Kang-Total-Byg and B.J. Entreprise, including the use/exchange of bid sheets and calculations. The contract value referenced in the proceedings was approximately DKK 17 million (USD 2.5 million). Another strand concerned tenders in Sisimiut, in which Permagreen Grønland and B.J. Entreprise were found to have coordinated, including via exchange of pricing information in connection with a tender where Permagreen's bid was lower by a set margin and B.J. Entreprise's bid became the lowest.

55. *Key legal issue: Competition law applicability notwithstanding procurement regulation.* A core defense argument across the set of cases was that Greenlandic tendering/procurement rules (the "licitation" framework) should be treated as *lex specialis* governing bid behavior in the construction sector, thereby limiting or displacing the Competition Act's application (or at least affecting the legal assessment). The Court rejected this approach. It held, in substance, that procurement rules regulate the tendering procedure, while competition law independently prohibits anticompetitive coordination between tenderers; accordingly, bid-rigging conduct remains caught by section 6(1).

56. In doing so, the Court also clarified that "bid cartels" fall squarely within the concept of anticompetitive agreements under the Competition Act, and that the prohibition is not limited to "hardcore" cartels in the narrow sense of explicit market sharing: coordination intended to restrict competition in tendering is sufficient.

57. *Outcome and sanctions.* The Court convicted all three undertakings (and imposed personal fines on four individuals). It set corporate fines significantly below the prosecution's

requests, which were in the million-kroner range and in part framed as up to 10% of the relevant contract values. The final corporate fines were: B.J. Entreprise, DKK 670,000; Kang-Total-Byg, DKK 480,000; and Permagreen Grønland, DKK 415,000. Individuals were fined DKK 25,000 each.

58. In its reasoning on fines, the Court relied on the legislative materials to the 2007 Competition Act (including guidance on seriousness, duration and gains, and on aggravating/mitigating factors such as cooperation with the authorities), while noting that Greenlandic enforcement practice was still developing and that proportionality considerations must reflect the specific conditions of the Greenlandic market.

59. *Significance.* The set of cases is a leading early example of criminal enforcement against bid rigging. It is particularly notable for confirming that sectoral/public procurement regulation does not "occupy the field": competition law applies in parallel and continues to prohibit collusion between tenderers even where tender procedures are governed by detailed administrative rules (see Anklagemyndigheden mod B.J. Entreprise A/S, 2012; Anklagemyndigheden mod Kang-Total-Byg Aps, 2012; and Anklagemyndigheden mod Permagreen Grønland A/S, 2012).

VII. Merger Control

60. Greenlandic merger control applies to "concentrations" (i.e., mergers, acquisitions of control, and full-function joint ventures). The notification and review system is mandatory and suspensory: a notifiable concentration may not be implemented before it has been notified and approved (or otherwise cleared) under the Act.

A. *Jurisdictional Thresholds*

61. Merger control applies where: (i) the undertakings concerned have a combined annual worldwide turnover of at least DKK 100 million (USD 14.8 million); (ii) at least two of the undertakings concerned each have an annual worldwide turnover of at least DKK 50 million (USD 7.4 million); and (iii) at least one of the undertakings concerned is located in Greenland.

B. *Review Timeframes*

62. The Greenlandic merger control procedure typically commences with voluntary pre-notification contacts, which are used to clarify jurisdictional issues, align on the appropriate filing route, and streamline the subsequent review. Once the parties submit a notification, the case proceeds under either an ordinary (full) notification or a simplified notification mechanism, depending on the transaction's competitive profile and the information requirements set out in the applicable notification rules.

63. For an ordinary notification, the Authority performs an initial completeness assessment; as reflected in practice-oriented guidance, this step is generally expected to be concluded within 10 working days of receipt, and an incomplete filing will typically prompt a request identifying the missing information. The statutory review periods are triggered only once a notification is considered complete.

64. Phase I constitutes the initial assessment phase. The competent decision-making body must adopt a decision within 40 working days from receipt of a complete notification. During Phase I, the Authority conducts a prima facie competition assessment and will either clear the concentration (unconditionally or on the basis that it raises no material concerns on the information available) or initiate an in-depth investigation (Phase II) where the transaction may significantly impede effective competition.

65. Where the case proceeds to Phase II, the competent body must adopt a final decision within an additional 90 working days after expiry of the Phase I period. The Phase II deadline may be extended in defined circumstances, most notably where the parties submit new or revised commitments late in the process (commonly described as ensuring sufficient time for the assessment of late remedies), and further extensions may be available with the parties' request or consent.

66. Throughout both phases, the Authority may request supplementary information to support the competitive assessment, while the notifying parties remain responsible for ensuring that the notification and subsequent submissions are accurate, complete, and internally consistent. Finally, the statutory review periods operate as hard decision deadlines; as a structural feature of the regime, failure to adopt a decision within the applicable deadlines results in the concentration being deemed approved.

C. *Merger of Pisiffik and Arctic Retail Group*

67. In 2020, the Competition Council cleared an acquisition by Pisiffik A/S of selected assets and activities of Arctic Retail Group ApS, subject to binding commitments offered by the notifying party. The decision concerns local retail grocery markets in Nuuk and Ilulissat.

1. Transaction and Procedure

68. The transaction was structured as an asset transfer. It covered (i) inventory and store fixtures, (ii) the transfer of employees, and (iii) the transfer of leases relating to three grocery stores (two in Ilulissat and one in Nuuk), as well as a related quick service restaurant location.

2. Relevant Markets and Counterfactual

69. The Authority assessed the transaction in the retail sale of groceries in Nuuk and Ilulissat. A key element of the assessment was the likely counterfactual: the Authority considered that Arctic Retail Group would likely exit the relevant grocery markets absent the transaction, and therefore assessed competitive effects against an "exit/failing firm-type" scenario rather than continued operation by the target.

3. Competitive Assessment

70. The Authority's analysis indicated that competitive concerns were primarily local and concentrated in Ilulissat:

- Ilulissat: Post-transaction, the merged entity's share was estimated at 70–80%, and the number of market participants would decrease from three to two. Concentration levels (Herfindahl–Hirschman Index – HHI) were estimated to increase from

5,000–5,500 to 5,500–6,000 (ΔHHI > 500), pointing to a risk of unilateral effects, including higher prices and/or reduced service and assortment.
- Nuuk: Under the exit counterfactual, the Authority considered the increment in concentration to be limited (HHI broadly stable; ΔHHI < 150), and did not identify a significant impediment to effective competition.

4. Outcome and Remedies

71. Although the Authority identified a distinct risk of harm in Ilulissat, the notifying party offered two commitments, which were accepted as conditions to the clearance. On that basis, the Competition Council concluded that the transaction, as conditioned, would not significantly impede effective competition in Nuuk or Ilulissat, and therefore approved the merger (see Merger between Pisiffik A/S and Artic Retail Group ApS, 2020).

VIII. Advocacy and Policy Initiatives

A. *The Market for Beer and Soft Drinks: Enforcement and Advocacy by the Competition Authorities*

72. Since the mid-1980s, the Greenlandic market for beer and soft drinks has developed into a highly concentrated, de facto monopolized structure, where one undertaking effectively controlled bottling/production for the Greenlandic market, while another undertaking performed wholesale and distribution functions. The structure was shaped by the establishment of Nuuk Imeq A/S as a bottling platform for products linked to Danish breweries, with KNI A/S acting as the principal distributor and wholesaler to retail channels across Greenland.

73. From the outset, the business model was supported by a combination of contractual arrangements and public regulation. In particular, Nuuk Imeq benefited from time-limited exclusivity and critical packaging rules that, in practice, constrained market access by requiring specific container types associated with the incumbent system. The competition authorities' engagement with the sector therefore evolved along two complementary tracks: enforcement against anticompetitive agreements and advocacy aimed at removing regulatory features that entrenched market foreclosure.

74. On the enforcement side, the Competition Council addressed the exclusivity embedded in distribution arrangements, including litigation that clarified the authorities' competence to intervene under competition law. The Council's decisions and subsequent court proceedings contributed to opening the distribution layer by limiting the scope for contractual exclusivity that insulated the incumbent structure from competitive entry.

75. On the advocacy side, the authorities progressively reframed the principal competition issue as a regulatory barrier, namely, packaging requirements that effectively preserved Nuuk Imeq's market position even as earlier exclusivity mechanisms expired. This advocacy was pursued through sustained engagement with political and administrative decision-makers, including contributions to the broader policy debate about whether the packaging regime could be liberalized without undermining environmental objectives. Inatsisartut's (Parliament of Greenland) debate materials explicitly linked the reform

discussion to the objective of introducing competition in a market characterized by a de facto monopoly in packaging for beer and soft drinks.

76. To support evidence-based reform, the competition authorities published analytical work highlighting the efficiency gains potentially achievable through deregulation, most notably by enabling imports of beverages in alternative packaging types and reducing the need for domestic bottling as a gateway to market access. This type of market study and policy-oriented analysis served as a central advocacy instrument to inform the government's subsequent assessment of societal and environmental trade-offs.

77. These advocacy efforts ultimately aligned with legislative and regulatory developments in 2022–2023, which culminated in a new framework allowing beer and soft drinks to be sold in a broader range of packaging, provided that the packaging is included in an approved return system. The new regime entered into force on January 1, 2024, alongside the implementation of the updated return system. In parallel, Nuuk Imeq's owners publicly stated that the new packaging rules materially affected the viability of the incumbent bottling model, and the bottling operation closed effective January 1, 2024.

78. Overall, the case illustrates how the Greenlandic competition authorities combined casework and institutional advocacy to address competition problems that were not solely driven by private conduct, but also by sectoral regulation. The authorities' interventions therefore extended beyond prohibiting restrictive agreements, towards promoting pro-competitive regulatory reform consistent with wider public policy objectives, including environmental protection through a functioning return-and-recycling framework.

B. *Market Study of the Grocery Retail Sector in Greenland (2023)*

79. In response to rising inflation in Greenland, the Consumer and Competition Authority initiated a market study of the grocery retail sector.[1]

80. The study examined developments in consumer prices in Greenland, with a particular focus on food prices in general and meat prices in particular. Price developments in Greenland were analyzed and compared with trends observed in selected other countries.

81. Based on the data collected, the Consumer and Competition Authority found no indication of excessive profits that would suggest abuse of a dominant position or coordination of food prices in the Greenlandic market.

82. The analysis showed that food price developments in Greenland are largely driven by price trends in Denmark and, to a lesser extent, the EU. There was no basis for concluding that the Greenlandic food price index had increased more than in Denmark.

83. On the contrary, the study found that price increases in Greenland over the past two years had been significantly lower than those observed in Denmark and the EU. This clearly contradicts the notion that Greenlandic grocery retailers have exploited the global crisis to raise prices or profit margins disproportionately.

---

[1] Consumer and Competition Authority, Market Study of the Grocery Retail Sector in Greenland 2023 [Markedsundersøgelse af Dagligvaremarkedet i Grønland 2023] (2024), https://aua.gl/wp-content/uploads/2024/02/Markedsundersoegelse-af-dagligvarepriser-.pdf.

84. Overall, the market study demonstrates that price developments in Greenland are closely linked to global market trends, which have inevitably influenced domestic price levels.

IX. Regional and International Cooperation

85. Greenland is a co-signatory to the Nordic Cooperation Agreement, which provides the framework for close cooperation between the Nordic competition authorities. This cooperation supports practical enforcement through mutual assistance with investigations and information-sharing, and it also serves as a platform for joint working groups and exchanges on common policy and enforcement issues.

86. In addition, the Authority is a member of the International Competition Network (ICN) and participates in selected working groups where resources permit and where the work is relevant in a Greenlandic context.

X. Challenges and Country-Specific Features

87. Several country-specific features influence the competitive process in Greenland and the operational realities of competition enforcement.

A. *Small-Scale and Concentrated Market Structures*

88. The small size of demand often limits the number of undertakings that can operate efficiently, particularly in markets with high fixed costs (e.g., logistics, infrastructure-related services, and network industries). As a result, high market shares and structurally concentrated outcomes may frequently reflect economies of scale rather than exclusionary conduct. This can complicate the assessment of dominance and competitive effects, as the relevant counterfactual may be constrained by limited prospects for rivals' entry or expansion.

B. *Geography, Logistics, and Local Market Definition*

89. Greenland's settlement pattern and transport conditions imply that competitive constraints are often local. Retail, services, and distribution markets may function as "town-by-town" markets, while wholesale and import channels are shaped by shipping schedules, capacity constraints, and seasonal variation. These features affect market definition, the assessment of competitive constraints, and the design of remedies in both behavioral cases and merger control, where local harm may arise even if national overlaps appear limited.

C. *Public Ownership and Mixed Policy Objectives*

90. A significant share of commercial activity is carried out by publicly owned or state-influenced undertakings, and public procurement is a major channel of demand in the economy. While the Greenlandic Competition Act applies to both public and private commercial activity, practical enforcement must often address the interface between competition law and sectoral regulation, supply obligations, or other public policy objectives. This interface can raise questions about the scope of competition law, the role of "special

legal basis" carve-outs, and the extent to which competition concerns should be addressed through enforcement, advocacy, or regulatory reform.

D. *Regulatory Barriers and the Role of Advocacy*

91. In a number of markets, the principal impediments to competition may stem from regulatory design (e.g., licensing frameworks, standards, exclusivities, or technical requirements) rather than overtly collusive conduct. In such settings, advocacy and analytical work (including market studies) can be decisive tools to support pro-competitive reform, especially where the Authority's intervention powers do not fully address the underlying driver of foreclosure or entry barriers.

E. *Evidence, Confidentiality, and Resource Constraints*

92. Investigations in small economies may be sensitive due to close business relationships, information asymmetries, and a limited number of market participants, which can heighten the risk of identifying complainants and reduce incentives to cooperate. At the same time, resource constraints, both within the Authority and among undertakings, may affect data availability, the feasibility of complex econometric analysis, and the pace of proceedings. This increases the importance of targeted information requests, pragmatic case prioritization, and clear procedural guidance to market participants.

F. *Remedies and "Fit" in Small Markets*

93. Structural remedies may be difficult to implement where there are few viable buyers, limited access to capital, and high dependency on logistics and premises. Behavioral commitments may therefore play a larger role than in larger economies, but require careful design, monitoring, and enforceability to ensure they effectively address identified competition concerns without imposing disproportionate administrative burdens.

94. Taken together, these features underline that competition enforcement in Greenland must be anchored in core legal principles while remaining attentive to small-economy realities: limited scale, high concentration, frequent regulatory overlays, and the need for proportionate, workable solutions.

XI. Author's Perspective

95. From a practitioner's standpoint, Greenland provides a clear illustration of how competition law in a small economy is less about replicating enforcement "templates" from larger jurisdictions and more about ensuring that the legal framework remains operational, credible, and proportionate under conditions of structural concentration and limited entry.

96. First, the most important contribution of competition policy is often not a high volume of cases, but the establishment of predictable rules and credible deterrence where harmful conduct does occur. This is particularly true in areas such as bid rigging and other hardcore restrictions that can materially harm public budgets and consumer welfare.

Ensuring that the enforcement system is able to detect, investigate, and sanction such conduct therefore remains central.

97. Secondly, competition problems in Greenland frequently arise at the intersection of market structure and regulation. In such cases, advocacy, market studies, and cooperation with policymakers can be as important as enforcement decisions. In practice, the most durable pro-competitive outcomes may come from targeted regulatory reform that reduces entry barriers or removes artificial foreclosure mechanisms, while still respecting legitimate public policy objectives (e.g., environmental protection, security of supply, and consumer protection).

98. Thirdly, small-economy enforcement places a premium on prioritization, procedural clarity, and pragmatic case handling. Limited resources require the Authority to focus on matters with the greatest likely welfare impact and to rely on streamlined processes where appropriate (including simplified merger review). At the same time, transparency in guidance and decision-making is essential to maintain legitimacy in a setting where market participants are few and institutional decisions are highly visible.

99. Finally, Greenland's experience underscores the value of regional and international cooperation. Access to peer exchange, best practices, and, where legally possible, mutual assistance can help compensate for limited domestic scale and support a robust competition regime that remains aligned with international standards while being tailored to local conditions.

XII. References and Resources

A. *Laws and Regulations*

- Competition Act (2020) [Inatsisartutlov nr. 8 af 19. november 2020 om ændring af Inatsisartutlov om konkurrence (Ændring af tærskelværdierne ved fusioner og indførelse af ordning med anonyme henvendelser samt administrative bødeforelæg)]
- Competition Act (2017) [Inatsisartutlov nr. 24 af 17. november 2017 om ændring af inatsisartutlov om konkurrence og landstingsforordning om telekommunikation og teletjenester]
- Competition Act (2014) [Inatsisartutlov nr. 1 af 15. maj 2014 om konkurrence (konkurrenceloven)]
- Competition Act (2007) [Landstingslov nr. 16 af 19. november 2007 om konkurrence]
- Competition Act (1992) [Landstingslov nr. 28 af 30. oktober 1992]

B. *Case Law*

- Anklagemyndigheden mod Permagreen Grønland A/S, KS 165 og 166/2011 (Retten i Grønland april 4, 2012)
- Anklagemyndigheden mod B.J. Entreprise A/S, KS 162, 163 og 164/2011 (Retten i Grønland april 4, 2012)
- Anklagemyndigheden mod Kang-Total-Byg Aps, KS 140 og 161/2011 (Retten i Grønland april 4, 2012)

- Greenland Venture A/S mod Styrelsen for Råd og Nævn, Konkurrencetilsynet, A 605/08 (Grønlands Landsret november 24, 2009)
- Konkurrencenævnet mod KNI A/S, B-1900-07 (Østre Landsret oktober 17, 2008)
- Konkurrencenævnet mod KNI A/S, B-1820-07 (Østre Landsret oktober 17, 2008)
- Merger between Pisiffik A/S and Arctic Retail Group ApS [Konkurrencenævnets afgørelse om Pisiffiks køb af Arctic Retail Group], 19/00780 (Konkurrencenævnet February 10, 2020)

C. *Public Reports*

- Consumer and Competition Authority, Market Study of the Grocery Retail Sector in Greenland 2023 [Markedsundersøgelse af dagligvaremarkedet i Grønland 2023] (2024), https://aua.gl/wp-content/uploads/2024/02/Markedsundersoegelse-af-dagligvarepriser-.pdf

100. To learn more about Greenlandic Consumer and Competition Authority:
    - Website: https://aua.gl/
    - Contact: aua@nanoq.gl

Guadeloupe

Odeya de La Mure, Jérôme Schall and Anne-Laure Vendrolini
French Competition Authority's Case Handlers

Supervised by Gwenaëlle Nouët
General Rapporteur at the French Competition Authority

I. Overview

1. The archipelago of Guadeloupe is located between the Caribbean Sea and the Atlantic Ocean in the Northern Hemisphere and forms part of the Lesser Antilles archipelago. It has a total surface area of approximately 1,628.43 square kilometers. Guadeloupe is an overseas department and region of France governed by Article 73 of the French Constitution[1] and is classified as an outermost region of the European Union[2]. The official language of Guadeloupe is French.

II. Demographics and Economy

2. Guadeloupe had a population of approximately 380,387 inhabitants in 2024, corresponding to a population density of about 234 inhabitants per square kilometer. The nominal gross domestic product (GDP) of Guadeloupe was estimated at approximately EUR 10.4 billion in 2023. The territory maintains a structural trade deficit, amounting to approximately EUR 3,551 million in 2024, reflecting a strong dependence on imports. In that year, imports totaled approximately EUR 3,928 million, while exports amounted to about EUR 377 million, resulting in a trade deficit that decreased by 2.2 percent between 2023 and 2024.

3. Guadeloupe's economy is predominantly service-oriented. In 2022, services accounted for approximately 84.4 percent of total value added, with public and non-market services playing a particularly significant role, representing around 38 percent of value added, while market services remained the principal contributors at approximately 46 percent. By contrast, the industrial sector accounted for only about 13.3 percent of total value added.

III. Legal Framework for Competition

4. Article 73 of the French Constitution establishes the principle of legislative identity. French competition law therefore applies automatically to overseas territories.

A. *Name and Date of First Competition Law*

5. Ordinance No. 86-1243 of December 1, 1986, on Freedom of Prices and Competition constitutes the first applicable competition statute.

6. This ordinance was subsequently codified in Book IV of the French Commercial Code.

B. *Subsequent Revisions or Updates*

7. Law No. 2001-420 of May 15, 2001, subsequently codified articles L. 420-1 and L. 420-2, which respectively prohibit anticompetitive agreements and abuse of a

---

1 Subject to the principle of legislative identity (French laws and regulations apply under the same conditions as in mainland France, unless otherwise specified by law or regulation).

2 These regions are an integral part of the EU. Therefore, EU law and all the rights and duties associated with EU membership apply to the outermost regions. In accordance with article 349 of the Treaty on the Functioning of the European Union, specific measures and provisions in EU legislation may be taken.

dominant position. According to articles L. 430-1 and L. 430-2, mergers must also be notified to the French Competition Authority (FCA) if they exceed the legal thresholds (see below section VII).

8. Law No. 2012-1270 of November 20, 2012, on Economic Regulation in the Overseas Territories, enacted new measures:
   - The government may intervene by decree in *wholesale markets and the supply chain* (art. L. 410-3).
   - The price of essential goods can be regulated, and the state representative may set the overall price of a *basket of essential products each year* if negotiations fail (arts. L. 410-4 and L. 410-5).
   - *Exclusive import agreements* are prohibited (art. L. 420-2-1).
   - Local authorities may refer cases directly to the FCA (art. L. 462-5), which can impose *structural or behavioral injunctions* and sanction dominant positions that raise competition concerns (art. L. 752-27).

9. Law No. 2017-256 of February 28, 2017, known as the "Lurel Law," reinforced this framework by:
   - Enhancing control over the creation or expansion of large retail outlets within catchment areas via the Departmental Commission for Commercial Development, which must take competitive aspects into account, with the possibility of referral to the FCA (art. L. 752-6-1).
   - Protecting local producers against *manifestly low prices* on competing imported products (art. L. 420-5).

C. *Scope*

10. French competition law applies to competitive agreements and abuse of dominance (see the above-mentioned elements) as well as to merger control (see section VII). State aid is regulated by the European Commission.

D. *Applicable Sectors*

11. French competition law applies to all sectors.

IV. Institutional Structure

A. *Competition Authority*

12. The Autorité de la concurrence (hereafter, the "French Competition Authority" or "FCA") was established in 2008 as a successor to the Conseil de la concurrence (French Competition Council).

B. *Supervising Body*

13. The FCA is an independent administrative authority.

C. *Organizational Structure*

14. The FCA is organized on the basis of functional separation (arts. L. 461-1 to L. 461-5).

15. Investigations are conducted by case handlers in the investigation services under the authority of the general rapporteur (*rapporteur general*).

16. Following adversarial proceedings, the decisions are adopted by an independent and impartial board (the "Collège") composed of 17 members (5 permanent members – the chair and 4 vice-presidents – and 12 non-permanent members). Their five-year term of office is irrevocable and is renewable once.

D. *Additional Regulatory Mandates*

17. Since 2015, the FCA has been entrusted with regulatory oversight of certain legal professions, notably notaries and judicial officers (formerly bailiffs and judicial auctioneers).

E. *Budget and Resources*

18. In 2024, the FCA's total budget amounted to EUR 25 million.

19. The total number of staff (including administrative and non-administrative staff) is around 200.

F. *Enforcement Powers*

20. The core mission of the FCA is to detect and repress anticompetitive practices, which include anticompetitive agreements and abuse of a dominant position, as well as exclusive import agreements, which are prohibited in the French overseas territories (arts. L. 420-1 to L. 420-7).

21. To achieve this goal, the FCA has been vested with extensive investigative and sanctioning powers. Investigative powers include the ability to send requests for information, to perform dawn raids and to receive leniency applications and whistleblower submissions (arts. L. 450-3 and L. 450-4).

22. As part of its decision-making powers, the FCA can impose fines. Alternatively, or in addition, the FCA can require undertakings to cease anticompetitive practices or make structural and/or behavioral commitments mandatory. Depending on the case, the FCA can also initiate a settlement procedure. In cases of urgency, the FCA has the power to issue interim measures at the request of third parties or *ex officio*, pending a decision on the merits (arts. L. 461-1 to L. 464-10).

23. In addition, the FCA is responsible for reviewing mergers (acquisitions, mergers, joint ventures, etc.) (arts. L. 430-1 to L. 430-10) above a certain size prior to their completion. After review, it may grant approval (with or without conditions) or veto the transaction. Lower notification thresholds apply in the French overseas departments and regions in consideration of the size of their markets (art. L. 430-3).

24. The FCA also plays an advisory role that consists of informing public authorities about draft legislation with implications for competition or studying the functioning of a sector in order to make recommendations (arts. L. 461-1 to L. 464-10).

V. Enforcement and Sanctions

A. *Fines and Sanctions*

25. *First*, the FCA can (i) require companies to stop anticompetitive practices within a set deadline; (ii) order corrective measures, either structural or behavioral, in order to put an end to prohibited practices; and (iii) accept commitments offered by companies (art. L. 464-2).

26. *Second*, fines may reach up to *10% of the undertaking's worldwide turnover*, excluding taxes. Turnover is calculated based on the highest worldwide turnover achieved during one of the financial years closed since the financial year preceding the year in which the practices were implemented (art. L. 464-2). This applies to anticompetitive agreements (art. L. 420-1) and abuse of a dominant position (art. L. 420-2).

27. *Third*, as for criminal liability, article L. 420-6 establishes *personal criminal liability* for individuals involved in cartel conduct. It provides that any natural person who plays a personal and decisive role in the conception, organization, or implementation of an anticompetitive agreement prohibited under articles L. 420-1, L. 420-2 and L. 420-2-2 may be held criminally liable. The offense requires intentional and fraudulent conduct and applies only to individuals, not to legal entities. Sanctions include up to four years' imprisonment and a EUR 75,000 fine. This liability exists in addition to the administrative sanctions imposed on undertakings by the FCA.

B. *Enforcement Track Record*

28. Since 2018, the FCA has issued approximately eight decisions involving Guadeloupe. These mainly concern anticompetitive agreements (one), abuse of a dominant position (two) and exclusive import rights (four). For instance:

- Decision 24-D-10 of December 4, 2024, concerning practices implemented in the inter-island passenger air transport sector (see below);
- Decision 23-D-02 of March 8, 2023, concerning practices implemented in the marketing of Canard-Duchêne champagne in the French West Indies and French Guiana (see "French Guiana" chapter);
- Decision 22-D-26, December 22, 2022, concerning practices implemented in the heavy goods vehicle technical inspection sector in Guadeloupe (see below);
- Decision 19-D-20 of October 8, 2019, concerning practices implemented in the distribution of perfumery and cosmetic products in the French West Indies, French Guiana, and Réunion: In this decision, the FCA fined several suppliers, importers and their parent companies for granting or benefiting from exclusive import rights for perfume and cosmetic products in the French overseas territories, in breach of article L. 420-2-1 of the French Commercial Code ("Lurel Law"). The infringements concerned products marketed by Procter & Gamble, Coty and Bourjois in Guadeloupe, Martinique, French Guiana and Réunion after March 22, 2013. The FCA imposed fines on both the suppliers that granted the exclusivities and the distributors that benefited from them, in accordance with the transaction procedure accepted by the parties;

- Decision 18-D-03 of February 20, 2018, regarding practices implemented in the marketing of biocidal termite traps in Réunion, the French West Indies, and French Guiana (see "French Guiana" chapter).

C. *Private Enforcement*

29. Article L. 481-1 of the Commercial Code stipulates that "any natural or legal person forming a company or organization referred to in article L. 464-2 shall be liable for any damage caused by engaging in anticompetitive practices."[3] Thus, victims may seek compensation for damages caused by a cartel or an abuse of a dominant position, as well as by an abuse of economic dependence, predatory pricing, or import exclusivity in overseas territories.

30. Regarding Guadeloupe, Orange brought an action for damages against Decision 14-DCC-15 of February 10, 2014, which, cleared, subject to a number of commitments, the exclusive takeover of Mediaserv by the Canal Plus Group through its Canal Plus Overseas subsidiary. In the decision of the Paris Court of Appeal of March 19, 2021, No. 18/19188, Canal Plus Antilles, Canal Plus International, and Canal Plus Réunion were *each ordered to pay EUR 50,000 to Orange in compensation for the moral damage caused by the commercial disruption resulting from the failure to comply with the commitments to which the FCA had made the merger conditional*. The appeal lodged by the Canal Plus subsidiaries was dismissed (Cass. com., November 16, 2022, No. 21-19.728).

VI. Noteworthy Cases

A. *Decision 24-D-10 of December 4, 2024, concerning practices implemented in the inter-island passenger air transport sector*

31. *Facts.* The FCA has fined two airlines operating in the inter-island passenger air transport sector in the Caribbean, as well as a consulting firm specializing in the air sector, for colluding on prices and services (time slots and frequencies).

32. More precisely, between 2015 and 2019, Compagnie Aérienne Inter Régionale Express (CAIRE, operating under the trade name Air Antilles), Air Caraïbes, and Miles Plus (a consulting firm operating under the name Aérogestion) implemented four agreements designed to allow Air Antilles and Air Caraïbes to significantly increase fares and reduce capacity while preserving their respective market shares.

33. The air links concerned were those connecting Pointe-à-Pitre and Fort-de-France, as well as those between each of these two cities and Saint-Martin, Saint Lucia and Santo Domingo.

34. *Legal issue.* Breach of article L. 420-1 of the Commercial Code prohibiting anticompetitive agreements/settlement procedure/financial penalty.

---

[3] Our translation.

35. Air Caraïbes and Miles Plus (Aérogestion) requested the benefit of the settlement procedure, and their respective fines were set by the FCA at EUR 13,000,000 and EUR 70,000.

36. Given the financial capacity of Air Antilles (CAIRE) and its parent company, Guyane Aéroinvest, the FCA, in accordance with established practice, determined that no financial penalty should be imposed on them. However, it imposed a fine of EUR 1,500,000 on their parent company, K Finance, on the basis of joint and several liability.

37. *Outcome.* No appeal was lodged within the legal time limits.

B. *Decision 22-D-26 of December 22, 2022, concerning practices implemented in the heavy goods vehicle technical inspection sector in Guadeloupe*

38. *Facts.* The FCA sanctioned the company Contrôle Technique Poids Lourds – Antilles Guyane (CTPL-AG) for having abused its dominant position in the market for the technical inspection of heavy goods vehicles (HGVs) in Guadeloupe between 2013 and 2018, by implementing two practices contrary to article L. 420-2 of the Commercial Code prohibiting abuse of a dominant position.

39. Firstly, CTPL-AG was found responsible for a series of discriminatory practices against companies operating in the related market of HGV inspections in Guadeloupe. CTPL-AG favored its sister company, Standard Tachy Achilles-Guyane, in this market by granting it more favorable prices, payment terms, appointment scheduling, and invoicing methods than its competitors.

40. Secondly, CTPL-AG relied on its dominant position to charge excessive prices for its HGV technical inspection services – prices not reasonably related to their economic value and which it could not have charged in a competitive market.

41. *Legal issue.* Breach of article L. 420-2 of the Commercial Code prohibiting abuse of a dominant position/settlement procedure/financial penalty.

42. CTPL-AG has requested the FCA to benefit from the settlement procedure pursuant to the provisions of paragraph III of article L. 464-2 of the Commercial Code. The FCA considered that a penalty of EUR 25,000 should be imposed on CTPL-AG.

43. *Outcome.* No appeal was filed within the legal time limits.

VII. Merger Control

44. As with antitrust law, French merger control applies in Guadeloupe. However, the French Commercial Code lays down specific rules for mergers concerning overseas territories in article L. 430-2, III.

A. *Notification Thresholds*

- National thresholds (art. L. 430-2, I): A concentration must be notified to the FCA if both of the following conditions are met: (i) the combined worldwide turnover of all parties exceeds EUR 150 million, and (ii) the individual turnover in France of at least two parties exceeds EUR 50 million.

- Retail threshold (art. L. 430-2, II): Where at least two of the parties to a concentration operate one or more retail outlets, a transaction meeting the following criteria must be notified: (i) the aggregate worldwide turnover of all parties exceeds EUR 75 million, and (ii) the aggregate worldwide turnover generated in France in the retail sector by at least two of the parties concerned exceeds EUR 15 million.
- Alternative thresholds (art. L. 430-2, III): Where at least one of the parties to the transaction carries out all or part of its activity in one or more overseas departments, the concentration must be notified if the following conditions are met: (i) the aggregate worldwide turnover of all parties exceeds EUR 75 million, and (ii) the aggregate turnover achieved in at least one of the overseas departments concerned by at least two of the parties exceeds EUR 15 million, or EUR 5 million in the retail trade sector, without it being necessary for that threshold to be reached by all undertakings concerned in the same department or territorial collectivity.

45. These provisions are applicable only if the transaction does not fall within the scope of Council Regulation (EC) No. 139/2004.

B. *Review Timeframes*

46. The review timeframes apply equally to concentrations notified on the basis of the general turnover thresholds (art. L. 430-2, I and II) and to those notified under the specific thresholds applicable to overseas territories (art. L. 430-2, III).

47. First, the FCA must make a decision on the concentration within 25 working days from the date of receipt of a complete notification (art. L. 430-5, I). Where the parties offer commitments, this period is extended by 15 working days, for a total of 40 working days (art. L. 430-5, II, second paragraph).

48. If the FCA considers that the transaction raises a serious risk of harm to competition, it may open an in-depth investigation. In that case, the FCA must adopt a decision within 65 working days from the opening of that procedure (art. L. 430-7, I).

49. Second, where commitments are submitted less than 20 working days before the end of the initial 25-day period referred to in L. 430-5, I, that period shall expire 20 working days after their receipt, without being allowed to exceed 85 working days from the opening of the in-depth investigation (art. L. 430-7, II). The provision also allows for the suspension of the time limits, either at the request of the parties (for up to 20 working days) or on the FCA's own initiative in the event of a failure to provide the requested information (art. L. 430-7, II, second paragraph).

50. Finally, following the FCA's decision, the Minister for the Economy may, within five working days, request the opening of an in-depth investigation (art. L. 430-7-1, I). The minister also has 25 working days to call in the case and rule on the transaction on public interest grounds other than the preservation of competition (art. L. 430-7-1, II, first and second paragraphs).

C. *Notified or Blocked Mergers*

51. Examples of notified mergers:
   - Decision 23-DCC-190 of September 25, 2023, concerning the acquisition of sole control of Guadeloupe Services Automobiles and Prestige Distribution Karaib by Citadelle: Thresholds of article L. 430-2, II / Automotive distribution sector / Clearance decision;
   - Decision 22-DCC-35 of April 27, 2022, regarding the acquisition of exclusive control of the company Bio Pôle Antilles by the Inovie group: Thresholds of article L. 430-2, III / Medical biology sector / Clearance decision subject to remedies;
   - Decision 16-DCC-155 of October 14, 2016, concerning the acquisition of sole control of Geimex by the Casino Group: Thresholds of article L. 430-2, I / Food distribution sector / Clearance decision subject to remedies;
   - Decision 14-DCC-15 of February 10, 2014, concerning the acquisition of sole control of Mediaserv, Martinique Numérique, Guyane Numérique, and La Réunion Numérique by Canal Plus Overseas: Thresholds of article L. 430-2, I / Telecommunication sector / Clearance decision subject to remedies.

VIII. Advocacy and Policy Initiatives

A. *Sectoral Studies or Market Inquiries*

52. Since 2008, the FCA has issued 18 opinions regarding French overseas territories, including two general opinions in 2009 and 2019 on the competitive functioning of the French overseas departments and regions, ten sector-specific opinions (e.g., fuel, telecommunication, regulated professions), five opinions on draft regulatory texts and one opinion at the request of a commercial court.

53. In its 2019 opinion (Opinion 19-A-12 of July 4, 2019), the FCA examined the factors explaining price differentials between mainland France and overseas territories, conducting an objective analysis of the cost structure of overseas distributors based on company accounts. Based on this assessment, the FCA made 20 recommendations concerning, in particular, dock dues (*octroi de mer*), structural injunction powers, vertical integration and online sales. This assessment was recently updated in an opinion issued in February 2026 on the margins of wholesale importers and distributors of food products in Martinique (Opinion 26-A-01 of February 10, 2026).

B. *Recent Policy Papers or Guidelines*

54. As in previous years, the FCA's roadmap for 2025–2026 sets the protection of purchasing power in the French overseas territories as an enforcement priority.

C. *Outreach to Businesses and Consumers*

55. The FCA has been undertaking a wide range of outreach activities to communicate on its missions and raise awareness of competition issues in the French overseas territories. This effort includes digital and physical publications (press releases and social media

posts on decisions and opinions, annual reports, studies and speeches of the chair available on the FCA's website) and frequent participation in parliamentary hearings and conferences focusing on island economies.

IX. Regional and International Cooperation

A. *Regional Organizations*

56. The French overseas departments and regions are outermost regions of the European Union. They are represented in the European Competition Network (ECN) via the FCA.

57. Moreover, Guadeloupe is an associate member of the Organisation of Eastern Caribbean States (OECS).

B. *Bilateral/MoUs with Other Competition Authorities*

58. The FCA maintains a constant and effective cooperation with EU and non-EU competition authorities, sharing experience and knowledge on the specific issues of island economies. The FCA, in particular, has built a close and fruitful relationship with the New Caledonian Competition Authority and the Polynesian Competition Authority. This collaboration relies not only on formal cooperation agreements but also on frequent informal exchanges.

C. *Participation in Global Networks*

59. The French overseas departments and regions are represented through the FCA in the main international competition fora (ICN, Organisation for Economic Co-operation and Development, United Nations Conference on Trade and Development, and G7).

X. Challenges and Country-Specific Features

A. *Small Market Size and High Concentration*

60. In its Opinion 09-A-45 of September 8, 2009, concerning the mechanisms for importing and distributing consumer goods in overseas departments, the FCA noted that the food distribution sector in three of the four French overseas departments studied at that time (namely, Guadeloupe, French Guiana and Réunion) exhibited relatively high levels of concentration, either across the entire department concerned or in one or more catchment areas.

61. In its Opinion 19-A-12 of July 4, 2019, regarding the functioning of competition in the French overseas territories, the FCA indicated:

> From a structural perspective, the food-dominated retail market in the DROM [overseas departments and regions] is still dominated by major national chains, which rely primarily on franchise and similar agreements. In this context, the competitive landscape has undergone contrasting changes: the French West Indies have seen the disappearance of several major distribution groups, while in Réunion and French Guiana, new brands have established themselves; in Mayotte,

> the situation has not changed significantly. Today, the competitive structure at the level of each DROM (without prejudice to an analysis by catchment area) appears to be more concentrated overall than in mainland France, though nuances exist between territories. Barriers to entry appear to be higher in the DROM than in mainland France. Generally speaking, new players have most often entered the market through the rebranding of existing stores rather than by creating new points of sale. Furthermore, the development of existing players typically involves external growth operations, which reinforces the importance of merger control in these territories. The narrowness of the markets, inherent in the geographical characteristics of these territories, is likely to discourage entry; therefore, the structure of these markets may, in some cases, prove to be less competitive than in mainland France.[4]

62. In the same opinion, the FCA also noted:

> [T]he small size of overseas markets leads local companies to concentrate their production and marketing resources in order to improve their productive efficiency, frequently resulting in the creation of duopolies or even monopolies, particularly when the production process requires the use of heavy equipment that generates economies of scale.[5]

B. *Dependence on Imports/Foreign Investment*

63. In its Opinion 19-A-12 of July 4, 2019, regarding the functioning of competition in the French overseas territories, the FCA indicated:

> Overseas departments are characterized by a structurally negative trade balance. The trade deficit is caused by the fact that these regions have a high level of imports relative to their exports. …The small size of local markets often prevents local businesses from reaching optimal production levels and achieving economics of scale, which affects their competitiveness and the prices of consumer goods. …For Martinique, Guadeloupe, and Réunion, this imbalance is not explained by the level of their imports, which is comparable to that of mainland France, but by the level of their exports, which is much lower than the national average. … Finally, despite the distance, the bulk of the French overseas departments' trade – both imports and exports – is conducted with mainland France.[6]

64. Local production represents only a minority share of the supply for wholesalers and distributors in the French overseas territories. This situation, which has persisted since 2009, can be explained, on the one hand, for certain categories of products, by the absence or insufficiency of local supply, and on the other hand, where such production does exist, by the lack of competitiveness of locally produced goods compared to imported substitute goods, despite the costs of access and the overseas

---

[4] FCA, Opinion 19-A-12 of July 4, 2019, at 5–6 (in French) (our translation).

[5] *Id.*, para. 367 (in French) (our translation).

[6] *Id.*, p. 8 and paras. 21–22 (in French) (our translation).

tax. As previously noted by the FCA in 2009, the primary cause of the lack of competitiveness in local production lies in the small size of overseas markets, which prevents local producers from achieving economies of scale. Several stakeholders point to the burden of fixed costs and the underutilization of production capacity. Producers also cite, among the factors hindering their competitiveness, the distances, which increase the cost of raw materials, and higher construction costs compared to mainland France.

65. According to IEDOM's 2024 annual report, due to its insularity, its relationship with mainland France, and its underdeveloped industrial base, Guadeloupe has a structurally negative trade balance (excluding services). With a highly service-oriented economy and a small market, a significant portion of Guadeloupe's demand is met by imports. At the same time, the island's main exports, particularly products from the agri-food and primary sectors, remain limited due to restricted production capacity.

66. Goods imported or produced in the French overseas departments and regions (DROM) are subject to the overseas tax regime, the rates of which are set by local public authorities for each DROM, with reference to the customs nomenclature. In French law, the overseas tax regime is governed by Law No. 2004-639 of July 2, 2004, on Overseas Taxes, as most recently amended by Ordinance No. 2023-1210 of December 20, 2023, and by Decree No. 2015-1077 of August 6, 2015.

67. Furthermore, the overseas tax regime gives local authorities the option of fully or partially exempting certain locally produced goods from overseas tax, within the limits of the differentials set by the European Union. It also provides for the possibility of exempting certain imported goods that constitute inputs for local production. The current overseas tax regime has been authorized at the European level until December 31, 2020.

68. The objectives of the overseas tax are, on the one hand, to protect local production (which remains uncompetitive compared to imported products due to the small size of overseas markets, which prevents local producers from achieving economies of scale) and, on the other hand, to finance the public authorities of the French DROM. However, in its Opinion 19-A-12 of July 4, 2019, regarding the functioning of competition in the French overseas territories, the FCA indicated:

> The overseas tax, initially designed to protect local production through differential rates, is no longer necessarily suited to this objective. The debate on its potential renewal could be an opportunity for public authorities to re-examine its mechanisms, refocus it on the objectives pursued in light of the realities of local production, territory by territory, and simplify its implementation, in order to improve its effectiveness and mitigate its impact on consumer prices.[7]

69. Also, in its Opinion 26-A-01 of February 10, 2026, concerning the margins of wholesale importers and distributors of essential food products in Martinique, the FCA recommended:

> In the absence of a more ambitious reform of overseas taxation, which would require identifying new sources of revenue for local authorities and alternative

---

7 *Id.* at 5 (in French) (our translation).

measures to support local production, the [FCA] recommends making the various overseas tax rates applied to goods entering Martinique, as well as the operators subject to them, simpler, more predictable, and more transparent. The [FCA] also recommends reviewing the overseas tax rates applicable to imported products and eliminating them if no equivalent exists in local production.[8]

XI. References and Resources

A. *Laws and Regulations*

- Book IV of the legislative part of the French Commercial Code: On Freedom of Prices and Competition (arts. L. 410-1 to L. 490-14) (in French)
- Book IV of the regulatory part of the French Commercial Code: On Freedom of Prices and Competition (arts. R. 410-1 to R. 490-10) (in French)

B. *Case Law*

- FCA, Decision 24-D-10 of Dec. 4, 2024, concerning practices implemented in the inter-island passenger air transport sector (in French)
- FCA, Decision 23-DCC-190 of Sept. 25, 2023, concerning the acquisition of sole control of Guadeloupe Services Automobiles and Prestige Distribution Karaib by Citadelle (in French)
- FCA, Decision 23-D-02 of Mar. 8, 2023, concerning practices implemented in the marketing of Canard-Duchêne champagne in the French West Indies and French Guiana (in French)
- FCA, Decision 22-D-26 of Dec. 22, 2022, concerning practices implemented in the heavy goods vehicle technical inspection sector in Guadeloupe (in French)
- FCA, Decision 22-DCC-35 of Apr. 27, 2022, regarding the acquisition of exclusive control of the company Bio Pôle Antilles by the Inovie group (in French)
- FCA, Decision 19-D-20 of Oct. 8, 2019, concerning practices implemented in the distribution of perfumery and cosmetic products in the French West Indies, French Guiana, and Réunion (in French)
- FCA, Decision 18-D-03 of Feb. 20, 2018, regarding practices implemented in the marketing of biocidal termite traps in Réunion, the French West Indies, and French Guiana (in French)
- FCA, Decision 16-DCC-155 of Oct. 14, 2016, concerning the acquisition of sole control of Geimex by the Casino Group (in French)
- FCA, Decision 14-DCC-15 of Feb. 10, 2014, concerning the acquisition of sole control of Mediaserv, Martinique Numérique, Guyane Numérique, and La Réunion Numérique by Canal Plus Overseas (in French)
- CA Paris [Paris Court of Appeal], Mar. 19, 2021, No. 18/19188 (in French)
  Cass. com. [Court of Cassation, Commercial Division], Nov. 16, 2022, No. 21-19.728 (in French)

[8] FCA, Opinion 26-A-01 of Feb. 10, 2026, at 4–5 (in French) (our translation).

C. *Public Reports*

- IEDOM, ANNUAL ECONOMIC REPORT OF GUADELOUPE 2024 (June 2025) (in French), https://www.iedom.fr/Rapport-annuel-economique-de-la-Guadeloupe-2024
- INSEE, ECONOMIC REVIEW 2024 – GUADELOUPE (June 2025) (in French), https://www.insee.fr/fr/statistiques/8567470?sommaire=8354895
- FCA, Opinion 26-A-01 of Feb. 10, 2026, concerning the margins of wholesale importers and distributors of essential food products in Martinique (in French)
- FCA, Opinion 19-A-12 of July 4, 2019, regarding the functioning of competition in the French overseas territories (in French)
- FCA, Opinion 09-A-45 of Sept. 8, 2009, concerning the mechanisms for importing and distributing consumer goods in overseas departments (in French)

70. To learn more about the French Competition Authority (FCA):
    - Website: https://www.autoritedelaconcurrence.fr/
    - Contact: communication@autoritedelaconcurrence.fr

Guernsey

Sarah Livestro
Legal Director at the Guernsey Competition and Regulatory Authority

Sonia Ragoopath
Regulatory Economist at the Guernsey Competition and Regulatory Authority

I. Overview

1. Guernsey is one of the Channel Islands, lying in the English Channel off the north-western coast of continental Europe. It is located to the south of the United Kingdom, approximately 30 miles (≈ 48 km) west of the Normandy coast of France. Guernsey covers approximately 62 square kilometers with a population density of approximately 1,015 persons/km^2.

2. The island of Guernsey is part of the Bailiwick of Guernsey, which also includes the islands of Alderney, Sark, and Herm. Guernsey is a Crown dependency of the British Crown, owing allegiance to the monarch (HM King Charles III) in his capacity as successor to the Dukes of Normandy. Guernsey is not part of the United Kingdom and is not represented in the UK Parliament. It has its own directly elected legislative assembly, legal system, fiscal system and administrative structure. The UK government is responsible for defense and international relations; the Crown (via the Privy Council) has ultimate constitutional responsibility for good governance.[1]

3. Guernsey's parliament is known as the States of Deliberation. It is a unicameral legislature composed of 38 elected deputies. Most day-to-day functions are carried out by Committees of the States. There is one senior committee (Policy and Resources) and seven principal committees, each of which is responsible for a specific policy area. The president of the Policy and Resources Committee is known as the Chief Minister.

4. The main language used in Guernsey is English. However, the island also has a local language, Guernésiais (also known as "Guernsey French" or "*patois*").[2] Guernésiais is spoken by only a small minority and is the subject of preservation efforts.

II. Demographics and Economy

5. On 31 December 2023, the population of Guernsey was 64,781.[3] The United Nations Conference on Trade and Development (UNCTAD) and Index Mundi report a 31% urbanization rate for Guernsey and Jersey cumulatively in 2021.[4]

6. Guernsey's total GDP for 2023 is estimated at USD 4,561 million, which is 5% higher than the 2022 estimate.[5] Total trade in goods and services (exports plus imports) between the UK and Guernsey was GBP 4.3 billion in the four quarters to the end of Q2 2025, an increase of 1.9% or GBP 81 million in current prices from the four quarters to the end of Q2 2024. Of this GBP 4.3 billion:
   - Total UK exports to Guernsey amounted to GBP 3.0 billion in the four quarters to the end of Q2 2025;

---

1 David Torrance, *The Crown Dependencies* (Commons Libr. Rsch. Briefing No. CBP8611, Sept. 12, 2025), https://commonslibrary.parliament.uk/research-briefings/cbp-8611/.

2 *About Guernésiais*, Guernsey Language Commission, https://language.gg/About_Guernesiais.

3 States of Guernsey Data & Analysis, Guernsey Quarterly Population, Employment and Earnings Bulletin (Oct. 29, 2024), https://www.gov.gg/CHttpHandler.ashx?id=183488&p=0.

4 *Guernsey Urbanization*, Index Mundi, https://www.indexmundi.com/guernsey/urbanization.html?utm_; *General profile: Guernsey*, UNCTAD, https://unctadstat.unctad.org/CountryProfile/GeneralProfile/en-GB/831/index.html?utm_.

5 States of Guernsey Data & Analysis, Guernsey Annual GVA and GDP Bulletin (Sept. 24, 2024), https://www.gov.gg/CHttpHandler.ashx?id=182351&p=0.

- Total UK imports from Guernsey amounted to GBP 1.2 billion in the four quarters to the end of Q2 2025 (an increase of 27.8% or GBP 268 million in current prices, compared to the four quarters to the end of Q2 2024).[6]

7. The main economic sectors in Guernsey are financial services, public administration, professional, scientific and technical services, and wholesale and retail trade.[7] Finance and professional services (legal and accountancy) firms make up 44% of Guernsey's economy. Traditional sectors (agriculture and manufacturing) account for a marginal share of gross value added. Other markets, such as tourism, restaurants, and hospitality, are minor compared to financial/business services.

III. Legal Framework for Competition

8. Aside from the enabling legislation, the Competition (Guernsey) Ordinance, 2012 was the first competition law to be enacted in Guernsey and remains in force. It was updated in 2014 to enable the Guernsey Competition and Regulatory Authority to carry out an investigation to comply with a request made by the Committee for Economic Development (the government committee to which the Authority reports) for a "report, market study or other document, advice, assistance or information."

9. The Competition Ordinance prohibits anti-competitive agreements and the abuse of a dominant position. It also establishes a merger control regime for Guernsey. There is no domestic prohibition on state aid. It applies to all economic sectors, with limited statutory exclusions, including public transport, air transport licensing and the Guernsey dairy. Other exceptions include certain planning matters, matters falling under the environmental pollution laws and certain matters relating to domestic waste collection.

IV. Institutional Structure

10. The Guernsey Competition and Regulatory Authority (GCRA or the "Authority") was established by the Guernsey Competition and Regulatory Authority Ordinance, 2012. It is both a competition authority and the sectoral regulator for telecommunications, postal services and electricity, replacing the previous Office of Utility Regulation in Guernsey with respect to those regulatory functions.

11. From its establishment, and until July 2020, the GCRA operated jointly with its Jersey counterpart, the Jersey Competition Regulatory Authority (JCRA), under the framework of the Channel Islands Competition and Regulatory Authorities (CICRA), sharing staff and resources. With effect from July 1, 2020, the GCRA and the JCRA reverted to operating as insular authorities.

12. The GCRA is accountable to the States of Guernsey via the Committee for Economic Development. The chair of the Authority is appointed by the Committee for Economic Development. Other members of the Authority are appointed by the

---

[6] UK Dep't Bus. & Trade, Trade and Investment Factsheet, https://assets.publishing.service.gov.uk/media/691345dd1fcc92b3f3496398/guernsey-trade-and-investment-factsheet-2025-10-31.pdf?utm_source=chatgpt.com.

[7] Guernsey Annual GVA and GDP Bulletin, *supra* note 5.

Committee after consultation with the chair. The Authority currently has seven permanent staff members.

13. Alongside its competition law functions, the GCRA is also responsible for economic regulation in the electricity, telecoms and postal sectors in Guernsey. The GCRA's competition law activity (excluding merger control work) is funded through a government grant, whereas utilities regulation is funded through operator license fees.

14. The GCRA may initiate a competition law investigation where it has reasonable grounds to suspect that a business has entered into an anti-competitive agreement or abused a dominant market position. It has a range of investigatory powers, including the power to require the provision of information, the power to enter business premises, take copies of documents and interview individuals, and the power to carry out interviews. The GCRA may also give interim directions during the course of an investigation if these are necessary to prevent irreparable harm, to protect the public interest or to protect or enhance the economic development and well-being of the Bailiwick.

15. The GCRA has merger control powers. "Prescribed" mergers, which are determined on the basis of financial thresholds,[8] may not be put into effect without the approval of the GCRA. The GCRA may not grant approval unless it is satisfied that the merger would not substantially lessen competition in any market in Guernsey for goods or services and would not be to the prejudice of consumers, the economic development and well-being of the Bailiwick, and the public interest.

16. Finally, the GCRA has the power to conduct an investigation into any business, undertaking or market in Guernsey where it has reasonable grounds to do so in order to comply with a request by the Committee for a report, market study or other document, advice, assistance or information.

V. Enforcement and Sanctions

17. If the GCRA finds that a business has breached the competition law, it can impose a financial penalty of up to 10% of an undertaking's annual turnover for each year of the infringement, capped at three years, and/or order that the wrongful conduct cease. There is no "cartel offence" in Guernsey, although the law does prescribe some criminal sanctions for matters such as failing to comply with the terms of an information request and obstructing an investigation.

18. Since its creation in 2012, the GCRA has brought two competition law infringement cases. One case related to post-term non-compete restrictions and was concluded with an infringement decision and a financial penalty in 2024.[9] The other relates to information exchange in the telecommunications sector. A final infringement decision was taken in 2021, and a penalty decision was adopted in 2022. An appeal to the Guernsey Court

---

8 A merger is "prescribed" if (i) the combined applicable turnover of the undertakings involved in the merger arising in the Channel Islands exceeds GBP 5 million, and (ii) two or more of the undertakings involved in the merger each have applicable turnover arising in Guernsey that exceeds GBP 2 million.

9 C1441G – Competition Law Investigation – The Medical Specialist Group, Guernsey Competition & Regulatory Authority, https://www.gcra.gg/case/c1441g-competition-law-investigation-medical-specialist-group.

of Appeal against a first instance judgment setting aside the decision on procedural grounds is currently pending.[10]

19. If a business abuses a dominant position, enters into an anti-competitive agreement or puts into effect a prescribed merger without the approval of the Authority, a private action for breach of statutory duty[11] may be brought by an "aggrieved person."[12] Such a private action may be brought both against the undertaking alleged to have committed the breach and against any officer of the undertaking with whose consent or connivance or as a result of whose neglect the breach was committed.[13] The Royal Court has the power to grant "such orders, reliefs and remedies as it considers appropriate,"[14] which includes an award of punitive or exemplary damages.

VI. Noteworthy Cases

20. In Case C1441G – *The Medical Specialist Group*, the GCRA found that the Medical Specialist Group (MSG) had infringed Guernsey competition law by entering into a five-year post-term non-compete clause with one of its consultants. The clause, which the MSG had sought to enforce against one of its former orthopedic surgeons who had gone on to establish a physiotherapy and musculoskeletal clinic in Guernsey, was held to constitute an anti-competitive agreement "by object" under Guernsey competition law.[15] As a result of the infringement, the GCRA imposed a financial penalty of GBP 96,635 on the MSG. The case had been remitted to the GCRA by the Royal Court following a successful appeal by the MSG against the GCRA's original finding that the MSG's post-term non-compete clauses with all of its consultants – ranging from 18 months to 5 years' duration – breached the prohibition on anti-competitive agreements. The case is significant because it highlights the relevance of competition law in labor markets, demonstrating that it can be used to challenge non-compete clauses where the worker concerned is also an "undertaking." An article on this topic was published in the *European Competition Law Review* in November 2025.

21. In Case C1471G – *JT and Sure*,[16] the GCRA found that JT (Guernsey) Limited and Sure (Guernsey) Limited, along with their respective direct parent companies, had engaged in a series of reciprocal contacts and exchanges of commercially sensitive information in relation to the deployment and roll-out of mobile networks and 5G services, which reduced competitive uncertainty between them. The GCRA concluded that this amounted to a restriction of competition by object. As a consequence of the infringement finding, it also imposed financial penalties on the parties. The Royal Court set aside the GCRA's substantive decision on procedural grounds, having already granted a stay of the parties'

10 C1471G – JT and Sure – Competition Investigation, Guernsey Competition & Regulatory Authority, https://www.gcra.gg/case/c1471g-jt-and-sure-competition-investigation.

11 The Competition (Guernsey) Ordinance, 2012, § 42(1).

12 The Competition (Guernsey) Ordinance, 2012, § 42(2).

13 The Competition (Guernsey) Ordinance, 2012, § 42(5).

14 The Competition (Guernsey) Ordinance, 2012, § 42(3).

15 Livestro, Sarah *Breaking the Chains in Labour Markets: The Application of Competition Law to Worker Non-Compete Clauses in Guernsey*, 46 E.C.L.R. 506 (2025)

16 C1471G – JT and Sure – Competition Investigation, *supra* note 10.

appeals against the penalty decision.[17] The GCRA has been granted leave to appeal to the Guernsey Court of Appeal against the Royal Court judgment.[18]

VII. Merger Control

22. Guernsey has a system of merger control. "Prescribed" mergers and acquisitions may not be put into effect without the approval of the GCRA. A merger is "prescribed" if the combined applicable Channel Islands turnover of the undertakings involved in the merger exceeds GBP 5 million and the applicable Guernsey turnover of two or more of the undertakings involved in the merger exceeds GBP 2 million.

23. The GCRA may not approve a merger unless it is satisfied that the merger would not lead to a substantial lessening of competition (SLC) in a market in Guernsey for goods or services and would not be to the prejudice of consumers, the economic development and well-being of the Bailiwick of Guernsey and the public interest.

24. Guernsey law sets out a two-stage review process for notified mergers. In Phase 1 (first detailed review), the Authority assesses the notified transaction. If it is satisfied that the merger fulfills the conditions described above, it approves the merger. If it requires further information to assess whether those conditions are met, the merger is placed into Phase 2 (second detailed review).

25. There is a separate procedure for merger assessment where the acquiring undertaking is a credit or a financial institution. Those mergers are initially assessed by way of preliminary review. Where further information is required to assess whether the conditions mentioned above are fulfilled, preliminary review mergers are transferred to the first detailed review (standard Phase 1) track.

26. The GCRA is required to publish details of any applications for merger clearance and to allow a period within which representations in respect of that merger may be made. The period allowed by the GCRA is ten working days for standard mergers and seven days for mergers on the preliminary review track.

27. There is no statutory timetable for the assessment of mergers in Guernsey. The GCRA works within an administrative timetable of 25 days for the conclusion of Phase 1 and 6 months for the conclusion of Phase 2. The average clearance time in the period 2024–2025 was less than 14 days, including the 10-day consultation period.

VIII. Advocacy and Policy Initiatives

28. The GCRA has carried out education and capacity-building work, such as a series of workshops for procurement officials working within the States of Guernsey and competition law training for Guernsey law firms. GCRA officers also undertake outreach work with business groups on an ad hoc basis.

29. The GCRA has published a series of guidelines on all aspects of its competition law work, including short practical guidance documents for businesses.

---

17 Sure and JT v. GCRA [2025] GRC016.

18 GCRA v. Sure and JT [2025] GCA072.

30. In 2025, the GCRA was asked by the States of Guernsey to undertake a market study in the construction sector, which is due to be completed by the end of Q1 of 2026.

IX. Regional and International Cooperation

31. The GCRA and the JCRA entered into a formal memorandum of understanding (MoU) in 2020 following the dissolution of CICRA. The MoU establishes a non-binding framework for cooperation between the two bodies, setting out principles for the exchange of information, coordination in cross-border investigations and mutual assistance in regulatory and competition law-related training. The MoU does not create any enforceable rights or alter the statutory duties of either authority. Rather, it provides for the sharing of research, policy developments, enforcement approaches and regulatory experience, subject to applicable confidentiality and data protection requirements.[19]

32. The GCRA is a member of the International Competition Network (ICN) and is a signatory to the ICN's Framework for Competition Agency Procedures (CAP). It is also a member of the International Institute of Communications (IIC).

33. As Guernsey is not a sovereign state but a Crown dependency, it is not a member of the Organisation for Economic Co-operation and Development (OECD). However, the OECD Convention was extended to the Bailiwick of Guernsey in 1990, meaning OECD decisions, standards, and obligations apply to Guernsey through the United Kingdom's membership.[20]

X. Challenges and Country-Specific Features

34. Guernsey faces a number of challenges in the competition sphere, which we anticipate are likely to be common across many small island jurisdictions. Certain local markets are highly concentrated, which makes dominance more likely and market entry less easy. There may be a higher cost of doing business, for example due to the cost of transporting goods to the island, which can both deter market entry and raise prices for consumers. Achieving economies of scale can be more difficult in small markets, which may again lead to higher prices for consumers.

XI. References and Resources

A. *Laws and Regulations*

- The Competition (Guernsey) Ordinance, 2012, https://www.guernseylegalresources.gg/CHttpHandler.ashx?id=77021&p=0
- OECD, *OECD Legal Framework*, https://www.oecd.org

---

19 Memorandum of Understanding Between Guernsey Competition and Regulatory Authority and Jersey Competition Regulatory Authority (July 16, 2020), https://www.gcra.gg/sites/default/files/publication/mou-gcrajcra-july 2020 final signed-by-all.pdf.

20 *OECD Legal Framework*, OECD, https://www.oecd.org/en/about/legal.html?utm.

B. *Case Law*

- Sure and JT v. GCRA [2025] GRC016, https://www.guernseylegalresources.gg/CHttpHandler.ashx?documentid=87061
- GCRA v. Sure and JT [2025] GCA072, https://www.guernseylegalresources.gg/CHttpHandler.ashx?documentid=87898
- Case C1441G – The Medical Specialist Group, https://www.gcra.gg/case/c1441g-competition-law-investigation-medical-specialist-group
- Case C1471G – JT and Sure, https://www.gcra.gg/case/c1471g-jt-and-sure-competition-investigation

C. *Public Reports*

- GUERNSEY LANGUAGE COMMISSION, *About Guernésiais*, https://language.gg/About_Guernesiais
- INDEX MUNDI, *Guernsey Urbanization*, https://www.indexmundi.com/guernsey/urbanization.html?utm_
- STATES OF GUERNSEY DATA & ANALYSIS, GUERNSEY ANNUAL GVA AND GDP BULLETIN (Sept. 24, 2024), https://www.gov.gg/CHttpHandler.ashx?id=182351&p=0
- STATES OF GUERNSEY DATA & ANALYSIS, GUERNSEY QUARTERLY POPULATION, EMPLOYMENT AND EARNINGS BULLETIN (Oct. 29, 2024), https://www.gov.gg/CHttpHandler.ashx?id=183488&p=0
- Torrance, David, *The Crown Dependencies* (Commons Libr. Rsch. Briefing No. CBP8611, Sept. 12, 2025), https://commonslibrary.parliament.uk/research-briefings/cbp-8611/.
- UK DEP'T BUS. & TRADE, TRADE AND INVESTMENT FACTSHEET, https://assets.publishing.service.gov.uk/media/691345dd1fcc92b3f3496398/guernsey-trade-and-investment-factsheet-2025-10-31.pdf?utm_source=chatgpt.com
- UNCTAD, *General profile: Guernsey*, https://unctadstat.unctad.org/CountryProfile/GeneralProfile/en-GB/831/index.html?utm_

D. *Academic Articles*

- Livestro, Sarah *Breaking the Chains in Labour Markets: The Application of Competition Law to Worker Non-Compete Clauses in Guernsey*, 46 E.C.L.R. 506

35. To learn more about the Guernsey Competition and Regulatory Authority:
    - Website: www.gcra.gg/
    - Contact: info@gcra.gg

Honduras

Suyen Muñoz Rivera
Commissioner President at the Commission for the Defense and Promotion of Competition

I. Overview

1. Honduras is located in the center of Central America, with a coastline on the Caribbean Sea and access to the Pacific Ocean through the Gulf of Fonseca. It has a total surface area of approximately 112,490 square kilometers.[1] Honduras had a population of approximately 10,825,703 inhabitants in 2024[2]. Politically, it is a sovereign state and constitutional republic. The official language of Honduras is Spanish. Economically, Honduras combines the characteristics of a small economy on the international scale with a domestic market that, due to its size, tends to concentrate supply in several sensitive sectors.

II. Demographics and Economy

2. In 2024, Honduras recorded a population of 10,825,703, corresponding to a density of approximately 96 inhabitants per square kilometer. Nearly 58.8% of the population lived in urban areas, indicating a high concentration in cities alongside significant dispersion across the rest of the country.[3]

3. In terms of economic scale, Honduras' nominal gross domestic product (GDP) was approximately USD 37.09 billion in 2024, with GDP per capita approximately USD 3,426 and real growth around 3.6%.[4]

4. From the perspective of stability and social conditions, year-on-year inflation as of December 2025 stood at 4.98% according to information published by the Central Bank of Honduras, while the unemployment rate was around 6.1% in 2024, and family remittances represented approximately 25.7% of GDP in 2024, which illustrates how price pressures and the importance of these inflows affect household income.[5]

5. From a productive perspective, value added was concentrated mainly in the services sector (58.4% of GDP), followed by industry (26.1%) and agriculture (11.2%), reflecting an economy whose performance depends largely on trade, transport and service provision activities.[6] Finally, external trade indicates dependence on imported final goods and inputs, with exports equivalent to 37.37% of GDP and imports to 61.42% of GDP, resulting in a trade deficit of – 24.05% of GDP.[7]

III. Legal Framework for Competition

6. Competition policy in Honduras is governed by the Law for the Defense and Promotion of Competition (LDPC or the "Law"), adopted through Legislative Decree No. 357-2005,

---

1 World Development Indicators: Honduras (selected indicators), World Bank (2024) (last visited Jan. 12, 2026), https://databank.worldbank.org/reports.aspx?source=2&country=HND.

2 *Id.*

3 *Id.*

4 *Id.*

5 *Id.*; BCH, 2025; ILO, 2024

6 World Bank, *supra* note 1.

7 Honduras: Exports and imports of goods and services (% of GDP) (data source: World Bank WDI), World Integrated Trade Solution (2024) (last visited Jan. 12, 2026), https://wits.worldbank.org/CountryProfile/en/HND.

a statute of public policy aimed at protecting the exercise of free competition and consumer welfare. In 2015, relevant amendments were introduced (e.g., provisions on exemption or reduction of fines linked to cooperation in investigations) through Legislative Decree No. 4-2015, which strengthened enforcement tools without altering the Restrictive Practices Prohibited by Their Nature (art. 5) and the Restrictive Practices to Be Prohibited According to Their Effects (art. 7).

7. As regards scope, the LDPC applies to all areas of economic activity, even where sectors are regulated by special laws, regulations or resolutions, and it also prevents conduct contrary to the Law from being justified on the basis of customs, usages or commercial stipulations, which is relevant in a country where certain "market practices" may become normalized unless the mechanism that reduces rivalry is stopped in time. In the same logic, the LDPC covers all economic agents (including associations and public entities when they act as active subjects) and even reaches persons domiciled outside Honduras when their acts produce effects in the national territory, which makes it possible to address cases and structures where conduct or transactions originate abroad but directly affect the domestic market (LDPC, arts. 3–4).

8. Operationally, the Regulations for the Implementation of the Law for the Defense and Promotion of Competition (LDPC Implementing Regulations) develop administrative procedures and standardize steps such as information requests and investigative measures, and the Law includes two mechanisms that increase practical effectiveness: (i) provisional measures to avoid serious and irreparable harm to the competitive process while the merits are decided (art. 40), and (ii) a civil action for damages, which allows affected parties to seek compensation by using final decisions of the Competition Defense and Protection Commission (CDPC) or final contentious-administrative judgments as evidence, adding real compliance pressure beyond the fine (art. 58).

IV. Institutional Structure

9. The competition authority in Honduras is the Commission for the Defense and Promotion of Competition (CDPC), whose establishment and powers are provided for in the LDPC, with the mandate to promote and protect competition, as well as to hear, process, and decide the matters set out in the Law and its Implementing Regulations. The CDPC is organized around a collegiate decision-making body (a board composed of three commissioners) and a technical and administrative structure that supports economic and legal analysis, administrative case processing and the enforcement of decisions. As of December 2025, the institutional payroll records 41 permanent positions, of which 18 make up technical staff, including directors, economists and lawyers.

10. With respect to the compliance with competition rules, the LDPC grants the CDPC authority powers specific to the subject matter, and its financing is structured through the inclusion of its annual budget in the general budget of the Republic, as well as quarterly transfers from own-source revenues, which makes resources a practical variable for investigative and follow-up capacity.

11. The CDPC does not perform consumer protection functions or sectoral regulation; instead, it focuses on enforcement of the LDPC and competition advocacy, which makes

coordination with public institutions and regulators particularly relevant when a sectoral provision may create barriers or result in market foreclosure.

12. Regarding enforcement powers, the LDPC enables the CDPC, in antitrust matters, to request information from economic agents and to support case processing with measures that ensure compliance with such requests, as well as a system of sanctions/fines for prohibited conduct and relevant procedural breaches. Additionally, the LDPC contemplates the conduct of inspections and verifications.

V. Enforcement and Sanctions

13. Article 37 of the LDPC establishes punitive fines applicable when the CDPC proves an anticompetitive practice under articles 5 or 7. Designed to neutralize the economic incentive of the conduct, the fine is set at up to three times the economic benefit obtained, or where that benefit cannot be determined, an objective cap of up to 10% of gross profit on sales in the preceding fiscal year applies. In all cases, the cessation of the conduct is mandatory. In practical terms, the LDPC seeks to ensure that infringement is not profitable, and therefore links the sanction to the benefit or, failing that, to a verifiable financial criterion (LDPC, art. 37).

14. In addition, there are procedural fines aimed at making the process effective and avoiding an investigation becoming a mere formality:

- article 41 allows successive daily fines (for up to 30 calendar days) to compel compliance with decisions, provisional measures and related remedies, and the ranges are updated by the consumer price index (CPI) so that the amount does not lose deterrent effect over time;
- article 42 reinforces the seriousness of procedural steps by sanctioning failure to attend summons and, upon repetition, opening the possibility of classifying the conduct as disobedience;
- article 46 protects the core of any investigation through the obligation to provide requested information and documentation, which is indispensable to support economic and legal analysis (LDPC, arts. 41, 42 and 46; CDPC, 2026).

15. As regards criminal liability, the LDPC does not provide criminal sanctions for administrative competition infringements; however, any civil and criminal liabilities that may arise are subject to the procedures before the competent authorities, pursuant to the Criminal Code in force (LDPC, art. 6; Criminal Code, Legislative Decree No. 130-2017).

16. The CDPC has conducted a limited number of investigations into alleged anticompetitive practices, averaging between one and two per year, and not all result in an administrative sanction. This reflects the evidentiary standard and due process: files are opened when there are elements that warrant verification, but some investigations end without a sanction because the analysis determines that the practice was not established or because the indicia do not reach a sufficient level to support moving the case towards a sanctioning decision.[8]

---

[8] Organisation for Economic Co-operation and Development & Inter-American Development Bank, Competition Law and Policy in Honduras: A Peer Review 34–35, 40 (2011), https://www.oecd.org/content/dam/oecd/en/publications/reports/2011/07/competition-law-and-policy-in-honduras-a-peer-review-2011_bf032f95/47c5f6a9-en.pdf.

17. Finally, the LDPC provides for judicial claims for damages: any party harmed by an infringement may bring an action before the competent jurisdiction once there is a final decision, which opens a complementary avenue for compliance and redress, especially when harm translates into prices, access or quality (LDPC, art. 58).

VI. Noteworthy Cases

A. *Cement Case (CENOSA and Lafarge – Resolution No. 22-2010)*

18. *Facts.* The CDPC initiated an *ex officio* investigation into the cement market to determine whether there was an agreement between CENOSA and Lafarge aimed at fixing prices and market allocation; both companies denied it and argued that parallel pricing was explained by government measures. The CDPC supported its conclusion with circumstantial evidence, including the use of state price-setting mechanisms as a channel for coordination and periodic communications between the companies through the Cement Institute Foundation.

19. *Key analytical issue.* Determining whether there was a hardcore anticompetitive practice through a horizontal agreement between competitors, pursuant to article 5 of the LDPC.

20. *Outcome.* The imposition of fines calculated at 8% of gross sales profit has led to subsequent contentious-administrative litigation.

21. *Impact/precedent.* The case consolidated the use of circumstantial evidence in concentrated markets and sent an institutional signal about the risk that certain "institutionalized" spaces or mechanisms may function as channels for coordination.[9]

B. *Sugar Case (Resolution No. 23-2010)*

22. *Facts.* The CDPC initiated an *ex officio* investigation into possible concerted practices among the main sugar mills/producers. Indirect evidence included price uniformity and correlation, simultaneous changes and different cost structures despite uniform prices, as well as structural elements such as concentration, lack of substitutes, product homogeneity and demand inelasticity.

23. *Key analytical issue.* Establishing whether there was unlawful price coordination among competitors, as a hardcore anticompetitive practice under article 5 of the LDPC, in a product of high sensitivity for consumers.

24. *Outcome.* Individual fines were imposed on several economic agents and participation in meetings aimed at regulating prices was prohibited, with reference to subsequent judicial review.

25. *Impact/precedent.* The file made clear that the "normalization" of coordination through meetings or administrative spaces does not make the conduct competitive, and that breaking that mechanism may be as relevant as the sanction itself.[10]

---

9 *Id.* at 30.

10 *Id.* at 31.

C. *Beer Case (Bay Island Brewery v. Cervecería Hondureña – Resolution No. 14-2010)*

26. *Facts.* Bay Island Brewery filed a complaint against Cervecería Hondureña regarding exclusivity clauses and conditions in the on-trade channel (bars and restaurants) on the island of Roatán, with the aim of preventing entry or expansion; the CDPC delineated the market by channel and territory, and considered a share close to 95% relevant to assess the ability to raise barriers.

27. *Key analytical issue.* Assessing exclusivities as conduct prohibited by its effects, pursuant to article 7 of the LDPC, in a market where the channel defines access.

28. *Outcome.* This file stands out as an example of exclusivity with the potential to foreclose the market.

29. *Impact/precedent.* It remains a methodological reference for analyzing vertical restraints in small localities, where access to points of sale is the central competitive asset and exclusivity can operate as a decisive barrier.[11]

30. *Section closing.* Beyond the cases mentioned above, the CDPC has also handled investigative case files concerning potentially anticompetitive conduct in markets such as telecommunications, port services, and clinical laboratories, thereby contributing to the protection of the competitive process and consumer welfare.

VII. Merger Control

31. In Honduras, merger control operates as a prior and mandatory review: when a transaction meets the notification criteria, the CDPC reviews it before it takes effect, with the purpose of determining whether it may significantly reduce or distort the competitive process in the market, whether because it eliminates competitive pressure between economic agents, facilitates coordination scenarios, or creates incentives and the ability to restrict access to inputs, channels or customers. Following the institutional assessment, the CDPC may authorize the proposed transaction, authorize it with conditions, or prohibit it, and during the review, it may also request information to complete the analysis.

32. Mandatory prior notification is triggered when at least one of the thresholds set by Normative Resolution is exceeded: (i) combined total assets equivalent to 4,000 monthly minimum wages, multiplied by 12; (ii) combined revenues/sales equivalent to 5,000 monthly minimum wages, multiplied by 12; or (iii) a combined share equal to or greater than 25% in the relevant market. With an average monthly minimum wage in 2025 of HNL 16,499.36 (USD 620), the asset threshold is equivalent to about USD 30 million and the revenue/sales threshold to USD 37 million. This scheme prevents potentially relevant transactions from falling outside prior review solely due to their accounting size.

33. As to procedural timelines, the LDPC Implementing Regulations provide that, if the filing is incomplete, the CDPC issues a notice to cure within ten working days; and

---

11 ID. at 35.

the 45 working-day period to decide is counted on the basis of a complete file, meaning it starts from the day after the cure and the submission of the requested information.

34. The following mergers have received conditional clearance:

- *Industria La Popular/Unilever de Centroamérica* (2025) – detergent brand portfolio (conditional): The transaction consisted of the transfer of a portfolio of brands from Unilever to Industria La Popular; the decision analyzed it as a horizontal concentration, as it consolidated brands that compete in the same relevant market, particularly household powder detergents. Although the asset transferred consists of brands, the impact is reflected in demand substitution, competitive pressure between portfolios and shelf and channel presence, so the analysis reviews market structure, barriers and potential discipline through imports or entry. As a structural condition, the buyer committed to keeping a key brand under independent distribution for at least three years, without operational control by its own network. Restrictions on prices, margins or the marketing of competing products are prohibited, and if the contract ends before four years, a new independent distributor must be appointed within six months, under the same conditions and for the remaining term plus two years, with notification to the Commission.
- *Delivery Hero SE/HugoTechnologies* (2025) – digital platform (conditional): The transaction consisted of Delivery Hero SE acquiring 100% of Hugo Technologies Intermediate LLC, resulting in an indirect change of control over the operating subsidiary in Honduras. Its relevance stems from the fact that Delivery Hero already participated in the country, so the transaction integrated two relevant platforms in the market under the same structure. The market share threshold triggered review and allowed the imposition of conditions; the case also shows that, in digital markets, risks tend to concentrate around networks, data and platform effects. As the main condition, the CDPC ordered the maintenance of separate and independent management for an initial period, with safeguards for sensitive information, to prevent coordination of commercial decisions or cross-use of data that could weaken effective rivalry between platforms.

VIII. Competition Advocacy

35. In Honduras, competition promotion is aimed at preventing unnecessary restrictions on competition that arise from public decisions, administrative practices or professional association rules. In that context, the CDPC carries out outreach and training activities, issues technical opinions to public institutions and produces studies and guidance instruments, with the objective of improving understanding, compliance and regulatory quality, and of preventing certain practices from becoming consolidated as market usages when they may limit options and affect the functioning of free competition.

36. Competition promotion and advocacy are organized through annual planning and are also activated upon request when a sector or institution requires guidance and there is capacity to address it, so these actions are carried out in person or virtually with a practical approach that explains which conduct tends to generate risks, what the CDPC assesses to consider it a restriction under the LDPC, and which alternatives allow the problem to be corrected without distorting the market.

37. With respect to technical instruments, by the end of 2025, the CDPC reached the final stage of preparing seven market sector studies, which are useful for identifying bottlenecks and proposing regulatory improvements, public policy measures or market-functioning enhancements. In the same period, work progressed on two guides: (i) a compliance guide, aimed at strengthening internal programs to prevent competition risks within economic agents, and (ii) a merger control guide, which systematizes relevant criteria and stages for notification and analysis under the LDPC, with an emphasis on clarity and institutional predictability.

38. Capacity building is also part of the advocacy approach. The CDPC receives training and technical assistance through virtual means, especially through RECAC (Central American Network of Competition Authorities), and complements that learning with exchanges and training with agencies and organizations such as INDECOPI (Peru), the CNMC (Spain) and the OECD (Organisation for Economic Co-operation and Development), depending on the availability of in-person or virtual opportunities for technical staff. This component helps sustain methodological consistency, improve the use of evidence and keep analytical criteria up to date in traditional and dynamic markets.

39. Against that background, a concrete example illustrates the practical role of advocacy in the country. In the Special Opinion Report concerning the College of Microbiologists (Case No. 265-D-6-2025), the CDPC analyzed the competitive effect of conditioning or suspending registration and renewal procedures for laboratories in relation to an economic agent, on the grounds that there was a complaint pending. The opinion concluded that suspending renewals and new registrations solely because a complaint was pending could, in practice, operate as an entry barrier and a continuing obstruction, and therefore recommended that the College immediately reconsider that decision and process the filings without delay, without conditioning the procedure on the existence or outcome of proceedings before the CDPC, and also refrain from adopting acts that, directly or indirectly, condition, delay or deny those applications due to the pending process.

IX. International Cooperation

40. Regional and international cooperation contributes to strengthening competition policy by enabling the alignment of technical standards, the exchange of methodological experience, and the maintenance of institutional consistency as markets integrate, economic agents operate in several countries, and relevant information is not always available immediately. In that logic, the CDPC combines formal cooperation (agreements and memoranda of understanding) with participation in regional fora, so that learning does not depend solely on internal experience but also on shared standards and continuous training.

41. On the bilateral front, the CDPC has signed technical cooperation instruments with peer authorities. For example, the agreement with ACODECO (Consumer Protection and Competition Defense Authority, Panama) establishes bases for coordination and exchange of experience in the application of competition rules, while the agreement with PROCOMPETENCIA (National Institute for the Promotion of Competition, Nicaragua) includes an emphasis that is particularly useful for Central America by linking competition with preserving the benefits of trade liberalization. Beyond the

immediate region, the agreement with CONACOM (National Competition Commission, Paraguay) includes training, exchange of best practices, and technical cooperation, which strengthens analytical and procedural capacity and helps build consistency in criteria and evidentiary standards.

42. In addition to bilateral agreements, the CDPC participates in regional coordination spaces and in global networks that facilitate coordination and capacity building. At the regional level, this is reflected in exchange dynamics among Central American authorities to discuss analytical criteria and common challenges, especially in markets with comparable structures and regulatory frameworks. At the global level, the CDPC relies on networks such as the ICN (International Competition Network) for access to technical workshops and best practices, and on UNCTAD (United Nations Conference on Trade and Development) initiatives for institutional strengthening and training, while the use of OECD comparative standards and assessments serves as a reference to organize methodologies, improve consistency and raise the technical quality of cases.

X. Challenges and Priorities

43. In Honduras, several markets operate with few relevant suppliers due to a combination of factors such as market size, logistical barriers, investment requirements and segmented demand, which limits how many competitors can be sustained on a stable basis. This reality increases the risk of coordination, exclusivity, and channel foreclosure, and requires that enforcement of the LDPC focus on mechanisms that reduce rivalry, particulary un markerts where the loss of competition translates into prices, availability, or quality.

44. An additional challenge arises when public objectives and economic activity converge, whether due to the presence of agents with state participation or sectoral regulation linked to essential services. The issue is to reconcile public policy objectives with effective competition, avoiding regulatory or contractual design that generates undue advantages, artificial barriers or discrimination beyond what is strictly necessary to fulfill the service purpose, which makes coordination with regulators and public entities under the criteria of necessity, proportionality and verifiable evidence critical.

45. Trade openness and dependence on imports add a practical challenge: competition from abroad does not always translate into domestic prices and conditions, as it may be constrained by logistical restrictions, unequal access to suppliers, distribution constraints or contractual clauses. For that reason, merger control and conduct analysis must focus on local effects and on effective market access, even where the transaction is structured outside the country or responds to regional strategies or foreign investment decisions.

46. At the institutional level, constraints are not limited to budget; they also include data, tools and specialized expertise for complex markets. This requires prioritization based on economic criteria, turning dispersed information into usable evidence, relying on cooperation and technical training where relevant, while balancing competition with development objectives, employment, supply security or investment attraction, and ensuring that any restriction has a verifiable justification and is the minimum necessary.

47. Finally, informality and certain practices that, in market dynamics, affect access to routes, permits, intermediation, points of sale or inputs can influence segments of different

markets and coexist with the formal sector, ultimately affecting the real conditions under which economic agents compete. In these scenarios, the challenge is to distinguish between structural conditions and avoidable barriers created by obstacles that close off options; therefore, in addition to sanctioning enforcement where appropriate, advocacy and institutional coordination help remove obstacles and improve market transparency.

XI. Author's Perspective

48. In Honduras, competition policy has the fundamental role of preserving rivalry and competitive dynamics where there can be freedom of entry and growth and where competition takes place under free-market conditions. When analysis focuses on the right variables (e.g., access to channels, inputs, information, distribution capacity or contractual conditions), the LDPC ceases to be seen as just another regulatory framework and becomes a practical tool to protect real options for consumers and for the competitive dynamics of the market.

49. From a medium- to long-term perspective, institutional strengthening should focus on three areas for improvement:
    - Consolidating the use of data and evidence to support decisions that are technically defensible, with particular priority given to the use of artificial intelligence to detect potential indicators of anticompetitive practices amid the expansion of digital markets;
    - Designing measurable and verifiable conditions and remedies so that they work in practice;
    - Maintaining competition advocacy that is more focused on removing administrative barriers or sectoral rules that close markets without providing a proportionate public benefit.

XII. References and Resources

A. *Laws and Regulations*

- Ley para la Defensa y Promoción de la Competencia [Law for the Defense and Promotion of Competition – LDPC] (2005), Decreto No. 357-2005, Diario Oficial La Gaceta (Honduras)
- Reglamento de la Ley para la Defensa y Promoción de la Competencia [Regulations for the Implementation of the Law for the Defense and Promotion of Competition] (2007), Acuerdo No. 001-2007, Diario Oficial La Gaceta (Honduras)

B. *Case Law*

- CDPC, Executive Summary – Concentrations in Digital Markets: Case Delivery Hero SE/Hugo Technologies Intermediate LLC (2025) (in Spanish)
- CDPC, Resolution, Case No. 276-NC-2-2025: Industria La Popular, S.A./Unilever de Centroamérica, S.A. (2025) (in Spanish)
- CDPC, Special Opinion Report: Case No. 265-D-6-2025, Colegio de Microbiólogos y Químicos Clínicos de Honduras (July 11, 2025) (in Spanish)

- CDPC, Resolution No. 22-2010 (Cement Case: CENOSA and Lafarge) (2010) (in Spanish)
- CDPC, Resolution No. 14-2010 (Beer Case: Bay Island Brewery v. Cervecería Hondureña) (2010) (in Spanish)

C. *Public Reports*

- CDPC, Honduras – edited ECMA revised CDPC (2020)
- OECD & IDB, Competition Law and Policy in Honduras: A Peer Review (2011), https://www.oecd.org/content/dam/oecd/en/publications/reports/2011/07/competition-law-and-policy-in-honduras-a-peer-review-2011_bf032f95/47c5f6a9-en.pdf
- World Bank, World Development Indicators: Honduras (selected indicators) (2024) (last visited Jan. 12, 2026), https://databank.worldbank.org/reports.aspx?source=2&country=HND
- World Integrated Trade Solution, Honduras: Exports and imports of goods and services (% of GDP) (data source: World Bank WDI), (2024) (last visited Jan. 12, 2026), https://wits.worldbank.org/CountryProfile/en/HND

50. To learn more about the Commission for the Defense and Promotion of Competition (CDPC):

Website: www.cdpc.hn

Contact: comision@cdpc.hn

Iceland

Páll Gunnar Pálsson
Director General of Icelandic Competition Authority

I. Overview

1. Iceland is a 103,000 square kilometers island in the North Atlantic Ocean, situated between North America and Europe, just southeast of Greenland. It is the world's 18th-largest island and the second largest in Europe, after Great Britain.[1]

2. A sovereign state organized as a parliamentary republic, Iceland is closely integrated with Europe through the European Economic Area (EEA) Agreement. It has also been a member of the Nordic Council, the North Atlantic Treaty Organization (NATO) and the Organisation for Economic Co-operation and Development (OECD) since their establishment.

3. The official language is Icelandic. Public authorities are required to ensure that it can be used in all areas of society. Moreover, all persons residing in Iceland must be given the opportunity to learn Icelandic and to use it for full participation in social life.[2]

II. Demographics and Economy

4. As of January 1, 2025, Iceland's population was estimated at 389,444 inhabitants, according to Statistics Iceland. Over recent decades, the country's demographic profile has changed significantly. Broadly speaking, the proportion of children has declined, while the share of older persons has increased. Over the past ten years, the number of individuals aged 0–19 has fallen from 46.6% to 40.7% relative to the working-age population. During the same period, the proportion of persons aged 65 and over has risen from 23.3% to 26.5%, the highest level recorded to date.[3]

5. Iceland is one of the most sparsely populated countries in the world, with a population density of roughly 3.78 people per square kilometer as of January 1, 2025. In this respect, it should be noted that around 10% of the country is covered by glaciers, and roughly half consists of uninhabited central highlands.

6. Settlement patterns are highly concentrated. Approximately 94.5% of the population lives in urban localities with 200 or more inhabitants, while only 5.5% (21,498 people) reside in rural areas. The Capital Region serves as a dominant urban hub and is home to 64% of the nation's total population.[4]

7. In 2024, Iceland's nominal gross domestic product (GDP) amounted to USD 33.3 billion.[5] The country's trade balance has historically been characterized by a deficit in goods trade and a surplus in services trade. Over the past two decades, the strength of service exports, notably tourism, has been decisive in sustaining an overall surplus in the combined balance of trade in goods and services, particularly from 2010 onward.

---

1 *Maps of Iceland*, WOLRDATLAS (Dec. 15, 2023), https://www.worldatlas.com/maps/iceland.

2 Act Respecting the Status of the Icelandic Language and Icelandic Sign Language (2011), https://www.government.is/media/menntamalaraduneyti-media/media/frettir2015/Thyding-log-um-stodu-islenskrar-tungu-og-islensks-taknmals-desember-2015.pdf.

3 News Release, Statistics Iceland, Iceland's population was 389,444 at the beginning of 2025 (Mar. 12, 2025), https://www.statice.is/publications/news-archive/inhabitants/the-population-on-1-january-2025/.

4 News Release, Statistics Iceland, Selfoss and surroundings exceeds 10,000 inhabitants (Oct. 7, 2025), https://www.statice.is/publications/news-archive/inhabitants/population-by-urban-nuclei-and-localites-2025/.

5 OECD, OECD ECONOMIC SURVEYS: ICELAND 2025 (June 2025), https://doi.org/10.1787/890dbe05-en.

8. The Icelandic economy rests on a few pillars: fisheries, tourism, aluminum smelting, and other power-intensive industries relying on domestic electricity generation. Fisheries remain a stable pillar of the economy, although their relative weight has declined gradually, with the share of marine exports falling from 26% in 2016 to 18% in 2025. By contrast, tourism is more cyclical. Revenue from foreign visitors accounted for around 38% of export earnings in 2016, fell sharply to 11–16% during the COVID-19 period, and has since recovered to approximately 34%. Aluminum smelting and other power-intensive industries have remained broadly stable, with their share moving from 22% in 2016 and 25% in 2025. At the same time, other sectors have gained ground, signifying a more diversified economy. This includes knowledge-based exports, which accounted for 13% of total export revenues in 2024, up from 7% in 2010.[6]

9. Given Iceland's small population and geographic isolation, many of its markets are characterized by high levels of concentration. The grocery retail and liner shipping markets are each dominated by two large firms, while the banking and telecommunications sectors are dominated by three principal operators. Electricity generation is largely controlled by a single major undertaking: the state-owned enterprise Landsvirkjun.

III. Legal Framework for Competition

10. On February 25, 1993, a modern competition law (No. 8/1993) entered into force in Iceland for the first time, replacing a framework more focused on price regulation. The enactment of the law was directly linked to Iceland's accession to the EEA, which came into effect on January 1, 1994. The EEA Agreement binds the 27 EU Member States and three European Free Trade Association (EFTA) nations – Iceland, Liechtenstein, and Norway – into a single, homogeneous market. With Act No. 2/1993, the competition rules and other provisions of the EEA Agreement were given legal effect in Iceland.

11. The Competition Act No. 8/1993 was amended on several occasions, most notably in 2000, when provisions on the abuse of a dominant position and merger reviews were strengthened considerably.

12. A new competition law entered into force on July 1, 2005 (No. 44/2005).[7] With the new act, the organizational structure of competition enforcement was bolstered by the establishment of Samkeppniseftirlitið (SKE), the Icelandic Competition Authority (ICA or the "Authority"). Additionally, the enforcement of rules on unfair trading practices and market transparency – previously handled by the former competition authorities – was transferred to a separate consumer authority. A primary objective of these changes was to strengthen the focus on competition enforcement at the new ICA.

---

6 Íslandsbanki Research, Economic Equinox: Macroeconomic Forecast 2025–2027 (Sept. 2025) https://cdn.islandsbanki.is/image/upload/v1/documents/MacroForecast-2025-09_EN.pdf; XXX *Selected Items of the Exports of Goods and Services 2013–2025*, Statistics Iceland, XXX https://px.hagstofa.is/pxen/pxweb/en/Efnahagur/Efnahagur__utanrikisverslun__3_voruthjonusta__voruthjonusta/UTA05003.px/table/tableViewLayout2/. XXX Please check the URL (no item selected) XXX

7 Competition Act (2005) (in Icelandic), https://www.althingi.is/lagas/nuna/2005044.html.

13. Since 2005, the Competition Act has been amended a few times, most notably: in 2007, with new provisions on the criminalization of cartel offenses by individuals; in 2008, with the strengthening of merger reviews; and in 2011, with the introduction of a market investigation regime.

14. The Competition Act applies to all types of economic activity – such as production, trade, and services – regardless of whether they are run by individuals, companies, public bodies or others. However, the Act does not apply to wages or other working conditions of employees according to collective agreements. With reference to the EEA Agreement, additional competition rules apply to certain sectors, such as energy and telecommunications, to enhance competition and safeguard consumer interests where market failure exists. In addition, extensive exemptions from competition rules apply to certain agricultural sectors, mainly concerning meat processing and the dairy industry.

15. The Competition Act prohibits cartels and other anti-competitive agreements between undertakings (art. 10), the abuse of a dominant position (art. 11) and restrictive practices by associations of undertakings (art. 12). Investigations are directed towards undertakings or associations of undertakings, and breaches are subject to administrative fines as well as decisions on structural or behavioral remedies. Serious cartel offenses by individuals carry criminal liability, which can result in custodial sentences of up to six years. It is the task of the ICA to assess whether the portion of a case concerning criminal liability should be reported to the police for a parallel investigation. To safeguard the ICA's leniency system, a criminal investigation can only commence upon a formal complaint from the ICA to the police. This means that the ICA can grant full immunity to both undertakings and their employees.

16. Furthermore, the ICA conducts merger reviews, enabling it to block mergers or approve mergers subject to remedies (art. 17 to 17(e)). The ICA is also empowered with a market investigation regime; this allows it to implement structural or behavioral remedies against circumstances or conduct that prevent or restrict competition, even if such restrictions do not derive from breaches of competition law.

17. The Competition Act also entails provisions enabling the ICA to take binding action against public bodies and protected undertakings. To this end, the Authority may decide on a financial separation between the activities of an undertaking benefiting from protection or public aid and its other activities in competition with other undertakings (art. 14). The ICA can also take action against public bodies to the extent that their acts may have a detrimental effect on competition, provided that special legislation does not contain specific rules for such actions (art. 16).

18. Furthermore, the Authority is tasked with advocating against actions by public bodies that restrict competition. To this end, the ICA may, inter alia, issue formal opinions to government ministers proposing amendments to legislation that restricts competition.

19. The ICA is authorized to make interim decisions if it is considered likely that conduct or circumstances under investigation are in breach of the provisions of the Competition Act or decisions taken on the basis thereof.

IV. Institutional Structure

20. The current institutional structure of competition enforcement and advocacy came into force on July 1, 2005, with the establishment of Samkeppniseftirlitið, the Icelandic Competition Authority.

21. The ICA is a separate administrative body. Responsibility for the implementation of the Competition Act lies with the Minister of Industries, under whose purview the ICA falls. The minister appoints a three-member non-executive board for a four-year term, which sets the Authority's priorities and monitors its activities. Major substantive decisions, such as administrative fines, merger annulments and structural or behavioral remedies, shall be submitted to the board for approval or rejection.

22. The director general of the ICA is appointed by the board. The director is responsible for the day-to-day operations of the Authority, makes decisions on its behalf and is its spokesperson.

23. Decisions of the ICA can be referred to a special administrative appeals body: the Competition Appeals Committee. The Committee is composed of three members appointed for a four-year term by the minister, following nomination by the Supreme Court. A written appeal shall be presented to the Committee within four weeks of the decision being notified to the parties to the case. Rulings of the Competition Appeals Committee may be referred by the ICA and the undertakings concerned to the general courts, i.e., the District Court of Reykjavík and the Court of Appeal, and, in significant cases and if that court subject to leave, to the Supreme Court. Parties may also choose to bring a decision of the ICA directly before the general courts, without first appealing to the Competition Appeals Committee.

24. The ICA is defined as an independent administrative authority. This independence is demonstrated by the fact that the Ministry of Industries is not involved in any decisions made by the ICA, nor does it review such decisions. The functions of the Competition Appeals Committee – along with the arm's-length relationship from political power provided by the board's appointment of the director general – secure a certain minimum level of independence. However, the ICA remains under the general responsibility of the Ministry and the government and is subject to budgetary decisions by the Parliament.

25. The ICA is solely responsible for competition enforcement and advocacy. Between 1993 and 2005, the competition authorities were also tasked with enforcing rules on unfair trading practices and market transparency. The rationale for the change was that a more focused competition authority would be a more effective enforcer and advocate for the objectives of competition law. This change has proven successful in a small economy like Iceland, as the new ICA has become more effective.

26. The ICA can require individual undertakings, groups of undertakings, and associations of undertakings to provide all information deemed necessary for the investigation of individual cases. Failure to provide correct and sufficient information is subject to administrative fines for the undertakings involved. Furthermore, managers, board members, or employees of undertakings or associations who destroy, falsify, or render unusable any information of significance to the ICA are liable to a fine or imprisonment for up to three years.

27. The ICA can conduct dawn raids at the premises of undertakings or associations of undertakings. However, this does not extend to other locations, such as managers' residences. In this respect, the Competition Act does not currently fulfill the requirements set out in the ECN+ Directive within the EEA.[8]

28. If the police, after receiving a complaint from the ICA, decide to investigate individuals' participation in a possible hardcore cartel, they can use all their criminal investigation tools, such as wiretapping. The Competition Act allows the police to share the resulting information with the ICA for its own cartel investigation. This has been of great value in some cases.

29. As previously stated, the ICA decides upon administrative fines, annulments of mergers, structural or behavioral remedies, and interim decisions. It can also impose daily fines on a party to a case that fails to comply with its decisions.

30. In addition to enforcing the Icelandic competition rules, the ICA is also responsible for the application of the competition rules of the EEA Agreement, mainly the prohibition rules on collusion (art. 53 of the Agreement) and abuse of a dominant position (art. 54). The Icelandic prohibition rules are in this respect identical to the EEA rules, allowing for the application of EU/EEA-law precedents.

31. The EFTA Surveillance Authority (ESA) ensures the uniform application of the competition rules within the EEA. Furthermore, the ESA can initiate its own investigations into breaches of the EEA rules by undertakings operating in Iceland. To this end, it can conduct dawn raids and other measures in Iceland to secure necessary information and documents, in cooperation with the ICA.

32. The ICA's budget in 2026 is ISK 690 million, approximately USD 5.6 million. As of February 2026, the ICA employed 27 staff members, including 8 economists, 15 lawyers, and 4 individuals with other educational backgrounds.

V. Enforcement and Sanctions

33. Competition law violations and breaches of prior decisions are subject to administrative fines imposed by the ICA. Fines may amount to up to 10% of the total turnover of the previous operating year of each undertaking or association of undertakings that is a party to the infringement.

34. Furthermore, the ICA can take action against agreements, terms and any activities that violate the prohibition rules of the Competition Act, as well as settlements or decisions made pursuant to the Act. Such actions may include any measures necessary to promote competition, cease infringements, or change conduct or structure.

35. According to the Competition Act, the ICA can conclude an investigation by a settlement with the undertakings under investigation.

---

8 Directive (EU) 2019/1 of the European Parliament and of the Council of Dec. 11, 2018, to Empower the Competition Authorities of the Member States to Be More Effective Enforcers and to Ensure the Proper Functioning of the Internal Market (ECN+), 2019 O.J. (L 11) 3.

36. Each year, the ICA allocates time to between 120 and 160 administrative cases. Of the 153 cases in 2025, 56 involved complaints and investigations concerning possible violations of the Competition Act or the ICA's earlier decisions.

37. In total, 93 undertakings have been fined since the entry into force of the first modern competition act in Iceland in 1993. Of these, 78 undertakings have been subject to administrative fines since the ICA was established in 2005. Of those fines, 37 were levied in cartel cases, 20 in cases regarding an abuse of a dominant position, and 22 concerned other violations, such as violations of earlier decisions or obligations to provide information and to notify a merger. Around half of the fines since 2005 have been determined through settlements with the parties, most of them for cartel violations.

38. The aggregate amount of administrative fines since 1993, taking into account reviews by the Competition Appeals Committee and the courts, is approximately ISK 24,710,000,000 (in real terms at year-end 2025), or approximately USD 201,172,000. Similarly, the aggregate amount of fines since 2005 is ISK 20,090,000,000, or around USD 163,600,000.

39. The ICA does not keep track of private enforcement arising from its enforcement decisions. In many instances, parties that have suffered loss because of violations seek information and documents from the ICA in order to assess possible damage claims. A few cases have been addressed in the courts, and compensation awarded. In addition, the ICA is aware of a few cases where damage claims have been settled privately.

40. It must be noted that Iceland has not implemented Directive 2014/104/EU, which facilitates damage claims arising from violations of competition law. Thus, claimants do not enjoy the same rights as claimants in EU countries.[9]

VI. Noteworthy Cases: Violations of Competition Law

A. *Serious Cartel Infringements in Transport Markets*

41. With a decision in August 2023 (No. 33/2023), the ICA completed an extensive cartel investigation into Samskip's collusion with its main competitor, Eimskip. Together, the companies hold an extensive market share in the markets for maritime and land transport. The decision itself is 3,600 pages long, which indicates the scope of the case.[10]

42. The investigation against Eimskip was concluded in June 2021, with the company's settlement with the ICA. With the settlement, Eimskip admitted violations, paid an administrative fine of ISK 1,500,000,000 (USD 12,200,000) and committed to take certain measures to prevent further violations and promote competition. At Samskip's request, the ICA engaged in settlement discussions with the undertaking, but the discussions did not lead to a settlement.

---

9 Directive 2014/104/EU of the European Parliament and of the Council of Nov. 26, 2014, on Certain Rules Governing Actions for damages Under National Law for Infringements of the Competition Law Provisions of the Member States and of the European Union, 2014 O.J. (L 349) 1.

10 News, ICA, Serious Infringements of Competition Law by Samskip (Aug. 31, 2023) (in Icelandic) https://www.samkeppni.is/utgafa/frettir/alvarleg-brot-samskipa-a-samkeppnislogum/.

43. In its 2023 decision, the ICA concluded that Samskip gravely violated the prohibition in article 10 of the Icelandic Competition Act and article 53 of the EEA Agreement by colluding unlawfully with Eimskip. It was also the ICA's conclusion that Samskip, during the case investigation, gravely violated article 19 of the Icelandic Competition Act with incorrect, misleading, and insufficient information and data delivery.

44. An administrative fine of ISK 4,200,000,000 (USD 32,200,000) was imposed for these violations. Furthermore, certain instructions were addressed to Samskip to prevent further violations and promote competition.

45. Regarding Samskip's violation, the decision states as follows:

> The collusion between Samskip and Eimskip as a whole was intended to enable the companies to significantly reduce competition and raise or maintain prices, e.g., by raising prices when contracts were being renewed, by raising prices and fees in price lists, by introducing new fees, by reducing discounts, etc. The strong position of Eimskip and Samskip in the market, the communication between the companies' managers, and other factors in the companies' collusion created ideal conditions for the companies to succeed in the collusion and profit at the expense of customers and society as a whole.

46. The breaches of Samskip (and Eimskip, according to the settlement) include the following:
   - Collusion regarding changes in shipping systems and to limit transport capacity.
   - Collusion to implement market sharing of larger customers in maritime and land transport (avoid competing for each other's larger customers).
   - Collusion on fees and discount terms in transport services and collusion to share important price and business information.
   - Collusion in land transport services involving market sharing on certain transport routes in Iceland.
   - Collusion on maritime transport between Iceland and other countries.
   - Collusion on stevedoring, mutual leasing or loan of containers.

47. Samskip appealed the decision. In its ruling in March 2025 (No. 7/2023), the Competition Appeals Committee confirmed that Samskip had engaged in illegal collusion with Eimskip between 2008 and 2013. The ruling imposes a fine of ISK 2,300,000,000 (USD 8,800,000) on Samskip for serious and extensive violations of article 10 of the Competition Act and article 53(1) of the EEA Agreement. Additionally, Samskip was fined ISK 100,000,000 (USD 603,000) for violating its duty to provide information under article 19 of the Act.[11]

48. The ruling confirms:

> [T]he appellant (Samskip) violated article 10 of the Competition Act and article 53(1) of the EEA Agreement with a multifaceted and long-term illegal collusion with Eimskip during the investigation period. This included collusion

---

[11] Competition Appeals Committee, Case No. 7/2023 (Mar. 19, 2025) (in Icelandic), https://www.samkeppni.is/wp-content/uploads/2025/07/Urskurdur-7-2023-19_03_2025.pdf.

> between the companies in 2008 as part of the "New Beginning" project, which started in June 2008 and was aimed at disrupting competition, as well as collusion regarding changes to Eimskip's shipping system that were implemented at the end of July of the same year… It is also proven that the companies engaged in market allocation (the "Piece") that involved avoiding competition for each other's key customers, which lasted from 2009 to 2012. …Additionally, the companies colluded on specific pricing matters and other sensitive competition issues.[12]

49. The Competition Appeals Committee's ruling states that specific collaboration between Samskip and Eimskip was not a violation, but "nonetheless the conclusion is to confirm the contested decision regarding its most significant aspects, as previously explained."[13]

50. The ruling has now been brought before the District Court of Reykjavík by both the ICA and Samskip.

B. *Cartel Offenses in the Market for Building Materials*

51. In Decision No. 11/2015, the ICA concluded that Byko, a large building material retailer, had colluded with its main competitor, Húsasmiðjan. This included price collusion on key building products, mainly through the long-standing, organized sharing of price information. The ICA considered this to be a serious violation of the Competition Act and the EEA Agreement and imposed a fine of ISK 650,000,000 (USD 5,330,000). The investigation into Húsasmiðjan's role in the case was concluded with a settlement in July 2014, where unlawful collusion was admitted and fines were paid.

52. Byko appealed the ICA's decision to the Competition Appeals Committee. In October 2015, the Committee concluded that Byko had participated in unlawful price fixing and had violated competition law. However, the committee did not agree with ICA's conclusion that the provisions of the EEA Agreement had been violated. The board also considered that Byko's violation was not as serious as the ICA had assumed, and reduced the fine by 90%.

53. The ICA brought the case before the Reykjavík District Court. In its judgment, the court agreed that Byko's violations had been serious and increased the company's fine. The court also agreed that the provisions of the EEA Agreement had been violated. Byko referred the case to the Court of Appeal, which concluded that Byko had committed serious violations of competition law. However, it considered the violations to be less extensive and that no violation of the EEA Agreement had been demonstrated. As a result, the fine was reduced.

54. The Supreme Court granted the Competition Authority permission to appeal the judgment. In its January 2021 judgment (No. 42/2021), the Supreme Court found that Byko's violation of article 10 of the Competition Act and article 53 of the EEA Agreement included regular and frequent communications between Byko and Húsasmiðjan, where among other things, information was obtained about prices, passed on to the companies' managers and discussed at meetings of the board of directors of Byko. The companies

---

[12] Our translation.

[13] Our translation.

also exchanged information about their performance, operations and ideas for changes in pricing policy. In addition, there was unlawful collusion between the companies in their attempt to get a smaller competitor to participate in the price collusion.[14]

55. The Court found that all the violations were serious and involved organized and systematic coordination between companies that held a near-monopoly in the relevant market. The Court considered an appropriate fine to be ISK 400,000,000 (USD 3,280,000).

56. In the initial stages of the investigation, the ICA reported possible violations by managers and employees of Byko and Húsasmiðjan to the police. In its judgment in Case No. 360/2015, the Supreme Court convicted eight employees of the companies.[15] During the investigation, the police conducted wiretapping and recorded telephone calls between the companies, which became important evidence in the investigations carried out by both the police and the ICA.

C. *Abuse of a Dominant Position in the Dairy Industry*

57. In its Decision No. 19/2016, the ICA concluded that the incumbent dairy company, MS, had seriously abused its dominant position by selling raw milk to its competitors for the production of dairy products at a much higher price than that paid by MS itself and its affiliated parties for the same raw milk.[16]

58. The ICA found that this had given MS and its affiliated parties a significant competitive advantage over competitors. In this way, the ability of such parties to compete with MS and its affiliated companies had been seriously impaired. For this serious breach, the ICA imposed a fine of ISK 440,000,000 (USD 3,607,740), as well as a fine of ISK 40,000,000 (USD 328,000) for violating the company's obligations to provide information to the ICA.

59. MS appealed the decision to the Competition Appeals Committee. The majority of the committee concluded that special exemptions for dairy companies to cooperate had set aside the Competition Act's prohibition on the abuse of a dominant position. As a result, MS's fine for violating article 11 of the Competition Act was annulled. On the other hand, the Committee confirmed that MS had violated the Competition Act's obligation to provide information.

60. After ICA's appeal, the Reykjavík District Court overturned the majority decision of the Competition Appeals Committee. MS appealed the District Court's judgment to the Court of Appeal, which upheld the decision. In March 2021 (No. 26/2020), the Supreme Court upheld the judgment of the Court of Appeal and imposed a fine of ISK 480,000,000 (USD 3,940,000) for serious abuse of a dominant position and violation of the company's disclosure obligations.[17]

---

14 Supreme Court of Iceland, Case No. 42/2019 (Jan. 7, 2021) (in Icelandic), https://www.haestirettur.is/domar/domur/?id=a1962b39-f939-4bdf-a1f6-9bb2fe439880.

15 Supreme Court of Iceland, Case No. 360/2015 (Dec. 1, 2016) (in Icelandic), https://www.haestirettur.is/default.aspx?pageid=0f2f6428-7b6a-11eb-947c-005056bc0bdb&id=3db316d5-9d3f-4477-93f1-02987bec8ecc.

16 ICA, Decision No. 19/2016 (July 7, 2016) (in Icelandic), https://www.samkeppni.is/wp-content/uploads/2025/07/Akvordun_19_2016_Brot-Mjokursamsolunar-ehf-a-samkeppnislogum.pdf.

17 Supreme Court of Iceland, Case No. 26/2020 (Mar. 4, 2021) (in Icelandic), https://www.samkeppni.is/media/frettir-2021/MS.pdf.

VII. Merger Control

A. *The Merger Rules and Statistics*

61. Merger control plays an important role in safeguarding competition in Iceland. Each year, the ICA allocates between 20% and 50% of its time to merger investigations, depending on the inflow and significance of merger notifications.

62. A merger shall be notified if the combined turnover of the companies concerned is ISK 3,000,000,000 (USD 24,600,000) or more in Iceland, and at least two of the companies involved in the merger have at least ISK 300,000,000 (USD 2,460,000) annual turnover in Iceland, respectively. These turnover thresholds may seem low in international comparison, but are, in reality, fairly high relative to Iceland's GDP.

63. Furthermore, since 2008, the ICA has been equipped with call-in powers if it considers that a merger below the aforementioned thresholds, but involving parties with a combined turnover above ISK 1,500,000,000 (USD 12,300,000), may significantly impede competition. The call-in option has no time limit; however, in a potential below-threshold merger case, the merging parties may take the initiative by making a transaction known to the Authority, thereby starting a 15-working-day time limit for call-in. In below-threshold merger cases called in by the Authority, the intervention ratio is high, demonstrating the usefulness of call-in powers in the jurisdiction.

64. A merger shall not be implemented during the ICA's investigation. The ICA shall, within 25 working days (Phase I), notify the merging parties if it considers that there are grounds for further investigation. A decision shall be taken no later than 90 working days (Phase II) after the earlier notification. In special circumstances stipulated in the Competition Act, these timeframes can be extended.

65. Due to the oligopolistic nature of most markets in Iceland, a significant percentage of notified mergers are subject to Phase II investigations. Until recent years, around 25–30% of mergers were subject to Phase II investigations. Following internal process improvements and enhanced procedural efficiency, this share declined to around 20% in recent year.

66. In its investigations into the effects of a merger, the ICA applies criteria based on EEA/EU law.

67. Since 2005, the ICA has reviewed close to 500 mergers. Of those, close to 20 have been annulled, or between 3% and 4% of the total number of investigations. In addition, between 1% and 3% of merger notifications are withdrawn by the merging parties after receiving the ICA's statement of objections or other initial assessment of the merger's effects. This has become more frequent in recent years.

68. Around 10% of mergers in the period since 2005 have been cleared with remedies following a settlement between the ICA and the merging parties. Of those remedies, close to 10% are structural only, around 75% are behavioral only and around 15% are mixed.

69. In the aftermath of the financial crisis and the banking collapse in Iceland in 2008, a large number of companies across various markets faced serious financial difficulties and were acquired by the new banks established on the ruins of the collapsed banks. More than 50 mergers with banks as acquirers were cleared with remedies, the objective

of which was to accelerate the divestment of shares and safeguard competition. If these remedies are included, the percentage of mergers cleared with remedies is around 20%, compared to 10% when these transactions are excluded.

B. *Noteworthy Merger Investigations*

1. Annulment of a Merger in the Market for Fertilizers

70. In a 2024 decision (No. 13/2024), the ICA annulled a merger in the market for fertilizers and other farming supplies. The case concerned the acquisition by Skeljungur – one of the larger competitors – of Búvís, a smaller competitor in the market. The investigation revealed that Búvís was an important competitor in the market for the import and sale of fertilizers and that the merger would have had a significant harmful effect on that market.[18]

71. The investigation showed that Búvís was established in response to significant increases in fertilizer prices and a lack of competition. Farmer testimonials obtained in the case also revealed that Búvís had changed the competitive landscape for the better, kept prices down, and improved service and terms of business for farmers.

72. The investigation also revealed that Búvís and Skeljungur were close competitors in the sale of fertilizers and that Búvís was an important competitor The investigation also revealed that Búvís and Skeljungur were close competitors in the sale of fertilizers and that Búvís was an important competitor exerting competitive pressure beyond what its market share alone would indicate. With the acquisition of Skeljungur, the important and powerful competitive constraint emanating from Búvís would have disappeared, and the number of viable competitors would have been reduced from four to three.

73. This merger case is important for Icelandic competition law as an SIEC (significant impediment to effective competition) "gap case" intervention, in which the merger did not create a dominant position but instead eliminated a competitor and removed important competitive constraints in an oligopolistic market.

2. Acquisition of a Local Pharmacy by a Larger Competitor Annulled

74. In a 2018 decision (No. 28/2018), the ICA annulled the acquisition of a small, localized pharmacy, Opna (Apótek MOS), by one of the two largest pharmacy chains, Lyf og heilsa (L&H). L&H operated 30 pharmacies across the country. Opna, on the other hand, operated one pharmacy in Mosfellsbær, a town close to Reykjavík, and the only local competitor was L&H.[19]

75. The ICA's investigation showed that Apótek MOS's entry had a very positive effect on competition in the area. Apótek MOS offered new services in the form of store layout and pharmacist assistance. Opening hours were also longer than had previously

---

[18] ICA, Decision No. 13/2024 (June 3, 2024) (in Icelandic), https://www.samkeppni.is/wp-content/uploads/2025/07/Akvordun-13-2024.pdf.

[19] ICA, Decision No. 28/2018 (Oct. 18, 2018) (in Icelandic), https://www.samkeppni.is/wp-content/uploads/2025/07/Kaup-Lyfja-og-heilsu-hf.-a-Opnu-ehf.-an-trunadar.pdf.

been customary in Mosfellsbær. The case data showed that consumers welcomed this new option and that competition from Apótek MOS had a significant impact on L&H's operations in Mosfellsbær.

76. The investigation also revealed that the pharmacy sector in Mosfellsbær is very local. A study of consumer purchasing behavior, along with other case data, showed that consumers generally prefer to do business with pharmacies closest to health centers/clinics or their homes.

77. L&H appealed the ICA's decision to the Competition Appeals Committee, maintaining that the investigation was flawed and that the ICA had made an incorrect assessment of the market definition and the merger's competitive impact. In ruling No. 7/2018, the ICA's decision was upheld.[20]

78. This merger case is an important example in Icelandic case law on the assessment of harmful local effects in retail markets.

3. Merger between a Large Grocery Chain and a Pharmacy Chain Annulled

79. In a 2017 decision (No. 28/2017), the ICA annulled the acquisition of one of the largest pharmacy retailers, Lyfja, by the largest grocery retailer, Hagar. The ICA concluded that by acquiring Lyfja, Hagar would have strengthened its dominant position in the grocery market and that harmful concentration would have occurred in the markets in which Hagar and Lyfja both operate, not least in the hygiene and cosmetics market. The merger would have led to the disappearance of the competition that existed between Hagar and Lyfja in that market.[21]

80. The ICA's investigation revealed that the companies were close competitors in the retail sale of hygiene and cosmetic products, the market for vitamins, supplements and minerals, and the market for food and beverages in the health-product category. The merged company would have had a significant competitive advantage over other competitors due to its economic strength and strong position in imports and distribution in certain areas, which would have been difficult to compete with.

VIII. Advocacy and Policy Initiatives

81. One of the roles of the ICA is to ensure that actions by public bodies do not restrict competition, to recommend to authorities ways to make competition more effective and to facilitate access to the market for new competitors. To this end, the Authority can issue a formal opinion addressed to ministers, drawing attention to laws and regulations that conflict with the objectives of the Competition Act.

82. Furthermore, and in addition to other roles of the ICA, it is responsible for monitoring the development of competition and business practices in individual markets and for

---

20 Competition Appeals Committee, Case No. 7/2018 (Mar. 8, 2019) (In Icelandic), https://www.samkeppni.is/wp-content/uploads/2025/07/Mal-7-2018-Urskurdur-8-mars-2019.pdf.

21 ICA, Decision No. 28/2017 (July 17, 2017) (In Icelandic), https://www.samkeppni.is/wp-content/uploads/2025/07/Akvordun_28_2017_Samruni-Haga-og-Lyfju.pdf.

examining management and ownership ties between companies. Such ties can have particularly detrimental effects on competition in small economies.

83. Since 2005, the ICA has issued close to 80 formal opinions and recommendations to ministries and other public authorities on ways to remove barriers to competition and make competition more effective. In addition, the ICA reviews between 40 and 80 drafts of legislation, regulations and other public policies each year at the request of the Parliament, ministries or public authorities.

84. Furthermore, the ICA has published around 50 reports on its website since 2005, covering market studies, the benefits of competition and other policy issues. The Authority also operates a website with extensive information intended to promote competition, provide transparency regarding the Authority's tasks and enhance awareness and know-how among market participants, politicians, the media and consumers alike. The ICA's presence on social media is intended to do the same.

85. The ICA also hosts meetings and conferences on competition-related issues.

86. The following are some examples of the ICA's advocacy and policy initiatives.

A. *Workshops and a Conference on Competition and the Public Sector*

87. In February 2026, the ICA, together with the OECD and the Icelandic government, organized two workshops and a conference on competition and the public sector.[22]

88. A workshop on competition assessment of rules and regulations was held on February 17, where representatives of almost all ministries and a number of other public authorities, together with the ICA and experts from the OECD, discussed the benefits of competition assessment, as explained in the OECD guidelines and recommendations.

89. A workshop on public procurement and the fight against bid rigging was held on February 18, during which representatives from ministries and procurement offices, together with the ICA and experts from the OECD, discussed tender design and the newly published OECD *Guidelines for Fighting Bid Rigging in Public Procurement* (2025). The OECD also issued the guidelines in Icelandic in relation to these events.

90. An open conference on competition and the public sector was held on February 19, during which the Minister of Finance and Economic Affairs, together with representatives from market participants, public authorities, the OECD, and the ICA, discussed the outcomes of the aforementioned workshops and policy issues going forward.

B. *Formal Opinion on Competition Barriers in the Transport Market*

91. In connection with an extensive investigation into the transport market, which followed from the above-mentioned *Eimskip/Samskip* cartel case, the ICA published an opinion (No. 1/2023), addressed to the Minister of Infrastructure, the operator of ports in the

---

22 ICA, Competition and the Public Sector – How Can We Boost Economic Activity While Getting More for Less? (Feb. 17–19, 2026) (in Icelandic), https://www.samkeppni.is/utgafa/frettir/samkeppni-og-hid-opinbera-hvernig-getum-vid-eflt-atvinnustarfsemi-og-fengid-um-leid-meira-fyrir-minna/.

Reykjavík area (Faxaflóahafnir), the City of Reykjavík, and other municipalities around the country.[23]

92. In the opinion, the ICA addressed the urgent need for the relevant public bodies to ensure that new and smaller competitors in maritime transport have access to adequate port facilities and ship handling. Furthermore, it recommended that the government create conditions for increased competition in land transport. Lastly, the ICA encouraged market participants to consider ways to increase restraint on new or specific charging in transport markets.

C. *Report on Ownership and Management Ties in the Economy*

93. In a 2021 report (No. 2/2021), the ICA addressed ownership and management ties in the economy. The report contains an extensive overview of decisions and policy publications in which ownership and management ties have been addressed. Furthermore, the report reflects on a few central issues, including concerns relating to ownership and management ties reflected in significant pension fund ownership in more than one competitor in several important markets (common ownership). The report also touches upon ownership and management ties in the fishing industry and investments related to the fishing industry in other markets.[24]

D. *Report on Competition in Fuel Markets*

94. In 2020, the ICA published a report (No. 2/2020) on competition barriers in fuel markets.[25] The report was a follow-up to an earlier report (No. 2/2015), in which the ICA published its preliminary assessment following a market investigation. The preliminary findings had, in the meantime, been addressed in merger investigations concerning two simultaneous fuel company mergers involving two of the largest grocery chains. The mergers were cleared with extensive remedies through settlements with the merging parties.

95. In the 2020 report, the ICA reviewed the competition barriers that were discussed in its preliminary assessment report and outlined changes that had occurred as a result of or in connection with that investigation.

IX. Regional and International Cooperation

96. With reference to the EEA Agreement, the ICA enforces the competition rules thereunder when applicable, together with the Icelandic competition rules. This entails

---

[23] ICA, Opinion No. 1/2023, Competition Barriers in the Transport Market: Ways to Strengthen Competition in the Transport Market (Sept. 1, 2023) (In Icelandic), https://www.samkeppni.is/wp-content/uploads/2025/07/Alit-1_2023-Samkeppnishindranir-i-flutningum.pdf.

[24] ICA, Ownership and Management Ties in the Economy: An Icelandic Competition Authority Project 2008–2021, No. 2/2021 (2021) (in Icelandic), https://www.samkeppni.is/wp-content/uploads/2025/07/Skyrsla 2 2021.pdf.

[25] ICA, Changes in the Fuel Market: Addressing Competition Barriers Identified in the Icelandic Competition Authority's Market Study, No. 2/2020 (2020) (in Icelandic), https://www.samkeppni.is/wp-content/uploads/2025/07/Markadsrannsokn-a-eldsneytismarkadi-skyrsla-18-12-20.pdf.

extensive cooperation with other competition authorities within the EEA, national competition authorities, as well as the EFTA Surveillance Authority and the European Commission. In this respect, the ICA participates in the European Competition Network (ECN).

97. The competition authorities of Iceland, Norway, Denmark, Sweden, Finland, the Faroe Islands, and Greenland have long-standing cooperation at the managerial and specialist levels. At regular meetings, the authorities discuss competition issues in general, changes in laws and regulations, and individual cases, decisions, and judgments of general relevance. Working groups are active in specific areas, and the Nordic Competition Authorities regularly publish joint reports on competition policy, the most recent being reports on competition and labor markets (2024)[26] and online pharmacy markets in the Nordics (2021).[27]

98. As part of this cooperation, the ICA has been a member of the Nordic Agreement on Cooperation in Competition Cases since 2017. The Agreement ensures efficient exchange of information between the authorities, as well as cooperation and assistance with respect to inspections.[28]

99. Furthermore, the ICA is a member and participates in the work of the Competition Committee of the OECD and is a member of the International Competition Network (ICN).

X. Challenges and Country-Specific Features

100. Competition law and competition enforcement have played a significant role in the development of the Icelandic economy in recent decades. Many sectors, such as telecommunications, air transport and tourism, have benefited from competition rules and competition enforcement. In concentrated markets, even an incremental improvement in market functioning can generate measurable welfare gains.

101. The ICA publishes annual reports on the calculated benefits of the ICA's interventions in the preceding decade. The assessment is based on OECD guidelines and is reviewed by an independent expert. According to the latest report (No. 1/2025), the estimated benefits from the ICA's interventions against collusion, abuse of a dominant position, and anti-competitive mergers during the years 2015–2024 amounted to 0.29–0.48% of Iceland's GDP over the period. This corresponds to an estimated 18–29 times the Authority's total budget during those years.[29]

102. The challenges moving forward remain structural features of the Icelandic economy. These include the small size of the economy, high concentration levels, high entry

---

26 Nordic Competition Authorities, Joint Nordic Report Competition and Labour Markets (2024), https://www.samkeppni.is/wp-content/uploads/2025/07/Competition-and-Labour-markets-Joint-Nordic-report-2024_0324.pdf.

27 Nordic Competition Authorities, Joint Nordic Report: Online pharmacy markets in the Nordics (Apr. 2021) https://www.samkeppni.is/wp-content/uploads/2025/07/Online-pharmacy-markets.pdf.

28 Agreement on Cooperation in Competition Cases, https://www.samkeppni.is/media/skjol/nordic-agreement-on-cooperation-in-competition-cases.pdf.

29 ICA, Calculated Benefits of the Icelandic Competition Authority's Interventions 2015–2024, No. 1/2025 (2025) (in Icelandic), https://www.samkeppni.is/wp-content/uploads/2025/07/Skyrsla-nr.-1-2025.pdf.

barriers, and the oligopolistic nature of many key markets. In its Economic Survey of Iceland, published in 2025, the OECD points:

> Prices are high in Iceland, reflecting the country's high income levels and possibly also resulting from market concentration… Over the past two decades, the costs of transport services and communication have risen and are markedly higher than in EU countries. These elevated costs translate into high business expenses in downstream industries… The issue of market concentration is well recognised by the authorities. Market concentration becomes an issue if it creates barriers to entry.[30]

103. The report goes on to state that "the key challenge for competition policy is to prevent barriers to entry or lack of foreign competition from allowing incumbents to abuse their market dominance, rather than to prevent market dominance *per se*."[31]

104. In a small economy like Iceland, issues related to the need for economies of scale are frequent in competition cases, particularly in merger cases. Public and political debates often highlight efficiency considerations and the perceived need for national champions. Under such circumstances, securing adequate funding for competition enforcement becomes a difficult challenge, particularly where enforcement actions face resistance from economically significant actors.

105. Each year, the board of the ICA sets the Authority's priorities for the forthcoming three-year period. According to its current priorities, the ICA will continue to use its powers to remove barriers to competition, open markets, and enforce competition rules in the sectors most important for consumers, the business environment, and the economy. In a small and concentrated market environment, sustained, credible enforcement remains a central pillar of economic policy.

XI. References and Resources

A. *Laws and Regulations*

- Competition Act (2005) (in Icelandic), https://www.althingi.is/lagas/nuna/2005044.html

B. *Case Law*

- Competition Appeals Committee, Case No. 7/2023 (Mar. 19, 2025) (in Icelandic), https://www.samkeppni.is/wp-content/uploads/2025/07/Urskurdur-7-2023-19_03_2025.pdf
- Competition Appeals Committee, Case No. 7/2018 (Mar. 8, 2019) (In Icelandic), https://www.samkeppni.is/wp-content/uploads/2025/07/Mal-7-2018-Urskurdur-8-mars-2019.pdf
- ICA, Decision No. 13/2024 (June 3, 2024) (in Icelandic), https://www.samkeppni.is/wp-content/uploads/2025/07/Akvordun-13-2024.pdf
- ICA, Decision No. 28/2018 (Oct. 18, 2018) (in Icelandic), https://www.samkeppni.is/wp-content/uploads/2025/07/Kaup-Lyfja-og-heilsu-hf.-a-Opnu-ehf.-an-trunadar.pdf

---

30 OECD, *supra* note 5, at 88.

31 *Id.*

– ICA, Decision No. 28/2017 (July 17, 2017) (In Icelandic), https://www.samkeppni.is/wp-content/uploads/2025/07/Akvordun_28_2017_Samruni-Haga-og-Lyfju.pdf
– ICA, Decision No. 19/2016 (July 7, 2016) (in Icelandic), https://www.samkeppni.is/wp-content/uploads/2025/07/Akvordun_19_2016_Brot-Mjokursamsolunar-ehf-a-samkeppnislogum.pdf
– Supreme Court of Iceland, Case No. 26/2020 (Mar. 4, 2021) (in Icelandic), https://www.samkeppni.is/media/frettir-2021/MS.pdf
– Supreme Court of Iceland, Case No. 42/2019 (Jan. 7, 2021) (in Icelandic), https://www.haestirettur.is/domar/domur/?id=a1962b39-f939-4bdf-a1f6-9bb2fe439880
– Supreme Court of Iceland, Case No. 360/2015 (Dec. 1, 2016) (in Icelandic), https://www.haestirettur.is/default.aspx?pageid=0f2f6428-7b6a-11eb-947c-005056bc0bd-b&id=3db316d5-9d3f-4477-93f1-02987bec8ecc

C. *Public Reports*

– ICA, Calculated Benefits of the Icelandic Competition Authority's Interventions 2015–2024, No. 1/2025 (2025) (in Icelandic), https://www.samkeppni.is/wp-content/uploads/2025/07/Skyrsla-nr.-1-2025.pdf
– ICA, Opinion No. 1/2023, Competition Barriers in the Transport Market: Ways to Strengthen Competition in the Transport Market (Sept. 1, 2023) (In Icelandic), https://www.samkeppni.is/wp-content/uploads/2025/07/Alit-1_2023-Samkeppnishindranir-i-flutningum.pdf
– ICA, Ownership and Management Ties in the Economy: An Icelandic Competition Authority Project 2008–2021, No. 2/2021 (2021) (in Icelandic), https://www.samkeppni.is/wp-content/uploads/2025/07/Skyrsla-2-2021.pdf
– ICA, Changes in the Fuel Market: Addressing Competition Barriers Identified in the Icelandic Competition Authority's Market Study, No. 2/2020 (2020) (in Icelandic), https://www.samkeppni.is/wp-content/uploads/2025/07/Markadsrannsokn-a-eldsneytismarkadi-skyrsla-18-12-20.pdf.
– Íslandsbanki Research, Economic Equinox: Macroeconomic Forecast 2025–2027 (Sept. 2025) https://cdn.islandsbanki.is/image/upload/v1/documents/MacroForecast-2025-09_EN.pdf
– Nordic Competition Authorities, Joint Nordic Report Competition and Labour Markets (2024), https://www.samkeppni.is/wp-content/uploads/2025/07/Competition-and-Labour-markets-Joint-Nordic-report-2024_0324.pdf.
– Nordic Competition Authorities, Joint Nordic Report: Online pharmacy markets in the Nordics (Apr. 2021) https://www.samkeppni.is/wp-content/uploads/2025/07/Online-pharmacy-markets.pdf.
– OECD, OECD Economic Surveys: Iceland 2025 (June 2025), https://doi.org/10.1787/890dbe05-en

106. To learn more about Icelandic Competition Authority:
   – Website: https://www.samkeppni.is/

Jamaica

David Miller
Executive Director Fair Trading Commission

I. Overview

A. *Geographical Location*

1. Jamaica is an island nation located in the Caribbean Sea and is part of the Greater Antilles in the western Atlantic Ocean. Situated south of Cuba and west of Haiti, Jamaica is geographically part of North America. The nation is known for its mountainous interior, coastal plains, and rich cultural heritage.[1]

B. *Surface Area*

2. Jamaica has a maximum length, from east to west, of about 235 kilometers (146 miles), while its maximum width is around 80 kilometers (50 miles). The total area of the nation is approximately 10,991 square kilometers (4,244 square miles). Recently designated an archipelagic state under the Maritime Areas Act, Jamaica's territory extends beyond its coastline to comprise some 66 islands, rocks, and cays.[2]

C. *Political Status*

3. Jamaica is a sovereign state with an independent system of governance, operating as a constitutional monarchy in which the king is head of state, represented locally by a governor-general. Under the Jamaican Constitution, the country exercises full political autonomy through its own executive, legislature, and judiciary.[3]

D. *Official Languages*

4. There are two main languages in Jamaica: English is the official language, but the majority of the population speaks an English-based Creole.[4]

II. Demographics and Economy

5. Honduras had a population of approximately 2,839,175 inhabitants in 2024[5], corresponding to a population density of about 262.2 inhabitants per square kilometer in 2023[6]. The nominal gross domestic product (GDP) of Honduras was estimated at approximately USD 22.01 billion in 2024[7]. The country maintains a trade deficit, amounting to approximately USD 5.42 billion in 2024[8]. Honduras's economy is

---

1 *Overview of Jamaica*, Jamaica Information Service, https://jis.gov.jm/information/parish-profiles/ (last visited Dec. 17, 2025).

2 *Id.*

3 *Overview of the Government of Jamaica*, Jamaica Information Service, https://jis.gov.jm/government/overview-government-jamaica/ (last visited Dec. 17, 2025).

4 Elaine Hartman Reckord, *UWI to Launch Discussion on Making Jamaican Language Official*, Jamaica Information Service (Sept. 10, 2019), https://jis.gov.jm/uwi-to-launch-discussion-on-making-jamaican-language-official/ (last visited Dec. 17, 2025).

5 *World Development Indicators: Jamaica*, World Bank, https://databank.worldbank.org/reports.aspx?source=2&country=JAM (last visited Dec. 17, 2025).

6 *Id.*

7 *Id.*

8 International Merchandise Trade, Statistical Institute of Jamaica, https://statinja.gov.jm/Trade-Econ%20Statistics/InternationalMerchandiseTrade/newtrade.aspx (last visited Dec. 17, 2025).

diversified across multiple sectors, including agriculture, mining and quarrying, manufacturing, construction, electricity, water supply and waste management, transport and storage, wholesale and retail trade (including repairs and installation of machinery and equipment), financial and insurance activities, as well as accommodation and food service activities.[9]

6. Level of market concentration:
   a. General insurance: The general insurance sector is served by 10 companies. Using revenue data from 2024 annual reports, the Fair Trading Commission found that the general insurance sector is unconcentrated. The two-firm concentration ratio was measured at 38%. Furthermore, the Herfindahl-Hirschman Index (HHI) was calculated at 1,361 percentage points.
   b. Deposit-taking institutions: The 2024 Annual Report published by the Bank of Jamaica (BOJ) showed that there were 11 deposit-taking institutions. Based on the report's data, the FTC found that the sector is moderately concentrated. The two-firm concentration ratio was measured at 57%.[10] Furthermore, the HHI was calculated at 2,017 percentage points.

III. Legal Framework for Competition

7. Jamaica's competition law regime is defined in the Fair Competition Act (FCA) of 1993, which established the Fair Trading Commission (FTC or the "Commission") as the primary agency responsible for promoting and maintaining competition in commercial activities. The FCA aims to preserve the benefits of a market economy – innovation, efficiency, consumer choice, and fair pricing – by preventing anti-competitive conduct.

A. *Evolution of the Legal Framework*

8. The FCA has evolved considerably since its enactment, reflecting the evolving needs of Jamaica's competitive marketplace.
9. The FCA has been subject to significant legislative developments:
   - In 2000, the Fair Competition (Notices and Procedures) Regulations were introduced to outline procedural rules governing investigations, hearings, and enforcement.
   - On August 20, 2001, an amendment to the FCA was passed, modernizing the framework to strengthen enforcement powers and improve alignment with international best practices.
10. These revisions reflect Jamaica's commitment to maintaining a competitive market environment responsive to global economic and regulatory changes.

---

9 Media Brief, Planning Institute of Jamaica, The Planning Institute of Jamaica's Review of Economic Performance, July–September 2025 (Nov. 25, 2025), https://www.pioj.gov.jm/wp-content/uploads/2025/11/DGs-QPB-30_2-Speaking-Notes_website_25.11.25.pdf (last visited Dec. 17, 2025).

10 Bank of Jamaica, Annual Report 2024 (2025), https://boj.org.jm/wp-content/uploads/2025/04/2024-BOJ-Annual-Report-final.pdf (last visited Jan. 2, 2026).

B. *Scope and Objectives*

11. The FCA serves three primary objectives:

- To encourage competition in trade and business throughout Jamaica;
- To ensure equal opportunity for all legitimate enterprises to participate in the economy; and
- To provide consumers with access to better products and services, a wider range of choices, and fair prices.

12. The FCA addresses two broad areas:

- Anti-competitive conduct: Prohibiting agreements that substantially lessen competition and abuse of dominance. This includes price fixing, bid rigging, collusion, resale price maintenance, and tied selling.
- Consumer protection: Preventing deceptive advertising and misleading representations that distort consumer decision-making.

C. *Sectoral Application*

13. The FCA covers most areas of the Jamaican economy, including both private and public businesses in goods and services. However, it does not apply to the coffee industry, collective bargaining for employment terms, or professional standards set by professional groups.

14. Some industries, like telecommunications, energy, financial services, and transportation, have their own regulators. In these cases, the FTC works with these agencies to create a consistent approach. The Office of Utilities Regulation (OUR), the Ministry of Science, Energy, Telecommunications and Transport (MSETT), the BOJ, the Broadcasting Commission of Jamaica (BCJ), and the Spectrum Management Authority (SMA) are examples of regulatory bodies. Through collaboration and the sharing of information and expertise, competition rules are incorporated into sector regulators' decisions without duplicating effort.

D. *Exemptions and Limitations*

15. While the FCA maintains a broad scope, certain exemptions and limitations exist:

- Government-mandated activities: Conduct expressly authorized or required by other legislation is exempt from the FCA. This includes specific functions carried out by state-owned enterprises or statutory bodies.
- Professional regulation: Activities of professions governed by statutory bodies may be subject to separate regulatory oversight, limiting the FTC's intervention unless competitive harm is demonstrable.
- Small and informal businesses: The FTC generally exercises discretion in enforcement against small-scale or informal enterprises where the competitive effect is negligible.
- Absence of merger control: Jamaica's competition law does not currently include formal merger control provisions, which limits its ability to review and prevent anti-competitive mergers. Ongoing policy discussions aim to address

this gap. Until a formal system is included in the FCA, the FTC assesses mergers under the provisions that address agreements that substantially lessen competition.

E. *Conclusion*

16. Jamaica's FCA represents a cornerstone of the country's market governance framework. Its universal application, supported by sectoral collaboration and evolving amendments, underscores Jamaica's commitment to a fair, transparent, and competitive marketplace. Continued modernization of the FCA, particularly through the introduction of merger control provisions and enhanced institutional coordination, will further strengthen Jamaica's competition regime and its contribution to sustainable economic development.

IV. Institutional Structure

A. *Competition Authority*

17. The FTC is Jamaica's national competition authority, established in 1993 under the FCA, and amended in 2001. The FTC is responsible for promoting and maintaining competition in trade and business and for preventing anti-competitive conduct that restricts the operation of markets in Jamaica. Since its inception, the FTC has functioned as Jamaica's competition law enforcement agency and the primary agency for competition policy and consumer protection matters, as defined in the FCA.

B. *Supervising Body*

18. The FTC is a statutory body within the portfolio of the Ministry of Industry, Investment and Commerce (MIIC). While it enjoys operational independence in conducting investigations and enforcement, the MIIC provides policy direction and budgetary support and facilitates coordination with other government entities. This structure ensures that the FTC remains autonomous in its decision-making while aligning with national economic and industrial policy objectives.

C. *Organizational Structure*

19. The FTC is governed by a commission composed of not fewer than three and not more than six commissioners, including an executive director, who shall be a member *ex officio* of the Commission. The commissioners are appointed by the MIIC and are responsible for policy direction, decision-making, and general oversight of the agency's operations.

20. The executive director oversees day-to-day administration, investigative and research operations, and project management. The executive director is supported by specialized divisions:

- The Competition Bureau, headed by the Competition Bureau chief, is responsible for investigations into restrictive agreements, abuse of dominance, merger assessments, and other anti-competitive practices.

- The Legal Services Division, headed by the senior legal counsel, provides legal advice, drafts enforcement decisions, and represents the Commission before the courts. It also investigates misleading advertising, unfair trading practices, and consumer complaints.
- The Administration and Finance Division consists of a general manager, an accountant, and other secretarial and support staff. Together, they handle human resources, budgeting, logistics, competition advocacy, and public awareness initiatives.
- The FTC maintains a professional staff of approximately 17 employees, including economists, attorneys, research officers, and administrative personnel.

D. *Enforcement Powers*

21. The FTC is vested with broad investigative and enforcement powers under the FCA. These include the authority to:
    - Conduct investigations into suspected breaches of the FCA, either on its own initiative or in response to complaints;
    - Compel the production of documents and other information relevant to an investigation;
    - Interview witnesses and interested parties pursuant to investigations;
    - Issue directions to cease and desist from anti-competitive conduct; and
    - Refer matters to the Supreme Court of Jamaica for enforcement, where necessary.
22. Although the FTC does not currently have direct fining authority, the Supreme Court may impose injunctions, orders for restitution, and other remedies when FCA violations are proven. The 2001 amendments to the FCA also strengthened the Commission's enforcement toolkit by improving investigatory procedures and clarifying the legal effect of its decisions.

E. *Additional Regulatory Mandates*

23. In addition to enforcing the FCA, the FTC has a dual mandate that extends to consumer protection. Under the FCA, the FTC investigates and takes action against false or misleading advertising and other unfair trade practices that harm consumers.
24. While the FTC does not directly regulate sectors such as telecommunications, energy, or financial services, it collaborates with sector regulators, notably the OUR, the MSETT, the BOJ, the BCJ, and the SMA, to promote the integration of competition principles within their regulatory frameworks. These collaborative efforts are often formalized through memoranda of understanding (MoUs) and interagency consultations.

F. *Budget and Resources*

25. The FTC's operations are financed through budgetary allocations from the government of Jamaica (GOJ), via the MIIC. The resource base, while modest, is strategically utilized to ensure efficient enforcement, continuous staff training, robust competition advocacy, and sustained public education campaigns. Ongoing efforts aim to enhance the FTC's

institutional capacity through improved data analytics, digital case management systems, and interagency cooperation.

V. Enforcement and Sanctions

26. Under the FCA, when the FTC determines that prohibited conduct has occurred and the offending enterprise fails to comply with directions, the FTC must apply to the Supreme Court of Jamaica for enforcement.

27. For each breach, the Court may impose a fine not exceeding JMD 1,000,000 or approximately USD 6,250 for individuals, and JMD 5,000,000 or approximately USD 31,250 for corporations or other entities.

28. The Court may also grant injunctions to restrain continuing anti-competitive conduct.

29. Regarding criminal or penal liability, the FCA provides for offenses related to obstruction of investigation. Those offenses may be prosecuted in court, and persons convicted can face a fine or imprisonment for up to five years (or both), depending on the seriousness of the offense.

30. However, for standard competition-law breaches (e.g., cartels, abuse of dominance, anti-competitive agreements), enforcement remains civil only. There is no criminal cartel offense under the FCA, nor are fines scaled as a percentage of turnover. There is no leniency or immunity program under the current regime. Thus, the Jamaican sanctions framework combines civil fines with the possibility of penal sanctions for obstruction or misleading representation during investigations, but lacks aggressive turnover-based fines or criminal cartel sanctions common in other jurisdictions.

A. *Enforcement Track Record*

31. The FTC retains the authority to initiate investigations on its own motion or in response to complaints concerning alleged violations of the FCA. From 2019 to 2025, the FTC investigated 209 matters across 32 relevant markets, focusing on "rule of reason" cases (i.e., non-cartel, non-per se hardcore cases), indicating modest but sustained enforcement activity during that period.

32. In 2024, the FTC filed a court claim seeking pecuniary penalties and injunctive relief against the largest gaming company and its subsidiary for alleged abuse of dominance in the lottery market. This demonstrates the FTC's willingness to use its competition mandate against dominant firms when warranted.

33. However, there exists a structural constraint; the FCA does not include a formal pre-merger notification regime or other merger control tools, which limits the FTC's ability to prevent anti-competitive consolidation before it occurs. The FTC assesses mergers under provisions that address agreements that substantially lessen competition. Additionally, the FCA does not provide for dawn raids or leniency programs.

34. Overall, enforcement has been more active in "conduct" cases (dominance, unfair practices) than in cartel or merger control matters. The enforcement record suggests a cautious but consistent use of the law, constrained by legal limitations such as caps on penalties and the absence of (i) turnover-based fines, (ii) a criminal cartel regime, (iii) a leniency program, and (iv) an explicit merger control system.

B. *Private Enforcement*

35. The FCA explicitly provides a private right of action: Any individual or enterprise harmed by an anti-competitive practice or other prohibited conduct may bring a claim before the courts for damages. The court may award damages to compensate for losses arising from anti-competitive conduct. However, when the FTC successfully obtains a court-imposed fine for a finding of violation, the fine is paid to the government (the Crown), not to the victim or consumer. For consumers or businesses to receive compensation, they must rely on their private action.

36. While the private right of action exists in theory, in practice, there are few publicly known successful damages claims under the FCA. The majority of enforcement is pursued via the public-regulator route, that is, the FTC, rather than through private litigation. Thus, private enforcement remains a legal option but appears underutilized in practice, likely due to litigation costs, evidentiary burdens, limited awareness, and the modest scale of potential recoveries under the penalty regime.

C. *Strengths, Gaps, and Reform Needs*

1. Strengths

37. The FCA provides a civil enforcement regime with the possibility of court-imposed fines and injunctions.

38. A private right of action exists, giving victims a direct route to redress and compensation.

39. The FCA includes penal sanctions for obstruction or misleading the authority, essential to support credible investigations.

40. The legal framework empowers the FTC to investigate and refer cases to court, demonstrating separation between investigatory and adjudicatory functions.

2. Gaps

41. The maximum fines are fixed and not scaled to enterprise size or market impact, likely insufficient to deter large or well-resourced firms.

42. There is no criminal cartel regime or turnover-based penalty model, which weakens deterrence against hardcore anti-competitive conduct such as cartelization.

43. There is no pre-merger notification or merger control, limiting the ability to assess and block anti-competitive consolidation before it harms markets.

44. There is no leniency program, making detection of cartels more difficult and reducing incentives for whistle-blowers or covert cooperation.

45. Private enforcement appears rare, suggesting practical barriers that limit its role in supplementing public enforcement.

3. Reform Considerations

46. Introduce turnover-based administrative fines (or penalties calculated as a percentage of revenues) to ensure penalties are proportionate and deterrent.

47. Introduce a leniency/immunization program to improve cartel detection and encourage reporting.

48. Establish a statutory merger notification and review regime to enable pre-emptive scrutiny of potentially anti-competitive mergers.

49. Strengthen procedural tools for private enforcement (discovery, class/collective actions) to make the private right of action more accessible and effective for victims.

VI. Noteworthy Cases

A. *Jamaica Stock Exchange v. Fair Trading Commission (Supreme Court Civil Appeal No. 92/97)*

50. *Facts.* The case of the *Jamaica Stock Exchange v. Fair Trading Commission* came before the Court of Appeal of Jamaica following the Supreme Court's refusal of the declaratory and injunctive relief sought by the Jamaica Stock Exchange (JSE). The JSE had brought a claim before the Supreme Court seeking certain declarations, inter alia, that it is expressly governed by the Securities Act and therefore does not fall within the purview of the FCA or the FTC, and further that the action taken by the FTC was ultra vires, in breach of the rules of natural justice, void, and contrary to the principles of separation of powers, on the basis that the FTC cannot properly perform the functions of investigator, interrogator, complainant and adjudicator.

51. The JSE therefore appealed to the Court of Appeal (CA) to determine whether the provisions of the FCA were applicable to the JSE, an entity operating within the securities market and subject to regulation under the Securities Act, and whether the FTC's exercise of its investigative and adjudicatory functions infringed constitutional principles, including the separation of powers and the rules of natural justice. The Court was therefore called upon to assess both the scope of the FCA in relation to securities-based activities and the lawfulness of the FTC's exercise of its statutory powers.

52. The relevant sections of the FCA are as follows:

- Section 2: Defines key terms used in the Act:
  a. "Goods" expressly excludes securities, money, and choses in action.
  b. "Market" includes markets for goods or services.
- Section 17: Prohibits agreements between enterprises that have as their purpose or effect the substantial lessening of competition in a market. Such agreements may include arrangements that restrict output, fix prices, or otherwise distort competitive conditions.
- Section 18: Addresses agreements that contain exclusionary provisions, namely provisions that restrict the supply of goods or services to particular persons or classes of persons. The provision is intended to prevent arrangements that unfairly exclude competitors or potential entrants from a market.
- Section 19: Defines a dominant position as a position of economic strength enjoyed by an enterprise that enables it to operate independently of competitive pressures or to appreciably influence a market.
- Section 20: Addresses the abuse of a dominant position by an enterprise, including conduct that has the effect of substantially lessening competition, subject to any applicable statutory defenses.

- Section 21: Empowers the FTC, upon a finding of abuse of dominance, to make determinations and issue directions where the conduct in question results in a substantial lessening of competition.
- Section 33: Authorizes the FTC to prohibit practices that contravene the FCA and to issue such directions as it considers necessary to remedy, mitigate, or prevent the continuation or recurrence of anti-competitive conduct.

53. *Legal issue(s) (on appeal)*:
    1. Applicability issue: Does the FCA apply to the JSE, given that the JSE operates exclusively within the securities market regulated by the Securities Act?
    2. Competition law issue: Can the JSE's membership rules and requirements amount to abuse of a dominant position or anti-competitive agreements under sections 17, 18, and 20 of the FCA?
    3. Constitutional issue: Would the doctrine of separation of powers be breached if the FTC were permitted to hear its complaint against the JSE?
    4. Is there likely a breach of the rules of natural justice if the hearing by the FTC is pursued, thereby invoking the FTC's investigatory and directive powers under the FCA?

54. The issues raised at 3 and 4 above are encompassed by the question whether the FTC has, or should have, the power to adjudicate matters that it has itself investigated and in which it has laid the complaint.

55. The relevant sections of the FCA are as follows:
    - The FCA regulates competition in *markets for goods and services*, but expressly excludes *securities* from the definition of "goods."
    - An abuse of dominance under section 20 requires conduct that substantially lessens competition in a defined market governed by the Act.
    - Where Parliament has enacted *specialized legislation* (the Securities Act) providing a comprehensive regulatory framework, general legislation (the FCA) will not apply unless clearly intended.
    - Administrative bodies may exercise investigative and directive powers without breaching the separation of powers, provided those powers are not judicial in nature.

56. *Outcome.* The Court of Appeal held that:
    - The *FCA does not apply to the JSE*, as securities are specifically covered by the provisions of the Securities Act, and the FCA expressly excludes them from its scope. Additionally, matters concerning JSE membership rules and compensation fund requirements fall within the *Securities Commission's exclusive regulatory authority* under the Securities Act.
    - The FCA does not contain provisions for delegating the investigative functions of the Commission to the staff, save for section 10. Although the Court of Appeal found a merger of the Commission's investigative and adjudicatory functions, it did not find a breach of the doctrine of separation of powers. However, the Court found that, by virtue of the FTC performing the functions of both complainant and adjudicator, it breached the rules of natural justice. Therefore, the action

and proceedings that had been taken and pursued by the FTC against the JSE were declared by the Court of Appeal to be void. The Court further granted an injunction to restrain the FTC from continuing the proceedings against the JSE.

57. *Impact or precedent.* Securities are expressly excluded from the scope of the FCA and additionally fall squarely within the purview of the JSE. Therefore, any matter concerning securities, whether or not it involves competition law, must be handled by the JSE and falls outside the jurisdiction of the FTC.

58. Since the FCA does not have a provision that delegates the investigative functions of the Commission to its staff, save for one provision, the staff must refer any matters to be adjudicated to the Court for determination of a breach under the FCA.

B. *Supreme Ventures Limited & Prime Sports (Jamaica) Limited v. Fair Trading Commission [2023] JMCC Comm. 24*

59. *Facts.* This case concerns an appeal brought by Supreme Ventures Limited (SVL) and Prime Sports (Jamaica) Limited (PSL) against the FTC's findings pursuant to section 49 of the FCA. The FTC's report concluded that SVL, as a dominant enterprise in the Jamaican lottery market, had engaged in conduct likely to contravene sections 19–21 of the FCA by abusing its dominant position in a manner that substantially lessened competition.

60. The appellants brought a claim in the Commercial Division of the Supreme Court that challenged the FTC's findings on both procedural and substantive grounds. Procedurally, the appellants' counsel submitted that the Commission failed to give the appellants proper or sufficient grounds to be heard before arriving at its findings, in breach of the Commission's statutory duties and/or the appellants' legitimate expectation that they would have been afforded such an opportunity to be heard before the report was finalized. It was contended that this failure undermined principles of procedural fairness applicable to the FTC's investigative process.

61. Substantively, the appellants argued that the Commission's conclusions, particularly in relation to the termination of contractual arrangements and the pursuit of higher/unprofitable lottery payout odds, were not supported by the material before the Commission and were inconsistent with the requirements of the FCA.

62. The Supreme Court, exercising its appellate jurisdiction, examined the scope of the FTC's investigative powers, the content and timing of procedural fairness obligations under the FCA, and whether the Commission's findings could properly stand having regard to the manner in which the investigation was conducted.

63. The Court's analysis was grounded primarily in the following provisions of the FCA:

- Section 4: Establishes the FTC as the statutory body charged with the administration and enforcement of the Act.
- Section 5: Prescribes the functions of the FTC, including the duty to investigate conduct that may contravene the FCA and to make findings in relation to anti-competitive behavior.
- Section 7: Confers investigative powers on the FTC, including the authority to require the production of information, summon persons, and conduct inquiries in furtherance of its statutory mandate.

- Section 19: Defines a dominant position as a position of economic strength enjoyed by an enterprise that enables it to operate independently of competitive pressures or to appreciably influence a market.
- Section 20: Addresses the abuse of a dominant position by an enterprise, including conduct that has the effect of substantially lessening competition, subject to any applicable statutory defenses.
- Section 21: Empowers the FTC, upon a finding of abuse of dominance, to make determinations and issue directions where the conduct in question results in a substantial lessening of competition.
- Section 49: Provides a statutory right of appeal to the Supreme Court against findings or decisions of the FTC.

64. *Legal issue(s).* The Court identified and addressed the following central issues:

65. Whether the Supreme Court had jurisdiction and power under section 49 of the FCA to interfere with or set aside the FTC's findings.

66. Whether the FTC failed to provide the appellants with a proper or sufficient opportunity to be heard, thereby breaching:

    a. statutory duties under the FCA, and/or

    b. principles of procedural fairness and legitimate expectation.

67. Whether the FTC's findings that SVL abused its dominant position, particularly through termination of retail contracts and pursuit of allegedly unprofitable 50:1 payout odds, were supported by the evidence and consistent with sections 19–21 of the FCA.

68. What relief, if any, was appropriate.

69. The Court applied the following legal principles:

    - Procedural fairness: There is a presumption that statutory powers will be exercised fairly. Fairness generally requires that a person who may be adversely affected by a decision be informed of the substance of the case against them and given an opportunity to respond.
    - Section 7(2) FCA: The Commission may hear affected persons orally during investigations, but shall do so where a written request for a hearing is made.
    - Legitimate expectation: A legitimate expectation may arise from an express promise or an established and consistent practice by a public authority, provided it is clear, unambiguous, and lawful.
    - Abuse of dominance (sections 20–21 FCA): Conduct by a dominant enterprise that restricts market entry or expansion and substantially lessens competition may constitute an abuse unless it results from superior competitive performance.
    - Appellate jurisdiction (section 49 FCA): The Court may confirm, modify, or direct reconsideration of the FTC's findings and is not confined to the narrow standards applicable in judicial review proceedings.

70. Opportunity to be heard – Contract terminations

    a. The Court found that, in relation to the investigation into termination of retail contracts and distribution arrangements, the FTC acted within its statutory remit.

The appellants were notified of the investigation, provided written responses to detailed queries, and participated in a meeting with the FTC. They did not request a formal hearing pursuant to section 7(2) of the FCA.

b. Accordingly, the Court held that the FTC did not breach procedural fairness in this respect, as the Act permits investigations to proceed on a documentary basis unless a hearing is requested.

71. Opportunity to be heard – 50:1 odds strategy: The Court reached a different conclusion regarding the FTC's findings on SVL's pursuit of approval for 50:1 payout odds. This aspect of the investigation arose partly from information obtained from the Betting, Gaming and Lotteries Commission (BGLC), yet the FTC failed to inform the appellants that this issue formed a material part of the investigation.

72. However, as the appellants would have an opportunity to be heard before a final decision was made, they would have an opportunity to be heard.

73. Legitimate expectation: The Court rejected the argument that a legitimate expectation arose from the Commission's conduct in a prior investigation. A single prior instance of sharing a draft report did not constitute a settled or consistent practice capable of grounding a legitimate expectation under Jamaican or public law principles. Additionally, it was found that the Commission's actions did not constitute a breach of procedural fairness.

74. Substantive findings under sections 19–21 FCA: Although the FTC's investigation into the 50:1 odds was not communicated to the appellant, the two components were found to be abusive, as, individually or collectively, they deterred competitors and potential competitors from engaging in competitive conduct in Jamaica's lottery market. It was therefore not established by the appellants that the FTC's decision in this regard was flawed, and it was found that the Commission's findings were consistent with the available evidence and provisions of the FCA.

75. *Conclusion/Holding.* The Court held that the FTC did not breach procedural fairness and its decision was consistent with the available evidence. It also found no basis to set aside, reverse, or modify the Commission's findings. The judge therefore affirmed the FTC's findings as set out at paragraph 161 of their report, which stated that the challenged conduct is likely to breach sections 19–21 of the FCA.

76. *Impact or precedent.* The matter is scheduled for hearing by the Court of Appeal in 2026; therefore, the impact or precedential value cannot be determined at this time.

C. *FTC v. D&G/Red Stripe*

77. *Facts.* In 2001, the FTC commenced an investigation into certain commercial practices of Desnoes & Geddes Ltd. (D&G), trading as Red Stripe, following a request for an opinion from D&G and a complaint from a new entrant to the beer market in Jamaica. The investigation was conducted to determine whether certain contractual, promotional, and other practices employed by D&G contravened the FCA. The inquiry focused on arrangements between D&G and on-trade and off-trade outlets and event organizers, as well as related sponsorship and promotional practices, with particular regard to their impact on competition, market access, and consumer choice.

78. The investigation covered certain contractual arrangements to which D&G was a party, primarily in relation to:

- Exclusivity in the promotion of brewed products in six outlets that D&G provides, among other facilities, a marketing rebate to be used for the promotion of D&G products; and
- Exclusivity in the sale and promotion of brewed products in events sponsored by D&G.

79. It specifically examined the following:

- The use of contractual clauses restricting the promotion and visibility of competing brewed products at on-trade outlets.
- Requirements that outlets provide exclusive or predominant point-of-sale advertising, signage, and brand visibility to D&G products.
- The inclusion of clauses obligating outlets to disclose sales data relating to competing brewed products to D&G.
- Event sponsorship arrangements that restricted or prohibited the sale and promotion of competing brewed products at sponsored events.
- Recommendations or requirements that competing alcoholic beverages be sold at premium prices and not promoted at sponsored events.
- The inclusion of post-term preferential clauses, including rights of first refusal, granting D&G priority access to future sponsorship opportunities.
- Full-line forcing provisions requiring outlets to stock a specified range of D&G brewed products – this was not found to impede effective competition in the relevant market.

80. *Relevant section(s) of the FCA: Section 20 (abuse of dominance).* The investigation commenced by looking at section 33, which inter alia deals with exclusive dealing arrangements, and section 20, which covers abuse of dominance. The investigation was later narrowed to section 20 only, as it was considered sufficiently broad to encompass any anti-competitive practice by a dominant enterprise.

81. Section 20: The primary substantive provision was applied in the investigation, which prohibits the abuse of a dominant position by an enterprise where such conduct impedes the maintenance or development of effective competition in a market.

82. Section 20(1): Sets out the general prohibition against abusive conduct by a dominant enterprise, including practices that restrict market access, deter competitive conduct, or impose unfair or unrelated contractual obligations.

83. Section 20(2): Establishes a statutory defense whereby conduct will not be regarded as abusive if it is exclusively directed towards promoting technical or economic progress and allows consumers a fair share of the resulting benefits. This provision was applied in assessing whether certain sponsorship and exclusivity arrangements could be objectively justified.

84. *Legal issue.* The FTC first had to determine the relevant market, then assessed dominance, and then assessed the anti-competitive impact to determine whether the above conduct had the effect, or was likely to have the effect, of substantially lessening competition in the relevant market.

85. Outcome. The Commission found that D&G/Red Stripe was dominant in Jamaica's brewed product (specifically, beer) market, as, inter alia, D&G held a very high market share and faced significant barriers to entry. In assessing the contractual provisions, the Commission found that several provisions breached the FCA and impeded effective competition in the relevant market, and thus had, or were likely to have, the effect of substantially lessening competition in the relevant market.

86. D&G/Red Stripe should:

- Remove or amend contractual clauses that restrict or prohibit the promotion and visibility of competing brewed products at on-trade outlets, where such restrictions are not objectively justified.
- Discontinue requirements obligating outlets or event organizers to provide sales data relating to competing brewed products, as such requirements confer an undue competitive advantage.
- Cease the use of event-based prohibitions on the sale and promotion of competing brewed products in circumstances where sponsorship funding is directly linked to D&G's advertising or brand promotion.
- Refrain from recommending or imposing premium pricing on competing alcoholic beverages, as such practices distort competitive conditions and limit consumer choice.
- Eliminate post-term preferential clauses, including rights of first refusal, which restrict competition for future sponsorship opportunities after the expiry of an agreement.
- Review and amend sponsorship agreements to ensure that any exclusivity provisions are proportionate, transparent, and compliant with section 20 of the FCA.
- Ensure ongoing compliance with the FCA by adopting contractual and promotional practices that do not impede the maintenance or development of effective competition.
- Submit to continued monitoring by the FTC, particularly in relation to exclusivity arrangements and sponsorship practices in the brewed beer market.

87. *Impact or precedent.* In concluding the investigation, the FTC emphasized that enterprises holding a dominant position bear a special responsibility to ensure that their conduct does not impair the development of genuine and effective competition. The FTC recommended removing or amending anti-competitive promotional and sponsorship clauses, discontinuing requirements for competitors' sales data, eliminating post-term preferential rights, and continuing to monitor exclusivity arrangements in highly concentrated markets to safeguard competition and consumer welfare.

88. *Outcome.* D&G/Red Stripe agreed with the FTC's position and accepted the recommendations. It implemented appropriate measures in accordance with the recommendations.

VII. Merger Control

89. The FTC examines and assesses mergers, acquisitions, and joint ventures pursuant to section 17 of the FCA. Section 17 of the FCA prohibits agreements that have as their purpose the substantial lessening of competition or are likely to have the effect

of substantially lessening competition for goods and services in Jamaica. The FTC's jurisdiction to investigate mergers based on section 17 was confirmed in *FTC v. Digicel Jamaica Limited and Anor* [2017] UKPC 28.[11]

A. *Notification Thresholds*

90. The FTC does not have a notification threshold. Section 5 of the FCA empowers the FTC to investigate conduct in Jamaica either on its own initiative or at the request of any person, to determine if an enterprise has contravened the FCA. The FTC currently investigates mergers either on its own initiative or when the parties notify the FTC of their intention to merge.

B. *Review Time Frames*

91. The review of a merger involves two phases. The Phase I review timeframe is 30 business days. If the FTC determines that the merger raises competition concerns at the conclusion of Phase I, then the review proceeds to Phase II. The Phase II timeframe for review is 60 business days. A merger review should be completed in 90 business days.

C. *Examples of Notified or Blocked Mergers*

1. Acquisition of Oceanic Digital (Jamaica) Limited by Digicel Jamaica Limited

92. One of the FTC's most prominent investigations, and the first merger it recommended blocking, was the acquisition of Oceanic Digital (Jamaica) Limited by Digicel Jamaica Limited.[12]

93. *Case Summary.* In this case, on March 11, 2011, Digicel Jamaica Limited ("Digicel") announced that it had signed an agreement with América Móvil (the parent company of Claro Jamaica Limited ("Claro")) to acquire Claro's business in Jamaica. As part of the transaction, Digicel would sell its business in El Salvador and Honduras to América Móvil. Notably, in 2011, the voice services market in Jamaica had three significant suppliers: Digicel, Claro, and Cable & Wireless Jamaica Ltd. (operating as LIME). Digicel and Claro were the most significant suppliers, and LIME was a distant third.

94. *Analytic review.* The investigation was undertaken pursuant to section 17 of the FCA. The agreement was examined generally under section 17 of the FCA and specifically under subsection 17(2)(b), which speaks to the limit or control of markets in Jamaica, and/or subsection 17(2)(c), which speaks to the sharing of markets. The investigation determined that the agreement did not expressly limit or control markets. The agreement also did not provide for the sharing of markets within Jamaica. It was further determined that neither Claro nor Digicel was barred from entering or entering the market by virtue of a non-compete clause or other condition or term of the agreement. Accordingly, it was

---

11 *See* FTC's Guideline to Reviewing Mergers, Acquisitions and Joint Ventures (2022), https://jftc.gov.jm/wp-content/uploads/2022/02/2022.02.22-FTC-Guideline-Review-of-Mergers-Acquistions-JVs-FINAL.pdf.

12 Case No. 6997-11 (Dec. 8, 2011).

concluded that the agreement did not have as its purpose the substantial lessening of competition. As a result, the FTC examined whether the agreement had, or was likely to have, the effect of substantially lessening competition.

95. Upon assessment, it was determined that Digicel offered voice and data services, while Claro offered voice, data, and video services. The parties overlapped in voice and data services. It was therefore resolved that the relevant product market was short messaging services (SMS) and voice services in Jamaica.

96. The investigation analyzed the market structure by examining the market share and concentration based on subscribers, voice traffic, and cell site ownership. This assessment used the HHI and found a highly concentrated market, with the concentration index increasing by more than 200 points. The transaction, therefore, raised significant concerns and was further explored.

97. The investigation indicated that the likelihood and sufficiency of effective entry were impacted by weak regulatory insight. This led Digicel to adopt a pricing strategy that reduced revenue opportunities for new entrants, as they would earn less from call origination and termination. Specifically, Digicel's pricing strategy made it relatively expensive for its subscribers to call other networks and for other networks to call Digicel's network. Consequently, it was concluded that entry was unlikely to be effective in mitigating the adverse competitive effects that were likely to arise from the transaction.

98. The investigation revealed that competition between Digicel and Claro led to frequent promotions and value-added offers. Promotions offered prizes such as call credit, cash, and mobile handsets, while value offers provided consumers with the opportunity to access bonus call credit, discounted calling rates, and mobile phones. The data indicate that Digicel's introduction of value offers coincided with Claro's entry in August 2007 and steadily intensified thereafter. It was concluded that Claro's participation in the market from 2007 to 2010 resulted in an average annual increase in consumer surplus of $4 billion and, on average, benefits of $37 million from promotion and value offerings. It was further concluded that incumbent suppliers and prospective entrants are likely to be harmed, as the transaction is expected to increase unilateral market power by eliminating a significant competitive constraint for Digicel.

99. It is important to note that the transaction allowed the market participant with the largest market share, with respect to cell site ownership, to acquire the participant with the second-largest market share. Claro represented a competitive constraint in the relevant market, and it was argued that Claro's absence would likely lead to the exercise of market power through unilateral anti-competitive effects.

100. The overall conclusion of the investigation was that Digicel's acquisition of Claro was likely to substantially lessen competition in the voice and text messaging service market in Jamaica. The transaction would allow Digicel's subscribers to access 3G mobile services sooner than they otherwise would. However, it was concluded that the efficiencies gained from the transaction were unlikely to offset its anti-competitive effects.

101. The Commission concluded that the challenged transaction be blocked, and proposed several remedies. Among them were:

- Making co-location agreements mandatory and regulating the rates, terms, and conditions of the agreements

- Regulating the interconnection rates for every network.
- Releasing Claro's subscribers from any contractual obligations so that they can choose their preferred provider.

2. Amalgamation of the businesses of The Gleaner Company Ltd., Radio Jamaica Ltd. and The Gleaner Company (Media) Ltd.

102. While the FTC does not have a mandatory legislative requirement that merging parties notify it of a merger, it has, on its own initiative under section 5 of the FCA, commenced investigations into mergers that have come to its attention. Merger investigations have spanned various industries, such as telecommunications, media, ice, insurance brokerage services, beverages, and the distribution of pharmaceutical and consumer products. One such merger investigation is the FTC's investigation into the amalgamation of the businesses of The Gleaner Company Ltd., Radio Jamaica Ltd. and The Gleaner Company (Media) Ltd.[13]

103. *Case summary.* On August 5, 2015, Radio Jamaica Ltd. ("RJR"), The Gleaner Company Ltd. ("Gleaner"), and the Gleaner Media Company Ltd. (the "Media Company") entered into an agreement which concerned a scheme of arrangement between RJR and Gleaner, and ultimately an amalgamation of the companies. Notably, RJR held controlling interests in media entities that operated radio, subscription television, and multimedia production. Gleaner had controlling interest in media (newspaper and radio) and non-media entities, both locally and overseas. The Media Company was a special-purpose vehicle incorporated for the transaction, namely the amalgamation of Gleaner and RJR.

104. Based on a proposed amalgamation agreement, the Media Company would become a wholly owned subsidiary of Gleaner. Gleaner would separate its media business as a going concern and keep the non-media elements. Once the scheme was effected, Gleaner would change the business's corporate name to become a company that holds and makes investments in other businesses or companies.

105. Additionally, Gleaner would transfer its media business to the Media Company, whereby, in consideration of the transfer, the Media Company would issue new ordinary shares to Gleaner. Gleaner would then sell its entire shareholding in the Media Company to RJR. In consideration of the sale, RJR would issue new ordinary shares in RJR to Gleaner shareholders.

106. *Analytic review.* The proposed agreement was reviewed pursuant to section 17 of the FCA. Notably, an agreement may be void under the FCA if:
    - The agreement has the purpose of substantially lessening competition in a market and/or
    - The agreement is likely to have the effect of substantially lessening competition in a market.

107. In assessing the agreement, the question was whether there was any efficiency justification under section 17(4) of the FCA. The finding of an efficiency justification permits an agreement that has as its purpose and/or effect of substantially lessening competition

---

[13] Case No. 7887-15 (Nov. 23, 2015).

in any market not to be treated as void if it generates sufficient economic or technical efficiencies to overcome the anti-competitive effects.

108. Upon review of the agreement, which contained a non-competition clause, the FTC found that the agreement did not have as its purpose the substantial lessening of competition in any market. Consequently, the agreement was assessed to determine whether it was likely to have the effect of substantially lessening competition in any market.

109. In analyzing the agreement's effect, the FTC examined the parties' industry and noted that RJR and Gleaner operated multisided platforms. The parties collectively held a significant share of the media audience across the major media platforms. RJR delivered content over the internet, television, and radio platforms, and Gleaner delivered content over the internet, radio, and newspaper platforms. Notably, RJR was not present on the newspaper platform, and Gleaner was not present on the television platform.

110. The investigation revealed that the amalgamation of Gleaner's and RJR's media assets would result in the creation of the only advertising service provider with a significant presence in television, newspapers, radio, and the internet. Accordingly, it was determined that the transaction was likely to have the effect of substantially lessening competition in the advertising market, including the radio and IP-based media platforms within the advertising media platform market.

111. The investigation assessed both horizontal and vertical effects arising from the transaction. Regarding horizontal effects, the amalgamation would significantly increase market concentration in the radio platform submarket and likely increase market power. Further, regarding the IP-based media platform within the advertising media platform market, it was reasoned that, as the transaction would eliminate Gleaner as a competitor in the future, it would likely reduce RJR's incentive to either acquire improved IT infrastructure or at least delay the acquisition of such infrastructure. It was concluded that the transaction was likely to have significant horizontal effects in the relevant markets.

112. With respect to vertical effects, the investigation focused on whether the amalgamated entity would increase incentives and/or opportunities to engage in anti-competitive foreclosure activities to the detriment of independent advertising agencies, specifically services provided via the internet, newspapers, radio, and television. Based on the facts of the transaction, the FTC opined that discrimination was more likely to be a rational strategy than outright foreclosure. Accordingly, it was posited that discriminatory conduct was likely to have the effect of substantially lessening competition by (i) harming independent advertising agencies in the market for advertising services; (ii) harming advertisers who are clients of independent advertising agencies, and (iii) harming some final consumers in the markets for goods and services produced by clients of independent advertising agencies.

113. Also, the investigation examined other potential public interest harms and concluded that the likely consequence of the transaction was reduced diversity of views on news items and a narrower variety of news items. Furthermore, there was the concern that, because of the transaction, fewer consumers would be likely to be informed about the products best suited to their tastes and needs. This would likely result in a reduction in consumer welfare in markets in the wider economy.

114. In the analysis of potential interest benefits, the investigation revealed that only the reduction in operating radio services as the only merger-specific public benefit. However,

it was determined that it was unlikely to offset the considerable harm posed by the anti-competitive effects in the advertising services and advertising media markets.

115. It was concluded that the transaction contravened section 17 of the FCA because it was likely to have the effect of substantially lessening competition in the markets for advertising services and in the radio and IP-based platform submarkets within the advertising media platform market. Additionally, the anti-competitive effects were unlikely to be offset by the potential benefits of the proposed transaction.

116. Several remedial measures were proposed to mitigate the likely anti-competitive effects of the transaction. Among them were the following:
   - The amalgamated entity commits to not engaging in discriminatory or anti-competitive practices in its advertising package;
   - The amalgamated entity commits to operating the newsrooms of the newspaper platform independently of the newsrooms for its television and radio platforms; and
   - The amalgamated entity commits to confining its creation of advertising content for television to "low budget production."

117. Gleaner/RJR agreed with the FTC's position and accepted the proposals. It implemented the remedial measures.

VIII. Advocacy and Policy Initiatives

118. Between 2020 and November 2025, the FTC consolidated its role as Jamaica's competition authority through a set of interlocking advocacy, analytical, and institutional-development initiatives. Operating in a period marked by pandemic-related disruptions, digital transformation, and heightened regulatory complexity, the FTC increasingly positioned its work within an evidence-based and preventative regulatory framework. Its approach combined stakeholder engagement, formal policy guidance, sectoral market analysis, and sustained capacity-building efforts, aimed at improving market outcomes while enhancing regulatory certainty and coherence. This section outlines the principal advocacy and policy-oriented activities undertaken during the period and situates them within the FTC's broader mandate to promote competition, consumer welfare, and sound economic regulation.

A. *Outreach to Businesses and Consumers*

119. Outreach to businesses and consumers remained a core component of the FTC's mandate and was pursued through sustained, structured, and targeted engagements. The FTC maintained regular interaction with micro, small, and medium-sized enterprises (MSMEs), professionals, and consumers through national and parish-level roadshows, trade expos, and sensitization sessions. Many of these activities were undertaken in collaboration with public- and private-sector partners, including the MIIC, the Inter-American Development Bank (IDB), the Jamaica Intellectual Property Office (JIPO), and the Jamaica Manufacturers & Exporters Association (JMEA), with outreach activities conducted across multiple parishes.

120. These engagements served a dual function: improving compliance with the FCA and strengthening market participants' understanding of competition principles, including merger notification thresholds, lawful pricing practices, and the identification of anti-competitive conduct. In parallel, the FTC pursued sector- and firm-specific outreach, including presentations to

Heineken Jamaica's senior management on competition law obligations, workshops for merchants focused on compliant pricing, and professional briefings, including continuing legal education sessions organized with the Jamaican Bar Association.

121. Public education efforts were reinforced through a sustained media strategy, comprising regular appearances on radio programs and the publication of analytical articles in mainstream and digital media. These contributions addressed competition issues across key sectors, including telecommunications and markets affected by COVID-19-related disruptions. The FTC also issued public advisories on topical consumer issues, addressing specific risks and rights – for example, the marketing of "unlimited" telecommunications plans and consumer guidance during periods of disruption to public transportation services. In several instances, these interventions were associated with observable adjustments in service providers' conduct.

122. Information dissemination was further supported through the FTC's social media pages (Instagram, Facebook, X, and LinkedIn), its quarterly electronic newsletter *FTC Newsline*, and its annual magazine *Compete*, which are circulated to both local and international stakeholders. Collectively, these tools were used to communicate enforcement outcomes, policy developments, and analytical insights on competition and consumer protection.

123. The FTC's public engagement program was complemented by thought-leadership initiatives such as the annual Shirley Playfair Lecture, which convened regional and international experts to examine contemporary issues, including post-pandemic competition dynamics, supply-chain disruptions, and the interaction between competition and consumer protection regimes.

B. *Recent Policy Papers or Guidelines*

124. In parallel with its outreach activities, the FTC advanced regulatory clarity through the development of policy papers and guidelines. A key milestone during the period was the publication of the *Guideline to Reviewing Mergers, Acquisitions and Joint Ventures* in 2022. Grounded in international best practices, including International Competition Network (ICN) recommendations, the guidelines articulated the FTC's analytical approach, procedural timelines, and information requirements under the FCA. This development materially enhanced predictability and transparency for businesses contemplating structural transactions.

125. The FTC also issued sector-specific and consumer-oriented guidance in response to observed market concerns. These included *Consumer Guidelines for Selecting a Nursing Home*, *Consumer Guidelines for Online Shopping*, proposed Guidelines on Valuator Empanelment, and proposed Guidelines on Panel Management intended to address restrictive practices in complementary service markets.

126. Beyond formal guidance instruments, the FTC fulfilled an active advocacy role within the broader policy framework by submitting technical position papers and conducting legislative reviews for other regulatory and policymaking bodies. These interventions included a position paper on spectrum screening for the SMA, recommendations to amend the Financial Services Commission Act to improve interagency information-sharing, and a review of the Land Surveyors Act aimed at reducing regulatory barriers to market entry. Similar contributions were made in relation to electricity licensing,

electronic transactions, and other regulatory regimes, reflecting the FTC's increasing integration within Jamaica's economic governance architecture.

C. *Sectoral Studies or Market Inquiries*

127. Sectoral studies and market inquiries constituted the empirical foundation of the FTC's advocacy and enforcement activities. Market studies were systematically used to diagnose structural impediments to competition, including high market concentration, entry barriers, information asymmetries, and regulatory distortions.

128. During the review period, the FTC undertook several major studies in financial services and the digital economy. It also contributed to and led the review of a major consultancy assessing the competitiveness of Jamaica's commercial banking sector. The BOJ was the other key contributor and reviewer of the assessment. The study identified, among other issues, persistent barriers to access faced by SMEs and retail consumers. Related work included a study on digital payment services, which examined competitive conditions and advanced policy recommendations on interoperability and market entry for fintech providers, as well as an assessment of the credit reporting market that informed proposals on data reciprocity and consumer safeguards.

129. In network industries, the FTC conducted multiple assessments of competition in telecommunications, including analyses of mobile market structure, spectrum caps, and allocation policies. These findings directly informed the SMA's proposed spectrum-holding policy. The Commission also examined several energy-related markets, including the regulatory framework governing the Jamaica Public Service, the liquefied petroleum gas market, imported motor-vehicle gasoline, and electrical inspection services.

130. Additionally, the FTC assessed emerging and sensitive sectors, including the cannabis industry, audit services, and nursing homes. These studies identified risks associated with premature regulatory restriction, persistent concentration, limited consumer choice, and information deficiencies. In the case of nursing homes, the analysis directly informed consumer guidance and engagement with the Ministry of Health and Wellness (MOHW). Several enforcement-initiated matters also evolved into broader market studies, including work on public transportation and ride-hailing, reinforcing steel bars in the construction sector, and the rum industry.

D. *Education and Capacity Building*

131. The FTC's advocacy and analytical work was supported by sustained investment in human and institutional capacity. FTC staff participated extensively in international and regional training programs hosted by institutions such as the Organisation for Economic Co-operation and Development (OECD), the ICN, the US Federal Trade Commission, the Caribbean Community (CARICOM) Competition Commission, CARIFORUM, INDECOPI, and the World Trade Organization. These programs covered advanced topics, including merger analysis, abuse of dominance, digital market regulation, and investigative techniques.

132. Internally, this external training was complemented by structured knowledge-sharing initiatives, including "lunch-and-learn" seminars at which staff presented on specialized analytical and enforcement topics. Institutional capacity was further strengthened through

the development of the Case Administration and Document System (CADS), a proprietary electronic case-management system funded under the World Bank's Foundations for Competitiveness and Growth Project. CADS modernized document management, case tracking, and record-keeping.

133. The FTC also remained actively engaged in international cooperation, including collaboration with the CARICOM Competition Commission (CCC) on regional market studies, participation in the CCC's COVID-19 Steering Committee, contributions to ICN working groups, and participation in study tours and conferences involving peer competition authorities.

134. Overall, the FTC's activities between 2020 and November 2025 reflect the institutional maturation of Jamaica's competition regime. Through integrated outreach, policy guidance, empirical market analysis, and sustained capacity building, the FTC strengthened compliance, improved regulatory predictability, and enhanced the analytical foundations of competition policy. While challenges remain – notably in monitoring the implementation of recommendations and expanding access to high-quality market data – the FTC's approach over the period positions it as a credible, analytically grounded authority within Jamaica and a constructive contributor to regional competition policy discussions.

IX. Regional and International Cooperation

A. *Regional Organizations*

135. In 1973, to advance regional integration among Caribbean countries, Jamaica signed the Treaty of Chaguaramas to become a member of CARICOM.

> CARICOM rests on four main pillars: economic integration; foreign policy coordination; human and social development; and security. These pillars underpin the stated objectives of our Community –

- to improve standards of living and work,
- the full employment of labor and other factors of production;
- accelerated, coordinated, and sustained economic development and convergence;
- expansion of trade and economic relations with Third States;
- enhanced levels of international competitiveness;
- organization for increased production and productivity;
- achievement of a greater measure of economic leverage;
- effectiveness of Member States in dealing with Third States, groups of States and entities of any description; and
- the enhanced coordination of Member States' foreign and foreign economic policies and enhanced functional cooperation.[14]

136. The Revised Treaty of Chaguaramas (RTC), which came into force in 2001, reflects the community structures that are necessary to improve the structure and management of CARICOM Member States towards an effective single market and economy that will respond to the challenges and opportunities in a globalized environment.

---

14 *Who We Are*, CARICOM, https://caricom.org/our-community/who-we-are/.

137. As a result of the CARICOM Single Market and Economy (CSME), it was expected that greater competition in and for the market would encourage businesses to engage in conduct geared towards preserving market share.

138. Chapter 8 of the RTC sets out the ground rules for business conduct in this new environment, with the aim of ensuring healthy competition and promoting consumer welfare. The goal of Community Competition Policy, as stated in article 169 of the RTC, is generally to ensure that the benefits expected from the establishment of the CSME are not frustrated by anti-competitive business conduct.

139. The CCC was established under article 171 of the RTC and is one of the key institutions supporting the CSME.[15] Jamaica, as a CARICOM Member State, was required to recognize and fulfill, in concrete terms, the obligations it assumed under article 176. Accordingly, the FTC has an established direct collaborative relationship with the CARICOM's CSME Unit, the CCC, and the other competition authorities within CARICOM, namely the Barbados Fair Trading Commission, the Trinidad and Tobago Fair Trading Commission, and the Competition and Consumer Affairs Commission of Guyana.

140. As the oldest and most experienced competition and consumer protection law enforcement authority within CARICOM, the FTC is instrumental and active in sensitizing Member States and assisting in establishing new authorities.

B. *Participation in Global Networks*

141. Over the years, the FTC has built relationships with many other competition agencies as well as with international organizations, such as the ICN, the United Nations Conference on Trade and Development (UNCTAD), and the OECD. The FTC maintains a strong working relationship with these organizations by participating in discussions, workshops, and seminars, and has benefited immensely in all areas of competition enforcement and advocacy.

142. The FTC routinely participates in several ICN working groups, which facilitate contact through which younger competition authorities can consult with more experienced authorities on investigative and advocacy techniques, case analyses, and related matters. This, together with the use of the ICN toolkit, supports cross-fertilization, strengthening the FTC's knowledge base and institutional memory.

X. Challenges and Country-Specific Features

A. *Small Market Size and High Concentration*

143. As a small island developing state (SIDS), Jamaica faces unique vulnerabilities and "diseconomies of scale," which add to production and distribution costs, undermine competitiveness, and limit diversification against external shocks. The small domestic market means that Jamaican firms often struggle to achieve the scale needed to be competitive in the global arena.[16]

---

15 History, CARICOM Competition Commission, https://caricomcompetitioncommission.com/en/about-us/history.

16 UNCTAD, Building Resilience in Small Island Developing States: A Compendium of Research Prepared by the UNCTAD Division for Africa, Least Developed Countries and Special Programmes (UNCTAD/ALDC/INF/2022/2, 2022), https://unctad.org/system/files/official-document/aldcinf2022d2_en.pdf.

144. The FTC (2017) noted that a small state might, by necessity, be more tolerant of higher levels of market concentration if significant domestic industries are to be competitive regionally and globally.[17] The current law proscribes abuse of dominance but does not include structural remedies such as mandatory merger controls, a policy choice linked to the specific context of a small economy.

B. *Dependence on Imports/Foreign Investment*

145. The GOJ considers foreign direct investment (FDI) a key driver for economic growth, and in recent years, it has reformed its economy to improve the investment climate.[18]

146. Similarly, Jamaica is heavily dependent on imports (especially food, fuel, and raw materials).[19]

C. *Lack of Resources or Expertise*

147. Jamaica faces significant challenges regarding the lack of resources and expertise across key sectors, including education, healthcare, and the broader workforce. These issues are often exacerbated by the migration of skilled professionals seeking better opportunities in overseas countries, leading to a persistent skills gap.[20]

D. *Balancing Competition and Development Goals*

148. Jamaica balances the need for competition to drive efficiency and attract investment with comprehensive national development goals outlined in its Vision 2030 Jamaica plan. This involves a delicate balancing act, as the country also grapples with significant challenges like high debt and vulnerability to external shocks.[21,22]

E. *Interplay with Traditional or Customary Economies*

149. The FTC[23] (2018) notes that Jamaica's economy features a significant informal sector (around 40% of GDP), coexisting with formal sectors like tourism, finance, mining, and agriculture, creating a complex interplay where traditional customs (like community resource use in fishing) meet modern market demands, driving both innovation

---

17 FTC, Bridling Market Dominance – A View from Jamaica (Dec. 22, 2017), https://jftc.gov.jm/wp-content/uploads/2017/10/Bridling-Market-Dominance-A-View-From-Jamaica-Mrs.-Barbara-Lee.pdf.

18 Investment Climate Statement (ICS), Int'l Trade Admin. (Feb. 29, 2024), https://www.trade.gov/country-commercial-guides/jamaica-investment-climate-statement-ics (last visited Dec. 22, 2025).

19 Ministry of Foreign Aff. & Foreign Trade, National Foreign Trade Policy: Positioning Jamaica to Increase Foreign Trade (Oct. 2017), https://mfaft.gov.jm/site/wp-content/uploads/2019/03/National-Foreign-Trade-Policy_2017-APPROVED-webversion_14Jan20193333.pdf (last visited Dec. 22, 2025).

20 *Closing the Skills Gap to Create More Jobs in the Caribbean*, Jamaica Observer (June 25, 2025), https://www.jamaicaobserver.com/2025/06/25/closing-skills-gap-create-jobs-caribbean/ (last visited Dec. 22, 2025).

21 Andrew Holness, Speaking Notes at the International Conference on Sustainable Development, Moving Forward: The SDGs in Practice, Columbia University (Sept. 21, 2026), https://opm.gov.jm/2-16-international-conference-on-sustainable-development/ (last visited Dec. 22, 2025).

22 Shavanne Smith, *Competition and Competition Policy Aiding the Economy*, FTC (Nov. 21, 2024), https://jftc.gov.jm/competition-and-competition-policy-aiding-the-economy/ (last visited Dec. 22, 2025).

23 David Miller, *Informal Economy in Latin America & the Caribbean: Implications for Competition Policy*, FTC (Sept. 12, 2018). Informal https://jftc.gov.jm/wp-content/uploads/2018/09/2018.09.12-FTC-submission-to-LACCF-on-Jamaicas-Informal-Economy.pdf (last visited Dec. 22, 2025).

(diaspora links) and challenges (crime, tax evasion), with government efforts focused on formalizing activity, improving infrastructure, and leveraging natural/cultural capital for sustainable growth.[24]

XI. References and Resources

A. *Laws and Regulations*

- Fair Competition Act of 1993

B. *Case Law*

- Supreme Ventures Limited & Prime Sports (Jamaica) Limited v. Fair Trading Commission [2023] JMCC Comm. 24
- Amalgamation of the businesses of The Gleaner Company Ltd., Radio Jamaica Ltd. and The Gleaner Company (Media) Ltd., Case No. 7887-15 (Nov. 23, 2015)
- Acquisition of Oceanic Digital (Jamaica) Limited by Digicel Jamaica Limited, Case No. 6997-11 (Dec. 8, 2011)
- FTC v. D&G/Red Stripe
- Jamaica Stock Exchange v. Fair Trading Commission (Supreme Court Civil Appeal No. 92/97)

C. *Public Reports*

- Bank of Jamaica, Annual Report 2024 (2025), https://boj.org.jm/wp-content/uploads/2025/04/2024-BOJ-Annual-Report-final.pdf (last visited Jan. 2, 2026)
- CARICOM Competition Commission, *History*, https://caricomcompetitioncommission.com/en/about-us/history
- CARICOM, *Who We Are*, https://caricom.org/our-community/who-we-are/.
- FTC, FTC's Guideline to Reviewing Mergers, Acquisitions and Joint Ventures (2022), https://jftc.gov.jm/wp-content/uploads/2022/02/2022.02.22-FTC-Guideline-Review-of-Mergers-Acquistions-JVs-FINAL.pdf.
- Int'l Trade Admin., Investment Climate Statement (ICS) (Feb. 29, 2024), https://www.trade.gov/country-commercial-guides/jamaica-investment-climate-statement-ics (last visited Dec. 22, 2025)
- Jamaica Information Service, *Overview of Jamaica*, https://jis.gov.jm/information/parish-profiles/ (last visited Dec. 17, 2025)
- Jamaica Information Service, *Overview of the Government of Jamaica*, https://jis.gov.jm/government/overview-government-jamaica/ (last visited Dec. 17, 2025)
- Ministry of Foreign Aff. & Foreign Trade, National Foreign Trade Policy: Positioning Jamaica to Increase Foreign Trade (Oct. 2017),

---

24 Ainsley Brown and Jahnoy Leith, *The Economic Structural Transformation of Jamaica using the LHI and SEZ Regime* (Jamaica Special Economic Zone Authority, 2022), https://www.pioj.gov.jm/wp-content/uploads/2023/03/The-Economic-Structural-Transformation-of-Jamaica-using-the-LHI-and-SEZ-Regime-Final.pdf (last visited Dec. 22, 2025).

https://mfaft.gov.jm/site/wp-content/uploads/2019/03/National-Foreign-Trade-Policy_2017-APPROVED-webversion_14Jan20193333.pdf (last visited Dec. 22, 2025)

- Statistical Institute of Jamaica, International Merchandise Trade, https://statinja.gov.jm/Trade-Econ%20Statistics/InternationalMerchandiseTrade/newtrade.aspx (last visited Dec. 17, 2025)
- UNCTAD, Building Resilience in Small Island Developing States: A Compendium of Research Prepared by the UNCTAD Division for Africa, Least Developed Countries and Special Programmes (UNCTAD/ALDC/INF/2022/2, 2022), https://unctad.org/system/files/official-document/aldcinf2022d2_en.pdf
- Wikimedia Commons, *Jamaica Regions map.png*, (2012, December 14), https://commons.wikimedia.org/wiki/File:Jamaica_Regions_map.png (last visited Dec. 17, 2025)
- World Bank, *World Development Indicators: Jamaica*, https://databank.worldbank.org/reports.aspx?source=2&country=JAM (last visited Dec. 17, 2025)

D. *Articles, Press Releases, Speeches*

- Brown, Ainsley, and Jahnoy Leith, *The Economic Structural Transformation of Jamaica using the LHI and SEZ Regime* (Jamaica Special Economic Zone Authority, 2022), https://www.pioj.gov.jm/wp-content/uploads/2023/03/The-Economic-Structural-Transformation-of-Jamaica-using-the-LHI-and-SEZ-Regime-Final.pdf (last visited Dec. 22, 2025)
- FTC, Bridling Market Dominance – A View from Jamaica (Dec. 22, 2017), https://jftc.gov.jm/wp-content/uploads/2017/10/Bridling-Market-Dominance-A-View-From-Jamaica-Mrs.-Barbara-Lee.pdf
- Hartman Reckord, Elaine, *UWI to Launch Discussion on Making Jamaican Language Official*, Jamaica Information Service (Sept. 10, 2019), https://jis.gov.jm/uwi-to-launch-discussion-on-making-jamaican-language-official/ (last visited Dec. 17, 2025)
- Holness, Andrew, Speaking Notes at the International Conference on Sustainable Development, Moving Forward: The SDGs in Practice, Columbia University (Sept. 21, 2026), https://opm.gov.jm/2-16-international-conference-on-sustainable-development/ (last visited Dec. 22, 2025)
- Jamaica Observer, *Closing the Skills Gap to Create More Jobs in the Caribbean* (June 25, 2025), https://www.jamaicaobserver.com/2025/06/25/closing-skills-gap-create-jobs-caribbean/ (last visited Dec. 22, 2025)
- Miller, David, *Informal Economy in Latin America & the Caribbean: Implications for Competition Policy*, FTC (Sept. 12, 2018). Informal https://jftc.gov.jm/wp-content/uploads/2018/09/2018.09.12-FTC-submission-to-LACCF-on-Jamaicas-Informal-Economy.pdf (last visited Dec. 22, 2025)
- Planning Institute of Jamaica, Media Brief, The Planning Institute of Jamaica's Review of Economic Performance, July–September 2025 (Nov. 25, 2025), https://www.pioj.gov.jm/wp-content/uploads/2025/11/DGs-QPB-30_2-Speaking-Notes_website_25.11.25.pdf (last visited Dec. 17, 2025)

- Smith, Shavanne, *Competition and Competition Policy Aiding the Economy*, FTC (Nov. 21, 2024), https://jftc.gov.jm/competition-and-competition-policy-aiding-the-economy/ (last visited Dec. 22, 2025)

150. To learn more about the Fair Trading Commission (FTC):
    - Website: https://jftc.gov.jm/
    - Contact: fairtrading@jftc.gov.jm

Jersey

Peter Hetherington
Chief Economist at the Jersey Competition Regulatory Authority

Sarah Price
Chief Operating Officer at the Jersey Competition Regulatory Authority

I. Overview

A. *Geographical Location and Surface Area*

1. Jersey (officially the Bailiwick of Jersey) is the largest of the Channel Islands and its surface area is 120 square kilometers (approximately 14.5 km by 8 km). It is located 22 kilometers from France and 137 kilometers from the southern coast of the United Kingdom (UK).

2. The capital and only town, St. Helier, is situated in Jersey's southeast. St. Helier includes two square kilometers of reclaimed land.

B. *Political Status*

3. Jersey is a self-governing dependency of the British Crown rather than part of the United Kingdom, a status that originates in the medieval Duchy of Normandy. When William, Duke of Normandy, became King of England in 1066, Jersey remained part of his Norman possessions, and when mainland Normandy was lost to the French Crown in 1204, the island chose to remain loyal to the English monarch. As a result, Jersey continued to be held by the monarch in their Norman capacity, which is why the British sovereign is recognized in Jersey as Duke of Normandy – regardless of gender – owing allegiance directly to the Crown.

4. As noted above, Jersey is not part of the United Kingdom, and decisions taken in the UK do not transfer to Jersey, and Jersey is not represented in the UK parliament. Instead, Jersey has its own democratically elected parliament, called the States Assembly. Jersey also has its own fiscal regime (tax), administrative and legal systems. Jersey's administrative units are called parishes, and there are 12 parishes in Jersey.

C. *Official Languages*

5. English is the primary, official language of Jersey, used for business and government. However, the island has its own traditional language, Jèrriais, a Norman-French dialect reflecting the island's historical links.

II. Demographics and Economy

A. *Population*

6. Jersey's population at the end of 2024 was estimated to be 104,540 people. In the past ten years, the population has increased by 4,480 people.

7. The age structure of Jersey's population has become older in recent years, with the largest five-year age group being 55–59 years old.

B. *Density*

8. Jersey had a population density of 859 inhabitants per square kilometer, with great variation by parish. St. Helier is the most densely populated, with 3,716 residents per square kilometer. Trinity has the lowest population density, with 267 residents per square kilometer.

C. *GDP (Nominal)*

9. Jersey's currency is the British pound sterling, although Jersey does print its own version of British pounds. Both can be used in Jersey, though Jersey pounds cannot be used in the United Kingdom.

10. In 2024, Jersey's GDP was GBP 6,905 million. This represents a slight decrease in real terms compared to 2023 (– 0.7%). GDP per capita was GBP 65,800 in 2024.

D. *Trade Balance*

11. Jersey represented the UK's 37th largest trading partner in the four quarters to the end of Q2 2025, accounting for approximately 0.4% of total UK trade. Total trade in goods and services (exports plus imports) between the UK and Jersey was GBP 7.8 billion in the four quarters to the end of Q2 2025.

E. *Main Economic Sectors*

12. Jersey is one of the most successful international finance centers in the world. The industry includes banking, trust and fiduciary services, wealth, asset and fund management. Jersey also represents an important jurisdiction for company administration, compliance, legal, accountancy and investment advisory services, with many highly skilled individuals and firms operating in this space. The financial sector employs approximately one in four of the island's workforce and represents a major contributor to Jersey's economy.

13. Tourism and hospitality also constitute an important economic feature of Jersey, with approximately 5,000–6,000 people employed.

14. Further, agriculture is a part of Jersey's history and heritage and accounts for over 50% of Jersey's land cover. The island's largest export is the Jersey Royal New Potato, with over 30,000 tonnes exported every year. Jersey is well known for its cows, the Jersey cow, and its seafood.

15. The government of Jersey is the largest employer on the island, employing teachers, civil servants, police, medical professionals and manual workers.

16. Finally, Jersey also has an emerging digital sector.

F. *Level of Market Concentration*

17. There are close links between Jersey and the United Kingdom, and many economic activities are functionally integrated. Others are more local in nature and are serviced by on-island resources. There are 8,500 businesses operating in Jersey's private sector, with the majority (59%) being sole traders. There are a small number of larger businesses, with just over 10% of businesses having more than ten staff.

18. The presence of small domestic markets, such as in Jersey, can limit the potential for competition and increase the scope for market dominance, as there may be limited opportunity to support multiple suppliers.

III. Legal Framework for Competition

19. Jersey has a long-established legal system, operating as a separate jurisdiction from the UK and the other Channel Islands, with its own competition framework aligned with best practice. The Jersey Competition Regulatory Authority (JCRA) oversees competition law in Jersey.

A. *Name and Date of First Competition Law*

20. Jersey's competition framework was first introduced through the Competition (Jersey) Law 2005 (hereinafter, the "Competition Law" or the "Law").

21. The Competition Law in Jersey is modeled on the competition provisions in the Treaty on the Functioning of the European Union (TFEU).

22. [1]Article 60 of the Law provides that, so far as possible, questions arising in relation to competition in Jersey must be dealt with in a manner that is consistent with the treatment of corresponding questions arising under EU law.

23. Relevant sources for the JCRA include judgments of the European Court of Justice or General Court, decisions and guidance published by the European Commission, and interpretations of EU law by courts and competition authorities in the EU Member States. Article 60, however, does not prevent the JCRA from departing from EU precedents where this is appropriate in light of the particular circumstances of Jersey.

B. *Subsequent Revisions or Updates*

24. In November 2025, changes to the Competition Law were approved to both enhance the operation of the island's mergers and acquisitions regime and to improve the JCRA's ability to conduct market studies. The JCRA also gained powers to accept legally binding 'commitments' from business regarding their future conduct to address any competition issues.

C. *Scope*

25. The Competition Law prohibits:

   - Anti-competitive agreements: Arrangements between businesses that may restrict competition (e.g., price fixing).
   - Abuse of dominance: When a business uses its market power to restrict or hinder competition, causing harm to competitors or consumers.
   - Harmful mergers: Mergers that reduce competition and limit consumer choice.

26. The JCRA can also conduct market studies, sectoral reviews and other types of in-depth market analysis.

Note: Jersey's Competition Law does not provide for state aid control, as subsidies and other forms of public financial support fall outside its scope and are instead governed through separate fiscal, budgetary and political oversight mechanisms.

---

1 Consolidated version of the Treaty on the Functioning of the European Union (TFEU), 2012 O.J. (C 326) 47, https://eur-lex.europa.eu/resource.html?uri=cellar:2bf140bf-a3f8-4ab2-b506-fd71826e6da6.0023.02/DOC_2&format=PDF.

D. *Applicable Sectors*

27. The Competition Law in Jersey applies universally across all markets, with a limited exception in relation to the government of Jersey. The government is subject to the Competition Law only when it is carrying out economic activity, and not when delivering services in the exercise of public functions, as provided for under the Competition Law.

E. *Exemptions and Limitations*

28. Exemptions to the Competition Law can be granted by the JCRA or the relevant minister. An example of an exemption is in force at the time of writing – this is allocated to Jersey Doctors on Call for the provision of after-hours medical care in Jersey.

29. If the arrangement is vertical, e.g., between a supplier and a buyer, and includes a vertical restraint, it may not require an exemption, as such arrangements can benefit from the Competition (Vertical Arrangements Block Exemption) (Jersey) Order 2023, which sets out the applicable conditions.

IV. Institutional Structure

A. *Competition Authority*

30. The JCRA is Jersey's competition and economic regulator. It was established by the States of Jersey in 2001.

B. *Supervising Body*

31. The JCRA is independent of the Minister for Sustainable Economic Development and the States of Jersey, and has a broad range of formal powers, as conferred under the JCRA's legal framework.

32. Formal meetings between the minister and the chair of the JCRA take place twice a year, and these meetings specifically discuss performance, internal controls and any other relevant information relating to the effective oversight of public funds.

C. *Organizational Structure*

33. The JCRA Board is comprised of three non-executive members, a chair and a chief executive. In addition to the chief executive, who also sits on JCRA's Board, there are eight other permanent staff members. The JCRA also makes use of external contractors and specialist legal advisors where needed.

D. *Additional Regulatory Mandates*

34. The JCRA's role is to promote competition in the supply of goods and services in Jersey, and to carry out economic regulation of port operations, postal services and the telecommunications sector.

E. *Budget and Resources*

35. In 2024, the Minister's Department provided GBP 747,000 in funding to the JCRA to finance the administration and enforcement of the Competition Law. The Minister's Department provided additional funding of GBP 150,000 in 2024 to support the JCRA's work around Jersey's Telecoms Security Framework.

Note: The JCRA also collects license fees from postal, telecoms and port licensees. It collects merger application fees. The JCRA can issue and collect fines following regulatory investigations, regulatory service incidents or breaches of license; however, these do not form part of the JCRA's income.

F. *Enforcement Powers*

36. The JCRA has legal powers to conduct market studies and regulatory investigations, to uphold commitments and undertakings in mergers and investigations, and to support Jersey's Telecoms Security Framework and its enforcement.

37. The JCRA can impose financial penalties of up to 10% of a business's turnover during the period of contravention, for a maximum of three years, for a breach of the Competition Law.

V. Enforcement and Sanctions

A. *Fines and Sanctions*

38. As noted above, financial penalties of up to 10% of a business's turnover during the period of contravention, for a maximum of three years, may be imposed by the JCRA for a breach of the Law. The JCRA can also fine companies for failing to provide information for market studies.

39. There is no criminal prosecution in Jersey for breaches of the Competition Law, but any parties harmed by anti-competitive arrangements have the possibility of bringing third-party claims to Jersey's Royal Court.

B. *Enforcement Track Record*

40. The JCRA conducts enforcement activities across all its areas of responsibility. In the competition sphere, investigations are carried out in accordance with the JCRA's investigation guidelines. At the time of writing, there was one active investigation in the transportation, logistics and storage sector. In previous years, the JCRA has also investigated a failure to notify a merger and conducted an inquiry into the telecoms market concerning market-sharing practices.

C. *Private Enforcement*

41. There is no private enforcement to date. The JCRA cannot award damages to any business or individual harmed as a result of anti-competitive arrangements.

VI. Noteworthy Cases

A. *Sure, Airtel merger (Case C-042)*

42. Sure and Airtel were competitors in Jersey's retail mobile services market. As direct rivals, the merger between them posed a risk of substantially lessening competition.

43. After assessment, the JCRA concluded that the merger was likely to reduce competition in the retail mobile market because:
    - Sure's market share would rise to around 47%; and
    - the number of mobile service providers would fall from three to two, removing Airtel, which had historically offered some of the lowest prices in the low- and mid-price segments.

44. After detailed consideration and the completion of a Phase II process, the merger was approved subject to conditions. First, a new mobile virtual network operator (MVNO) entrant was required: the Co-op, a Channel Islands cooperative, agreed to operate as an MVNO using Sure's network, enabling independent competition in the retail market. Second, Sure was required to make pricing commitments to protect consumers for 36 months post-merger. This included withdrawing any Sure and Airtel tariffs active at the time of clearance.

45. The transaction was complex, with the merger timetable paused multiple times to gather additional information, verify facts, and assess the commitments proposed by the merging parties.

B. *School Uniforms Market Study (Case M-006)*

46. A market study is used by the JCRA to explore whether a market, or feature of a market, is working well for Jersey consumers. This market study was requested by the EducationMinister and explored the school uniform market in Jersey. The study estimated that the value of the market was approximately GBP 1.6 million with 42 island primary and secondary schools. While school uniform requirements and policies vary between schools on the island, school uniforms are clearly a strong feature of Jersey schools.

47. The study found that there is scope to improve the school uniform market for the benefit of consumers. This conclusion was based on several factors:
    - Demand for school uniforms represents a sizeable potential market.
    - Supply of school uniforms remains relatively concentrated.
    - For a number of schools, the proportion of branded and compulsory items appears high.
    - Current market practices do not fully align with the JCRA's previous guidance.

48. The study made three key recommendations to enhance competition, improve market discipline and help ensure consumers get a fair deal:
    - The government should further consider policy developments and practices in other jurisdictions.
    - Schools should conduct regular reviews of all contracts and supply arrangements relating to school uniforms.

- The JCRA will work with the government to develop more specific guidance on the design and operation of competitive tenders for school uniforms.

49. The market study was well received, and with the government's support, new guidelines have been introduced limiting the number of branded and compulsory items. This demonstrates that even in small local markets, competition policy can have a positive impact.

VII. Merger Control

50. The JCRA operates a mandatory clearance regime for specific mergers and acquisitions. Approval is granted only if the JCRA is satisfied that the merger is unlikely to substantially lessen competition in the market.

Note: This merger framework is in the process of being updated and the jurisdictional thresholds are expected to change in 2026.

A. *Notification Thresholds*

51. Under the Competition (Mergers and Acquisitions) (Jersey) Order 2010, a merger cannot proceed without prior approval from the JCRA where it meets certain thresholds:

- Horizontal mergers: The merging parties are active in the same market, and the merger would result in, or increase, a share of supply or purchase of 25% or more.
- Vertical mergers: One party has a share of supply or purchase of 25% or more, and the other party operates upstream or downstream of that supply.
- Conglomerate mergers: One party has a share of supply or purchase of 40% or more, with no horizontal or vertical relationship.

52. The JCRA participates in pre-notification discussions and endeavors to assist parties submitting a merger application form.

53. As noted above, this merger framework is in the process of being updated and the jurisdictional thresholds will be changing in 2026/2027 to be turnover-based with the addition of a call-in power for the JCRA to consider transactions below the revenue threshold.

B. *Review Timeframes*

54. The JCRA's administrative target timeframe for a Phase I merger is 25 working days from publication of the Notice of Application on the JCRA website (including a 10-working-day public consultation period).

Note: If, during the assessment of the application, issues arise that may lead to the refusal of approval for the merger or approval with conditions, the JCRA will conduct a second detailed review. There is no statutory deadline for the conclusion of a second detailed review. However, the JCRA's practice, by way of an administrative target, is to endeavor to reach a final decision within six months from the date of first registration of the application (i.e., the commencement of Phase I).

C. *Examples of Notified or Blocked Mergers*

55. The JCRA has not blocked any mergers to date; however, some applications are withdrawn following discussion with the JCRA.

VIII. Advocacy and Policy Initiatives

A. *Outreach to Businesses and Consumers*

56. The JCRA uses a range of tools to communicate with businesses and consumers. This includes the use of media releases to publicize key decisions and LinkedIn. This sits alongside the publication of draft decisions for feedback and other forms of engagement.

57. With respect to businesses, the JCRA uses the full range of tools available to it, which includes formal statutory tools, such as market studies or investigations, alongside open, advisory and warning letters.[2] These aim to:
   - raise awareness of the competition law;
   - encourage compliance with the law; and/or
   - identify and stop anti-competitive behavior.

58. In 2024, the JCRA also participated in the Jersey Consumer Council Fair. This was aimed at helping Jersey's consumers and spreading good practice around businesses competing fairly.

B. *Recent Policy Papers or Guidelines*

59. The JCRA occasionally releases policy papers on areas it oversees – two recent examples cover sustainability in the regulated sector and reflections from a strategic review of postal services completed in 2024:
   - *Sustainability in the Regulated Sectors in Jersey*
   - *Strategic Review of Postal Services: Reflections on the Review*

60. The JCRA maintains a full set of guidelines, which are regularly reviewed and updated – these are available at https://www.jcra.je/competition-law/legislation-and-guidelines/.

C. *Sectoral Studies or Market Inquiries*

61. In general, the JCRA carries out studies of individual markets rather than sectors. An overview of market studies completed can be found at https://www.jcra.je/competition-law/market-studies/.

62. One exception to this is the JCRA's work in the construction sector, which commenced with a sector review: Construction Sector Review (Case C-070).

D. *Education and Capacity Building*

(See Overview of Outreach to Businesses and Consumers)

IX. Regional and International Cooperation

A. *Bilateral/MoUs with Other Competition Authorities*

63. The JCRA has one memorandum of understanding (MoU) in place with the Guernsey Competition and Regulatory Authority (GCRA).[3]

---

2 *See Open, Advisory and Warning Letters*, JCRA, https://www.jcra.je/competition-law/open-advisory-and-warning-letters/.

3 JCRA Memorandum of Understanding with the GCRA (2020), https://www.jcra.je/other-documents/strategic-plans/governance-framework/jcra-memorandum-of-understanding-with-the-gcra/.

64. On an informal basis, the JCRA engages with the Gibraltar Regulatory Authority, the Isle of Man Communications and Utilities Regulatory Authority, Ofcom and the UK's Competition and Markets Authority (CMA).

B. *Participation in Global Networks*

65. The JCRA is a member of the International Competition Network (ICN). For telecoms, it is also a member of the International Institute of Communications (ICC) and plays an active role in the Small Nations Regulatory Forum (SNRF).

X. Challenges and Country-Specific Features

66. Competition law and economic regulation seek to achieve economic efficiency and sustainable competition. This allows consumers to have the benefits of fair prices, desirable goods and services and the opportunity to choose what they want to buy. This can be challenging at times in a small market, such as Jersey, given the understandable economic constraints. But equally, this can present opportunities to consider pragmatic approaches tailored to market needs. For example:

- Small domestic markets: Limit the potential for competition and increase the scope for market dominance, as there may be limited opportunity to support multiple suppliers. But being small also offers opportunities for groundbreaking market developments. For example, an all-island fiber to the premises network, which, if well regulated, provides significant benefits to consumers and businesses.
- Informal and complex relationships between individuals: Individuals may try to resolve issues in ways other than engaging with the JCRA through formal procedures. Through close connections with the local business community, however, there is the opportunity to inform and educate on the need to constructively engage with the JCRA.
- Small population and administrative constraints: It is more difficult to find the required technical expertise to support competition and regulatory policy. Conversely, there are opportunities to build a broad and strong breadth of knowledge within the local team, rather than create narrowly focused expertise.

67. Overall, these challenges and opportunities are reflected in the stated purpose of the JCRA, which is "*To make markets work for everyone in Jersey.*"

XI. References and Resources

A. *Laws and Regulations*

- Air and Sea Ports (Incorporation) (Jersey) Law 2015
- Competition (Jersey) Law 2005
- Postal Services (Jersey) Law 2004
- Telecommunications (Jersey) Law 2002

B. *Case Law*

- JCRA, Case C-069 Competition Law Investigation – transportation, logistics and storage sector (2025)

- JCRA, Case C-070, Construction Sector Review (2025)
- JCRA, Case C-042 – Sure, Airtel (2024)

C. *Public Reports*

- GOV.JE, *Annual Report and Accounts for Government of Jersey*, https://www.gov.je/Government/PlanningPerformance/BudgetAccounts/Pages/index.aspx
- GOV.JE, *Government, History and Culture*, https://www.gov.je/LifeEvents/MovingToJersey/WhyChooseJersey/Pages/Government.aspx
- JCRA, JCRA ANNUAL REPORT AND ACCOUNTS 2024 (2025), https://www.jcra.je/other-documents/annual-reports/jcra-annual-report-and-accounts-2024/
- JCRA, SUSTAINABILITY IN THE REGULATED SECTORS IN JERSEY (Jan. 18, 2024), https://www.jcra.je/cases-documents/cases/2024/sustainability-in-the-regulated-sectors-in-jersey/
- JCRA, STRATEGIC REVIEW OF POSTAL SERVICES: REFLECTIONS ON THE REVIEW (Jan. 11, 2024), https://www.jcra.je/media/598878/strategic-review-of-postal-services-reflections-on-the-review.pdf
- JCRA, CASE M-006 – SCHOOL UNIFORMS MARKET STUDY (Dec. 12, 2023), https://www.jcra.je/cases-documents/cases/2022/m-006-school-uniforms-market-study/
- OXERA, TELECOMS STRATEGY FOR JERSEY: FINAL OXERA REPORT (Jan. 2018) https://www.gov.je/Industry/TelecomsStrategy/Pages/FinalOxeraReportOnTelecomsStrategyForJersey.aspx
- POLICY CENTRE JERSEY, JERSEY'S POPULATION (Feb. 25, 2026), https://www.policy.je/papers/jerseys-population
- POLICY CENTRE JERSEY, JERSEY'S ECONOMY (Oct. 5, 2025), https://www.policy.je/papers/jerseys-economy
- STATISTICS JERSEY, JERSEY'S ECONOMY 2024: GDP AND GVA (Oct. 3, 2025), https://stats.je/wp-content/uploads/2025/10/R-Jerseys-Economy-2024-SJ20251003.pdf
- STATISTICS JERSEY, *Population*, https://stats.je/statistic/population/
- UK DEP'T BUS. & TRADE, TRADE AND INVESTMENT FACTSHEETS, JERSEY (DEC. 17, 2025), https://assets.publishing.service.gov.uk/media/6940064c33c7ace9c4a421b6/jersey-trade-and-investment-factsheet-2025-12-17.pdf

68. To learn more about the the Jersey Competition Regulatory Authority:
    - Website: https://www.jcra.je/
    - Contact: info@jcra.je

Martinique

Odeya de La Mure, Jérôme Schall and Anne-Laure Vendrolini
French Competition Authority's Case Handlers

Supervised by Gwenaëlle Nouët
General Rapporteur at the French Competition Authority

I. Overview

1. The island of Martinique is situated between the Caribbean Sea and the Atlantic Ocean, in the Northern Hemisphere, and forms part of the Lesser Antilles archipelago. It has a total surface area of approximately 1,128 square kilometers. Politically, Martinique is a French overseas collectivity governed under Article 73 of the French Constitution[1]. The island is administered by a single assembly that exercises the powers devolved to overseas departments and regions and is recognized as an outermost region of the European Union[2]. The official language of Martinique is French.

II. Demographics and Economy

2. Martinique had a population of approximately 355,459 inhabitants in 2024, corresponding to a population density of about 315 inhabitants per square kilometer. The nominal gross domestic product (GDP) of Martinique was estimated at approximately EUR 10.1 billion in 2023. The territory maintains a structural trade deficit, amounting to approximately EUR 3,002 million in 2024, reflecting a strong dependence on imports. In that year, imports totaled approximately EUR 3,399 million, while exports amounted to about EUR 397 million, resulting in a trade deficit that remained largely stable, decreasing by only 0.1 percent between 2023 and 2024.

3. Martinique's economy is predominantly service-oriented. In 2020, services accounted for approximately 86.5 percent of total value added, with public and non-market services representing around 39.9 percent of value added, while market services contributed approximately 46.6 percent. By contrast, the industrial sector accounted for only about 3.4 percent of total value added.

III. Legal Framework for Competition

4. Article 73 of the French Constitution establishes the principle of legislative identity. French competition law therefore applies automatically to overseas territories.

   (For further details, please refer to the "Guadeloupe" chapter.)

IV. Institutional Structure

5. The Autorité de la concurrence (hereafter, the "French Competition Authority" or "FCA") was established in 2008 as a successor to the Conseil de la concurrence (French Competition Council).

   (For details regarding the supervising body, organizational structure, additional regulatory mandates, budget, resources, and enforcement powers, please refer to the "Guadeloupe" chapter.)

---

1 Subject to the principle of legislative identity (French laws and regulations apply under the same conditions as in mainland France, unless otherwise specified by law or regulation).

2 These regions are an integral part of the EU. Therefore, EU law and all the rights and duties associated with EU membership apply to the outermost regions. In accordance with article 349 of the Treaty on the Functioning of the European Union, specific measures and provisions in EU legislation may be taken.

V. Enforcement and Sanctions

6. Since 2018, the FCA has issued approximately nine decisions involving Martinique. These mainly concern anticompetitive agreements (two), abuse of a dominant position (two), failing to comply with its commitments (one) and exclusive import rights (three). For instance:

- Decision 25-D-05 of November 3, 2025, concerning compliance with the commitments annexed to Decision No. 22-DCC-254 of December 22, 2022, regarding the acquisition of sole control of the Géant Casino La Batelière hypermarket and H Immobilier by the Parfait Group (see below);
- Decision 24-D-10 of December 4, 2024, concerning practices implemented in the inter-island passenger air transport sector (see the "Guadeloupe" chapter);
- Decision 19-D-20 of October 8, 2019, concerning practices implemented in the distribution of perfumery and cosmetic products in the French West Indies, French Guiana, and Réunion: In this decision, the FCA fined several suppliers, importers and their parent companies for granting or benefiting from exclusive import rights for perfume and cosmetic products in the French overseas territories, in breach of article L. 420-2-1 of the French Commercial Code ("Lurel Law"). The infringements concerned products marketed by Procter & Gamble, Coty and Bourjois in Guadeloupe, Martinique, French Guiana and Réunion after March 22, 2013. The FCA imposed fines on both the suppliers that granted the exclusivities and the distributors that benefited from them, in accordance with the transaction procedure accepted by the parties;
- Decision 18-D-03 of February 20, 2018, regarding practices implemented in the marketing of biocidal termite traps in Réunion, the French West Indies, and French Guiana (see the "French Guiana" chapter);
- Decision 18-D-02 of February 19, 2018, concerning practices implemented in the green space maintenance sector in Martinique: In 2011, two social housing bodies in Martinique launched a public tender for the maintenance of green areas. Several companies belonging to Groupe Fontaine submitted separate but coordinated bids, as evidenced by their strong similarities, in order to circumvent the rules governing the allocation of lots. The FCA found this conduct to constitute a cartel in a public procurement procedure and imposed fines of EUR 60,000 on Madianet, and EUR 10,000 each on Groupe Fontaine and Les Bougainvillées.

7. Regarding Martinique, Outremer Télécom brought an action for damages against Decision 09-D-36 of December 9, 2009, relating to practices implemented by Orange Caraïbe and France Télécom in various electronic communications service markets in the departments of Martinique, Guadeloupe and French Guiana. The Paris Court of Appeal, in a ruling issued on June 17, 2020, No. 17/23041, ordered Orange Caraïbe SA and Orange SA jointly to pay Digicel Antilles Françaises Guyane SA EUR 173.64 million in compensation for lost profits. Orange Caraïbe SA is ordered to pay Digicel Antilles SA EUR 7.12 million in compensation for the additional costs incurred as a result of the exclusivity agreements it imposed on distributors, as well as compensation for its financial loss. Orange Caraïbe SA is ordered to pay

Digicel Antilles SA EUR 737,500 in compensation for the additional costs incurred as a result of the exclusive repair agreement it entered into, as well as compensation for its financial loss.

(For information on fines, sanctions, and private enforcement, please refer to the "Guadeloupe" chapter.)

VI. Noteworthy Cases

A. *Decision 25-D-05 of November 3, 2025, concerning compliance with the commitments annexed to Decision No. 22-DCC-254 of December 22, 2022, regarding the acquisition of sole control of the Géant Casino La Batelière hypermarket and H Immobilier by the Parfait Group*

8. *Facts.* The FCA sanctioned the Parfait Group, which is active in particular in the food distribution sector in Martinique, for failing to comply with three commitments annexed to Decision 22-DCC-254 of December 22, 2022, regarding the acquisition of sole control of the Géant Casino La Batelière hypermarket and H Immobilier by the Parfait Group.

9. The Parfait Group failed to meet its commitments. First, it did not sell the business assets of the target hypermarket by the sale deadline, but only on September 9, 2025, nearly two years late. Secondly, the Parfait Group failed to preserve the value of either the target hypermarket's business or that of the shopping center's real estate complex, both of which suffered significant deterioration. Finally, the Parfait Group obstructed the agent's work, both in the commitment monitoring phase and in its mandate to sell the target hypermarket's business.

10. *Legal issue.* Failure to fulfill commitments (art. L. 430-8 of the Commercial Code)/ financial penalties.

11. The cumulative amount of penalties imposed on the Parfait Group is EUR 7.6 million.

12. *Outcome.* This decision is the subject of an appeal (case pending).

13. *Impact or precedent set.* Decision 22-DCC-254 of December 22, 2022, regarding the acquisition of sole control of the Géant Casino La Batelière hypermarket and H Immobilier by the Parfait Group.

B. *Decision 14-D-16 of November 18, 2014, concerning practices implemented in the military relocation services sector in Martinique*

14. *Facts.* The FCA sanctioned three removal companies for presenting cover quotes in order to distort competition in the military relocation market.

15. The investigation established that, in many cases, the companies were not competing with each other and, in fact, were sharing customers. They cooperated to submit cover quotes (quotes deliberately inflated) so that one of them would definitely secure the business for the relocation of the military personnel in question.

16. The FCA deemed these practices serious because their object and effect were to create an artificial allocation of the market between the removal companies and to prevent prices from being set by the free play of competition.

17. *Legal issue.* Violation of article L. 420-1 of the Commercial Code prohibiting anticompetitive agreements/financial penalty/implementation of paragraph III of article L. 464-2 of the Commercial Code (non-contestation of objections).

18. Of the six companies active in this sector, three – AGS Martinique (and its parent company Mobilitas), Martinique Déménagements and SMDTE – were fined a total of EUR 237,840.

19. Martinique Déménagements committed to setting up a compliance program.

20. *Outcome.* The decision was subsequently upheld by both the Paris Court of Appeal on May 19, 2016, and the Court of Cassation on October 18, 2017, with both courts dismissing the respective appeals.

21. *Impact or precedent set.* Similar behaviors have already been sanctioned by the FCA in this sector (in particular, Decisions 09-D-19 of June 10, 2009; 07-D-48 of Dec. 18, 2007; 02-D-62 of Sep. 27, 2002; 01 D 63 of Oct. 9, 2001; and 99-D-50 of July 13, 1999).

VII. Merger Control

22. As with antitrust law, French merger control applies in Martinique. However, the French Commercial Code lays down specific rules for mergers concerning overseas territories in article L. 430-2, III.

23. Examples of notified mergers:
    - Decision 20-DCC-74 of May 26, 2020, concerning the acquisition of sole control of two food-focused businesses by Ah-Tak: Thresholds of article L. 430-2, III / Food distribution sector / Clearance decision;
    - Decision 14-DCC-15 of February 10, 2014, concerning the acquisition of sole control of Mediaserv, Martinique Numérique, Guyane Numérique, and La Réunion Numérique by Canal Plus Overseas: Thresholds of article L. 430-2, I / Telecommunication sector / Clearance decision subject to remedies.

(For information on notification thresholds and review timeframes, please refer to the "Guadeloupe" chapter.)

VIII. Advocacy and Policy Initiatives

(See the "Guadeloupe" chapter)

IX. Regional and International Cooperation

24. Martinique is an associate member of the Organisation of Eastern Caribbean States (OECS).

(For information on regional organizations, bilateral MoUs and participation in global networks, please refer to the "Guadeloupe" chapter.)

X. Challenges and Country-Specific Features

A. *Small Market Size and High Concentration*

25. In its various opinions (issued in 2006, 2009, and 2019), the FCA noted the small size of the local market in Martinique, which often prevents local businesses from reaching optimal production scale and achieving economies of scale, thereby affecting their competitiveness and the prices of consumer goods.

26. In its Opinion 26-A-01 of February 10, 2026, concerning the margins of wholesale importers and distributors of essential food products in Martinique, the FCA highlighted the lack of competition in the maritime freight sector, even though Martinique is heavily dependent on imports from mainland France:

> Since the successive withdrawals of shipping companies Horn Line (2009), WEC Lines (2014), Geest Line (2018), and Maersk (2022), the link between Europe and the French West Indies has been served by three shipping companies: CMA CGM, Marfret, and Seatrade. Marfret does not operate its own vessels on these routes but benefits from a slot charter agreement (SCA) on CMA CGM's vessels. ...CMA CGM vessels transported 96% of the containers destined for Martinique, 20–30% of which were transported by CMA CGM on behalf of Marfret.[3]

(For further details, please refer to the "Guadeloupe" chapter.)

B. *Dependence on Imports/Foreign Investment*

27. In its Opinion 19-A-12 of July 4, 2019, regarding the functioning of competition in the French overseas territories, the FCA indicated:

> Overseas departments are characterized by a structurally negative trade balance. The trade deficit is caused by the fact that these regions have a high level of imports relative to their exports. ...The small size of local markets often prevents local businesses from reaching optimal production levels and achieving economies of scale, which affects their competitiveness and the prices of consumer goods... For Martinique, Guadeloupe, and Réunion, this imbalance is not explained by the level of their imports, which is comparable to that of mainland France, but by the level of their exports, which is much lower than the national average. ...Finally, despite the distance, the bulk of the French overseas departments' trade – both imports and exports – is conducted with mainland France.[4]

28. Local production represents only a minority share of the supply for wholesalers and distributors in the French overseas territories. This situation, which has persisted since 2009, can be explained, on the one hand, for certain categories of products, by the absence or insufficiency of local supply, and on the other hand, where such production

---

3 FCA, Opinion 26-A-01 of Feb. 10, 2026, p. 8 and paras. 83 and 90 (in French) (our translation).

4 FCA, Opinion 19-A-12 of July 4, 2019, paras. 21–22 (in French) (our translation).

does exist, by the lack of competitiveness of locally produced goods compared to imported substitute goods, despite the costs of access and the overseas tax. As previously noted by the FCA in 2009, the primary cause of the lack of competitiveness in local production lies in the small size of overseas markets, which prevents local producers from achieving economies of scale. Several stakeholders point to the burden of fixed costs and the underutilization of production capacity. Producers also cite, among the factors hindering their competitiveness, the distances, which increase the cost of raw materials, and higher construction costs compared to mainland France.

29. In its *Annual Economic Report of Martinique 2024*, IEDOM has indicated:

> Martinique maintains little trade with its regional neighbors [and] North American imports are 80% sourced from the United States, consisting primarily of petroleum products (80%) and charcoal (9%). Imports from South America come mainly from Chile (heavy fuel oil) and Brazil (industrial machinery). Caribbean imports account for 4.4% of the total: Trinidad and Tobago supplies kerosene, gas, and nitrogen fertilizers; the Dominican Republic provides agricultural products, agri-food products, and candles; and Jamaica supplies seafood (almost entirely conch).[5]

30. In its Opinion 26-A-01 of February 10, 2026, concerning the margins of wholesale importers and distributors of essential food products in Martinique, the FCA confirmed:

> The majority of products consumed in Martinique are still imported by sea from France. …According to the evidence gathered during the investigation, consumer goods sold in Martinique come mainly from Europe and more specifically from mainland France… Given its dependence on imports and an unfavorable international context for its exports (such as rum and bananas), Martinique suffers from a large and persistent trade deficit. This deficit decreased by EUR 50 million and EUR 106 million in 2023 and 2024, respectively. For the second consecutive year, Martinique's trade deficit narrowed, with a decrease of EUR 106 million, following a reduction of EUR 50 million in 2023, reaching EUR 2.5 billion. This trend is mainly explained by the decline in imports of goods and services (– 4.7% in volume between 2023 and 2024), linked to weaker private demand.[6]

(The balancing of competition with development goals is addressed in the "Guadeloupe" chapter.)

XI. References and Resources

A. *Laws and Regulations*

- Book IV of the legislative part of the French Commercial Code: On Freedom of Prices and Competition (arts. L. 410-1 to L. 490-14) (in French)

[5] IEDOM, Annual Economic Report of Martinique 2024, 51 (June 2025) (in French) (our translation), https://www.iedom.fr/Rapport-annuel-economique-de-la-Martinique-2024.

[6] FCA, Opinion 26-A-01 of Feb. 10, 2026, paras. 63–64, 68, 75 (in French) (our translation).

- Book IV of the regulatory part of the French Commercial Code: On Freedom of Prices and Competition (arts. R. 410-1 to R. 490-10) (in French)

B. *Case Law*

- FCA, Decision 25-D-05 of Nov. 3, 2025, concerning compliance with the commitments annexed to Decision 22-DCC-254 of December 22, 2022, regarding the acquisition of sole control of the Géant Casino La Batelière hypermarket and H Immobilier by the Parfait Group (in French)
- FCA, Decision 24-D-10 of Dec. 4, 2024, concerning practices implemented in the inter-island passenger air transport sector (in French)
- FCA, Decision 20-DCC-74 of May 26, 2020, concerning the acquisition of sole control of two food-focused businesses by Ah-Tak (in French)
- FCA, Decision 19-D-20 of Oct. 8, 2019, concerning practices implemented in the distribution of perfumery and cosmetic products in the French West Indies, French Guiana, and Réunion (in French)
- FCA, Decision 18-D-03 of Feb. 20, 2018, regarding practices implemented in the marketing of biocidal termite traps in Réunion, the French West Indies, and French Guiana (in French)
- FCA, Decision 18-D-02 of Feb. 19, 2018, concerning practices implemented in the green space maintenance sector in Martinique (in French)
- FCA, Decision 14-D-16 of Nov. 18, 2014, concerning practices implemented in the military relocation services sector in Martinique (in French)
- FCA, Decision 14-DCC-15 of Feb. 10, 2014, concerning the acquisition of sole control of Mediaserv, Martinique Numérique, Guyane Numérique, and La Réunion Numérique by Canal Plus Overseas (in French)
- FCA, Decision 09-D-36 of Dec. 9, 2009, relating to practices implemented by Orange Caraïbe and France Télécom in various electronic communications service markets in the departments of Martinique, Guadeloupe and French Guiana (in French)
- CA Paris [Paris Court of Appeal], June 17, 2020, No. 17/23041 (in French)

C. *Public Reports*

- IEDOM, Analysis of Margins in the Food Distribution Chain in Martinique (Feb. 2026) (in French), https://www.iedom.fr/Analyse-des-marges-dans-la-chaine-de-la-distribution-alimentaire-en-Martinique-11571?lang=fr
- IEDOM, Annual Economic Report of Martinique 2024 (June 2025) (in French), https://www.iedom.fr/Rapport-annuel-economique-de-la-Martinique-2024
- Insee, Economic Review 2024 – Martinique (June 2025) (in French), https://www.insee.fr/fr/statistiques/8570568?sommaire=8354931
- FCA, Opinion 26-A-01 of Feb. 10, 2026, concerning the margins of wholesale importers and distributors of essential food products in Martinique (in French)
- FCA, Opinion 19-A-12 of July 4, 2019, regarding the functioning of competition in the French overseas territories (in French)

- FCA, Opinion 09-A-45 of Sept. 8, 2009, concerning the mechanisms for importing and distributing consumer goods in overseas departments (in French)

31. To learn more about the French Competition Authority (FCA):
    - Website: https://www.autoritedelaconcurrence.fr/
    - Contact: communication@autoritedelaconcurrence.fr

Mauritius

Vipin Naugah
Executive Director at the Competition Commission

I. Overview

1. Mauritius is strategically located in the Indian Ocean on a network of air and sea routes between Asia, Europe and Africa. It is the main island of the Republic of Mauritius, which also comprises several smaller outer islands, including Rodrigues, Agalega and Chagos Archipelago. The total land surface area of the main islands of Mauritius is about 2,040 square kilometers, and the country has an exclusive economic zone of approximately 2,000,000 square kilometers. It is a mature and stable democracy that pursues a liberal and open economic policy.

2. Whilst English is the official language, French and Creole (the local dialect) are the most widely spoken languages.[1]

II. Demographics and Economy

3. The population of the Republic of Mauritius was 1.24 million in July 2025.[2] The population density is about 620 per square kilometer,[3] with around 40% of the population living in urban areas.[4]

4. The country is classified as an upper-middle-income economy by the World Bank,[5] with a gross domestic product (GDP) per capita of USD 12,520 for 2025.[6] The economy is largely diversified, with the main pillars being manufacturing, contributing to around 13% of the country's economic output, followed by financial and insurance services (12%), tourism (7%), and information and communication technology (6%) in 2024.[7] It should be noted that Mauritius is heavily dependent on imports and experiencing persistent trade deficits.[8]

III. Legal Framework for Competition

5. The Competition Act 2007[9] (the "Act"), fully proclaimed on November 25, 2009, establishes the competition law regime in Mauritius. It provides for the various forms of anti-competitive practices and merger control. The law also provides for a framework to assess the competitive impact of public policies and advise the government accordingly.

---

[1] General Information about the Republic of Mauritius, Embassy of the Republic of Mauritius, https://mauritius-moscow.govmu.org/Pages/Mauritius-Russia/General-Information-about-the-Republic-of-Mauritius.aspx.

[2] Statistics Mauritius, Population and Vital Statistics, Jan.–June 2025, No. 1879, 2 tbl. 3.1 (Aug. 2025) https://statsmauritius.govmu.org/Pages/Statistics/ESI/Population/Pop_Vital_Jan-Jun25.aspx.

[3] *Id.* at 2 tbl. 3.2.

[4] Statistics Mauritius, Digest of Demographic Statistics, tbl. 1.9 (2024), https://statsmauritius.govmu.org/Pages/Statistics/By_Subject/Population/SB_Population.aspx.

[5] *Mauritius*, World Bank Group, https://www.worldbank.org/ext/en/country/mauritius.

[6] Datasets, Mauritius, GDP per capita, current prices, International Monetary Fund, https://www.imf.org/external/datamapper/NGDPDPC@WEO/MUS?zoom=MUS&highlight=MUS (last visited Jan. 14, 2026).

[7] Statistics Mauritius, National Accounts Estimates 2022–2025, Issue No. 1901, 16 tbl. 5 (Dec. 2025), https://statsmauritius.govmu.org/Documents/Statistics/ESI/2025/EI1901/NAE_Dec25_191225.pdf.

[8] Tableau de Bord, Statistics Mauritius (Mar. 2026), statsmauritius.govmu.org/Pages/Statistics/Tableau-de-Bord.aspx.

[9] Competition Act 2007, https://competitioncommission.mu/wp-content/uploads/2025/08/Competition-Act-2007-200825.pdf.

6. The main provisions of the Act provide for the framework:
   - to assess collusive agreements such as horizontal agreements, bid rigging and resale price maintenance (sections 41–43);
   - to review and remedy other non-collusive agreements (sections 44 and 45), abuse of a monopoly situation (section 46), and merger situations (sections 47 and 48);
   - to advise the minister responsible for competition matters (currently the Minister of Commerce and Consumer Protection) on state action (including any public body) that may adversely affect competition in the supply of goods and services (section 19).

7. It should be noted that under the Act, collusive agreements are the only type of restrictive business practices for which financial penalties can be imposed. The Act provides for immunity and leniency for collusive agreements, subject to prescribed circumstances.

8. There is no sectoral exemption under the Act; however, petroleum products (motor gasoline, gas oil, and liquefied petroleum gas) are excluded only insofar as they relate to the fixing of their prices and their importation. The following are also excluded:
   - any employer practice or any agreement by which employers are parties insofar as it relates to the remuneration, terms or conditions of employment of employees;
   - any agreement insofar as it contains provisions relating to the use, license, or assignment of rights under or existing by virtue of laws relating to copyright, industrial design, patents, trademarks or service marks;
   - any practice or agreement approved or required under an international agreement to which Mauritius is a party.

9. Since its entry into force, there have been some ancillary amendments to the Act to reinforce the existing provisions or introduce new ones related to, inter alia, the protection of informers/whistleblowers and powers to grant leniency/immunity from fines. In September 2025, a major amendment was introduced to the Act to establish a framework for the conduct of market inquiries to identify and address issues arising from market features, including the structure, regulatory environment, and general conduct of operators (section 51B).

10. A law review process is also underway to propose further amendments aimed at strengthening the competition regime and addressing legal loopholes that may hinder the effective enforcement of the Act.

IV. Institutional Structure

11. The Act establishes the Competition Commission (the "Commission") as an independent body corporate to enforce the law. While it remains independent in its operations, it falls under the aegis of the Ministry of Commerce and Consumer Protection for budget governance purposes.

12. The Competition Commission comprises two distinct organs: the investigative and adjudicative arms.

A. *The Investigative Arm*

13. The investigative function is entrusted to the executive director, who is the chief executive officer of the institution and is appointed by the president of the Republic of Mauritius upon the advice of the prime minister after consultation with the leader of the opposition. The Act explicitly provides that the executive director shall not be subject to direction or control by any other person or authority in the exercise of investigative powers.

14. The executive director heads the institution, which is currently departmentalized as follows:
    - Legal and Cartel Department: Conducts investigations into collusive agreements and provides legal support;
    - Economics, Research and Advocacy Department: Provides economic analysis, conducts market studies and inquiries and leads advocacy initiatives;
    - Enforcement Strategy, Merger and Monopoly Department: Reviews mergers and abuse of monopoly situations;
    - Corporate Services Department: Provides operational support across departments on such matters as finance, human resources, procurement, IT and general administration.

15. The executive director holds broad powers in relation to the enforcement mandate. The Act confers mandatory information gathering for the conduct of investigations and market inquiries. These powers include the issuance of orders for the production of information, the conduct of inspections, and the compulsion of any person to attend for oral examination or to furnish statements in writing on oath.

B. *The Adjudicative Arm*

16. The adjudication function rests with the Commission, which consists of five commissioners: a chairperson, a vice-chairperson and three commissioners. The law provides for the appointment of commissioners by the president of the Republic of Mauritius, on the advice of the prime minister following consultation with the leader of the opposition, based on their qualifications and experience in law, economics, accountancy, or commerce within the public sector, private sector, and academia.

17. The role of the Commission is to conduct hearings, determine competition matters, and issue reasoned decisions. In case of breaches of the Act, the Commission is empowered to issue directions to parties to implement behavioral and/or structural remedies and, where applicable, to impose financial penalties.

18. The Competition Commission is not the competent authority to look into consumer protection issues, as the scope of the Act is limited to the regulation of competition in Mauritius. It should be noted that the Commission has purview over all sectors of the economy, including regulated sectors. In this regard, section 66 of the Act provides that the Competition Commission shall enter into memoranda of understanding (MoUs) with sector regulators for governing the effective exercise of respective responsibilities and establishing a mechanism for practical cooperation. To that effect, the Competition Commission has entered into MoUs with several regulatory bodies.[10]

---

[10] *Memoranda of Understanding*, COMPETITION COMMISSION, https://competitioncommission.mu/memoranda-of-understanding/.

C. *Budget and Resources*

19. The Competition Commission is funded mainly by a government grant, with an average annual budget of approximately USD 1.6 million (MUR 75.2 million). In terms of human resources, there are 33 established positions, of which 25 are dedicated to enforcement-related functions, representing about three-quarters of the total workforce.

V. Merger Control

20. There is no mandatory merger notification requirement in Mauritius. The Act caters for a voluntary regime where parties can notify the Commission of their merger transaction. The executive director is also empowered to open an investigation into prospective or completed merger situations, *proprio motu*. A merger transaction is subject to review where relevant market share thresholds are met and reasonable grounds exist to believe that the creation of the merger situation has resulted in, or is likely to result in, a substantial lessening of competition within any market for goods or services.

21. The Commission can impose directions on parties in relation to a merger situation where it harms competition. Such directions can be structural or behavioral. The Commission can also accept undertakings (commonly referred to as "commitments" in other jurisdictions) from parties to the merger situation.

22. While there are no statutory timeframes for reviewing merger situations, the Competition Commission sets indicative timeframes for reviewing notified mergers.

23. Where a transaction is notified to the Competition Commission or where the latter believes a transaction could fall within the purview of the Act, the Competition Commission conducts a Phase I assessment (pre-investigation) to determine whether the transaction qualifies as a merger situation, meets the 30% market share threshold, and whether it has resulted or may result in a substantial lessening of competition in any market in Mauritius. Phase I assessments are usually completed within a maximum of 30 working days following receipt of complete notification.

24. If there are no competition concerns with the merger transaction, the matter closes at Phase I. If competition concerns have been identified, an in-depth assessment in the form of an investigation is launched. The executive director has up to six months to complete the investigation and submit a report to the Commission. In the investigation phase, the executive director may engage with the parties to discuss undertakings under section 63 of the Act to address competition concerns. If satisfactory undertakings are offered in a timely manner, the investigation may be concluded in less than six months.

VI. Enforcement and Sanctions

25. Since coming into operation in November 2009, the Competition Commission has handled more than 1,100 complaints and issues generated internally from market screening exercises. About 400 of these matters moved to pre-investigation assessment (i.e., inquiries that assess whether there are reasonable grounds to launch investigations into those matters). In total, 76 investigations have been initiated by the Competition Commission to date, covering various sectors of the economy. These include information

and communication technologies, food and beverages, insurance, banking and finance, health, and construction and property development. In terms of case distribution, around 42% of the matters relate to collusive agreements, 36% to abuse of monopoly situations, and 22% to mergers.

26. The Act establishes an enforcement regime that is administrative in nature. As such, no criminal sanctions are provided under the Act for competition breaches. For abuse of monopoly situation and merger cases, the Commission has the power to issue directions imposing structural and behavioral remedies to address the competition concerns identified. Only cartel infringements (sections 41, 42 or 43) can be sanctioned through financial penalties, notwithstanding that the breach was committed negligently or intentionally. The Commission can impose financial penalties of up to 10% of the infringing undertaking's annual turnover for the period of infringement, capped at a maximum duration of five years.

27. Since 2009, the Commission has imposed fines in seven cartel cases totaling around EUR 2 million. In most cases, the parties benefited from a reduction in fines from leniency applications. The Act provides for both leniency and immunity under prescribed conditions for cartel cases. The Competition Commission's leniency policy is prescribed in *CC 3 Guidelines – Collusive Agreements.*

28. For abuse of monopoly situation, the Competition Commission has so far completed 15 investigations, imposing directions in 12 cases and finding no evidence of breach in 3 matters. In addition, two cases were discontinued following a material change in circumstances. It should be noted that the Commission accepted undertakings in 10 out of 12 cases and issued infringement decisions in 2 matters.

29. Mergers that are believed to be problematic are reviewed through formal investigations. The Competition Commission has issued nine merger decisions so far and, in most cases, merging parties offered undertakings to satisfactorily address the competition concerns identified.

30. The Competition Commission has not blocked any merger transactions so far. However, pursuant to section 61 of the Act, the Commission has imposed divestment remedies.

VII. Noteworthy Cases

A. *Cartel: Venison*

31. In March 2023, the Competition Commission concluded an investigation against producers of venison (deer meat) for price fixing in breach of section 41 of the Act. The collusive practice was in relation to the supply of venison to a meat processor and wholesale distributor. The agreement arose through the parties' participation in a cooperative society, which was used to commercialize venison until it became dormant in 2014. The investigation found that the cooperative society served as a platform for joint discussions and negotiations with the processor and distributor, eliminating price competition and constituting collusive conduct.

32. All the parties to the investigation were fined a total of EUR 30,000. The case sets an important precedent for businesses in their capacity as members of trade associations or cooperatives. Businesses remain legally and financially liable for past collusive conduct

even if their association or cooperative society is defunct at the time of investigation. This case also highlights that cartel conduct, even if it involves a buyer's knowledge and/or participation, remains prohibited under the Act.

B. *Abuse of Monopoly Situation: Merchant Discount Rate of CIM Finance Ltd.*

33. In 2017, the Competition Commission investigated an alleged abuse of monopoly situation by CIM Finance Ltd., a major provider of hire-purchase facilities, in relation to merchant fees. The anti-competitive concern was that CIM Finance Ltd. practiced discriminatory pricing by charging higher merchant fees to smaller merchants than to larger merchants, for reasons not entirely associated with cost differentials. The practice potentially distorted competition in the downstream retail market by providing an unfair advantage to larger merchants.

34. During the investigation, CIM Finance Ltd. undertook to review its pricing structure by limiting the gap between the fees charged to smaller and larger merchants to an extent that can be justified by economies of scale and other factors. The Commission accepted those undertakings.

C. *Notified Mergers: Acquisition of Engen Ltd. by Vitol Emerald Bidco Propriety Ltd.*

35. Vitol Emerald Bidco (part of the Vitol Group) proposed acquiring Engen Ltd., a company in South Africa. Engen Ltd. owned Engen Petroleum (Mauritius) Ltd. in Mauritius. The acquirer, Vitol, already controlled Vivo Energy Mauritius Ltd. The petroleum sector in Mauritius is highly concentrated, with Engen Petroleum (Mauritius) Ltd. and Vivo Energy Mauritius Ltd. being two of the four main players. As such, the Commission was concerned that the merger would result in a substantial lessening of competition in several markets in Mauritius, particularly in the supply of motor gasoline and diesel used mainly by vehicles and commercial users, jet fuel for aviation, marine gasoil and fuel oil for ships and vessels.

36. The parties to the merger were required to divest Engen Petroleum (Mauritius) Ltd. to an independent purchaser to maintain competition in the said markets. The divestment has been completed, with the buyer satisfying the conditions that it can sustain the business in a manner that ensures effective competition post-divestment.

37. Other recent notified mergers include that of: (i) Swan Securities Ltd. and Capital Markets Brokers Ltd., two licensed investment dealers providing stockbroking and execution services on the Stock Exchange of Mauritius; and (ii) the acquisition of the majority stake in MC Vision Ltd., a local pay-TV service provider, by Canal+ International S.A.S.

VIII. Advocacy and Policy Initiatives

38. Alongside enforcement, the law mandates the Competition Commission to promote competition through advocacy initiatives, including market studies and policy reviews. These functions are in addition to the Competition Commission's general mandate of promoting the provisions of the Act and its activities.

A. *Market Studies and Policy Review*

39. Pursuant to section 30 of the Act, the executive director is empowered to conduct market studies and, where relevant, make recommendations to address structural or regulatory impediments. Since its inception, the Competition Commission has completed eight market studies into various sectors of the economy, including construction, telecommunications, aviation, digital services, agro-industry, pharmaceuticals, and ports. These studies have contributed to bringing regulatory reforms aimed at promoting competition in markets. For instance, the Competition Commission's first market study on the supply of cement led to the liberalization of the market. Similarly, the pharmaceutical market study identified various concerns and proposed recommendations to incentivize competition for the benefit of patients. These included:

- the implementation of industry best practices to promote transparency and good governance and thus ease entry;
- an alternative pricing mechanism to ensure affordability;
- regulatory reforms to the Intellectual Property Rights regime to foster intrabrand competition.

40. With regard to policy reviews, section 19 of the Act provides that the Competition Commission can advise the government on any action taken or proposed to be taken that may adversely affect competition in the supply of goods and services. In pursuance of this function, the Commission has advised the government on various policy matters relating to sugar, cement, scrap metal, cattle and pork sectors in Mauritius.

41. The advice on pork addressed the regulatory distortion to competition in the supply of processed pork in Mauritius. The issue related to a discriminatory import licensing regime whereby import permits for processing-grade pork were contingent upon processors purchasing an equivalent volume of slaughtered pigs from local breeders.

42. The measure was applicable to all local pork processors except the dominant operator. The regulatory measure was intended to protect local breeders and to secure a channel for them to sell excess produce. However, it distorted competition and led to the exit of some local pork processors. The Commission recommended that the above policy be abolished and invited the government to consider other regulatory measures to protect local pig breeders.

B. *Outreach to Stakeholders*

43. With the aim of raising awareness of competition law enforcement and promoting a culture of competition among the various stakeholders, the Competition Commission has been conducting various outreach activities since it commenced operations in November 2009. These include press articles, media campaigns, guidelines and workshops on competition for business, trade associations, professionals, consumer organizations, public officials, students and the general public. A few of these initiatives are highlighted below.

44. To fight collusive practices in public procurement, the Competition Commission has embarked on a continuous program to educate public procurement officials on bid rigging and how to flag collusion in tenders. The key objective is to capacitate government officials engaged in tender design and processes through relevant training on competitive

bidding processes, as well as screening for bid-rigging practices among suppliers. This initiative also serves as an information-sharing platform between procurement officials and the investigative staff at the Competition Commission in the detection of potential bid-rigging cases.

45. In collaboration with the Institute for Judicial and Legal Studies of Mauritius and the Common Market for Eastern and Southern African (COMESA) Competition and Consumer Commission, the Competition Commission led capacity-building workshops in the field of competition law and economics intended for barristers and other law practitioners. The objective is to enable law practitioners to assist their clients in complying with the Act and to share knowledge of restrictive business practices and the latest developments in competition law and regulation in the region.

46. Cognizant of the important role that accountancy firms play in mergers and acquisitions, the Competition Commission organized a series of workshops to raise awareness of merger control provisions. These workshops targeted the major accountancy firms that advise on mergers and acquisitions and deal with the administration and receivership of companies.

47. Other initiatives include interactive sessions with senior officials of ministries on the importance of undertaking competitive assessment in policy making; working sessions with consumer organizations to gather their perspectives on potential competition issues; and an essay contest and seminars for secondary and tertiary students on the importance of competition law enforcement.

48. The Competition Commission has also published several guidelines or guidance notes pertaining to competition law in general, abuse of dominant position, merger review, merger notifications, collusive practices, recommended practices for trade associations, resale price maintenance, and bid rigging. These are accessible on the Competition's website.[11]

IX. Regional and International Cooperation

49. The Republic of Mauritius is a party to several regional treaties, including the COMESA, the Southern African Development Cooperation (SADC), and the African Continental Free Trade Area (AfCFTA). The Competition Commission has close working relationships with relevant regional competition bodies established under these regional organizations.

50. The Competition Commission has been actively collaborating with the COMESA Competition and Consumer Commission to enforce regional competition law (the COMESA Competition and Consumer Regulations), as well as to build capacity and raise awareness of competition law in COMESA member states. To date, the Competition Commission has assisted the COMESA Competition and Consumer Commission on more than 300 notified mergers at the COMESA level. The collaboration between the COMESA Competition and Consumer Commission and the Competition Commission

---

11 *Competition Law Flash Guides Archives*, COMPETITION COMMISSION, https://competitioncommission.mu/publication-category/flash-guides/.

was formalized through the signing of an MoU in 2017. The Competition Commission has partnered with the COMESA Competition and Consumer Commission on various advocacy events. Among other projects, the Competition Commission hosted the Third COMESA Regional Judges Workshop in Mauritius in 2024, alongside a dedicated capacity-building workshop for legal practitioners.

51. The Competition Commission is also active at the SADC regional level, being part of its Competition and Consumer Policy and Law Committee. This forum fosters cooperation and dialogue among competition authorities in SADC. In 2016, the heads of SADC competition authorities entered into a multilateral MoU to formalize their cooperation in promoting competition law enforcement in the region. The Competition Commission has other bilateral MoUs in place with national competition agencies from Seychelles, South Africa and India.

52. The Competition Commission has been playing a leading role within the African Competition Forum (ACF), a regional network of 37 national and regional competition agencies in Africa. It served as co-chair of the ACF from 2014 until October 2023, when it took over the helm of the institution as the chair. Several milestones have been achieved by the ACF under the Competition Commission's chairmanship, which, among others, include:
- the launch of a dedicated ACF website;
- the formalization of working groups for structured deliverables;
- and the publication of two key research works:[12] *Trade Flow Patterns and Regional Value Chains in the Agriculture and Agro-Processing Sector* and *Digital Platforms Landscaping Study*.

53. On the international front, the Competition Commission is an active member of the International Competition Network (ICN). It previously served as co-chair of the ICN Advocacy Working Group and contributed to the development of competition advocacy tools, as well as hosted the Working Group's annual conference in 2013. The Commission has been the co-chair of the ICN Merger Working Group since November 2023, and it hosted the ICN Merger Workshop 2025 in Mauritius.

X. Challenges and Country-Specific Features

54. Some features of the Mauritian economy pose significant challenges and call for robust competition law enforcement and policy actions to ensure market contestability. These include:
- the dominance by a few large conglomerates in terms of ownership or control of enterprises in key sectors;
- state monopolies in strategic sectors, limiting scope for the entry of new firms;
- the adoption of the national exhaustion regime limiting parallel imports.

55. According to the World Bank 2021 report,[13] many sectors of the Mauritian economy (462 of 672 sectors, representing around 70%) are highly concentrated, including key upstream ones like information and communication technology, financial services,

---

12 *Publications*, African Competition Forum, https://african-competition-forum.org/project-details/.

13 World Bank Group, Mauritius: Through the Eye of a Perfect Storm: Coming Back Stronger from the COVID Crisis – A World Bank Group Country Economic Memorandum (2021), https://documents.worldbank.org/en/publication/documents-reports/documentdetail/586691621628367648.

transport and tourism. While a high degree of concentration can be expected in a small economy like Mauritius, it raises potential risks of anti-competitive practices.

56. The issue of concentrated markets is compounded by the strong presence of a few large conglomerates in various key sectors with vertically integrated enterprises across the value chains. While vertical integration brings benefits such as efficiency gains from reduced transaction costs and security of supply, it can also raise potential competition concerns. For instance, high levels of cross-directorships and multi-market contracts may facilitate collusion and reduce price rivalry.[14] Moreover, purchasing goods and services within groups can foreclose other players from the relevant markets, particularly the smaller ones.

57. Another feature of the Mauritian economy that poses potential challenges for market competition is state control of strategic sectors, including public utilities, telecommunications, ports, and aviation. While public interest issues might justify state participation in these sectors, the scope for entry and competition is limited.

58. The Mauritian economy has a high degree of import concentration despite being a comparatively open economy. The issue could potentially be due to the national exhaustion regime adopted by the country,[15] which limits parallel imports while favoring exclusive territorial distribution agreements. The Competition Commission, in the context of its market study into the pharmaceutical sector, recommended authorizing parallel imports to lower the price of pharmaceutical products in Mauritius while ensuring adequate drug traceability for health safety considerations. However, the import regime that restricts parallel imports is still in place.

XI. References and Resources

A. *Laws and Regulations*

- COMPETITION ACT 2007, https://competitioncommission.mu/wp-content/uploads/2025/08/Competition-Act-2007 200825.pdf

B. *Case Law*

- Competition Commission (2017), INV 035 MERCHANT DISCOUNT RATE OF CIM FINANCE LTD, https://competitioncommission.mu/wp-content/uploads/2019/08/inv025-decision-170717-1.pdf
- Competition Commission (2023), INV 050 HORIZONTAL COLLUSIVE AGREEMENT(S) IN THE SUPPLY OF DEER/VENISON IN MAURITIUS, https://competitioncommission.mu/wp-content/uploads/2023/04/INV050-Comm-Decision.pdf
- Competition Commission (2024), INV 067 Undertakings in relation to acquisition of Engen Limited by Vivo Group, https://competitioncommission.mu/commission-decision/undertakings-in-relation-to-acquisition-of-engen-limited-by-vivo-group

---

14 OECD, Roundtable on Ex officio Cartel Investigations and Use of Screens to Detect Cartels – Background Note by the Secretariat (DAF/COMP(2013)14, Nov. 4, 2013), https://one.oecd.org/document/DAF/COMP(2013)14/en/pdf.

15 Surishta Chetamun & Marius Schneider, *Mauritian Supreme Court Confirms National Exhaustion of IP Rights*, 13 J. Intell. Prop. L. & Prac. 599 (2018), https://academic.oup.com/jiplp/article-abstract/13/8/599/5045929.

C. *Public Reports*

- ACF, Digital Platforms Landscaping Study (Nov. 2024) https://www.compcom.co.za/wp-content/uploads/2025/06/ACF-Digital-Platform-Study.pdf
- ACF, Trade Flow Patterns and Regional Value Chains in the Agriculture and AGRO-Processing Sector (Sept. 2024), https://www.compcom.co.za/wp-content/uploads/2024/12/ACF-Agricultural-Report_Full.pdf
- Competition Commission, CC 3 – Guidelines on Collusive Agreements (2009) (last amended Dec. 2017), https://competitioncommission.mu/cc3-guidelines-collusive-agreements/
- COMPETITION COMMISSION, COMPETITION LAW FLASH GUIDES ARCHIVES, https://competitioncommission.mu/publication-category/flash-guides/.
- EMBASSY of the Republic of Mauritius, GENERAL INFORMATION ABOUT THE REPUBLIC OF MAURITIUS, https://mauritius-moscow.govmu.org/Pages/Mauritius-Russia/General-Information-about-the-Republic-of-Mauritius.aspx.
- International MONETARY Fund, DATASETS, MAURITIUS, GDP PER CAPITA, CURRENT PRICES, https://www.imf.org/external/datamapper/NGDPDPC@WEO/MUS?zoom=MUS&highlight=MUS; accessed Jan. 14, 2026.
- Statistics Mauritius (Mar. 2026), TABLEAU DE BORD, https://statsmauritius.govmu.org/Pages/Statistics/Tableau-de-Bord.aspx
- Statistics Mauritius, Population and Vital Statistics, Jan.–June 2025, No. 1879 (Aug. 2025) https://statsmauritius.govmu.org/Pages/Statistics/ESI/Population/Pop_Vital_Jan-Jun25.aspx
- Statistics Mauritius, Digest of Demographic Statistics (2024), https://statsmauritius.govmu.org/Pages/Statistics/By_Subject/Population/SB_Population.aspxStatistics Mauritius, National Accounts Estimates 2022–2025, Issue No. 1901 (Dec. 2025), https://statsmauritius.govmu.org/Documents/Statistics/ESI/2025/EI1901/NAE_Dec25_191225.pdf
- World Bank Group, MAURITIUS : THROUGH the Eye of a Perfect STORM: COMING Back STONGER FROM the COVID Crisis – A World Bank Group Country Economic Memorandum (2021), https://documents.worldbank.org/en/publication/documents-reports/documentdetail/586691621628367648
- World Bank Group, OVERVIEW : MAURITIUS, https://www.worldbank.org/ext/en/country/mauritius

D. *Academic Articles or Books*

- Chetamun, Surishta & Marius Schneider, *Mauritian Supreme Court Confirms National Exhaustion of IP Rights*, 13 J. Intell. Prop. L. & Prac. 599 (2018), https://academic.oup.com/jiplp/article-abstract/13/8/599/5045929
- OECD, Roundtable on Ex officio Cartel Investigations and Use of Screens to Detect Cartels – Background Note by the Secretariat (DAF/COMP(2013)14, Nov. 4, 2013), https://one.oecd.org/document/DAF/COMP(2013)14/en/pdf

59. All competition legislation can be found on the Mauritius Competition Authority's website. To learn more about the Competition Commission of Mauritius:

- Website: www.competitioncommission.mu
- Email : info@competitioncommission.mu

Mayotte

Odeya de La Mure, Jérôme Schall and Anne-Laure Vendrolini
French Competition Authority's Case Handlers

Supervised by Gwenaëlle Nouët
General Rapporteur at the French Competition Authority

I. Overview

1. The island of Mayotte is located in the Indian Ocean, in the Southern Hemisphere, and forms part of the Comoros archipelago. It is situated in the northern part of the Mozambique Channel, northwest of Madagascar. Mayotte has a total surface area of approximately 375 square kilometers. Politically, Mayotte is a French overseas department and region, governed under Article 73 of the French Constitution[1], and is recognized as an outermost region of the European Union[2]. The official language of Mayotte is French.

II. Demographics and Economy

2. Mayotte had a population of approximately 329,000 inhabitants in 2024, corresponding to a population density of about 690 inhabitants per square kilometer. The nominal gross domestic product (GDP) of Mayotte was estimated at approximately EUR 3.1 billion in 2023. The territory maintains a structural trade deficit, amounting to approximately EUR 857.7 million in 2023, reflecting a strong dependence on imports. In that year, imports totaled approximately EUR 870.4 million, while exports amounted to about EUR 12.7 million, resulting in a trade deficit that decreased by 19.4 percent between 2023 and 2024.

3. Mayotte's economy is predominantly service-oriented. In 2022, the tertiary sector accounted for approximately 77.4 percent of total value added, while the industrial sector contributed about 15.7 percent and agriculture represented around 3.5 percent of the island's value added in 2023.

III. Legal Framework for Competition

4. Article 73 of the French Constitution establishes the principle of legislative identity. French competition law therefore applies automatically to overseas territories (see arts. L. 924-1 to L. 924-6 and R. 924-1 to R. 924-4 for any applicable adjustments).

   (For further details, please refer to the "Guadeloupe" chapter.)

IV. Institutional Structure

5. The Autorité de la concurrence (hereafter, the "French Competition Authority" or "FCA") was established in 2008 as a successor to the Conseil de la concurrence (French Competition Council)

   (For details regarding the supervising body, organizational structure, additional regulatory mandates, budget, resources, and enforcement powers, please refer to the "Guadeloupe" chapter.)

---

[1] Subject to the principle of legislative identity (French laws and regulations apply under the same conditions as in mainland France, unless otherwise specified by law or regulation).

[2] These regions are an integral part of the EU. Therefore, EU law and all the rights and duties associated with EU membership apply to the outermost regions. In accordance with article 349 of the Treaty on the Functioning of the European Union, specific measures and provisions in EU legislation may be taken.

V. Enforcement and Sanctions

6. Since 2018, the FCA has issued very few decisions involving Mayotte:

- Decision 21-D-28 of December 9, 2021, relating to the implementation of paragraph V of article L. 464-2 of the French Commercial Code concerning the obstruction by Mayotte Channel Gateway SAS of the investigation by the FCA's services (see below);
- Decision 16-D-07 of April 19, 2016, concerning compliance with the commitment to divest the mobile telephony activities of Outremer Telecom in Réunion and Mayotte, as set forth in the decision authorizing the acquisition of SFR by the Altice Group (see below);
- Decision 15-D-17 of November 30, 2015, relating to practices implemented in the mobile telephony market for non-residential customers in Réunion and Mayotte (see below);
- Decision 14-D-05 of June 13, 2014, regarding practices implemented in the mobile telephony sector for residential customers in Réunion and Mayotte: The FCA has fined SFR and its subsidiary SRR in Réunion a total of EUR 15.9 million for implementing and maintaining abusive price differentials between on-net calls – calls made between customers of the same mobile network – and off-net calls – calls made to customers of competing networks. These practices lasted for more than twelve years in Réunion and over three years in Mayotte. The FCA found that charging higher prices for calls to competitors' networks distorted competition and harmed consumers.

(For information on fines, sanctions, and private enforcement, please refer to the "Guadeloupe" chapter.)

VI. Noteworthy Cases

A. *Decision 21-D-28 of December 9, 2021, relating to the implementation of paragraph V of article L. 464-2 of the French Commercial Code concerning the obstruction by Mayotte Channel Gateway SAS of the investigation by the FCA's services*

7. *Facts.* By deliberately and repeatedly failing to respond to the FCA's December 14, 2020, request for information, Mayotte Channel Gateway SAS (MCG) obstructed an investigative measure by the investigating authorities. The FCA also considered that this practice was attributable to MCG's parent company, Nel Import Export.

8. *Legal issue.* Breach of paragraph V of article L. 464-2 of the French Commercial Code/Injunction. The FCA imposed a joint penalty of EUR 100,000 on MCG and Nel Import Export. The FCA also ordered the Nel Group to respond to the FCA's request for information within one month of notification of the decision.

9. *Outcome.* In its judgment of December 21, 2023, the Paris Court of Appeal dismissed the appeal lodged by Mayotte Channel Gateway and Nel Import Export against the decision of the FCA.

B. *Decision 16-D-07 of April 19, 2016, concerning compliance with the commitment to divest the mobile telephony activities of Outremer Telecom in Réunion and Mayotte, as set forth in the decision authorizing the acquisition of SFR by the Altice Group*

10. *Facts.* On October 30, 2014, the FCA authorized the Altice/Numericable group to acquire sole control of SFR. To address the significant market power that Numericable and Altice would have acquired in the mobile telephony sector in the Indian Ocean (66% market share in Réunion, 90% in Mayotte), Altice and Numericable committed to divesting Outremer Telecom's mobile telephony operations in Réunion and Mayotte. Specifically, pending the divestiture, Altice and Numericable pledged to maintain the economic viability, market value, and competitiveness of these operations until their sale. They also committed to refraining from interfering in the management of the divested business.

11. By increasing the price of Outremer Telecom's mobile phone plans in Réunion and Mayotte, the Altice/Numericable Group has failed to meet its obligations.

12. *Legal issue.* Failure to fulfill commitment related to the sale of Outremer Telecom's mobile telecommunications activities in Réunion and Mayotte was noted. This commitment was a condition of the FCA's Decision 14-DCC-160 of October 30, 2014, concerning the acquisition of sole control of SFR by the Altice Group.

13. A financial penalty of EUR 15 million was imposed jointly and severally on Altice Luxembourg and Numericable-SFR.

14. *Outcome.* Decision of the Council of State of March 31, 2017: rejection. On March 31, 2017, the Council of State rejected the petition filed by Altice and Numericable-SFR.

C. *Decision 15-D-17 of November 30, 2015, relating to practices implemented in the mobile telephony market for non-residential customers in Réunion and Mayotte*

15. *Facts.* SFR and its Réunion-based subsidiary SRR have, in the mobile telephony market for business customers, established and maintained (12 years in Réunion and 6 years in Mayotte) excessive price differences between calls made to other customers on the SRR network (on-net calls) and those made to its competitors' networks (off-net calls), which were charged at a higher rate.

16. From 2000 to 2013 in Réunion and from 2007 to 2013 in Mayotte, SFR, the leading operator in both markets with a 60% market share in Réunion and 85% in Mayotte, marketed offers with significant price differences between on-net and off-net calls. This particularly affected the Pro, Flotte, Intégrale Entreprise and Evidence packages.

17. In this case, price differences in Mayotte were up to nearly three times higher than cost differences. These offers strongly encouraged companies to join the most developed network and made competing networks appear more expensive to call.

18. *Legal issue.* Breach of article L. 420-2 of the French Commercial Code and article 102 of the Treaty on the Functioning of the European Union (abuse of dominant position/ settlement procedure/financial penalty).

19. The FCA imposed a fine of EUR 10.7 million on SFR and SRR.

20. *Outcome.* The decision is final and has not been appealed within the legal time limits.

21. *Impact or precedent set.* This decision follows an initial decision handed down in 2014, fining SFR and SRR nearly EUR 46 million for the same practices implemented in the mobile telephony market for private individuals (Decision 14-D-05 of June 13, 2014, regarding practices implemented in the mobile telephony sector for residential customers in Réunion and Mayotte).

VII. Merger Control

22. As with antitrust law, French merger control applies in Mayotte. However, the French Commercial Code lays down specific rules for mergers concerning overseas territories in article L. 430-2, III.

23. Examples of notified mergers:

   - Decision 24-DCC-26 of February 15, 2024, regarding the acquisition of control of ten companies belonging to the Capriona Group by United Basalt Products: Thresholds of article L. 430-2, III / Precast concrete sector / Clearance decision;
   - Decision 19-DCC-11 of January 23, 2019, regarding the acquisition of sole control of Mayotte Motor Corporation Distribution and Hamaha Rent by Citadelle: Thresholds of article L. 430-2, III / Automotive distribution sector / Clearance decision;
   - Decision 15-DCC-142 of October 20, 2015, regarding the joint acquisition of control of Telecom Réunion Mayotte by Iliad and the Hiridjee Group: Thresholds of article L. 430-2, I / Telecommunications sector / Clearance decision.

(For information on notification thresholds and review timeframes, please refer to the “Guadeloupe” chapter.)

VIII. Advocacy and Policy Initiatives

24. With particular regard to the Indian Ocean region, the FCA issued an opinion in 2018 on construction materials in Réunion and Mayotte (Opinion 18-A-09 of October 3, 2018).

(For information on sectoral studies or market inquiries, recent policy papers or guidelines, and outreach to businesses and consumers, please refer to the “Guadeloupe” chapter.)

IX. Regional and International Cooperation

(See the “Guadeloupe” chapter)

X. Challenges and Country-Specific Features

A. *Dependence on Imports/Foreign Investment*

25. In its Opinion 19-A-12 of July 4, 2019, regarding the functioning of competition in the French overseas territories, the FCA indicated:

> Overseas departments are characterized by a structurally negative trade balance. The trade deficit is caused by the fact that these regions have a high level of

> imports relative to their exports. . . . The small size of local markets often prevents local businesses from reaching optimal production levels and achieving economies of scale, which affects their competitiveness and the prices of consumer goods.[3]

26. According to IEDOM's annual report for 2024, "[l]ike other small island economies, Mayotte imports most of the goods it consumes, and its exports remain very low. The territory's trade balance is therefore structurally in deficit, and its coverage ratio is very low. In 2024, the trade deficit amounted to EUR 857.7 million."[4]

B. *Lack of Resources or Expertise*

27. In its Opinion 18-A-09 of October 3, 2018, the FCA analyzed the competitive situation in the construction materials markets in Mayotte and Réunion. The FCA observed significant price differentials compared to mainland France for construction materials, as well as very high profit margins for certain products. It concluded that the additional costs identified could be explained, for all the materials concerned, by the high cost of transportation, the specific tax on imported goods (*octroi de mer*), storage difficulties linked in particular to land scarcity, and the requirements for standardization and certification of processes and materials, which are sometimes poorly adapted to the specificities of the French overseas territories. It also noted the existence of other more specific factors, such as high degrees of horizontal concentration and vertical integration in certain markets.

(Small market size, high concentration, and the balancing of competition with development goals are addressed in the "Guadeloupe" chapter.)

XI. References and Resources

A. *Laws and Regulations*

- Book IV of the legislative part of the French Commercial Code: On Freedom of Prices and Competition (arts. L. 410-1 to L. 490-14) (in French)
- Book IV of the regulatory part of the French Commercial Code: On Freedom of Prices and Competition (arts. R. 410-1 to R. 490-10) (in French)

B. *Case Law*

- FCA, Decision 24-DCC-26 of Feb. 15, 2024, regarding the acquisition of control of ten companies belonging to the Capriona Group by United Basalt Products (in French)
- FCA, Decision 21-D-28 of Dec. 9, 2021, relating to the implementation of paragraph V of article L. 464-2 of the French Commercial Code concerning the obstruction by Mayotte Channel Gateway SAS of the investigation by the FCA's services (in French)

---

3 FCA, Opinion 19-A-12 of July 4, 2019, paras. 339 and following (in French) (our translation).

4 IEDOM, Annual Economic Report of Mayotte 2024, p. 49 (June 2025) (in French) (our translation), https://www.iedom.fr/Rapport-annuel-economique-de-Mayotte-2024.

- FCA, Decision 19-DCC-11 of Jan. 23, 2019, regarding the acquisition of sole control of Mayotte Motor Corporation Distribution and Hamaha Rent by Citadelle (in French)
- FCA, Decision 16-D-07 of Apr. 19, 2016, concerning compliance with the commitment to divest the mobile telephony activities of Outremer Telecom in Réunion and Mayotte, as set forth in the decision authorizing the acquisition of SFR by the Altice Group (in French)
- FCA, Decision 15-D-17 of Nov. 30, 2015, relating to practices implemented in the mobile telephony market for non-residential customers in Réunion and Mayotte (in French)
- FCA, Decision 15-DCC-142 of Oct. 20, 2015, regarding the joint acquisition of control of Telecom Réunion Mayotte by Iliad and the Hiridjee Group (in French)
- FCA, Decision 14-D-05 of June 13, 2014, regarding practices implemented in the mobile telephony sector for residential customers in Réunion and Mayotte (in French)
- CE [Council of State], Mar. 31, 2017, No. 401059 (in French)
- CA Paris [Paris Court of Appeal], Dec. 21, 2023, n° 22/00474 (in French)

C. *Public Reports*

- IEDOM, Annual Economic Report of Mayotte 2024 (June 2025) (in French), https://www.iedom.fr/Rapport-annuel-economique-de-Mayotte-2024
- FCA, Opinion 26-A-01 of Feb. 10, 2026, concerning the margins of wholesale importers and distributors of essential food products in Martinique (in French)
- FCA, Opinion 19-A-12 of July 4, 2019, regarding the functioning of competition in the French overseas territories (in French)
- FCA, Opinion 18-A-09 of Oct. 3, 2018, concerning the competitive situation in the construction materials markets in Mayotte and Réunion (in French)
- FCA, Opinion 09-A-45 of Sept. 8, 2009, concerning the mechanisms for importing and distributing consumer goods in overseas departments (in French)

28. To learn more about the French Competition Authority (FCA):

- Website: https://www.autoritedelaconcurrence.fr/
- Contact: communication@autoritedelaconcurrence.fr

New Caledonia

Stéphane Retterer
President of the New Caledonia Competition Authority

Chloé Racine
Head of Legal service of the New Caledonia Competition Authority

I. Overview

1. New Caledonia is an insular territory located in the South Pacific, approximately 1,500 kilometers east of the Australian coast. It belongs to the southern region of Melanesia and is divided into three provinces endowed with their own powers: the South Province, the North Province and the Loyalty Islands Province. The total surface area of the territory is 18,576 square kilometers.

2. From an institutional standpoint, New Caledonia constitutes a *sui generis* overseas collectivity of the French Republic, with a specific constitutional status and a high degree of autonomy. Its institutional organization is based on the provisions of the Nouméa Accord of May 5, 1998, enshrined in the Constitutional Law of July 20, 1998,[1] which provides for a gradual transfer of powers from the State to local institutions. New Caledonia is also one of the thirteen overseas countries and territories (OCT) associated with the European Union.

3. The official language of the territory is French. The legal tender is the Pacific franc (XPF), which is pegged to the euro at a fixed exchange rate: one euro is equal to XPF 119.33.

II. Demographics and Economy

4. In 2025, New Caledonia had an estimated population of around 264,000 inhabitants.[2] The average population density remains relatively low, at around 14.6 inhabitants per square kilometer, but this figure conceals significant territorial disparities. The South Province concentrates the majority of the population, with a density of around 29 inhabitants per square kilometer, whereas population density stands at around 9 inhabitants per square kilometer in the Loyalty Islands and 5 inhabitants per square kilometer in the North Province. This uneven distribution of the population contributes to the fragmentation of markets and to a reduction in their effective size.

5. From an economic perspective, New Caledonia's nominal gross domestic product is estimated at XPF 943 billion (approximately USD 9 billion), which corresponds to a GDP per capita of XPF 3.5 million (approximately USD 34,000),[3] placing the territory among the high-income economies of the Pacific region. However, the New Caledonian economy remains structurally dependent on external trade and is characterized by a chronic trade deficit. In 2024, against a backdrop of severe economic and social crisis, the trade deficit widened significantly, reaching XPF 115 billion (approximately USD 1.1 billion), representing nearly 10% of GDP. This imbalance reflects a heavy dependence on imports, especially for consumer goods, energy products and industrial inputs.

6. New Caledonia's economy has traditionally been based on the nickel sector, which plays a central role in terms of exports, industrial activity and public finances, while simultaneously exposing the territory to fluctuations in international commodity prices.

---

1 Constitutional Law No. 98-610 of July 20, 1998, relating to New Caledonia (in French).
2 ISEE-NC, 2025.
3 ISEE-NC, 2024.

Other sectors also contribute significantly to the local economy, notably agriculture, fisheries and aquaculture, manufacturing industries, tourism, as well as the construction and public works sector, whose relative weight has increased in recent years in the context of reconstruction and economic recovery.

7. Market structures in New Caledonia are characterized by a high degree of concentration, resulting from the small size of the domestic market, geographic isolation and the existence of significant barriers to entry. Several strategic sectors are organized around public monopolies, in particular telecommunications and mobile telephony infrastructure and services, provided by the Office des postes et télécommunications (OPT-NC); electricity transmission, entrusted to ENERCAL; and the importation and marketing of certain agricultural products, such as meat and potatoes, which fall under the responsibility of the Office de commercialisation et d'entreposage frigorifique (OCEF). Beyond these monopolies, many markets are dominated by a limited number of private operators, giving rise to recurring oligopolistic structures, which raise specific issues in terms of competition and economic regulation.

III. Legal Framework for Competition

8. Competition law in New Caledonia is based on an autonomous legal framework. In line with the recommendations issued in 2012 by the French Competition Authority,[4] New Caledonia adopted two *lois du pays* in 2014 entrusting an independent administrative authority with the responsibility of implementing the full range of competition enforcement and regulatory instruments within the territory. This framework is founded, first, on Country Law No. 2014-7 of February 14, 2014, which established a competition law specific to New Caledonia, and, second, on Country Law No. 2014-12 of April 24, 2014, which created the New Caledonia Competition Authority (Autorité de la concurrence de la Nouvelle-Calédonie – ACNC).

9. The legal framework was further supplemented by Country Law No. 2019-10 of April 19, 2019, which amended several provisions of Book IV of the Commercial Code applicable in New Caledonia, in particular with regard to anti-competitive practices, merger control and procedural rules.

10. New Caledonian competition law covers a broad material scope. It prohibits cartels, abuses of a dominant position, abuses of economic dependence and exclusive import rights. It also establishes a system for controlling mergers and transactions affecting the retail sector. In addition, Book IV of the Commercial Code prohibits various restrictive commercial practices likely to undermine the balance of commercial relationships.

11. These rules are intended to apply to all economic sectors and to all operators, whether public or private, carrying out an economic activity within the territory in markets subject to the forces of competition.

12. The scope of application of these rules is nevertheless subject to limitations when the legislator grants exclusive rights to an operator for the performance of specific tasks,

---

4 Report of the French Competition Authority of Sept. 21, 2012, on the mechanisms for importing and distributing consumer goods in New Caledonia (in French).

thereby placing it in a situation of legal monopoly.[5] Furthermore, the New Caledonian legislator has not provided for any specific mechanism for the control of public aid under competition law.

IV. Institutional Structure

13. The New Caledonia Competition Authority (ACNC) is the authority responsible for the enforcement of competition law within the territory. Although it was established in 2014, it only began to exercise its full powers on March 2, 2018, when it became fully operational.

14. The ACNC is an independent administrative authority, devoid of any hierarchical link to the government of New Caledonia or any ministerial administration. This status is intended to guarantee its functional independence in the exercise of its missions.

15. From an organizational standpoint, the ACNC is based on a dichotomous structure ensuring the separation of investigative and decision-making functions, in accordance with constitutional requirements. It comprises an investigation service and administrative services (administrative and financial services, procedural services, legal services and IT services).

16. The ACNC is composed of a five-member board, including a full-time chair and four non-permanent members. The board is responsible for ruling on the cases brought before the ACNC, on the basis of the investigations and proposals prepared by the investigation service, which operates under the authority of a general rapporteur. In addition, the chair of the ACNC is solely responsible for the organization and functioning of the institution and takes all necessary decisions to this end.

17. The ACNC has a total staff of thirteen. Its annual budget amounts to approximately XPF 186 million, i.e., EUR 1.5 million.

18. Pursuant to Book IV of the Commercial Code, the ACNC is entrusted with ensuring free functioning of competition and market competition throughout the territory. It is therefore competent to review mergers and transactions affecting the retail sector that meet the thresholds set by the Code. It also performs an enforcement function consisting in sanctioning anti-competitive and restrictive commercial practices. To that end, it is vested with extensive investigative and sanctioning powers: it may conduct investigations, carry out on-site inspections and seizures, impose behavioral or structural injunctions, and levy pecuniary sanctions in the event of established anti-competitive practices.

19. The ACNC also has advisory powers enabling it to give an opinion on any matter relating to competition. In this capacity, it may be consulted by public authorities and issue recommendations to the government and Congress of New Caledonia. Finally, beyond its strictly adjudicatory and advisory missions, the ACNC carries out active awareness-raising and information activities targeting institutions, businesses and the general public. This mission aims to promote the benefits of effective and balanced competition, as well as to disseminate knowledge of the legal framework, methods and procedures applicable to competition in New Caledonia.

---

5 The Court of Cassation reiterated the ACNC's lack of jurisdiction to control the actions of OPT-NC in a situation of legal monopoly in a ruling dated June 22, 2022 (Court of Cassation, Commercial Division, No. 20-22.438) (in French).

V. Enforcement and Sanctions

20. Since becoming fully operational in 2018, the ACNC has developed a sustained decision-making activity. To date, it has issued more than 200 decisions (an average of around 30 decisions per year) covering the full scope of its powers. More than half of these decisions fall within its preventive function and relate to the review of mergers and operations in the retail sector.

21. New Caledonian competition law provides for a set of administrative sanctions designed to ensure the effectiveness of the rules laid down in the Commercial Code. In the event of established anti-competitive practices, the ACNC may impose an administrative fine of up to XPF 175 million (approximately EUR 1,465,000) on a natural person and up to 5% of the highest worldwide turnover, net of taxes, achieved by the undertaking or group to which it belongs, in case of legal persons.

22. In addition, article Lp. 471-7 of the Commercial Code provides for a specific pecuniary sanction against natural persons who have played a personal and decisive role in the design, organization or implementation of anti-competitive practices, with fines of up to XPF 8,500,000 (approximately EUR 71,000). This mechanism aims to strengthen the effectiveness of enforcement by directly holding accountable the executives or decision-makers involved in unlawful practices.

23. The legal framework also provides for specific pecuniary sanctions in the event of infringements of the rules governing merger and retail expansion control, in particular in cases of failure to notify, early implementation of a transaction, or non-compliance with commitments or injunctions.

24. With regard to restrictive commercial practices, the penalty regime varies depending on the nature of the infringement. Administrative fines can range from XPF 1 million to XPF 8.5 million (approximately EUR 8,000 to EUR 71,000) for natural persons and from XPF 5 million to XPF 45 million (approximately EUR 42,000 to EUR 377,000) for legal persons.

25. For all infringements, in addition to pecuniary sanctions, the ACNC may order the publication or dissemination of its decisions.

26. Finally, New Caledonian competition law provides for the possibility of private enforcement, as economic operators may, in principle, bring actions for damages before the judicial courts in order to obtain compensation for harm caused by anti-competitive practices. In practice, recourse to such actions remains limited, as the effectiveness of competition law relies mainly on public enforcement carried out by the ACNC.

VI. Noteworthy Cases

A. *Decision No. 2023-PAC-04 of September 27, 2023, on practices implemented in the pyrotechnics sector in New Caledonia*

27. Interdis held a monopoly position in the upstream market for the supply of pyrotechnic products in New Caledonia. From September 2014 onwards, it progressively ceased to supply, under normal conditions, Plein Les Yeux, a company active in the downstream

market for pyrotechnic displays. The contested practices included late or non-existent responses to orders, failure to offer substitute products when the requested references were unavailable, and differential treatment compared to other customers.

28. The issue was therefore whether such conduct constituted an abuse of a dominant position, within the meaning of article Lp. 421-2 of the Commercial Code, characterized by an implicit refusal to supply and discriminatory treatment, resulting in the foreclosure of a competitor in a related market.

29. The ACNC found the existence of a single and continuous practice of abuse of a dominant position, extending over a six-year period. It held that the products refused were objectively necessary for Plein Les Yeux's activity, that Interdis had sufficient stocks or substitute solutions available, and that the practices were not objectively justified. Interdis was fined XPF 4,050,000 (approximately EUR 34,000) and ordered to publish the decision. Injunctions were also imposed in order to ensure non-discriminatory treatment of orders in the future.

B. *Decision No. 2022-PAC-06 of August 29, 2022, on practices implemented in the medical devices sector in New Caledonia*

30. Several medical device suppliers entered into exclusive import agreements with Medi-Services for New Caledonia, thereby making it the exclusive distributor of their products within the territory. These agreements had the effect of excluding other local wholesale importers from distributing the brands in question, in a sensitive sector related to public health. The practices were implemented in parallel by several suppliers, conferring on Medi-Services a monopolistic position for certain product ranges.

31. The ACNC held that the exclusive importation agreements at issue constituted a per se infringement of New Caledonian competition law, the characterization of which is independent of their actual or potential effects on competition. It recalled that the burden of proof as regards the conditions for exemption lies with the undertakings concerned, and found that Medi-Services had failed to demonstrate that exclusivity was indispensable or that it generated efficiency gains benefiting end users.

32. Taking into account the nature of the practices, their particular seriousness in a sector affecting public health, the harm caused to the New Caledonian economy, as well as mitigating circumstances and the commitments offered by certain suppliers, the ACNC imposed pecuniary sanctions on all the undertakings concerned, including a principal fine of XPF 47,425,000 imposed on Medi-Services (approximately EUR 397,000), together with publication sanctions intended to ensure a deterrent effect.

33. In a recent ruling,[6] the Paris Court of Appeal upheld the ACNC's legal analysis, validating in particular the per se qualification of the exclusive importation agreements and the refusal to grant an exemption. The court nevertheless revised the fine, reassessing its quantum.

---

6 Paris Court of Appeal, Dec. 18, 2025, No. 22/16187 (in French).

C. *Opinion No. 2020-A-07 of December 28, 2020, on the price formation mechanism for consumer goods in New Caledonia*

34. In 2020, at the request of the government of New Caledonia, the ACNC conducted an in-depth analysis of the mechanisms governing the formation of prices for consumer goods. At that time, price differentials with mainland France were estimated at an average of 33%, reaching more than 70% for certain products. The analysis focused on a representative basket of consumer goods, corresponding to the categories included in the "quality-price shield" schemes applicable to large food retailers.

35. The ACNC thus sought to determine the extent to which the observed price levels could be justified by structural constraints inherent in a remote, small-scale insular economy, or whether they also resulted from regulatory, structural or behavioral factors affecting market competition throughout the supply and distribution chain.

36. It concluded that while insularity, geographic remoteness and the narrowness of markets inevitably entail higher supply and distribution costs, these factors alone are insufficient to explain the magnitude of the observed price differentials. The Opinion highlights the existence of regulatory and behavioral factors specific to New Caledonia, such as import restrictions, weakly regulated monopoly or oligopoly situations in certain upstream markets, strong intermediation by wholesale importers, overlapping taxes, and pricing strategies based on consumers' willingness to pay. The ACNC also emphasized that the additional costs borne throughout the value chain were more heavily passed on to retail prices than in mainland France or in the overseas departments.

37. The Opinion concluded with eighteen interdependent recommendations aimed at strengthening competition and reducing price distortions throughout the entire consumer goods supply chain, from upstream import and local production markets to downstream distribution markets.

VII. Merger Control

38. Competition law in New Caledonia provides for a merger control regime designed to address the high level of structural concentration of local markets. This regime is supplemented by a specific framework applicable to the retail sector. In this sector, the commercial surface area and turnover of operators may, on their own, confer significant market power within a given catchment area, regardless of the traditional concentration thresholds. This specificity is particularly noticeable in the mass distribution sector, given its importance for the supply of consumer goods and basic necessities.

39. Notifiable merger transactions include acquisitions or mergers of undertakings, as well as the creation of joint ventures, where the aggregate turnover generated in New Caledonia by the undertakings or groups of natural or legal persons involved in the transaction exceeds XPF 1.2 billion, and where at least two of the undertakings or groups of natural or legal persons concerned individually generate, directly or indirectly, a turnover equal to or exceeding XPF 200 million in New Caledonia (art. Lp. 431-2 of the Commercial Code).

40. By way of derogation, a transaction that has no effect on the markets of New Caledonia is not subject to merger control.

41. Transactions in the retail sector subject to notification include projects to open a retail store, extensions of sales areas, changes of commercial brand or business activity, as well as the takeover of an existing store by a new operator, where the sales area is or becomes greater than 600 square meters (art. Lp. 432-1 of the Commercial Code).

42. By way of derogation, any transaction in the retail sector must be notified, regardless of the sales area, when, following the transaction, the operator or future operator holds a market share equal to or greater than 25% in the relevant catchment area and has a turnover exceeding XPF 600 million.

43. Notified transactions are examined by the ACNC within time limits laid down by the Commercial Code. In merger control, a simplified procedure allows the ACNC to issue its decision within 25 working days where the transaction:

- does not give rise to any overlap of activities between the undertakings concerned and does not result in the elimination of a potential competitor; or
- gives rise to one or more overlaps of activities without any affected market.[7]

44. In other cases, the transaction is reviewed within 40 working days, which may be extended by 15 working days if commitments are finalized. When the ACNC decides to open an in-depth review phase, the time limit for adopting a decision may be extended to a maximum of 100 working days.

45. With regard to the control of transactions in the retail sector, the review periods vary depending on the market share held by the undertaking concerned in the relevant catchment area. Where that share is below 25% following the transaction, the notification is eligible for a simplified procedure and the decision must be adopted within 25 working days of receipt of a complete filing. Where the market share is equal to or greater than 25%, the ACNC has a maximum of 40 working days to adopt a decision, at the end of which it may decide to open an in-depth review. In such cases, it has a maximum of 100 working days to issue its decision.

46. The vast majority of notified transactions have resulted in clearance decisions. However, approximately 20% of the authorized transactions were cleared subject to commitments.

47. The ACNC has also adopted a prohibition decision in Decision No. 2023-DCC-06.[8] In that case, SELAS Bioclinic, a subsidiary of the Calédobio group, itself majority-controlled by the Cerba group, notified a proposed acquisition of sole control over SPFPL-SARL Biolabo NC, a holding company owning several medical biology laboratories located in the South Province. The transaction would have led the

---

[7] *See* Decree No. 2018-41/GNC of Jan. 9, 2018, adopted pursuant to art. Lp. 431-9 of the Commercial Code applicable in New Caledonia, concerning the terms and conditions of application and the content of the notification file for a merger (in French).

[8] ACNC, Decision No. 2023-DCC-06 of Nov. 17, 2023, on the acquisition of exclusive control of SPFPL-SARL Biolabo NC by SELAS Bioclinic (in French).

Calédobio group to indirectly hold a majority stake in several competing laboratories active in the markets for medical biology testing in New Caledonia. The transaction was likely to harm competition given the horizontal overlaps between the parties in the downstream markets for medical biology tests and the presence of the Cerba group in the upstream markets for the supply of equipment, reagents and consumables for medical biology.

48. The ACNC rejected the application of the failing firm defense, finding that the target was not facing proven financial difficulties and that an alternative acquisition scenario involving a credible competitor was plausible. Moreover, it found that the transaction would have led to the creation of a quasi-monopoly situation, with very high market shares in the downstream markets for medical biology testing, and would have strengthened the dominant position of the Calédobio group.

49. Finally, the analysis identified significant anti-competitive risks, both price-related and non-price-related, including harm to the competitive market structure, a risk of price increases for non-regulated medical acts, a potential deterioration in the quality and diversity of services, as well as negative effects on public procurement markets for the subcontracting of medical biology tests. Risks of vertical foreclosure were also identified, in particular to the detriment of the territorial hospital center.

50. The commitments proposed by the notifying party, which were exclusively behavioral in nature, were considered insufficient and inappropriate to remedy the competition concerns identified. In the absence of effective corrective measures, the ACNC therefore decided to prohibit the transaction.

VIII. Advocacy and Policy Initiatives

51. Alongside its preventive and enforcement functions, the ACNC also carries out a significant advocacy mission aimed at promoting a culture of competition and raising awareness among economic and institutional stakeholders of the competition issues specific to the territory.

52. To that end, the ACNC conducts ongoing awareness-raising activities targeting undertakings, legal professionals and, more broadly, the general public. In this context, it has, since 2023, introduced the Authority's Breakfast Meetings, which provide regular opportunities for dialogue with economic operators. These meetings, organized in an informal and interactive setting, make it possible to address targeted topics, to explain and discuss the decisions and opinions issued by the ACNC, and to respond to participants' questions regarding the practical application of competition law in New Caledonia. The ACNC also carries out communication activities through its website and social media channels aimed at the general public, to explain the rationale for its action and the benefits of effective competition for consumers.

53. As part of this advocacy mission, the ACNC publishes and regularly updates a number of educational and forward-looking documents. In particular, it issues procedural notices intended to clarify the rules applicable to undertakings and to enhance legal certainty for economic operators. It also prepares economic notes addressing structural issues affecting the New Caledonian economy. Recent work includes analyses of price and

margin regulation and the conditions for their economic effectiveness,[9] as well as economic development models and the effects of protectionism on market competition.[10] These notes aim to provide public authorities with economic analysis tools for defining and evaluating economic policies.

54. The ACNC has also carried out numerous sector inquiries as part of its advisory role. These studies have focused on key sectors of the New Caledonian economy, such as international and domestic air transport,[11] the pharmaceutical sector,[12] and competition in the travel and tourism agency sector.[13] These sector inquiries make it possible to identify structural market failures and to formulate recommendations aimed at improving market functioning in the long term.

55. Finally, the ACNC pays particular attention to capacity building and training in the field of competition law. In this respect, it benefits from regular support from the French Competition Authority, particularly in terms of investigative powers, procedures and sanctions. The ACNC also organizes training activities for professionals and local institutions. Lastly, it develops awareness-raising initiatives targeting students, with a view to increasing knowledge of its missions and contributing to the emergence of a sustainable culture of competition within the territory.

IX. Regional and International Cooperation

56. New Caledonia does not belong to any regional competition organization vested with normative or decision-making powers comparable to those existing in other regions of the world, such as the Caribbean Community (CARICOM) or the West African Economic and Monetary Union (WAEMU). As an OCT of the European Union, it is neither part of the EU internal market nor subject to EU competition law. The ACNC's cooperation therefore relies primarily on informal and functional regional networks, foremost among which is the Pacific Island Network of Competition Consumer and Economic Regulators (PINCCER).

57. Established in May 2023, PINCCER is an informal network bringing together competition authorities, consumer protection authorities and economic regulators from the Pacific region, such as French Polynesia, Australia, New Zealand, Fiji and Vanuatu. The network was designed to address shared challenges, in particular those relating to competition, the high cost of living, market concentration and consumer protection. Its objective is to strengthen the capacities of member authorities by providing a structured framework for cooperation, experience sharing and capacity building.

---

9 ACNC, *Price and Margin Regulation in New Caledonia: When and How to Regulate?*, Econ. Note No. 2 (June 2024) (in French).

10 ACNC, *Protectionism and Economic Development Models in New Caledonia*, Econ. Note No. 3 (Oct. 2024).

11 ACNC, Opinion No. 2022-A-04 of Dec. 13, 2022, on competition in the aviation sector in New Caledonia (in French).

12 ACNC, Opinion No. 2022-A-01A of Feb. 28, 2022, on the supply and distribution of reimbursed and non-reimbursed medicinal products for human use in New Caledonia (in French).

13 ACNC, Opinion No. 2025-A-01 of Feb. 10, 2025, on competition in the tourism and travel agency sector (in French).

58. Beyond the regional framework, the ACNC also participates in the work of international competition networks. In particular, it is a member of the International Competition Network (ICN).

X. Challenges and Country-Specific Features

59. Competition law in New Caledonia operates within an economic and institutional environment shaped by several structural constraints inherent in small insular economies, compounded by specific features linked to the territory's economic, social and political history.

60. The limited size of the New Caledonian market and the narrowness of economic outlets favor structural market concentration across numerous sectors. The small number of operators, combined with the absence of significant economies of scale, frequently leads to the emergence of monopoly or oligopoly situations. This configuration makes the application of competition law particularly delicate, insofar as certain concentrated market structures may appear economically rational while nevertheless presenting high risks for the competitive process.

61. The New Caledonian economy is also characterized by a significant presence of public undertakings, as well as by historically strong public intervention, including in markets open to competition, which may give rise to competitive distortions to the detriment of private operators. The ACNC is therefore progressively addressing such situations, both through its advisory action and, where appropriate, through the enforcement of abuse of dominance rules when undertakings vested with exclusive rights operate in downstream or related competitive markets.

62. Moreover, New Caledonia remains heavily dependent on imports, which limits local operators' ability to exert competitive pressure on prices. Foreign direct investment remains relatively low, in particular due to geographic remoteness, market size and political uncertainty.

63. The constraints weighing on the New Caledonian economy have been exacerbated by the major crisis that began on May 13, 2024, which resulted in a significant contraction of tax revenues, a deterioration in economic activity and a loss of skills. In this context, the territory faces an increased need for economic, human and technical resources, which may be mobilized as part of a State reconstruction and support plan. Improving the attractiveness of the territory therefore constitutes a central challenge, which presupposes not only economic and regulatory reforms, but also the stabilization of the institutional and political framework, an essential condition for investor confidence and for economic actors more broadly.

64. Another major challenge lies in reconciling competition objectives with economic development goals. In a transitioning insular economy, competition policy cannot be conceived in isolation, but must be articulated with a trade policy oriented towards the Pacific region, as well as with an industrial or productivity policy tailored to local specificities. In this respect, the ACNC, notably through its advocacy actions, seeks to promote a framework in which public interventions and aid to undertakings are embedded in a logic that is consistent with competition principles. At this stage,

the absence of a genuine system for controlling public subsidies highlights the need for a state aid framework tailored to local constraints, while minimizing distortions of competition.

XI. Author's Perspective

65. The experience of New Caledonia highlights the specific challenges that a newly established competition authority may face in a small insular economy. When it was established, the ACNC had to operate within an economic environment characterized by historically entrenched practices and by significant public intervention in certain markets. Nevertheless, thanks to the volume and diversity of decisions adopted across all areas of its jurisdiction, as well as to an active information and awareness policy, the ACNC is now better identified and more firmly integrated into the New Caledonian economic landscape.

66. The New Caledonian experience also confirms the central role of *ex ante* control of market structures in a small insular economy. In a context where market size is limited and the entry of new players is rare, a single merger or retail establishment project may be sufficient to lock in a sector on a long-term basis. In this respect, merger control and, even more so, the specific control regime applicable to the retail sector constitute essential levers for preserving competition.

67. The effects of this *ex ante* policy can already be observed in certain sectors, particularly in the mass distribution sector. Over the last decade, the number of operators active in this market has increased, and the market shares of the two main players have decreased significantly, reflecting increased competitive intensity.

68. Finally, the ACNC, now fully operational, is engaged in a process of continuous improvement of public action in the fields of competition and economic regulation. Institutional developments may therefore need to be considered. For example, the government of New Caledonia could envisage evolving the ACNC into an independent authority responsible for both competition enforcement and telecommunications regulation, thereby enhancing the coherence of public action in strategic markets characterized by high barriers to entry and significant technological challenges.

XII. References and Resources

A. *Laws and Regulations*

- Constitutional Law No. 98-610 of July 20, 1998, relating to New Caledonia (in French)
- Decree No. 2018-41/GNC of Jan. 9, 2018, adopted pursuant to art. Lp. 431-9 of the Commercial Code applicable in New Caledonia, concerning the terms and conditions of application and the content of the notification file for a merger (in French)

B. *Case Law*

- ACNC, Decision No. 2023-DCC-06 of Nov. 17, 2023, on the acquisition of exclusive control of SPFPL-SARL Biolabo NC by SELAS Bioclinic (in French)
- ACNC, Decision No. 2023-PAC-04 of Sept. 27, 2023, on practices implemented in the pyrotechnics sector in New Caledonia (in French)
- ACNC, Decision No. 2022-PAC-06 of Aug. 29, 2022, on practices implemented in the medical devices sector in New Caledonia (in French)
- Paris Court of Appeal, Dec. 18, 2025, No. 22/16187 (in French)
- Court of Cassation, Commercial Division, June 22, 2022, No. 20-22.438 (in French)

C. *Public Reports*

- ACNC, Opinion No. 2025-A-01 of Feb. 10, 2025, on competition in the tourism and travel agency sector (in French)
- ACNC, *Protectionism and Economic Development Models in New Caledonia*, Econ. Note No. 3 (Oct. 2024), https://awards.concurrences.com/IMG/pdf/acnc_economic_white_paper_-_protectionism_and_economic_development_2_.pdf?134791/367b55dcc8480eed763b8c12eabca0fa698767a96105dd27d3d7c2fb09e76cbc
- ACNC, *Price and Margin Regulation in New Caledonia: When and How to Regulate?*, Econ. Note No. 2 (June 2024) (in French).
- ACNC, Opinion No. 2022-A-04 of Dec. 13, 2022, on competition in the aviation sector in New Caledonia (in French)
- ACNC, Opinion No. 2022-A-01A of Feb. 28, 2022, on the supply and distribution of reimbursed and non-reimbursed medicinal products for human use in New Caledonia (in French)
- ACNC, Opinion No. 2020-A-07 of Dec. 28, 2020, on the price formation mechanism for consumer goods in New Caledonia (in French)
- FCA, Report of the French Competition Authority of Sept. 21, 2012, on the mechanisms for importing and distributing consumer goods in New Caledonia (in French).

69. To learn more about the New Caledonia Competition Authority:

Website: https://site.autorite-concurrence.nc/

Contact: contact@autorite-concurrence.nc

Papua New Guinea

Steven Iraitogo Sugl
Executive Manager at the Competition Law Enforcement Division

I. Overview

1. Papua New Guinea (PNG) is an island nation in Melanesia, located in the South Pacific Ocean. It occupies the eastern half of the island of New Guinea and includes numerous offshore islands, such as the Bismarck Archipelago and Bougainville. The country lies north of Australia and east of Indonesia. Papua New Guinea has a total land area of approximately 462,840 square kilometers. Politically, it is an independent sovereign state, formally known as the Independent State of Papua New Guinea, operating as a parliamentary democracy and a Commonwealth realm, with the British monarch serving as head of state. The official languages of PNG are English, Tok Pisin, and Hiri Motu, and the country is noted for its exceptional linguistic diversity, with over 800 indigenous languages.

II. Demographics and Economy

A. *Population*

2. Whilst different sources have varying figures, according to a government profile, the population is approximately 11.78 million (2025 estimate).

B. *Density*

3. With a density of approximately 25.5 people per square kilometer, the urban population accounts for about 13.25% of the total; the majority live in rural, village-based communities.

C. *GDP (Nominal)*

- Nominal GDP (2025 estimate): approximately USD 32.7 billion to USD 32.8 billion, according to the International Monetary Fund's (IMF) *World Economic Outlook* for 2025. This is based on recent international financial estimates.
- GDP growth: Growth is projected at around 4.6–4.7% in 2025, reflecting recovery and ongoing expansion in resource sectors (such as liquefied natural gas and mining) and agriculture.
- GDP per capita: approximately USD 2,565 in 2025 (nominal), also from IMF projections. Local official GDP figures for 2024 are still being finalized by PNG's National Statistical Office (NSO), with full 2024 GDP data scheduled for formal release in early 2026.

D. *Trade Balance*

- Merchandise trade data (2024): Exports grew to about PGK 52 billion in 2024, while imports rose to about PGK 26 billion, giving a *positive trade balance* (approx. PGK 28 billion).
- Balance of trade (2025 quarterly): PNG continued to record *trade surpluses throughout 2025*, with quarterly figures showing a surplus of approximately PGK 10,680 million in Q3 2025.
- Current account: Persistently strong, with a surplus relative to GDP reported at around 17.4% in 2024.

4. *Conclusion.* Exports significantly outweigh imports in recent years, giving Papua New Guinea a *sustained trade surplus* – especially in resource and commodity exports. Current figures from official NSO classifications and trade statistics are *most recent through 2024*, with 2025 data trending similarly by available quarterly updates.

E. *Main Economic Sectors*

1. Resource Sector (Mining, Oil & Gas)

5. The resource sector remains a core driver of PNG's economy, especially LNG (liquefied natural gas), gold and other minerals.

6. LNG exports accounted for a large share of total export earnings in 2024, and new projects (e.g., Papua LNG, Wafi-Golpu Mine) are expected to sustain growth. Resource production and export earnings continue to strongly influence GDP and trade performance.

2. Agriculture, Forestry & Fisheries

7. *Agriculture is one of the largest contributors to the economy*, supporting the livelihoods of the majority of the population and generating significant export revenue through crops such as *coffee, cocoa, palm oil and copra, as well as fishery products.*

8. It remains a *priority sector for government development plans*, and in 2025 its performance – particularly coffee and cocoa exports – has been highlighted as a major growth engine.

9. The Food and Agriculture Organization (FAO) and other recent sources indicate that *agriculture contributes around 26–30 % of GDP* and employs most people, especially in rural areas.

3. Services Sector

10. The *services sector – including retail, transport, and tourism – is expanding*, contributing to non-resource economic growth and domestic demand. Retail and transport services are performing well in urban centers.

4. Construction and Manufacturing

11. *Construction has grown with infrastructure spending*, tied to both public works and resource-project investments.

12. Manufacturing remains smaller relative to agriculture and mining, but is growing gradually, often linked to processing and value-adding activities.

5. Telecommunications & ICT

13. The telecommunications and information and communication technology (ICT) sector is one of the *faster-growing parts of the services economy*, with expansion in digital connectivity and mobile services supporting business and consumer markets.

F. *Level of Market Concentration*

14. Some key industries in PNG are highly concentrated. Whilst concentration in some industries is due to the nature of the markets, in others it is due to a lack of effective competition from existing players to erode the market share of the largest players. Some of those highly concentrated markets are in the aviation industry (the provision of airport terminals and air transport services), the telecommunications industry (calls, broadband, and pay TV services), the electricity industry (distribution, transmission, and retail services), the seaport industry (terminal operations, stevedoring, handling, and coastal shipping), the water industry (water and sewerage services), and poultry supply markets.

III. Legal Framework for Competition

15. In the early 2000s, the government of PNG undertook major structural changes, including the privatization of state-owned enterprises (SOEs) in key sectors such as ports, electricity, postal services, and telecommunications. As part of the reforms, the Independent Consumer and Competition Commission (ICCC) was established to carry out functions of economic regulation of state-owned monopolies, protect consumer interests, and promote effective competition in the markets.

16. The ICCC was established through the enactment of the Independent Consumer and Competition Commission Act 2002 (ICCC Act). The ICCC became operational in January 2003 after the ICCC Act was passed in 2002.

A. *Name and Date of First Competition Law*

17. The first competition law of PNG is titled the Independent Consumer and Competition Commission Act 2002 ("ICCC Act"). The ICCC Act covers competition, consumer protection, and economic regulation of state-owned utilities.

B. *Subsequent Revisions or Updates*

18. The ICCC Act was amended in 2018 to change the merger notification regime from voluntary to mandatory, with the inclusion of notification thresholds. If proposed transactions meet the notification thresholds, the acquiring party is required to notify the ICCC and get prior approval before completing the transaction. Failure to notify carries a default penalty of PGK 750,000.00.

C. *Scope*

19. With respect to competition law provisions, the ICCC Act covers all three pillars – anti-competitive agreements, abuse of dominance, and merger control. It does not cover state aid.

D. *Applicable Sectors*

20. The application of the competition provisions is universal, including SOEs.

E. *Exemptions and Limitations*

21. There are no exemptions in its application to any industry or specific sectors of the economy unless it is limited by another law. The same ICCC Act applies to SOEs, small businesses, and the informal sector.

IV. Institutional Structure

A. *Competition Authority*

22. The agency is called the Independent Consumer and Competition Commission (ICCC). It was established through the passing of the ICCC Act in 2002 and became operational in January 2003.

B. *Supervising Body*

23. The ICCC is independent in its decision-making and is not subject to any ministerial or government directions. However, it gets its annual budgetary grants from the government in addition to its small internally generated revenues.

C. *Organizational Structure*

24. The ICCC is governed by a three-member commission, comprising the commissioner (as the chair) and two associate commissioners. It is required by law that one associate commissioner be a non-resident of PNG with vast experience in the areas of competition law, consumer protection and/or utilities regulation.

25. The chair/commissioner, who is also the chief executive officer, oversees daily operational matters and is supported by a general manager.

26. Various key mandates of the ICCC are performed by separate divisions headed by their respective executive managers. The two support divisions perform the respective functions of legal and corporate affairs services. The ICCC also has four regional branches that mainly focus on consumer protection work, but report to the head office if they notice or suspect any issues relating to competition and utilities regulation. The total number of staff (including commissioners) permitted under the current organization structure is 79. The competition division has 11 technical officers who handle all competition-related work, including merger applications, investigations into anticompetitive agreements and abuse of dominance.

D. *Additional Regulatory Mandates*

27. The additional mandates of the ICCC include consumer protection, economic regulation in the port industry (including service standards and tariff setting) and premiums for third-party motor vehicle insurance. The ICCC also regulates prices for water and sewerage services, public motor vehicle (PMV) and taxi services, and fuel prices at the service stations.

E. *Budget and Resources*

28. The estimated annual budget of the ICCC is close to PGK 20 million, but the government funding is less than PGK 15 million.

F. *Enforcement Powers*

29. Regarding its competition function, the ICCC has investigative powers in cases of suspected breaches, including search and entry, compulsory information-gathering, and the ability to seek injunctions. All penalties for breaches are imposed by the courts.

V. Enforcement and Sanctions

A. *Fines and Sanctions*

30. The pecuniary penalties for any breach are imposed by the court. The maximum penalties for any competition law breach are PGK 10 million for corporations and PGK 500,000 for individuals. Individuals implicated in a breach can be banned from holding managerial positions for a maximum period of five years. There is no criminal liability for any breach. In addition to the penalties for breach, damage claims by aggrieved parties can be brought against the offenders.

B. *Enforcement Track Record*

31. On average, the ICCC has carried out about three investigations so far in a year. The types of cases range from all three main areas of competition law.

C. *Private Enforcement*

32. The ICCC Act actually provides for damages claims, but this is yet to be tested, as the ICCC has yet to bring a successful competition law case.

VI. Noteworthy Cases

33. Since its inception, the ICCC has recorded just one case that has gone through the full court process. This was on allegations of breaches of merger laws under the ICCC Act.

A. *Independent Consumer and Competition Commission v. Freedom Apex Limited (2023)*

34. *Facts.* Prior to the transaction, Dae Won Trading Limited (Dae Won), the seller, and Freedom Apex Limited (Freedom Apex), the purchaser, operated grocery businesses in both the retail and wholesale segments in the Highlands Region of PNG. In 2021, the parties completed the transaction worth more than PGK 50 million. Section 81 of the ICCC Act requires that, for any acquisition exceeding PGK 50 million (or with a combined market share of more than 50%), the acquiring party must notify the ICCC and obtain prior approval before concluding the transaction. The transaction was concluded without prior approval from the ICCC.

35. *Legal issue.* The ICCC alleged that the value of Freedom Apex's acquisition of Dae Won's retail and wholesale businesses exceeded the mandatory notification threshold, and that Freedom Apex did not obtain prior approval to complete the transaction. Therefore, Freedom Apex failed to notify and obtain prior approval before proceeding with the acquisition. The ICCC instituted the court proceedings in 2023.

36. *Outcome.* In July 2025, the National Court of PNG issued its decision in favor of the ICCC. In August 2025, Freedom Apex appealed the decision (of the lower courts).

37. *Impact or precedent set.* Whilst the matter is not the test of any substantive competition concerns, it is a precedent case in the history of the ICCC. It has been observed that there has been an increase in the number of notifications after the amendment to section 81 of the ICCC Act.

VII. Merger Control

38. As alluded to above, the ICCC Act has provisions for merger control. The merger laws cover all industries, including SOEs and small local businesses. The law prohibits mergers and acquisitions that would have the effect of substantially lessening competition in any market. The real test for any competition concerns is on the grounds of substantial lessening of competition. Besides this, the law also allows for mandatory prior notification for transactions that exceed either of the notification thresholds.

A. *Notification Thresholds*

39. The two thresholds relate to the transaction value (especially the purchase price) and the market share. Any transactions that are likely to exceed the value of PGK 50 million – and/or resulting in a combined market share greater than 50% – must seek and obtain prior approval (through clearance or authorization) before proceeding. The law requires the acquiring party to give notice by applying for clearance.

B. *Review Timeframes*

40. Under the ICCC Act, there are two processes that are employed for all merger notifications received and processed. They are called "clearance" and "authorization." Under the ICCC Act, it is required that clearance, which is more of a Phase I assessment, must be completed and a decision is handed down within 20 days from the date of registration. The authorization process, which is a Phase II assessment, takes up to 72 days. These respective timeframes can be extended on mutual agreement (between the ICCC and the applicant) and/or delays in the response from the applicant on any further information requests issued by the ICCC.

C. *Examples of Notified or Blocked Mergers*

41. The two major merger applications blocked by the ICCC were in the banking and aviation industries, respectively. The merger application in the aviation industry involved the proposed acquisition of an airline by its competitor on the grounds of the failing firm defense. Six years after that decision, the airline that claimed to be failing is still operating in the market.

42. The merger in the banking industry was blocked on the grounds of substantial lessening of competition concerns. At the time of the proposed transaction in 2021, the selling party claimed that it was exiting the market, hence selling to the proposed acquirer. At that time, only three commercial banks were operating in the country. After the decision, the proposed seller remained in PNG and expanded its operations. The banking industry has since grown, and there are currently seven banks in PNG.

VIII. Advocacy and Policy Initiatives

A. *Outreach to Businesses and Consumers*

43. This is one of the key activities planned and undertaken every year. The ICCC hosts two annual forums called Consumer Protection and Competition Consultative Committee Meetings. The ICCC also seeks opportunities to speak on radio stations and to publish advertisements in newspapers. When announcing a determination on clearance and/or authorization applications, the ICCC also explains the relevant provisions and conduct in question. The ICCC also conducts specific awareness campaigns in various towns on cartels, bid rigging in public procurement, leniency policy, abuse of dominance, etc.

B. *Recent Policy Papers or Guidelines*

44. The ICCC has published a Leniency Policy, Business Acquisition Review Guidelines, and Confidentiality Claims Guidelines (on the process of handling confidential information submitted to the ICCC).

C. *Sectoral Studies or Market Inquiries*

45. The ICCC has recently undertaken a study into the aviation industry to assess the competitiveness of various supply chain segments and identify necessary actions to correct any market failures. The ICCC has recently released its draft report for public comment.

D. *Education and Capacity Building*

46. The ICCC provides support to its staff in accessing short training programs offered in workshops held by the International Competition Network (ICN), the Organisation for Economic Co-operation and Development (OECD), and Asia-Pacific Economic Cooperation (APEC), as well as through technical support from the Asian Development Bank (ADB).

IX. Regional and International Cooperation

A. *Regional Organizations*

47. The ICCC is a member of the PINCCER (Pacific Island Network of Competition Consumer and Economic Regulators). The Australian Competition and Consumer Commission (ACCC), together with the New Zealand Commerce Commission, serves as the Secretariat to the PINCCER.

B. *Bilateral/MoUs with Other Competition Authorities*

48. Through the PINCCER, the ICCC entered into a memorandum of understanding (MoU) with the Fiji Competition and Consumer Commission in 2023. This is the only bilateral MoU the ICCC has with other countries.

C. *Participation in Global Networks*

49. The ICCC is a member of the ICN and, at times, attends its workshops and webinars, especially for capacity-building purposes. The ICCC also attends OECD workshops for training purposes, mostly those hosted by the Korea Policy Center. Since PNG is an APEC member economy, the ICCC also attends and participates in workshops relating to competition, consumer protection and economic regulation.

X. Challenges and Country-Specific Features

A. *Small Market Size and High Concentration*

50. Highly concentrated markets include aviation, electricity, shipping and ports, poultry, and oil palm. Petroleum fuel product imports and refineries are also highly concentrated in PNG. The biggest challenge in some of these industries is the market size. For example, the aviation industry has two players providing domestic services, but only one that competes on international routes due to the limited inbound and outbound traffic volume. Potential new entrants did not find it attractive to enter because the incumbents have taken up the small size of the "pie." In other industries, such as telecommunications, it is the lack of innovation and growth among players that allows a single dominant player to control the market. This industry was once dominated by an SOE operator, but the ICCC introduced competition in 2007 when it issued operating licenses to potential new entrants.

B. *Dominance of Public Enterprises*

51. The SOEs dominate the electricity, ports and aviation industries. When the electricity industry was under the regulatory oversight of the ICCC, deregulation occurred in the generation segment. There are currently various independent power producers (IPPs) generating power and supplying it to PNG Power Limited (which is the dominant SOE). It purchases electricity and retails it to consumers through its established distribution centers and grids.

C. *Dependence on Imports/Foreign Investment*

52. PNG relies heavily on imports for almost all consumer goods. For local production, manufacturers import all producing plants and machines as well as the main ingredients for their production. The country also needs more foreign direct investment (FDI), and successive governments have maintained support for FDI. Such investments provide benefits, including employment opportunities and tax revenues, although the government sometimes grants tax incentives to attract FDI.

D. *Lack of Resources or Expertise*

53. Among the persistent challenges facing the ICCC are: (i) the financial support needed to implement its work plan in accordance with its mandates; and (ii) a lack of experienced and readily available local individuals who can be operational immediately upon recruitment. For officers recruited to the competition division in particular, it takes time to master the technical nature of assessing cases, planning and progressing investigations, and carrying out merger analysis. It also takes time for the ICCC to train and develop staff capacity. As the legal team is drawn from a general law background, it has been a real challenge to retain them after they have beend upskilled to a level where they can handle competition matters with limited guidance or supervision.

E. *Balancing Competition and Development Goals*

54. One of the areas where the government has tried to bypass competition law is FDI. Foreign investors want certain certainties and incentives for their investments, and they mostly ask for exemptions. Besides other laws, such as taxation, FDI at times asks for exclusivity. Since the ICCC Act is silent on FDI, the government sometimes comes up with legislation to exempt the application of the competition provisions of the ICCC Act. A case in point is in the petroleum fuel import and refinery market.

F. *Interplay with Traditional or Customary Economies*

55. Most small local businesses operate in informal markets. They trade by privately importing products and posting their goods on social media platforms and through networks of sales agents. One of the industries with a large number of market participants is the PMV. They sometimes go on strike, refraining from providing services, or collude to increase fares, and it is very challenging to apply competition law to the operators.

XI. Author's Perspective

56. It is my opinion that having more cases in court (regardless of the outcome) would really send a strong and clear message to everyone, especially policymakers, that competition is a great tool to improve consumer welfare and contribute to economic growth. However, to bring a case to court, the ICCC needs well-trained officers who can be able to (i) conduct a thorough investigation to collect relevant evidence, and (ii) analyze and provide sound economic analysis to support the case. I also think the provisions of competition laws should be simplified to ensure the burden of proof is placed more on the defendants.

XII. References and Resources

A. *Laws and Regulations*

- Independent Consumer and Competition Commission Act 2002

B. *Case Law*

(The ICCC v. Freedom Apex case is yet to be published)

C. *Public Reports*

- ENCYCLOPAEDIA BRITANNICA, *Papua New Guinea Summary*, https://www.britannica.com/summary/Papua-New-Guinea
- FAO, *Papua New Guinea Investment Proposal* (2025), https://www.fao.org/hand-in-hand/previous-editions/hih-investment-forum-2025/png/en
- GEORANK, *Papua New Guinea Statistics: Country Profile & Rankings* (Jan. 3, 2026), https://georank.org/facts/papua-new-guinea
- ICCC, PNG AVIATION SECTOR INQUIRY: DRAFT REPORT (NOV. 2025), https://iccc.gov.pg/wp-content/uploads/2025/12/Aviation-Industry-Inquiry_Draft-Report.pdf
- IMF data via Worldometer, https://www.worldometers.info/gdp/papua-new-guinea-gdp/
- NEW ZEALAND FOREIGN AFF. & TRADE, *Papua New Guinea: Trade and Economic Update as at December 2025* (2025), https://www.mfat.govt.nz/en/trade/mfat-market-reports/papua-new-guinea-trade-and-economic-update-as-at-december-2025
- NSO, *PNG GDP Rescheduled* (Nov. 4, 2025), https://www.nso.gov.pg/2025/11/04/release-of-2024-png-gdp-rescheduled/
- PNG OSAKA EXPO, *PNG Country Profile* (2025), https://www.pngosaka2025.gov.pg/papua-new-guinea-country-profile/
- TRADING ECONOMICS, *Papua New Guinea Balance of Trade* (2025), https://tradingeconomics.com/papua-new-guinea/balance-of-trade

D. *Articles or Books*

- Erehe, Roselyn, *PNG's Economic Outlook: Strong Growth Between Inflationary Challenges and Trade Surplus Surge*, PNG BUSINESS NEWS (Mar. 9, 2025) https://www.pngbusinessnews.com/articles/2025/3/png-s-economic-outlook-strong-growth-between-inflationary-challenges-and-trade-surplus-surge?utm_source=chatgpt.com

57. To learn more about the ICCC:
    - Website: www.iccc.gov.pg.
    - Contact: infor@iccc.gov.pg

Réunion

Odeya de La Mure, Jérôme Schall and Anne-Laure Vendrolini
French Competition Authority's Case Handlers

Supervised by Gwenaëlle Nouët
General Rapporteur at the French Competition Authority

I. Overview

1. The island of Réunion is located in the Indian Ocean, in the Southern Hemisphere, and forms part of the Mascarene Islands. It lies between Madagascar and Mauritius. Réunion has a total surface area of approximately 2,512 square kilometers. Politically, Réunion is a French overseas department and region, governed under Article 73 of the French Constitution[1], and is recognized as an outermost region of the European Union[2]. The official language of Réunion is French.

II. Demographics and Economy

2. Réunion had a population of approximately 896,200 inhabitants in 2024, corresponding to a population density of about 352 inhabitants per square kilometer. The nominal gross domestic product (GDP) of Réunion was estimated at approximately EUR 23.2 billion in 2024. The territory maintains a structural trade deficit, amounting to approximately EUR 6,724 million in 2024, reflecting a strong dependence on imports. In that year, imports totaled approximately EUR 7,137 million, while exports amounted to about EUR 413 million, resulting in a trade deficit that increased by 0.7 percent between 2023 and 2024.

3. Réunion's economy is predominantly service-oriented. In 2022, market services – including the digital economy, transportation, tourism, and personal and business services – accounted for approximately 49.8 percent of total value added, while non-market services such as health, education, and social services contributed around 36.2 percent. Construction and public works represented 6.1 percent, industry 4.6 percent, agriculture 1.7 percent, and energy 1.6 percent of the island's value added.

III. Legal Framework for Competition

4. Article 73 of the French Constitution establishes the principle of legislative identity. French competition law therefore applies automatically to overseas territories.

(For further details, please refer to the "Guadeloupe" chapter.)

IV. Institutional Structure

5. The Autorité de la concurrence (hereafter, the "French Competition Authority" or "FCA") was established in 2008 as a successor to the Conseil de la concurrence (French Competition Council).

(For details regarding the supervising body, organizational structure, additional regulatory mandates, budget, resources, and enforcement powers, please refer to the "Guadeloupe" chapter.)

---

1 Subject to the principle of legislative identity (French laws and regulations apply under the same conditions as in mainland France, unless otherwise specified by law or regulation).

2 These regions are an integral part of the EU. Therefore, EU law and all the rights and duties associated with EU membership apply to the outermost regions. In accordance with article 349 of the Treaty on the Functioning of the European Union, specific measures and provisions in EU legislation may be taken.

V. Enforcement and Sanctions

6. Since 2018, the FCA has issued approximately 10 decisions involving Réunion. These mainly concern anticompetitive agreements (2), abuse of a dominant position (3) and exclusive import rights (3). For instance:

   - Decision 22-D-21 of November 16, 2022, concerning practices implemented in the fisheries and aquaculture sector in Réunion (see below);
   - Decision 21-D-25 of November 2, 2021, concerning practices implemented in the molasses supply sector in Réunion (see below);
   - Decision 20-D-05 of March 23, 2020, concerning practices implemented in the military personnel relocation sector from Réunion: In this decision, the FCA sanctioned several moving companies for engaging in bid-rigging practices in the market for military relocations in Réunion. The investigation showed that the companies submitted "cover bids" rather than genuinely competing, in order to circumvent the regulatory requirement for military personnel to obtain two competing quotes for reimbursement purposes. Five companies and the parent companies of two of them were fined a total of EUR 162,000, with penalties set according to the seriousness of the conduct, the harm to the economy, and the individual situation of each company;
   - Decision 19-D-20 of October 8, 2019, concerning practices implemented in the distribution of perfumery and cosmetic products in the French West Indies, French Guiana, and Réunion: In this decision, the FCA fined several suppliers, importers and their parent companies for granting or benefiting from exclusive import rights for perfume and cosmetic products in the French overseas territories, in breach of article L. 420-2-1 of the French Commercial Code ("Lurel Law"). The infringements concerned products marketed by Procter & Gamble, Coty and Bourjois in Guadeloupe, Martinique, French Guiana and Réunion after March 22, 2013. The FCA imposed fines on both the suppliers that granted the exclusivities and the distributors that benefited from them, in accordance with the transaction procedure accepted by the parties;
   - Decision 18-D-03 of February 20, 2018, regarding practices implemented in the marketing of biocidal termite traps in Réunion, the French West Indies, and French Guiana (see "French Guiana" chapter).

7. Regarding Réunion, Parabole Réunion, Mediacom Ltd., and Radio Télévision brought an action for damages against Decision 11-D-12 of September 20, 2011. In the decision of the Paris Court of Appeal of June 16, 2025, No. 23/06193, Groupe Canal+, Canal+ France, and Canal+ Distribution were ordered to compensate Parabole Réunion, Mediacom Ltd., and Radio Télévision par Satellite for operating losses over two distinct periods, as well as for moral harm and damage to their reputation.

   (For information on fines, sanctions, and private enforcement, please refer to the "Guadeloupe" chapter.)

VI. Noteworthy Cases

A. *Decision 22-D-21 of November 16, 2022, concerning practices implemented in the fisheries and aquaculture sector in Réunion*

8. *Facts.* The FCA sanctioned the Réunion Interprofessional Fisheries and Aquaculture Association (ARIPA) for implementing practices contrary to article L. 420-1 of the Commercial Code. ARIPA member operators jointly set fish prices in the form of price guidelines applicable to all stages of the value chain, except – with a few exceptions – the end consumer. This practice was encouraged from the outset by ARIPA, regularly validated by its management committees and controlled in various ways, within the statutory bodies of both the professional families that are members of ARIPA and ARIPA itself.

9. In addition, ARIPA has undertaken to regulate Réunion's fish market by imposing a series of constraints on operators, which it describes as structuring measures. These measures include, in particular, a strict definition of authorized transactions according to the professional group to which operators belong, prior consultation and collective implementation of promotional operations, and various categories of interprofessional aid granted to member operators intended, as the case may be, to restrict or promote the sale of fish landed on the local market.

10. The FCA considered that all these measures constituted a complex and ongoing infringement whose purpose was to restrict the commercial autonomy of operators in this sector.

11. *Legal issue.* Breach of article L. 420-1 of the Commercial Code prohibiting anti-competitive agreements/settlement procedure/financial penalty. ARIPA requested that the FCA grant it the benefit of the settlement procedure, pursuant to the provisions of paragraph III of article L. 464-2 of the Commercial Code.

12. The FCA considered that a penalty of EUR 60,000 should be imposed on ARIPA.

13. *Outcome.* The decision is final and has not been appealed within the legal time limits.

B. *Decision 21-D-25 of November 2, 2021, concerning practices implemented in the molasses supply sector in Réunion*

14. *Facts.* The FCA sanctioned Tereos Océan Indien (hereafter "TOI"), a subsidiary of the Tereos Group, for abusing its dominant position in the market for the supply of molasses produced from sugar cane from Réunion to local distilleries.

15. Molasses is a by-product of sugar production. It is used in particular by distilleries in Réunion to produce rum, which is known as traditional rum or sugar-mill rum. TOI owns the only two sugar factories on Réunion Island. As such, it is the sole supplier of molasses produced from local sugar cane.

16. The FCA concluded that TOI abused its dominant position by including, in its supply contracts with two of the distilleries, including DSAV, restrictive clauses that undermine free competition. The FCA considered that these clauses contributed to locking up the

market and preventing distilleries from renegotiating the terms of their molasses supply and therefore constituted an abuse of a dominant position on the part of TOI.

17. *Legal issue.* Breach of article L. 420-2 of the Commercial Code prohibiting abuse of a dominant position/simplified procedure.

18. The FCA therefore imposed a fine of EUR 750,000 on TOI, jointly and severally with its two subsidiaries, Sucrière de La Réunion and Sucrerie de Bois Rouge, after having applied the legal ceiling then provided for in article L. 464-5 of the Commercial Code for simplified procedures.

19. *Outcome.* The Paris Court of Appeal upheld the FCA's decision by judgment of July 3, 2025. An appeal to the Court of Cassation is pending.

VII. Merger Control

20. As with antitrust law, French merger control applies in Réunion. However, the French Commercial Code lays down specific rules for mergers concerning overseas territories in article L. 430-2, III.

21. Examples of notified mergers:
    - Decision 20-DCC-34 of March 4, 2020, relating to the acquisition of sole control of Teralta Ciment Réunion and Teralta Granulat Béton Réunion by Entreprise Audemard: Thresholds of article L. 430-2, I / Construction materials sector / Clearance decision;
    - Decision 15-DCC-142 of October 20, 2015, regarding the joint acquisition of control of Telecom Réunion Mayotte by Iliad and the Hiridjee Group: Thresholds of article L. 430-2, I / Telecommunications sector / Clearance decision;
    - Decision 15-DCC-104 of July 30, 2015, concerning the acquisition of sole control of Société Réunionnaise de Produits Pétroliers by Rubis: Thresholds of article L. 430-2, I / Petroleum-product storage and liquefied petroleum gas filling sectors / Clearance decision subject to remedies.

(For information on notification thresholds and review timeframes, please refer to the "Guadeloupe" chapter.)

VIII. Advocacy and Policy Initiatives

22. With particular regard to the Indian Ocean region, the FCA issued an opinion in 2018 on construction materials in Réunion and Mayotte (Opinion 18-A-09 of October 3, 2018).

(For information on sectoral studies or market inquiries, recent policy papers or guidelines, and outreach to businesses and consumers, please refer to the "Guadeloupe" chapter.)

IX. Regional and International Cooperation

(See the "Guadeloupe" chapter)

X. Challenges and Country-Specific Features

A. *Small Market Size and High Concentration*

23. In its Opinion 18-A-09 of October 3, 2018, concerning the competitive situation in the construction materials markets in Mayotte and Réunion, the FCA noted, with regard to Réunion:

Regardless of the material considered, the number of significant operators is small, often limited to two (for cement, for example) or three. These long-standing players enjoy an economic and cultural advantage over potential new entrants. While this concentration can be explained in part by the market's insularity and narrowness, according to the DGCCRF [Directorate General for Competition Policy, Consumer Affairs and Fraud Control] investigation report, it is undoubtedly also linked to "barriers that may be erected to access certain markets." Such concentration is conducive to closing markets to new players and restricting the flow of information, a situation further exacerbated by capital and family ties.[3]

(For further details, please refer to the "Guadeloupe" chapter.)

B. *Dependence on Imports/Foreign Investment*

24. According to IEDOM's annual report for 2024, "[l]ike other overseas departments and most island economies, the economy of Réunion relies heavily on imports for its supplies of goods and raw materials. Its trade balance is therefore structurally in deficit. Mainland France is also its primary trading partner."[4]

25. In its Opinion 19-A-12 of July 4, 2019, the FCA indicated:

> Martinique, Guadeloupe, French Guiana, and Réunion continue to suffer from a significant trade imbalance. For Martinique, Guadeloupe, and Réunion, this imbalance is not explained by the level of their imports, which is comparable to that of mainland France, but by the level of their exports, which is much lower than the national average. . . . Finally, despite the distance, the bulk of the French overseas departments' trade – both imports and exports – is conducted with mainland France.[5]

26. Local production represents only a minority share of the supply for wholesalers and distributors in the French overseas territories. This situation, which has persisted since 2009, can be explained, on the one hand, for certain categories of products, by the absence or insufficiency of local supply, and on the other hand, where such production does exist, by the lack of competitiveness of locally produced goods compared to imported substitute goods, despite the costs of access and the overseas tax. As previously noted by the FCA in 2009, the primary cause of the lack of competitiveness in local

---

3 FCA, Opinion 18-A-09 of Oct. 3, 2018, para. 85 (in French) (our translation).

4 IEDOM, Annual Economic Report of Réunion 2024, p. 48 (June 2025) (in French) (our translation), https://www.iedom.fr/Rapport-annuel-economique-de-La-Reunion-2024.

5 FCA, Opinion 19-A-12 of July 4, 2019, paras. 21–22 (in French) (our translation).

production lies in the small size of overseas markets, which prevents local producers from achieving economies of scale.

27. Several stakeholders point to the burden of fixed costs and the underutilization of production capacity. Producers also cite, among the factors hindering their competitiveness, the distance, which increases the cost of raw materials, and higher construction costs compared to mainland France. In Réunion, where the industrial sector is more developed than in the other French overseas departments and regions (DROM), the lack of local alternatives mainly concerns certain product categories (for example, hygiene and cleaning products and certain food products such as canned goods, frozen foods, and organic products). However, an association of producers in Réunion believes that the local industry's situation has deteriorated compared to 2009, particularly due to the gradual withdrawal of several favorable tax measures.

C. *Lack of Resources or Expertise*

28. In its Opinion 18-A-09 of October 3, 2018, the FCA analyzed the competitive situation in the construction materials markets in Mayotte and Réunion. The FCA observed significant price differentials compared to mainland France for construction materials, as well as very high profit margins for certain products. It concluded that the additional costs identified could be explained, for all the materials concerned, by the high cost of transportation, the specific tax on imported goods (*octroi de mer*), storage difficulties linked in particular to land scarcity, and the requirements for standardization and certification of processes and materials, which are sometimes poorly adapted to the specificities of the French overseas territories. It also noted the existence of other more specific factors, such as high degrees of horizontal concentration and vertical integration in certain markets.

(The balancing of competition with development goals is addressed in the "Guadeloupe" chapter.)

XI. References and Resources

A. *Laws and Regulations*

- Book IV of the legislative part of the French Commercial Code: On Freedom of Prices and Competition (arts. L. 410-1 to L. 490-14) (in French)
- Book IV of the regulatory part of the French Commercial Code: On Freedom of Prices and Competition (arts. R. 410-1 to R. 490-10) (in French)

B. *Case Law*

- FCA, Decision 22-D-21 of Nov. 16, 2022, concerning practices implemented in the fisheries and aquaculture sector in Réunion (in French)
- FCA, Decision 21-D-25 of Nov. 2, 2021, concerning practices implemented in the molasses supply sector in Réunion (in French)
- FCA, Decision 20-D-05 of Mar. 23, 2020, concerning practices implemented in the military personnel relocation sector from Réunion (in French)

- FCA Decision 20-DCC-34 of Mar. 4, 2020, relating to the acquisition of sole control of Teralta Ciment Réunion and Teralta Granulat Béton Réunion by Entreprise Audemard (in French)
- FCA, Decision 19-D-20 of Oct. 8, 2019, concerning practices implemented in the distribution of perfumery and cosmetic products in the French West Indies, French Guiana, and Réunion (in French)
- FCA, Decision 18-D-03 of Feb. 20, 2018, regarding practices implemented in the marketing of biocidal termite traps in Réunion, the French West Indies, and French Guiana (in French)
- FCA, Decision 16-D-09 of May 12, 2016, concerning practices implemented in the sectors of metal reinforcements and welded mesh on Réunion Island (in French)
- FCA, Decision 15-DCC-142 of Oct. 20, 2015, regarding the joint acquisition of control of Telecom Réunion Mayotte by Iliad and the Hiridjee Group (in French)
- FCA, Decision 15-DCC-104 of July 30, 2015, concerning the acquisition of sole control of Société Réunionnaise de Produits Pétroliers by Rubis (in French)
- FCA, Decision 14-DCC-15 of Feb. 10, 2014, concerning the acquisition of sole control of Mediaserv, Martinique Numérique, Guyane Numérique, and La Réunion Numérique by Canal Plus Overseas (in French)
- FCA, Decision 11-D-12 of Sept. 20, 2011, on the fulfillment of the commitments set out in the decision authorizing the acquisition of TPS and CanalSatellite by Vivendi Universal and the Canal Plus Group (in French)
- CA Paris [Paris Court of Appeal], June 16, 2025, No. 23/06193 (in French)

C. *Public Reports*

- IEDOM, Annual Economic Report of Réunion 2024 (June 2025) (in French), https://www.iedom.fr/Rapport-annuel-economique-de-La-Reunion-2024
- IEDOM, Large-scale Food Retailing in Réunion (July 2020) (in French), https://www.iedom.fr/La-grande-distribution-alimentaire-a-La-Reunion-de-bonnes-performances
- FCA, Opinion 26-A-01 of Feb. 10, 2026, concerning the margins of wholesale importers and distributors of essential food products in Martinique (in French)
- FCA, Opinion 19-A-12 of July 4, 2019, regarding the functioning of competition in the French overseas territories (in French)
- FCA, Opinion 18-A-09 of Oct. 3, 2018, concerning the competitive situation in the construction materials markets in Mayotte and Réunion (in French)
- FCA, Opinion 09-A-45 of Sept. 8, 2009, concerning the mechanisms for importing and distributing consumer goods in overseas departments (in French)

29. To learn more about the French Competition Authority (FCA):
Website: https://www.autoritedelaconcurrence.fr/
Contact: communication@autoritedelaconcurrence.fr

Saint-Barthélemy

Odeya de La Mure, Jérôme Schall and Anne-Laure Vendrolini
French Competition Authority's Case Handlers

Supervised by Gwenaëlle Nouët
General Rapporteur at the French Competition Authority

I. Overview

1. The island of Saint-Barthélemy is located between the Caribbean Sea and the Atlantic Ocean, in the Northern Hemisphere, and forms part of the Lesser Antilles archipelago. It has a total surface area of approximately 21 square kilometers. Politically, Saint-Barthélemy is a French overseas collectivity, governed under Article 74 of the French Constitution[1]. In 2007, it transitioned from being a commune in the department of Guadeloupe to a French overseas collectivity. The official language of Saint-Barthélemy is French.

II. Demographics and Economy

2. Saint-Barthélemy had a population of approximately 10,562 inhabitants in 2021, corresponding to a population density of about 503 inhabitants per square kilometer. The nominal gross domestic product (GDP) of the island was estimated at approximately EUR 367 million in 2014. The territory maintains a structural trade deficit, reflecting its reliance on imports. The economy of Saint-Barthélemy is predominantly tourism-oriented. In 2024, the main employment sectors were accommodation and food services (33.6%), construction (19.4%), other market services (21.7%), and retail (15.4%).

III. Legal Framework for Competition

3. According to article LO 6213-1 of the General Code for Local Authorities, "[l]egislative and regulatory provisions are automatically applicable in Saint-Barthélemy, with the exception of those relating to matters governed by organic law pursuant to article 74 of the Constitution or falling within the jurisdiction of the local authority pursuant to article LO 6214-3."[2] As competition law does not fall within the reserved jurisdiction of Saint-Barthélemy, the French Commercial Code is automatically applicable there.

   (For further details, please refer to the "Guadeloupe" chapter.)

IV. Institutional Structure

4. The Autorité de la concurrence (hereafter, the "French Competition Authority" or "FCA") was established in 2008 as a successor to the Conseil de la concurrence (French Competition Council).

   (For details regarding the supervising body, organizational structure, additional regulatory mandates, budget, resources, and enforcement powers, please refer to the "Guadeloupe" chapter.)

---

1. It has an ad hoc status defined by organic law, and its own normative power in certain areas covered by law or regulations (French laws and regulations are not automatically applicable under the same conditions as in mainland France).
2. Our translation.

V. Enforcement and Sanctions

5. Since 2009, the FCA has issued only a few decisions involving Saint-Barthélemy:
   - Decision 20-D-16 of October 29, 2020, concerning practices implemented in the champagne marketing sector in the French West Indies and French Guiana (see the "Saint-Martin" chapter);
   - Decision 16-D-15 of July 6, 2016, relating to practices implemented in the distribution sector for consumer goods in overseas territories (see below);
   - Decision 15-D-14 of September 10, 2015, on the practices implemented by Bolton Solitaire SAS, Danone SA, Johnson & Johnson Santé et Beauté France SAS, and Pernod-Ricard SA in the distribution of consumer goods overseas: Following two *ex officio* referrals, the FCA has obtained from several manufacturers (Bolton Solitaire, Danone, Johnson & Johnson Santé et Beauté France, and Pernod-Ricard) the removal of all exclusivity in the distribution of their products overseas;
   - Decision 13-D-15 of June 25, 2013, concerning practices implemented in the maritime freight transport sector between Northern Europe and the French West Indies (see below).

(For information on fines, sanctions, and private enforcement, please refer to the "Guadeloupe" chapter.)

VI. Noteworthy Cases

A. *Decision 16-D-15 of July 6, 2016, relating to practices implemented in the distribution sector for consumer goods in overseas territories*

6. *Facts.* The FCA fines Henkel and several importers of its products in La Réunion, the Antilles, Guiana and the Wallis and Futuna Islands approximately EUR 615,000 for implementing exclusive import contracts between March 2013 and February 2016.

7. The extension of exclusive import contracts beyond the date set by law – namely, March 22, 2013 – in contracts between Henkel and its wholesalers led the FCA to impose fines.

8. *Legal issue.* Breach of article L. 420-2-1 of the Commercial Code/financial penalties.

9. The fine is divided as follows: (i) EUR 250,000 for Henkel, (ii) EUR 210,000 for importers of Henkel products in La Réunion, (iii) EUR 140,000 for importers of Henkel products in the Antilles and Guiana, and (iv) EUR 15,000 for the importer of Henkel products in the Wallis and Futuna Islands.

10. Companies involved have not issued a statement of objection and have been able to benefit from the settlement procedure introduced in 2015 by the Law of August 6, 2015.

11. *Outcome.* This decision is final; no appeal was filed within the legal time limits.

12. *Impact or precedent set.* Opinion 13-A-20 of November 7, 2013, concerning the project to expand the main food distribution store in Saint-Barthélemy

13. *Facts.* The prefect delegated to the French State Representative in Saint-Barthélemy and Saint-Martin, president of the Territorial Commission for Commercial Development, has submitted a request to the FCA for an opinion regarding the proposed expansion of the main food retail store in Saint-Barthélemy, pursuant to article L. 752-6-1 of the Commercial Code.

14. *Legal issue.* The competitive risks associated with this expansion therefore appear very limited and cannot justify its *ex ante* prohibition on this basis.

B. *Decision 13-D-15 of June 25, 2013, concerning practices implemented in the maritime freight transport sector between Northern Europe and the French West Indies*

15. *Facts.* Maritime freight transport between Northern Europe, particularly French ports, and the Caribbean is the primary route for imports and exports. On this route, 90% of trade (excluding fuel) is handled by CMA-CGM, which shares its transport capacity with its competitors. Specifically, CMA-CGM leases space on its vessels to other companies to transport their containers. CMA-CGM has signed space leasing agreements with Maersk, Marfret, and WEC Lines.

16. During the investigation, it emerged that certain contractual clauses between CMA-CGM and Maersk, Marfret, and WEC Lines were highly restrictive and led to sluggish competition. These clauses limited the companies' ability to adapt to demand and may have hindered the entry of new operators into the market. The combined effect of all these restrictive clauses could result in prices 10% to 25% higher than the average rates charged by companies operating on similar routes.

17. In particular, the FCA considered the following to be problematic:
   - the exclusivity clauses between Maersk, Marfret, and WEC Lines and CMA-CGM, which prohibited them from loading their containers onto a vessel competing with CMA-CGM;
   - the lack of transparency in the capacity allocation mechanism;
   - the inability of Maersk, Marfret, and WEC Lines to resell unused reserved capacity to third parties; and
   - the indefinite duration of the contracts binding the companies to CMA-CGM.

18. *Legal issue.* Application of article L. 464-2 of the Commercial Code providing for a commitment procedure. After receiving the FCA's competition concerns, CMA-CGM, Maersk, Marfret, and WEC Lines proposed to modify their practices. The four companies presented joint commitments, which were improved during discussions with the FCA.

19. In particular, the companies committed to:
   - removing all exclusivity clauses;
   - ensuring that CMA-CGM allocates leasing capacity according to predefined rules;
   - allowing CMA-CGM's co-contractors to resell unused capacity to third parties;
   - preempting unused capacity – if CMA-CGM has the option and under certain conditions – with this right being strictly regulated under the supervision of an independent agent;

- limiting the duration of contracts to two years with the possibility of terminating or renegotiating the terms of the contract at any time; and
- informing any new entrants of available capacity.

VII. Merger Control

20. As with antitrust law, French merger control applies in Saint-Barthélemy. However, the French Commercial Code lays down specific rules for mergers concerning overseas territories in article L. 430-2, III.

21. Examples of notified mergers:
    - Decision 24-DCC-11 of February 5, 2024, concerning the acquisition of sole control of Centre auto SBH, Turbe car rental, and Turbe car rental II by Socipar: Thresholds of article L. 430-2, III / Automotive distribution sector / Clearance decision;
    - Decision 23-DCC-243 of December 19, 2023, relating to the acquisition of sole control of PBS Auto by Socipar: Thresholds of article L. 430-2, III / Automotive distribution sector / Clearance decision
    - Decision 22-DCC-35 of April 27, 2022, concerning the acquisition of sole control of Bio Pôle Antilles by the Inovie Group: Thresholds of article L. 430-2, III / Medical biology sector / Clearance decision subject to remedies.

(For information on notification thresholds and review timeframes, please refer to the "Guadeloupe" chapter.)

VIII. Advocacy and Policy Initiatives

22. With particular regard to Saint-Barthélemy, the FCA issued an opinion in 2011 on regulatory measures issued by the French Telecommunications and Posts Regulator (ARCEP) regarding access to the submarine cables (Opinion 11-A-08 of June 10, 2011).

(For information on sectoral studies or market inquiries, recent policy papers or guidelines, and outreach to businesses and consumers, please refer to the "Guadeloupe" chapter.)

IX. Regional and International Cooperation

(See the "Guadeloupe" chapter)

X. Challenges and Country-Specific Features

A. *Dependence on Imports/Foreign Investment*

23. According to IEDOM's annual report for 2024:

> Due to its status as an OCT (Overseas Country and Territory), Saint-Barthélemy's foreign trade is not subject to European Union rules. Thus, customs statistical services do not track the territory's imports and exports, except those with France. However, a large portion of Saint-Barthélemy's foreign trade is with the United States. …Goods imported into Saint-Barthélemy come primarily

from the United States, via Tropical Shipping, and from mainland France, via CMA-CGM, whose goods first transit through Guadeloupe. In addition, Saint-Barthélemy receives imports from the ports of Saint-Martin.[3]

XI. References and Resources

A. *Laws and Regulations*

- Book IV of the legislative part of the French Commercial Code: On Freedom of Prices and Competition (arts. L. 410-1 to L. 490-14) (in French)
- Book IV of the regulatory part of the French Commercial Code: On Freedom of Prices and Competition (arts. R. 410-1 to R. 490-10) (in French)

B. *Case Law*

- FCA, Decision 24-DCC-11 of Feb. 5, 2024, concerning the acquisition of sole control of Centre auto SBH, Turbe car rental, and Turbe car rental II by Socipar (in French)
- FCA, Decision 23-DCC-243 of Dec. 19, 2023, relating to the acquisition of sole control of PBS Auto by Socipar (in French)
- FCA, Decision 22-DCC-35 of Apr. 27, 2022, concerning the acquisition of sole control of Bio Pôle Antilles by the Inovie Group (in French)
- FCA, Decision 20-D-16 of Oct. 29, 2020, concerning practices implemented in the champagne marketing sector in the French West Indies and French Guiana (in French)
- FCA, Decision 16-D-15 of July 6, 2016, relating to practices implemented in the distribution sector for consumer goods in overseas territories (in French)
- FCA, Decision 15-D-14 of Sep. 10, 2015, on the practices implemented by Bolton Solitaire SAS, Danone SA, Johnson & Johnson Santé et Beauté France SAS, and Pernod-Ricard SA in the distribution of consumer goods overseas (in French)
- FCA, Decision 13-D-15 of June 25, 2013, concerning practices implemented in the maritime freight transport sector between Northern Europe and the French West Indies (in French)

C. *Public Reports*

- IEDOM, Annual Economic Report of Saint-Barthélemy 2024 (Oct. 2025) (in French), https://www.iedom.fr/Rapport-annuel-economique-de-Saint-Barthelemy-2024
- FCA, Opinion 26-A-01 of Feb. 10, 2026, concerning the margins of wholesale importers and distributors of essential food products in Martinique (in French)

---

[3] IEDOM, Annual Economic Report of Saint-Barthélemy 2024, p. 39, 76 (Oct. 2025) (in French) (our translation), https://www.iedom.fr/Rapport-annuel-economique-de-Saint-Barthelemy-2024.

- FCA, Opinion19-A-12 of July 4, 2019, concerning the functioning of competition in the French overseas territories (in French)
- FCA, Opinion 13-A-20 of Nov. 7, 2013, concerning the project to expand the main food distribution store in Saint-Barthélemy (in French)
- FCA, Opinion 11-A-08 of June 10, 2011, concerning a request for an opinion from the Electronic Communications and Postal Regulatory Authority (ARCEP) on the wholesale markets for inter-territorial long-distance services relating to the local authorities of Saint-Martin and Saint-Barthélemy (in French)
- FCA, Opinion 09-A-45 of Sept. 8, 2009, concerning the mechanisms for importing and distributing consumer goods in overseas departments (in French)

24. To learn more about the French Competition Authority (FCA):

Website: https://www.autoritedelaconcurrence.fr/

Contact: communication@autoritedelaconcurrence.fr

Saint-Martin

Odeya de La Mure, Jérôme Schall and Anne-Laure Vendrolini
French Competition Authority's Case Handlers

Supervised by Gwenaëlle Nouët
General Rapporteur at the French Competition Authority

I. Overview

1. The island of Saint-Martin is located between the Caribbean Sea and the Atlantic Ocean in the Northern Hemisphere and forms part of the Lesser Antilles archipelago. The island is divided between two countries by a 10-kilometer border, with the French side in the north and the Dutch side in the south, the latter being an autonomous state within the Kingdom of the Netherlands since October 10, 2010. The French part of Saint-Martin covers approximately 53 square kilometers of the island's total 93 square kilometers. Politically, Saint-Martin is a French overseas collectivity, governed under Article 74 of the French Constitution[1], and is recognized as an outermost region of the European Union. It changed its status from a commune of the department of Guadeloupe to a French overseas collectivity in 2007. The official language of Saint-Martin is French.

II. Demographics and Economy

2. Saint-Martin had a population of approximately 31,500 inhabitants in 2021, corresponding to a population density of about 594.3 inhabitants per square kilometer in 2022. The nominal gross domestic product (GDP) of the island was estimated at approximately EUR 550 million in 2022. The territory maintains a structural trade deficit, reflecting its dependence on imports. Saint-Martin's economy is predominantly service-oriented, with a strong focus on tourism. Non-market services contribute about one-third of total value added, while sectors partially linked to tourism – such as transportation, accommodation and food services, and trade – account for approximately 19.3 percent. The real estate and construction sectors represent 12.3 percent and 6.5 percent of value added, respectively.

III. Legal Framework for Competition

3. According to article LO 6313-1 of the General Code for Local Authorities, "[l]egislative and regulatory provisions are automatically applicable in Saint-Martin, with the exception of those relating to matters governed by organic law pursuant to article 74 of the Constitution or falling within the jurisdiction of the local authority pursuant to article LO 6314-3."[2] As competition law does not fall within the reserved jurisdiction of Saint-Martin, the French Commercial Code is automatically applicable there.

(For further details, please refer to the "Guadeloupe" chapter.)

IV. Institutional Structure

4. The Autorité de la concurrence (hereafter, the "French Competition Authority" or "FCA") was established in 2008 as a successor to the Conseil de la concurrence (French Competition Council).

---

1 It has an ad hoc status defined by organic law, and its own normative power in certain areas covered by law or regulations (French laws and regulations are not automatically applicable under the same conditions as in mainland France).

2 Our translation.

(For details regarding the supervising body, organizational structure, additional regulatory mandates, budget, resources, and enforcement powers, please refer to the "Guadeloupe" chapter.)

V. Enforcement and Sanctions

5. Since 2018, the FCA has issued only two decisions involving Saint-Martin:
   - Decision 24-D-10 of December 4, 2024, concerning practices implemented in the inter-island passenger air transport sector (see the "Guadeloupe" chapter);
   - Decision 20-D-16 of October 29, 2020, concerning practices implemented in the champagne marketing sector in the French West Indies and French Guiana (see below).

(For information on fines, sanctions, and private enforcement, please refer to the "Guadeloupe" chapter.)

VI. Noteworthy Cases

A. *Decision 20-D-16 of October 29, 2020, concerning practices implemented in the champagne marketing sector in the French West Indies and French Guiana*

6. *Facts.* The FCA first condemned the Centre Vinicole Champagne Nicolas Feuillatte (hereinafter "CVC-NF") and Financière Martin for having, from March 22, 2013, to January 1, 2015, in the case of the former, granted exclusive import rights for its "Nicolas Feuillatte" and "Palmes d'Or" champagnes and, in the case of the latter, benefited from these rights on the islands of Saint-Martin and Saint-Barthélemy.

7. These rights, which resulted from an exclusive distribution agreement concluded in 2011, continued to be contractually stipulated after March 22, 2013, in violation of article L. 420-2-1 of the Commercial Code, inserted by Law No. 2012-1270 of November 20, 2012, on overseas economic regulation, known as the "Lurel" law, which prohibits agreements or concerted practices having the object or effect of granting exclusive import rights to an undertaking or group of undertakings in the overseas collectivities.

8. The FCA also condemns CVC-NF and Distillerie Dillon, as perpetrators, and Bardinet SAS and Compagnie Européenne de Prises de Participation (hereinafter "COFEPP SA"), in their capacity as parent companies, for having, from March 22, 2013, to December 31, 2014, in the case of the former, granted – under a contract concluded in 2010 – exclusive import rights for its "Nicolas Feuillatte" and "Palmes d'Or" champagnes, and, in the case of the latter, having benefited from these rights in the territory of Martinique.

9. The case file also revealed that following the entry into force of a new agreement that did not include an exclusive import clause, CVC-NF and Distillerie Dillon agreed to maintain, from January 1, 2015, to June 28, 2016, the exclusive right to import Nicolas Feuillatte products into Martinique for the benefit of the former, again in violation of article L. 420-2-1 of the Commercial Code.

10. These agreements and practices were not eligible for the exemption provided for in paragraph III of article L. 420-4 of the Commercial Code, as the companies in question failed to provide evidence that consumers could derive a fair share of the profit that would result from such exclusive import rights.

11. *Legal issue.* Breach of article L. 420-2-1 of the Commercial Code/financial penalties

12. The following financial penalties were imposed: (i) on CVC-NF, a penalty of EUR 216,600; (ii) on Financière Martin, a penalty of EUR 5,200; (iii) on Distillerie Dillon, jointly and severally with Bardinet SAS and COFEPP SA, in their capacity as parent companies, a fine of EUR 421,000.

13. *Outcome.* In its judgment of June 9, 2022, the Paris Court of Appeal confirmed the decision in substance while partially reversing it by reducing the amount of the penalty.

14. *Impact or precedent set.* This is the eighth decision issued by the FCA concerning exclusive import practices in overseas territories.

VII. Merger Control

15. As with antitrust law, French merger control applies in Saint-Martin. However, the French Commercial Code lays down specific rules for mergers concerning overseas territories in article L. 430-2, III.

16. Examples of notified mergers:

   - Decision 22-DCC-35 of April 27, 2022, concerning the acquisition of sole control of Bio Pôle Antilles by the Inovie Group: Thresholds of article L. 430-2, III / Medical biology sector / Clearance decision subject to remedies;
   - Decision 16-DCC-155 of October 14, 2016, concerning the acquisition of sole control of Geimex by the Casino Group: Thresholds of article L. 430-2, I / Food distribution sector / Clearance decision subject to remedies.

(For information on notification thresholds and review timeframes, please refer to the "Guadeloupe" chapter.)

VIII. Advocacy and Policy Initiatives

17. With particular regard to Saint-Martin, the FCA issued an opinion in 2011 on regulatory measures issued by the French Telecommunications and Posts Regulator (ARCEP) regarding access to the submarine cables (Opinion 11-A-08 of June 10, 2011).

(For information on sectoral studies or market inquiries, recent policy papers or guidelines, and outreach to businesses and consumers, please refer to the "Guadeloupe" chapter.)

IX. Regional and International Cooperation

18. Saint-Martin is an associate member of the Organisation of Eastern Caribbean States (OECS).

(For information on regional organizations, bilateral MoUs and participation in global networks, please refer to the "Guadeloupe" chapter.)

X. Challenges and Country-Specific Features

A. *Dominance of Public Enterprises*

19. The Energy Code of the Collectivity of Saint-Martin recognizes EDF as the sole operator for the supply and distribution of electricity.

20. Moreover, since 2006, the Saint-Martin Water and Sanitation Authority (EEASM) has been responsible for water and collective and non-collective sanitation on the territory of Saint-Martin. It owns the infrastructure (plants, stations and networks) and is responsible for investments. The EEASM is a public industrial and commercial establishment (EPIC) of the Collectivity of Saint-Martin, created in 2006.

21. Finally, the Saint-Martin mixed-economy company (SEMSAMAR), of which the local authority of Saint-Martin is the main shareholder, is responsible for land-use planning.

B. *Lack of Resources or Expertise*

22. Saint-Martin is a non-interconnected zone (ZNI), dependent on hydrocarbon imports, particularly by sea. The size of the electrical grid, as well as the specific technologies used for its implementation and management, is a factor that leads to electricity production and supply costs that are consistently higher than in mainland France.

23. Despite the availability of numerous jobs, Saint-Martin's tourism sector suffers from a shortage of skilled local labor due to a lack of appropriate training on the island. Training programs, most of which are offered in Guadeloupe, do not always meet the specific needs of the region or those of its residents, who are predominantly English-speaking. This labor shortage, combined with an insufficient supply of hotel rooms, puts the French part of the island at a disadvantage compared to the Dutch part, whose accommodation better meets the expectations of an increasingly demanding clientele, mainly of North American origin.

XI. References and Resources

A. *Laws and Regulations*

- Book IV of the legislative part of the French Commercial Code: On Freedom of Prices and Competition (arts. L. 410-1 to L. 490-14) (in French)
- Book IV of the regulatory part of the French Commercial Code: On Freedom of Prices and Competition (arts. R. 410-1 to R. 490-10) (in French)

B. *Case Law*

- FCA, Decision 24-D-10 of Dec. 4, 2024, concerning practices implemented in the inter-island passenger air transport sector (in French)
- FCA, Decision 22-DCC-35 of Apr. 27, 2022, concerning the acquisition of sole control of Bio Pôle Antilles by the Inovie Group (in French)
- FCA, Decision 20-D-16 of Oct. 29, 2020, concerning practices implemented in the champagne marketing sector in the French West Indies and French Guiana (in French)

- FCA, Decision 16-DCC-155 of Oct. 14, 2016, concerning the acquisition of sole control of Geimex by the Casino Group (in French)
- CA Paris [Paris Court of Appeal], June 9, 2022 RG n° 20/16288(in French)

C. *Public Reports*

- IEDOM, ANNUAL ECONOMIC REPORT OF SAINT-MARTIN 2024 (Oct. 2025) (in French), https://www.iedom.fr/Rapport-annuel-economique-de-Saint-Martin-2024?lang=fr
- FCA, Opinion 26-A-01 of Feb. 10, 2026, concerning the margins of wholesale importers and distributors of essential food products in Martinique (in French)
- FCA, Opinion19-A-12 of July 4, 2019, concerning the functioning of competition in the French overseas territories (in French)
- FCA, Opinion 11-A-08 of June 10, 2011, concerning a request for an opinion from the Electronic Communications and Postal Regulatory Authority (ARCEP) on the wholesale markets for inter-territorial long-distance services relating to the local authorities of Saint-Martin and Saint-Barthélemy (in French)
- FCA, Opinion 09-A-45 of Sept. 8, 2009, concerning the mechanisms for importing and distributing consumer goods in overseas departments (in French)

24. To learn more about the French Competition Authority (FCA):
Website: https://www.autoritedelaconcurrence.fr/
Contact: communication@autoritedelaconcurrence.fr

Saint-Pierre and Miquelon

Odeya de La Mure, Jérôme Schall and Anne-Laure Vendrolini
French Competition Authority's Case Handlers

Supervised by Gwenaëlle Nouët
General Rapporteur at the French Competition Authority

I. Overview

1. The archipelago of Saint-Pierre and Miquelon is located in the Atlantic Ocean, off the coast of Newfoundland, near North America. It has a total surface area of approximately 242 square kilometers. Politically, Saint-Pierre and Miquelon is a French overseas collectivity, governed under Article 74 of the French Constitution[1]. Over time, it changed its status from a French overseas territory to an overseas department in 1976, then to a collectivity with special status in 1985, before becoming a French overseas collectivity in 2007. The official language of Saint-Pierre and Miquelon is French.

II. Demographics and Economy

2. Saint-Pierre and Miquelon had a population of approximately 5,819 inhabitants in 2024, corresponding to a population density of about 24.3 inhabitants per square kilometer. The archipelago is characterized by a very low overall population density, with a marked difference between Saint-Pierre (201 inhabitants per square kilometer) and Miquelon-Langlade (3 inhabitants per square kilometer). The nominal gross domestic product (GDP) of the archipelago was estimated at approximately EUR 0.24 billion in 2023.

3. The territory maintains a structural trade deficit, amounting to approximately EUR 94 million in 2024, reflecting a strong reliance on imports. In that year, imports totaled approximately EUR 97.6 million, while exports amounted to about EUR 3.6 million, with a decrease in the trade deficit observed between 2023 and 2024. Saint-Pierre and Miquelon's economy is predominantly service-oriented. In 2015, the tertiary sector accounted for approximately 88 percent of total value added, with public administration contributing 45.3 percent and commerce 11.4 percent. The energy and industrial sectors represented 5.6 percent of value added, while primary sectors, including agriculture, livestock, and fishing, generated less than 1 percent.

III. Legal Framework for Competition

4. According to article LO 6413-1 of the General Code for Local Authorities, "[l]egislative and regulatory provisions are automatically applicable in Saint-Pierre and Miquelon, with the exception of those relating to matters governed by organic law pursuant to article 74 of the Constitution or to matters falling within the jurisdiction of the local authority pursuant to article LO 6414-1(II)."[2]As competition law does not fall within the reserved jurisdiction of Saint-Pierre and Miquelon, the French Commercial Code is automatically applicable there (see arts. L. 914-1 to L. 914-2 and R. 914-1 to R. 914-3 for any applicable adjustments).

(For further details, please refer to the "Guadeloupe" chapter.)

---

1 It has an ad hoc status defined by organic law, and its own normative power in certain areas covered by law or regulations (French laws and regulations are not automatically applicable under the same conditions as in mainland France).

2 Our translation.

IV. Institutional Structure

5. The Autorité de la concurrence (hereafter, the "French Competition Authority" or "FCA") was established in 2008 as a successor to the Conseil de la concurrence (French Competition Council).

(For details regarding the supervising body, organizational structure, additional regulatory mandates, budget, resources, and enforcement powers, please refer to the "Guadeloupe" chapter.)

V. Enforcement and Sanctions

6. Since 2009, only a few decisions have been issued regarding Saint-Pierre and Miquelon. For instance:

- Decision 22-D-09, March 10, 2022, relating to practices implemented in the aggregates sector and downstream markets in Saint-Pierre and Miquelon: Le Béton Contrôlé referred practices in the aggregates sector and downstream markets in Saint-Pierre and Miquelon to the FCA. The company accused Société d'Exploitation des Carrières of violating certain commitments made mandatory by Decision 12-D-06 of January 26, 2012, concerning practices implemented in the aggregates sector and downstream markets in Saint-Pierre and Miquelon. The FCA rejected the referral by Le Béton Contrôlé on the grounds that it was partially inadmissible and was not supported by sufficient evidence.
- Decision 12-D-06 of January 26, 2012, concerning practices implemented in the aggregates sector and downstream markets in Saint-Pierre and Miquelon (see below).

(For information on fines, sanctions, and private enforcement, please refer to the "Guadeloupe" chapter.)

VI. Noteworthy Cases

A. *Decision 12-D-06 of January 26, 2012, Concerning Practices Implemented in the Aggregates Sector and Downstream Markets in Saint-Pierre and Miquelon*

7. *Facts.* The supply of aggregates in Saint-Pierre and Miquelon is essentially concentrated around an economic interest group (EIG), "Exploitation des carrières," which operates the island's only quarry (the Fauteuil quarry) and sells the aggregates to its member companies: Allen-Mahé, Atelier Fer, Guibert Frères, and Saint-Pierraise de Transport (SSPT). These companies then resell a portion of the processed aggregates back to the EIG.

8. A series of agreements and abuses have stifled competition in the sector. Between 1994 and 2009, the EIG and its members implemented four types of agreements: (i) they agreed on the conditions of membership and the operating procedures of the EIG, in order to limit the arrival of new members, thus closing access to the Fauteuil quarry to third parties; (ii) the prices for all processed aggregates that the EIG members sold back to the EIG were set jointly; (iii) three of these companies agreed to share among

themselves, in an "equitable" manner, the revenue from supplying aggregates to the EIG as well as the subcontracted work carried out on its behalf; and (iv) the EIG and its members agreed that the EIG would be the sole bidder in calls for tenders issued by local authorities for the supply of asphalt.

9. In addition to these agreements, the EIG and its members abused their collective dominant position by refusing to sell riprap to third-party companies, which was necessary for the latter to respond to certain calls for tenders.

10. *Legal issue.* Breach of articles L. 420-1 and L. 420-2 prohibiting agreements and abuses of dominant position/settlement procedure/financial penalty.

11. The FCA has issued a decision sanctioning five entities (the EIG "Exploitation des carrières" and the companies Allen-Mahé, Atelier Fer, Guibert Frères and SSPT) with a fine of EUR 381,400.

12. The EIG "Exploitation des carrières," Allen-Mahé, Atelier Fer, Guibert Frères and SSPT requested the benefit of the provisions of paragraph III of article L. 464-2 of the Commercial Code, which governs the settlement procedure.

13. *Outcome.* No appeal was filed within the legal time limits.

14. *Impact or precedent set.* The anti-competitive practices condemned took place in the building and public works sector over a long period of time, with significant market foreclosure even though the market in question is very small – namely, that of Saint-Pierre and Miquelon, an overseas collectivity with only a few inhabitants.

VII. Merger Control

15. As with antitrust law, French merger control applies in Saint-Pierre and Miquelon. However, the French Commercial Code lays down specific rules for mergers concerning overseas territories in article L. 430-2, III.

(For information on notification thresholds and review timeframes, please refer to the "Guadeloupe" chapter.)

VIII. Advocacy and Policy Initiatives

(See the "Guadeloupe" chapter)

IX. Regional and International Cooperation

(See the "Guadeloupe" chapter)

X. Challenges and Country-Specific Features

A. *Dependence on Imports/Foreign Investment*

16. According to IEDOM's annual report for 2024, like other small island economies, the economy of Saint-Pierre and Miquelon is characterized by a predominance of imports and weak exports. Its trade balance is therefore structurally in deficit. Furthermore, with local production remaining relatively low, the archipelago is heavily dependent on external factors. In 2024, Saint-Pierre and Miquelon imported EUR 97.6 million worth

of goods and exported EUR 3.6 million. Total imports in value decreased by 4.4% compared to 2023. Exports saw a significant increase of 106.0% compared to 2023. It should be noted that fishery products landed in Canada are not recorded by French customs. This applies to almost all catches.

B. *Lack of Resources or Expertise*

17. According to IEDOM's annual report for 2024, the harsh climate and limited territory constrain the development of the agricultural and livestock sectors. Fishing, traditionally a mainstay of the archipelago's economy, now accounts for only a minimal share of its total value added. Thus, the agriculture, livestock, and fishing sectors represented 0.6% of total value added in 2015. All economic sectors in the archipelago are also experiencing recruitment difficulties.

XI. References and Resources

A. *Laws and Regulations*

- Book IV of the legislative part of the French Commercial Code: On Freedom of Prices and Competition (arts. L. 410-1 to L. 490-14) (in French)
- Book IV of the regulatory part of the French Commercial Code: On Freedom of Price and Competition (arts. R. 410-1 to R. 490-10) (in French)

B. *Case Law*

- FCA, Decision 22-D-09 of Mar. 10, 2022, relating to practices implemented in the aggregates sector and downstream markets in Saint-Pierre and Miquelon (in French)
- FCA, Decision 12-D-06 of Jan. 26, 2012, concerning practices implemented in the aggregates sector and downstream markets in Saint-Pierre and Miquelon (in French)

C. *Public Reports*

- IEDOM, Annual Economic Report of Saint-Pierre and Miquelon 2024 (June 2025) (in French), https://www.iedom.fr/Rapport-annuel-economique-de-Saint-Pierre-et-Miquelon
- FCA, Opinion 26-A-01 of Feb. 10, 2026, concerning the margins of wholesale importers and distributors of essential food products in Martinique (in French)
- FCA, Opinion19-A-12 of July 4, 2019, concerning the functioning of competition in the French overseas territories (in French)
- FCA, Opinion 09-A-45 of Sept. 8, 2009, concerning the mechanisms for importing and distributing consumer goods in the overseas departments (in French)

18. To learn more about the French Competition Authority (FCA).

Website: https://www.autoritedelaconcurrence.fr/

Contact: communication@autoritedelaconcurrence.fr

Singapore

Alvin Koh
Chief Executive at the Competition and Consumer Commission

I. Overview

1. Singapore is a city-state in Southeast Asia with a total land area of 736.3 km^2.[1] One of the smallest countries in the world by land area, Singapore is located at the southern tip of the Malay Peninsula between Malaysia and Indonesia, at the junction of the Strait of Malacca and the South China Sea.

2. Singapore is a sovereign state with a parliamentary system. Despite its small size, the country has developed into a major global financial and trading hub. The official languages are English, Chinese, Malay, and Tamil, with English serving as the primary language of business and administration. As a former British colony, Singapore's legal system is rooted in the common law tradition and the country ranks highly in rule-of-law indices.

II. Demographics and Economy

3. Singapore has a population of approximately 6.11 million people as of 2025.[2] It is one of the most densely populated countries in the world, with approximately 8,300 people per square kilometer. The population is entirely urban, with no distinct, large-scale rural population.

4. Singapore's nominal gross domestic product ("GDP") was approximately USD 547 billion in 2024,[3] with a per capita GDP of approximately USD 90,674. Despite its small domestic market, Singapore remains a major trading hub.

5. Singapore is one of the world's most open economies and trades with a diverse range of partners around the world across a wide range of goods and services.[4] Singapore's main economic sectors[5] include wholesale trade, manufacturing, financial services, transportation and storage, information and communications, and professional services.

III. Legal Framework for Competition

6. Passed in October 2004, the Competition Act 2004 (the "Act") is the primary piece of legislation setting out Singapore's competition law with the goal of promoting fair competition and preventing anti-competitive activities in markets. The Act contains three main prohibitions, targeting different types of anti-competitive conduct (the "Prohibitions"). First, section 34 prohibits agreements between undertakings, decisions by associations of undertakings or concerted practices that have as their object or effect the prevention, restriction or distortion of competition in Singapore ("Anti-Competitive Agreement Prohibition"). Second, section 47 prohibits conduct on the part of one or

---

1 *Environment*, Singapore Department of Statistics, https://www.singstat.gov.sg/find-data/get-latest-data#environment.

2 *Population and Population Structure*, Singapore Department of Statistics, https://www.singstat.gov.sg/find-data/get-latest-data#population-and-population-structure.

3 *GDP (current US$)*, World Bank, https://data.worldbank.org/indicator/NY.GDP.MKTP.CD?locations=SG.

4 *Sustainable Non-Inflationary Economic Growth*, Monetary Authority of Singapore, https://www.mas.gov.sg/who-we-are/mas-gallery/explore-our-gallery/zone-b/sustained-non-inflationary-economic-growth/a-very-open-economy.

5 *Singapore Economy*, Singapore Department of Statistics, https://www.singstat.gov.sg/infographics/singapore-economy

more undertakings that amounts to the abuse of a dominant position in any market in Singapore ("Abuse of Dominance Prohibition"). Third, in relation to merger control, section 54 prohibits mergers that result in a substantial lessening of competition in Singapore ("Merger Control Prohibition").

7. The Prohibitions are applicable to economic and commercial activity carried out by individuals, businesses or other entities unless excluded or exempted under the Act. For example, the Anti-Competitive Agreement and Abuse of Dominance Prohibitions do not apply to economic activities generating pro competitive benefits that outweigh any potential anti-competitive effects, such as (i) vertical agreements between parties at different levels of the production or distribution chain, or (ii) agreements that generate net economic benefit (technical or economic progress). Agreements and conduct required by written law or necessary to comply with international obligations are also excluded from the Act, as are activities carried on by the Singapore government or statutory boards.

8. Competition in certain sectors and in relation to certain specified activities has also been excluded from the Act and placed within the jurisdiction of sectoral regulators – e.g., telecommunications and media, financial services and the supply of piped potable water.

9. The above examples are not exhaustive of the exclusions and exemptions under the Act, which are set out in full under the Third and Fourth Schedules of the Act.

IV. Institutional Structure

10. Singapore's competition regulator was first established on January 1, 2005, as a statutory board under the Ministry of Trade and Industry. On April 1, 2018, the statutory board was renamed to its current name, the Competition and Consumer Commission of Singapore ("CCS"), as its mandate was broadened to cover consumer protection (in particular fair trade practices), in relation to the enforcement of the Consumer Protection (Fair Trading) Act ("CPFTA"). On July 1, 2025, CCS had its mandate expanded to include consumer product safety and legal metrology.

11. CCS is an independent statutory body constituted by a board consisting of a chairperson and other members appointed by the Minister for Trade and Industry (the "Board"). Operationally, CCS is led by a chief executive, who reports to the Board and is responsible for CCS's overall management and administration. The chief executive also sits on the Board. The organization is structured into divisions, broadly divided along functional lines, such as legal, enforcement, consumers, economics, policy, data, international cooperation and communications. There is also a corporate and administrative division that supports the organization's overall operations, such as finance, human resources, and information technology.

12. To effectively investigate and address anti competitive conduct, CCS has been granted substantial enforcement powers under the Act. CCS is empowered under the Act to issue notices to any person (including businesses and their owners, managers, employees or third parties) to require the production of information and documents. In certain circumstances, CCS has the power to enter and inspect premises (with or without a court-ordered warrant) to obtain evidence in the form of documents, equipment or information. CCS may also issue interim directions it considers necessary to prevent any

action that may prejudice an investigation, or give directions to stop any infringement or remedy the effects of such an infringement, or to prevent serious, irreparable damage to a particular person or category of persons or protect the public interest.

13. CCS operates a leniency programme, allowing participants engaged in cartel activities to come forward early, cooperate with CCS and provide information and evidence of the infringement in return for immunity from or a reduction in financial penalties. Cartel activities include, among other things, price fixing, bid rigging, output restrictions, and market-sharing agreements.

14. CCS also has a fast-track procedure whereby parties who admit liability for infringing either the Anti-Competitive Agreement Prohibition or the Abuse of Dominance Prohibition will be eligible for a fixed percentage reduction in the amount of financial penalty they may be directed to pay.

V. Enforcement and Sanctions

15. Upon the conclusion of an investigation, CCS has various options in its toolkit. CCS is empowered to issue directions to require the undertaking to stop or modify any infringing conduct. The undertaking may also be directed to take specific actions to remedy the effects of the infringing conduct on competition. CCS may also impose a financial penalty for infringements, amounting to up to 10% of the applicable turnover of the undertaking's business in Singapore for each year of infringement, up to a maximum of three years, where the infringement has been committed intentionally and negligently. In merger cases, CCS has powers to investigate mergers, prohibit the relevant transaction, unwind completed mergers, approve a merger subject to conditions, or grant unconditional approval.

16. Undertakings that have notified a transaction to CCS, or undertakings under investigation, may offer commitments to CCS at any time before CCS has made a decision. Such commitments may involve taking or refraining from taking such actions as CCS considers appropriate for the purpose of remedying, mitigating or preventing any identified anti-competitive harm. CCS has the discretion to decide whether to accept commitments on a case-by-case basis and does not generally accept commitments in cases involving restrictions of competition by object with no accompanying net economic benefit.

17. Parties have the right to appeal CCS's decisions to an independently appointed Competition Appeal Board (CAB). Decisions of the CAB may also be appealed to the High Court and subsequently to the Court of Appeal on points of law, or the amount of a financial penalty. Appeals to the courts are by way of rehearing, and the court, in determining an appeal, may exercise all the powers and duties of the CAB.

18. Over the past two decades since its formation, CCS has had a substantial enforcement record across all three prohibitions. As at the date of this publication, CCS has issued 23 infringement decisions addressing anti-competitive conduct across varied economic sectors such as manufacturing, transport and hospitality in relation to the Anti-Competitive Agreement and Abuse of Dominance Prohibitions.

19. In terms of the Merger Control Prohibition, merger parties may choose to notify CCS of their merger situation by applying for a decision as to whether the merger situation infringes, or will infringe, the Merger Control Prohibition. Not notifying a merger situation carries the risk that if it does raise competition concerns, CCS may investigate the merger on its own initiative and give directions to remedy the competition concerns. Notwithstanding the voluntary merger regime, CCS is regularly notified of mergers by applicants seeking a decision from CCS regarding whether their merger substantially lessens competition. CCS has issued 106 merger decisions to date.

20. CCS has also issued 19 guidance decisions and 25 decisions that relate to either the Anti-Competitive Agreement Prohibition or the Abuse of Dominance Prohibition. These notification decisions follow from applications made to receive either guidance or a decision from CCS as to whether the applicant's conduct is likely to infringe the aforesaid prohibitions. The effect of receiving guidance or a decision is that the applicants have immunity from enforcement action by CCS in relation to the notified conduct, save where the information provided by the applicant and on which CCS based its guidance or decision was incomplete, false or misleading in a material particular. Like the merger notification process, having the guidance/decision process allows businesses to notify their conduct to seek CCS's view, thereby providing greater certainty as to the legality of their conduct.

21. Section 86 of the Act also allows for private entities to bring a civil competition law ("follow-on" action) claim before the courts, but only when there has already been a final infringement decision by CCS (or by the CAB, or the courts on appeal, as the case may be). As such, private claims are complementary to public enforcement.

VI. Noteworthy Cases

A. *Abuse of Dominance Case: SISTIC v. CCS [2010] SGCAB 1*

22. On June 4, 2010, CCS issued its first abuse of dominance decision under the Abuse of Dominance Prohibition. SISTIC.com Pte Ltd. ("SISTIC"), a ticketing services provider in Singapore, was found by CCS to be dominant in the ticketing services market. SISTIC imposed exclusivity restrictions on event promoters and venue operators, and further induced them to continue with SISTIC via individualized discounts and incentives. The exclusivity restrictions essentially forced event promoters and venue operators to use SISTIC as their sole ticketing service provider and foreclosed competition from alternative ticketing providers. Upon conclusion of its investigation, CCS issued an infringement decision on SISTIC and imposed a financial penalty of SGD 989,000 on it.

23. SISTIC's appeal to the CAB was eventually dismissed, although the quantum of the financial penalty imposed on SISTIC was reduced to SGD 769,000.

24. Critically, the CAB held that the test for abuse of dominance in Singapore is similar to that in the United Kingdom and European Union, that an abuse will be established where CCS demonstrates that a practice by a dominant entity has, or is likely to have, an adverse effect on competition. It is sufficient for CCS to show a likely effect and it is not necessary for it to demonstrate an actual effect on the process of competition.

25. Finally, it is notable that, at the time of the infringement decision and subsequent appeal, SISTIC was a company indirectly owned by the Singapore government.[6] The CAB did not overrule CCS's conclusion that the Act was applicable to companies owned by the government provided they engaged in commercial and economic activity. The intent of competition law is to regulate the conduct of market players, and the exclusion in section 33(4) of the Act only excluded the government and statutory bodies that performed public and statutory functions.

B. *International Cartel Case: Nachi-Fujikoshi Corporation v. CCS [2016] SGCAB 1*

26. On May 27, 2014, CCS issued an infringement decision against four Japanese companies and their Singapore subsidiaries for engaging in anti-competitive agreements and unlawful exchanges of information in respect to the price and sale of ball and roller bearings ("bearings") sold to aftermarket customers in Singapore. CCS commenced an investigation after receiving two separate leniency applications from JTEKT Corporation ("JTEKT") and NSK Ltd. ("NSK Japan") relating to anti-competitive agreements that they had entered into with other manufacturers of bearings in respect of the sale, distribution and prices of such bearings. CCS found that all four of the Japanese companies were engaged in a long-standing arrangement consisting of regular meetings on and the systematic exchange of strategic information as to future pricing intentions from as early as 1980 or 1990 until March 2011. The parties were ordered to pay financial penalties amounting to SGD 9.3 million, with JTEKT being granted immunity and NSK Japan a discount on the penalty quantum, due to their participation in CCS's leniency programme. As Nachi-Fujikoshi Corp ("Nachi") also applied for leniency after CCS conducted an inspection without notice, it too received a discount on the quantum of penalty.

27. On Nachi's appeal to the CAB against the quantum of financial penalty ordered by CCS, the CAB agreed with CCS that the infringing conduct harmed competition in Singapore, irrespective of whether the sale of the bearings was invoiced in Japan or the bearings delivered in Singapore. The quantum of financial penalty was, however, reduced to SGD 4.7 million, as the CAB found that the turnover from a different financial year should have been used to calculate the quantum of financial penalties.

28. This case demonstrates how international cartel conduct can impact competition in a Singapore market and is an example of how CCS's leniency programme has been effective in helping to detect cartel conduct.

C. *Merger Infringement: Uber Singapore Technology Inc. v. CCS [2018] SGCAB 2*

29. On September 24, 2018, following investigations, CCS issued an infringement decision against Uber Technologies Inc. (including certain subsidiaries) ("Uber"), and Grab Inc. (including certain subsidiaries) ("Grab"), arising from the acquisition by Grab of Uber's

---

6 AXS, an American ticketing services company, acquired a majority stake in SISTIC.com Pte Ltd. in October 2025.

Southeast Asian business ("the Transaction"). CCS found that the Transaction would lead to a substantial lessening of competition in the market for two-sided platforms matching drivers and riders for the provision of booked chauffeured point-to-point transport services ("CPPT Services") in Singapore.

30. Notably, the Transaction was not initially notified to CCS. This resulted in CCS issuing interim measure directions to the merger parties in order to help ensure that the market remained open and contestable while CCS carried out investigations into the merger's impact in the CPPT Services market. Upon the conclusion of its investigation, CCS imposed financial penalties on Uber and Grab amounting to approximately SGD 13 million, as well as directions that included requiring Grab and Uber to remove all exclusivity obligations, lock-in periods and termination fees on drivers, as well as exclusive arrangements with taxi operators. Grab was also required to maintain its pre-transaction pricing policies, product options and algorithm pricing matrix. Grab and Uber were also required to appoint a monitoring trustee to monitor their compliance with the directions. Uber appealed the infringement decision to the CAB, while Grab chose not to do so.

31. On appeal, the CAB upheld the infringement decision and the financial penalties. It affirmed CCS's decision that the Transaction would result in the substantial lessening of competition in Singapore's ride-hail market and that Uber and Grab must have been aware that the Transaction would have the effect of restricting competition in Singapore.

32. Notably, the CAB held that in investigating a merger, CCS should first determine whether the transaction resulted or may be expected to result in a substantial lessening of competition in a relevant market, apart from and before considering the appropriateness of voluntary commitments offered by the parties. CCS has discretion whether to accept voluntary commitments, even if these were sufficient to remedy or prevent any substantial lessening of competition from the transaction being considered.

D. *Largest Cartel Case: Gold Chic and Ors. v. CCS [2020] SGCAB 1*

33. On September 12, 2018, CCS issued an infringement decision against 14 undertakings for their participation in anti-competitive price discussions in relation to the supply of fresh chicken products on numerous occasions from 2000 to 2014. These 14 undertakings were estimated to have a combined share of more than 90% of the market for fresh chicken products in Singapore.

34. CCS found that these meetings took place at locations such as karaoke bars and restaurants, and that the undertakings discussed price movements, including the quantum and timing of the increases, and implemented these price movements accordingly (the "Anti-Competitive Discussions"). Further, CCS also found that the undertakings had an understanding not to compete with each other, which was implemented as a general industry practice (the "Non-Aggression Pact"). Four of the undertakings applied to CCS for leniency following two separate dawn raids. These undertakings were granted discounts on the quantum of their financial penalties. CCS ultimately imposed financial penalties ranging from SGD 5,000 to SGD 3.3 million on the undertakings, with a total combined penalty of SGD 26.9 million.

35. Ten of the entities appealed against the infringement decision, including one of the leniency applicants, who appealed only on the quantum of financial penalties imposed on it.

36. The CAB upheld CCS's finding that the undertakings had participated in the Anti-Competitive Discussion, but found that there was insufficient evidence to prove the existence of the Non-Aggression Pact. As a result, the CAB reduced the quantum of the financial penalties for the appellant undertakings to SGD 10.8 million. The total penalties after the appeal amounted to SGD 20 million.

37. This case is notable for being the infringement decision with the largest penalties imposed to date and the complexities of a very large investigation involving many undertakings.

VII. Merger Control

38. Merger control in Singapore operates as a voluntary notification system where merger parties are responsible for assessing whether their merger would infringe the Act by substantially lessening competition. CCS publishes detailed guidelines on mergers to assist merger parties with their self-assessment. Should merger parties be concerned that their merger will result in or has resulted in a substantial lessening of competition in a Singapore market, the merger can be notified to CCS (paying the applicable fee) for a decision as to whether the merger would infringe the Act. CCS regularly undertakes scans for unnotified mergers and will investigate such mergers where there is a reasonable suspicion that they will substantially lessen competition.

39. Singapore's voluntary notification system balances regulatory oversight with business flexibility, enabling businesses to innovate and operate efficiently without imposing excessive regulatory burden. This supports Singapore's position as the regional hub for mergers and acquisitions, accounting for 39% of the total transaction volume and 52% of the total transaction value in Southeast Asia in 2025.[7]

40. CCS is generally of the view that competition concerns are unlikely to arise in a merger situation unless the merged entity has or is expected to have (i) at least 40% market share, or (ii) 20% to 40% market share with the top three firms holding at least 70% in combined market share, post-merger.

41. CCS currently adopts a two-phase approach in assessing applications. CCS will generally first undertake a preliminary Phase 1 review, which is expected to be completed within 30 working days, for mergers that clearly do not raise competition concerns. However, if CCS is unable to conclude in Phase 1 that the merger situation does not raise competition concerns, it will carry out a more in-depth Phase 2 review, which is expected to be completed within 120 working days.

42. At the time of writing, CCS is reviewing its guidelines on merger procedures to introduce a streamlined track to its merger assessment process, which aims to: (i) assess low-risk mergers by day 25 of the 30 working day timeline; (ii) reduce the regulatory burden

---

[7] *Philippine M&A Trends in 2025*, PwC (Dec. 22, 2025), https://www.pwc.com/ph/en/deals-corporate-finance/deals-publications/2025-ap-ma-report.html.

on merger parties and third parties in submitting information to CCS; and (iii) provide greater clarity for merger parties at an earlier stage on CCS's assessment outcomes.

43. During its merger assessment or investigation, CCS may consider interim measures to prevent the merger parties from taking any action that might prejudice its ability to consider the merger situation further or to impose appropriate remedies. If there is a finding of infringement, CCS has powers to issue directions to remedy the anti-competitive effects, including requiring the merger to be unwound or modified. CCS may also require merger parties to pay a financial penalty if the infringement was committed intentionally or negligently.

VIII. Advocacy and Policy Initiatives

44. In administering and enforcing the Act, CCS adopts a two-pronged approach that integrates enforcement with advocacy to cultivate a robust competitive ecosystem. This multifaceted approach encompasses strategic engagement with government agencies, the business community, legal practitioners, academia and the broader public to embed pro-competition principles while fostering a deep rooted culture of competition throughout Singapore's economic landscape.

45. CCS's enforcement of the Act is based on an evidence-based economics approach whereby economic analysis and empirical data are used to explain market dynamics, explore potential theories of harm, and assess the effects of a given conduct on competition in the market. With the rise of digital markets, CCS is keeping pace by developing its expertise in various areas, including data science, data engineering, technology insight and behavioral insight, and developing computational tools to improve its enforcement capabilities. To this end, CCS established its Data and Digital ("D2") Division, which specializes in harnessing technology to improve CCS's effectiveness in its enforcement and advocacy work with respect to competition and consumer protection issues in digital markets and beyond.

46. To further strengthen its internal enforcement capabilities, a key focus of CCS's D2 Division is to develop tools that rely on machine learning ("ML")/artificial intelligence ("AI"). One such tool developed by the D2 Division is the Complaint Analytics Tool, a topic modeling tool that uses natural language processing and ML techniques to cluster complaints into common themes for further analysis and sense-making. The Complaint Analytics Tool automates the analysis of complaints received by CCS, thus streamlining the identification of potential anti-competitive conduct in markets. The D2 Division is also actively exploring opportunities for AI to expedite existing tools, such as the Bid Rigging Detection Tool, which currently uses a rule-based methodology to flag suspicious tender documents for government projects that suggest bid rigging. The incorporation of ML/AI into enforcement tools can help CCS improve its efficiency and reduce human error while expanding its investigative coverage. CCS also possesses a digital forensics team to aid in its evidence collection, especially during raids.

47. Beyond its enforcement mandate of addressing anti-competitive activities with significant adverse impact on the economy, CCS has developed a comprehensive advocacy framework that proactively shapes market behavior and regulatory thinking

across Singapore's economy. As part of CCS's functions, CCS advises the Singapore government and other public sector authorities (collectively, "Public Sector Agencies") on national needs and policies in respect of competition matters. In this regard, CCS provides advice to Public Sector Agencies on a myriad of competition issues, including the impact of specific public policy initiatives on competition in the affected markets, the structure of public procurement to encourage greater competition between suppliers, the supply of goods and services by the government, and the competition impact of government divestments. In the course of doing so, CCS shares its assessment of the proposed initiative's impact on competition in affected market(s) and identifies ways to remove or mitigate competition concerns. Public Sector Agencies are thus able to appreciate and evaluate competition concerns when formulating and implementing their policy initiatives. Since its establishment, CCS has issued over 350 advisories to various Public Sector Agencies.

48. CCS also partners with Public Sector Agencies to conduct market studies that facilitate a better understanding of markets under their purview or to identify potential obstacles that may hamper industry development or transformation goals. This is another way in which CCS supports Public Sector Agencies in their work.

49. As part of a multi-stakeholder working group, CCS enhanced the Technical Reference 76 on Guidelines for electronic commerce ("e-commerce") transactions ("E-commerce Voluntary Guidelines") in 2025 to address emerging challenges in Singapore's e-commerce market. First published in 2020, the E-commerce Voluntary Guidelines equip e-commerce businesses with industry best practices on key activities relating to online transactions. The E-commerce Voluntary Guidelines were last revised in 2022 to include additional anti-scam guidelines for e-retailers and e-marketplaces,[8] to offer better protection for consumers transacting online. The latest updates to the guidelines aim to enhance consumer trust and promote market competitiveness. With merchants increasingly depending on e-marketplaces to reach consumers, the way in which e-marketplaces interact with merchants on their platforms can significantly impact merchants' businesses and affect the ability of new and existing e-marketplaces to enter and compete fairly and effectively. For instance, e-marketplaces may restrict their merchants' ability to sell their products on competing platforms or impose onerous and unfair listing conditions for merchants. E-marketplaces may also accord preferential treatment to their own product or service listings, or those of their affiliates, creating an uneven playing field that disadvantages other merchants on their platforms. The E-commerce Voluntary Guidelines provide guidance for e-marketplaces and e-retailers on engaging merchants fairly (such as fair listing conditions and allowing businesses to use multiple e-marketplaces), promoting transparency in their dealings with merchants and providing effective dispute resolution mechanisms. The E-commerce Voluntary Guidelines also guide industry players on the appropriate use of automated tools and AI. In deploying such tools, e-marketplaces and e-retailers should ensure these systems

---

8 "E-marketplaces" refer to online intermediaries or platforms that allow participating merchants to exchange information about products or services with customers to enter into an electronic commerce transaction, which may or may not provide information or services about payments and logistics.

operate transparently and fairly, and consider how to manage any risks appropriately (such as compliance with competition, data protection, cybersecurity and other related laws).

50. CCS regularly engages Public Sector Agencies in Singapore via the Competition and Consumer Regulators Community ("C2RC"), an interagency platform enabling Public Sector Agencies to learn about the latest local and overseas competition developments and to share best practices and experiences on competition and regulatory issues.[9] This collaborative approach is particularly useful in small economics where government policies may have a significant impact on market dynamics and competition. Through C2RC, CCS seeks to raise Public Sector Agencies' awareness of competition issues and the need to consider competition impact in government policies at an early stage of the policymaking or review process. This enables Public Sector Agencies to identify and address potential competition issues to avoid unintended consequences that may otherwise undermine their policy objectives.

51. In collaboration with another Public Sector Agency, CCS also developed a toolkit for AI model developers and deployers. Comprising 49 self-assessment process checks and two technical tests, the AI Markets ("AIM") Toolkit helps AI developers and deployers self-assess whether their AI models and business practices comply with the Act.

52. In addition, CCS's stakeholder engagement strategy reflects a nuanced understanding of how competition awareness must be embedded across different segments of society. Through carefully designed conferences and targeted workshops for businesses and industry associations, educational seminars for university students, digital platforms and social media engagement, regular electronic newsletters, strategic public materials, and active media engagement, CCS creates multiple touchpoints that reinforce competitive principles. This multi-channel approach ensures that competition consciousness becomes ingrained in business decision-making processes whilst simultaneously educating the broader public about the benefits of competitive markets through both traditional and digital channels.

53. The biannual Stakeholder Perception Survey represents CCS's commitment to evidence-based strategic planning, gathering insights from businesses, competition law practitioners, and consumers to inform its evolving approach. This data-driven methodology ensures that CCS's advocacy efforts remain responsive to actual market needs rather than theoretical frameworks, enabling CCS to continuously refine its outreach priorities and address identified gaps in Singapore's competition culture.

IX. Regional and International Cooperation

54. Given the increasingly globalized world where competition cases often transcend national boundaries, CCS has positioned itself not merely as a participant in international forums but as a thought leader that shapes global best practices whilst advancing Singapore's strategic interests.

---

9 C2RC was previously known as the Community of Practice for Competition and Economic Regulations (COPCOMER).

55. CCS is an active member of the International Competition Network (ICN), which is formed by competition regulators dedicated towards developing recommended best practices, manuals, and frameworks to guide competition authorities on enforcement, advocacy, and agency effectiveness. In particular, CCS is part of the ICN's Steering Group, which is the elected body that guides the ICN's work and priorities. CCS is currently the ICN Advocacy Working Group co-chair (term 2024–2027), and CCS's chief executive, Mr. Alvin Koh, has been appointed as ICN vice chair from 2025. Apart from participating in the ICN Annual Conferences and regular thematic workshops that facilitate dialogue among ICN members, CCS contributes to various working group projects that facilitate the development of best practices in competition enforcement and regulation. For example, as co-chair of the ICN Advocacy Working Group, CCS is organizing the ICN Advocacy Workshop in 2026 for ICN members to discuss notable developments and best practices in the area of competition advocacy. CCS is also part of the ICN Secretariat team tasked with updating the ICN website.

56. Under the Association of Southeast Asian Nations (ASEAN) Economic Community ("AEC") Blueprint 2030, ASEAN Member States ("AMS") aim to foster fair markets in the region to enable businesses to compete on a level playing field, within a transparent, equitable, and conducive ecosystem. As part of the ASEAN community, Singapore works with other AMS to develop sound competition policies and best practices for the region. CCS represents Singapore at the ASEAN Experts Group on Competition ("AEGC"), which is the official platform to discuss and cooperate on competition policy and law issues in ASEAN. CCS is currently leading an AEGC study on AI and its impact on competition, with the aim of improving awareness of AI and its impact on markets in the region. In 2025, CCS hosted the 11th ASEAN Competition Conference to discuss emerging competition developments in ASEAN and to raise awareness of competition issues among relevant stakeholders in the region. CCS also actively participates in other platforms that discuss competition policy and law issues, such as the Organisation for Economic Co-operation and Development ("OECD") and the Asia-Pacific Economic Cooperation ("APEC") Competition Policy and Law Group, among others.

57. In addition, CCS has established a comprehensive network of bilateral cooperation arrangements with competition authorities worldwide. For instance, CCS has entered into memoranda of understanding ("MoUs") with key overseas partners, including the Japan Fair Trade Commission, the Indonesia Competition Commission, the Competition Bureau Canada, the Philippine Competition Commission, and the State Administration for Market Regulation of the People's Republic of China. These MoUs facilitate various forms of cooperation, including information sharing, technical assistance, staff exchanges, mutual notification and coordination in cross-border competition cases. At the national level, Singapore has also entered into free trade agreements ("FTAs") with other jurisdictions, which typically include provisions on competition enforcement and cooperation. Similar to CCS's MoUs, the FTAs greatly facilitate CCS's cooperation with its overseas counterparts.

58. CCS's comprehensive approach towards international engagements highlights how small economies can overcome geographical and market-size limitations through

strategic partnerships and active participation in international networks. Indeed, CCS's active participation across various networks underscores its commitment to promoting competition policy and law beyond a domestic focus. In this regard, as a reputable competition authority, CCS also provides technical assistance and capacity-building support to other developing competition authorities, sharing its experience in implementing and enforcing competition law. For example, in 2024, CCS organized a five-day workshop for participants from ASEAN under the Singapore-United States Third Country Training Programme to build up the capacity of competition authorities in the region.

X. Challenges and Country-Specific Features

59. As a small economy with no natural resources, Singapore relies heavily on global trade and on the confidence of investors, businesses and consumers. Furthermore, Singapore is a highly digitalized nation, with its digital economy contributing 18.6% of the nation's GDP in 2024.[10] A key focus for CCS is to ensure its competition policy remains relevant and enforcement remains credible in the face of emerging market challenges.

60. Rapidly evolving market trends and technological advancements in Singapore's fast-growing digital economy will make competition regulation increasingly complex. For instance, a market study by CCS has found that the increased use of AI systems and algorithms to make pricing decisions may increase the risk of collusion between competitors on digital platforms.[11] For effective regulation, CCS would require enhanced resources for market studies into digital markets and to build up sufficient technical competencies to address nascent issues arising from emerging or developing technologies. For example, the advancements in generative AI and its effects on traditional or even emerging markets are unclear and untested. Technical expertise in algorithms, AI, data science and data forensics would be required in navigating these challenges. However, like other smaller jurisdictions, CCS's limited resources make it challenging to build up and sustain all these capabilities.

61. Nevertheless, to better deal with emerging challenges in digital markets, CCS is committed to further strengthening its technical competencies in data science and engineering. CCS officers in the D2 Division regularly undergo external training to develop basic skill sets and know-how on web scraping, data analytics, and ML/AI applications. This has enabled CCS to develop tools in partnership with other public sector agencies, such as the AIM Toolkit, which helps businesses self-assess whether their AI models and business practices are compliant with the Act. At the same time, CCS officers are regularly exposed to experts in behavioral economics, regulation, personal data, etc.

---

10 Lee Li Ying, *Singapore's digital economy contributed 18.6% to GDP, generated 214,000 tech jobs in 2024*, The Straits Times (Oct. 8, 2025), https://www.straitstimes.com/tech/singapores-digital-economy-contributes-18-6-to-gdp-generates-241000-tech-jobs-in-2024.

11 CCS, E-commerce Platforms Market Study: Findings and Recommendations (Sept. 10, 2020), https://isomer-user-content.by.gov.sg/45/f8f8ec3b-40c3-4b4f-8884-3fcb640ae7f7/CCCS%20Ecommerce%20Platforms%20Market%20Study%20Report.pdf.

XI. Author's Perspective

62. The administration and regulation of competition law can and should transcend traditional enforcement boundaries. If worked on properly, it can provide a critical steer for economic growth, even in small economies. In a time of commercial uncertainty at a global level, competition authorities have an opportunity to re-examine their functions and possibly cast themselves not just as effective enforcers, but also as strategic partners of other parts of government and even industry to drive competition and consumer protection in markets.

63. Separately, strong competition enforcement and advocacy need to be complemented with equally effective consumer protection laws and policies. CCS believes that markets work well when businesses compete on the merits. This is not solely dependent on the competitive process, but also requires ensuring that businesses do not attempt to gain market share through unfair business practices (such as misleading consumers), the supply of unsafe products or the use of non-conforming measuring instruments. It is therefore apt that these key functions are part of the toolkit CCS now possesses to ensure that Singapore's markets function efficiently and drive national growth.

64. In the coming years, CCS will strive to be a thought leader among the giants in the competition and consumer landscape. In the international space, having benefited in its earlier years from more developed regimes, Singapore hopes to share its experiences and work with like-minded jurisdictions and other small economies facing their own challenges to collectively build sustainable, efficient and resilient competition regimes.

XII. References and Resources

- The Competition Act 2004 and subsidiary legislation, https://sso.agc.gov.sg/act/ca2004
- Published decisions of the Competition Appeal Board, https://www.mti.gov.sg/resources/laws-and-regulations/summary-of-appeals-received-by-the-competition-appeal-board-cab/
- CCS's Public Register of infringement decisions, market studies, advisories, merger notifications and commitments and remedies, https://www.ccs.gov.sg/case-register/public-register/

65. To learn more about the Competition and Consumer Commission:
Website: https://www.ccs.gov.sg/

Trinidad and Tobago

Krystle S. Maharaj
Senior Legal Counsel, Trinidad and Tobago Fair Trading Commission

Bevan Narinesingh
Executive Director, Trinidad and Tobago Fair Trading Commission

I. Overview

A. *Geographical Location*

1. The Republic of Trinidad and Tobago is a twin-island nation that lies off the northeastern coast of Venezuela, approximately 11 kilometers (7 miles) from the Venezuelan mainland. Geographically, it is situated between the Caribbean Sea and the Atlantic Ocean, making it an important crossroads for trade and maritime activities in the region.

B. *Surface Area*

2. Trinidad covers 4,768 square kilometers, making it the larger island, while Tobago is significantly smaller at 300 square kilometers

3. The combined surface area of the entire Republic of Trinidad and Tobago is 5,128 square kilometers.

C. *Political Status*

4. Trinidad and Tobago is a sovereign state, an independent country that gained independence from the United Kingdom on August 31, 1962. It became a republic in 1976 and is a member of the Commonwealth of Nations and the Caribbean Community (CARICOM). The country is a democratic republic, with a President as the Head of State and a Prime Minister as the Head of Government.

D. *Official Languages*

5. English is the official language of Trinidad and Tobago. While it is the dominant language, several local languages and dialects are spoken across the country, including Trinidadian Creole, Tobagonian Creole, and regional languages such as French Creole (*patois*) and Spanish, reflecting historical influences.

II. Demographics and Economy

6. Trinidad and Tobago is a twin-island nation with a population of approximately 1.51 million people. This nation boasts a strong oil- and gas-driven economy, rich cultural heritage, and stable parliamentary democracy – factors that have shaped its unique growth and development. Trinidad and Tobago is one of the higher-income Caribbean countries owing to its energy sector; its gross domestic product (GDP) was USD 26.43 billion in 2024, according to official World Bank data. The economy is open, with a substantial export component (notably petroleum and gas) and import dependency for many goods. The trade balance may fluctuate with global energy prices.

7. Main economic sectors include energy (oil and gas), petrochemicals, manufacturing, and services (including finance and tourism in Tobago), as well as smaller-scale agriculture.

8. As a small economy, many sectors are characterized by a few large players (both domestic and foreign), considerable state involvement, and significant structural barriers to entry. This creates a higher risk of dominance or oligopoly than in larger economies.

III. Legal Framework for Competition

9. In 1998, the need for a national competition agency was first conceptualized by the government, highlighting *inter alia* that, as a small island economy, Trinidad and Tobago possesses distinctive needs and as such its laws should be shaped by these distinctive features, in particular:

- In a small economy, competition policy must not entail elaborate administration or burdensome compliance procedures;
- The pattern of competition in the local home market will increasingly be shaped by open and liberalized regimes for foreign trade and inward foreign investment; and
- Competition policy must not freeze Trinidad and Tobago's industrial structure into a pattern of small businesses. Its concern must not be the number of producers situated in Trinidad and Tobago, but rather the competitive functioning of the market.

10. The journey toward establishing a comprehensive competition regime shaped by global trends and a growing recognition of the role of competition in promoting fair markets, economic growth, and consumer welfare continued with the passage of the Fair Trading Act (FTA), Ch. 81:13. The Act was passed by Parliament in 2006 and partially proclaimed in 2007 and 2014, enabling the establishment of the Trinidad and Tobago Fair Trading Commission (TTFTC), the agency responsible for implementing and administering the FTA.

11. On February 10, 2020, the FTA was fully proclaimed, which enabled the TTFTC's enforcement powers. These powers include, but are not limited to, the regulation of anti-competitive agreements and practices, abuses of monopoly power, and mergers and acquisitions. The FTA generally applies to all economic activities across all economic sectors in Trinidad and Tobago, regardless of an enterprise's nationality, place of incorporation, domicile, or principal place of business. It covers all agreements and conduct that affect the local market, even if the activities occur outside Trinidad and Tobago.

12. However, the following are exempt from the FTA's provisions:[1]

- Combinations or activities of employees for their own reasonable protection as employees;
- Arrangements for collective bargaining on behalf of employers for the purpose of fixing terms and conditions for employment;
- Agreements related to the use, license, or assignment of intellectual property rights, as well as the application of such provisions. In this case, only the relevant provisions related to such rights will be exempt, and not the remaining stipulations of the agreement;
- Activities of professional associations directly related to the development or enforcement of professional standards of competition reasonably necessary for the protection of the public;
- Activities expressly authorized or required under international treaties or agreements to which Trinidad and Tobago is a party,

[1] Section 3(1) FTA

- Companies that fall within the purview of the Telecommunications Authority Act; and
- Banks and non-bank financial institutions falling within the purview of the Securities Act or declared as such by the Minister by Order subject to affirmative resolution of Parliament.

13. Nevertheless, the TTFTC remains dedicated to upholding the principles of competition across all industries. The TTFTC, by proactively providing guidance and support, assists other regulators in navigating the complexities of competition law, fostering a collaborative environment that ensures fair practices. This commitment extends to exempted sectors, ensuring that they operate in ways that benefit consumers, encourage innovation, and sustain a dynamic market.

IV. Institutional Structure

A. *Competition Authority*

14. The Trinidad and Tobago Fair Trading Commission (TTFTC or the "Commission") is an independent statutory authority established under the FTA.

B. *Supervising Body*

15. The TTFTC is independent, though it operates within the national legal/regulatory environment; its line ministry is the Ministry of Trade, Investment and Tourism.

C. *Organizational Structure*

16. The Act provides for a commission (comprising a chairperson and commissioners) and an executive director. Staff size includes a senior legal counsel, an investigator, and administrative and marketing staff.

D. *Additional Regulatory Mandates*

17. The TTFTC operates within a framework of shared responsibility with several local regulators in Trinidad and Tobago, ensuring comprehensive enforcement of competition laws across different sectors of the economy.

18. Key regulators that collaborate with the TTFTC include:
    - The Central Bank of Trinidad and Tobago, which plays a crucial role in overseeing competition in the financial sector. It works alongside the TTFTC to ensure that mergers and acquisitions in the banking and financial services sectors do not result in anti-competitive concentrations.
    - The Telecommunications Authority of Trinidad and Tobago: The telecommunications sector is subject to specific regulations aimed at promoting competition and consumer protection. The Telecommunications Authority collaborates with the TTFTC to monitor and address competition issues in this dynamic and rapidly evolving industry.
    - The Regulated Industries Commission, which oversees sectors such as water and electricity, which have unique competition challenges. By working together,

the TTFTC and the Regulated Industries Commission ensure that competition laws are effectively enforced in these essential sectors.

19. While the primary focus of the FTA is on competition, it also includes provisions aimed at safeguarding consumer interests. The TTFTC works in tandem with other regulatory bodies, such as the Consumer Affairs Division of the Ministry of Trade, Investment and Tourism, to address consumer complaints and ensure that businesses adhere to fair trading practices. This integrated approach enhances the overall regulatory environment and promotes consumer confidence.

E. *Budget and Resources*

20. The TTFTC's annual budget for the last three years has been TTD 2,580,000 (approximately USD 380,000). The TTFTC has also received assistance from the European Commission and the Inter-American Development Bank (IDB) to assist in the implementation of certain projects and initiatives.

V. Enforcement and Sanctions

A. *Fines and Sanctions*

21. As of now, the TTFTC has not yet imposed any fines or sanctions. The FTA provides for civil penalties of up to 10% of a company's annual turnover in the relevant market, with the intent of deterring anti-competitive practices. However, due to the nascent stage of enforcement, no cases have reached the point where these penalties have been necessary. For the time being, enforcement has largely been absent penalties. However, this is expected to change as the TTFTC continues to build its investigative capacity and deepen its understanding of market dynamics.

B. *Enforcement Track Record*

22. The TTFTC's enforcement track record is still in its early stages. As of now, no formal investigations have been launched, nor has any action been taken regarding anti-competitive behavior such as price fixing, market division, or abuse of dominance. This absence of formal investigations or enforcement actions is largely due to resource constraints, the institution's youth, and the lack of significant cases since the establishment of the TTFTC. In this context, the TTFTC's focus has been on building its institutional capacity, monitoring market conditions, and engaging in advocacy and education to ensure compliance with competition principles.

C. *Private Enforcement*

23. Currently, private enforcement through damages claims has not been a significant feature of competition law in Trinidad and Tobago. While the FTA allows private parties to seek redress for harm caused by anti-competitive behavior, there has been little use of this provision to date. The lack of private enforcement can be attributed to several factors, including low awareness of the right to claim damages, the complexity and cost of litigation, and the absence of major enforcement cases that would set precedents for private parties to follow.

24. The lack of formal investigations, sanctions, or private enforcement thus far reflects the early phase of the TTFTC's development. However, as the TTFTC's capacity grows and more market dynamics are understood, enforcement is likely to become more active. The TTFTC has signaled its intent to strengthen its investigative framework, increase public awareness, and eventually begin enforcing the law through targeted cases, which could set important legal precedents.

VI. Noteworthy Cases

25. To date, the TTFTC has not formally concluded any investigations or issued decisions regarding breaches of the FTA. This is reflective not of inactivity but of the TTFTC's measured and proactive approach to developing a culture of competition compliance in a small, highly concentrated market still becoming familiar with the principles of competition law. In lieu of enforcement action, the TTFTC has placed strategic emphasis on monitoring market conduct, engaging stakeholders, and educating the public on businesses' obligations under the FTA. This has included:

- Sector engagements: The TTFTC regularly meets with representatives from key industries, including professional associations, distributors, and trade bodies, to discuss pricing practices, membership rules, and other structural behaviors that could raise competition concerns. These engagements aim to clarify legal obligations and prevent anti-competitive conduct before it arises.
- Public notices and advocacy: The TTFTC has published advisories and press notices to raise awareness about competition law compliance. For example, in 2024, the TTFTC issued a public warning to professional associations, cautioning against conduct such as price fixing, restrictive entry rules, or information sharing among competitors. These notices serve as soft enforcement tools to encourage voluntary compliance and deter potential breaches.
- Monitoring of market conditions: The TTFTC continually monitors sectors prone to limited competition, such as construction materials, telecommunications, and essential services. By analyzing market trends and consumer complaints, the Commission maintains a state of readiness to act should conduct cross the legal threshold for intervention.

VII. Merger Control

26. Section 14 of the FTA prohibits anti-competitive mergers and requires merging parties to obtain the TTFTC's permission before completion. A "merger" is defined in section 13(1). Under section 14(1)(b), mandatory notification applies where:

- the parties' combined assets exceed TTD 50 million; and
- at least one party carries on or intends to carry on business in Trinidad and Tobago.

27. While there is no statutory definition of "carries on business," the TTFTC may consider indicators such as managing local property, holding meetings or bank accounts, maintaining business systems, enforcing legal rights, investing locally, or engaging in continuous profit-seeking activity. Both thresholds must be met.

28. There are no exemptions from mandatory notification, nor restrictions on voluntary notification below thresholds. When reviewing transactions, the TTFTC must ensure that a merger does not substantially lessen competition, harm consumers, or negatively affect the economy. Notified mergers cannot close without approval. Under section 14(2), the TTFTC must issue a decision within one month of receiving a complete application; delays may arise from incomplete filings. Decisions are subject to court review or deferment under section 16. If parties fail to notify a notifiable merger or implement a merger prior to clearance, the TTFTC may investigate and impose penalties of up to 10% of annual turnover, and may seek divestment orders. Breaches may include premature information-sharing, coordination of competitive behavior, or early transfer of ownership or control.

29. Since the full proclamation of the FTA in 2020, merger review has been a major component of the TTFTC's work. To date, the TTFTC has reviewed and approved more than 40 merger transactions spanning various sectors, such as information and communication technology (ICT), food and beverage, energy and energy services, pharmaceuticals, transportation, commercial/real estate, and aviation, involving local as well as international enterprises. To date, the TTFTC has not blocked any merger transaction.

VIII. Advocacy and Policy Initiatives

A. *Outreach to Businesses and Consumers*

30. Advocacy is a key function of the TTFTC, aimed at promoting awareness and understanding of competition law among businesses, consumers, and policymakers. Through its advocacy efforts, the TTFTC fosters a culture of fair competition and compliance. On numerous occasions, the TTFTC has been specifically selected to participate in high-level meetings/workshops – serving both as moderator and speaker – and has contributed to written work products organized or facilitated by international bodies such as the National Institute for the Defense of Competition and the Protection of Intellectual Property (INDECOPI) of Peru, the International Competition Network (ICN), the Organisation for Economic Co-operation and Development (OECD), the US Federal Trade Commission (FTC), Canada's Competition Bureau, CADE Brazil, and the CARICOM Competition Commission.

31. The successes of this high-level involvement have been used by the TTFTC in the following ways:

- as a benchmark for legislative or regulatory reforms;
- as a benchmark for assessing/evaluating changes to its practices, guidelines or policies; and
- as a resource for competition advocacy or studies.

32. The TTFTC also engages in collaborative efforts with other national competition authorities.

B. *Recent Policy Papers or Guidelines*

1. Merger Guidelines

33. The Merger Guidelines issued by the TTFTC[2] provide detailed guidance on the evaluation of mergers and acquisitions under the FTA. These guidelines are designed to clarify how the TTFTC assesses the competitive impact of mergers, and when such transactions may need to be notified to the Commission for review. The guidelines help businesses understand:

- Thresholds for filing: When a merger or acquisition must be reported to the TTFTC, based on the turnover or market share of the companies involved.
- Competitive analysis: How the TTFTC will assess whether the merger will lead to a substantial lessening of competition in any relevant market.
- Remedies: Possible actions that companies may need to take to mitigate anti-competitive effects.

34. The TTFTC's Merger Guidelines align with international standards but are tailored to Trinidad and Tobago's unique market conditions. They help ensure that companies engage in fair competition while also promoting efficient business operations and innovation.

2. Guide to the Fair Trade Act

35. The Guide to the Fair Trading Act[3] provides an overview of Trinidad and Tobago's competition law, primarily focusing on how the law applies to business conduct, including but not limited to:

- Cartels and anti-competitive behavior: This section provides information about illegal practices such as price fixing, bid rigging, and market division.
- Abuse of market power: Guidance on how the TTFTC views and handles dominant firms that may abuse their market power to the detriment of competition.
- Unfair trade practices: The guide details what constitutes unfair business practices and how such practices are prosecuted under the FTA.
- Sanctions and penalties: Information on penalties for companies found in violation of the law.

36. This is a comprehensive resource for understanding the TTFTC's approach to fair competition, covering everything from basic principles to enforcement and compliance.

C. *Sectoral Studies or Market Inquiries*

37. The TTFTC has conducted and concluded but not yet published internal market studies in the following sectors: pharmaceuticals, food and beverage, shipping, maritime and related industries, and the micro, small and medium enterprise (MSME) industry.

---

2 TTFTC, Draft Merger Guidelines 2020 https://www.tandtftc.org/laws-policies/merger-guidelines/.

3 TTFTC, Guide to the Fair Trade Act, 2020 https://www.tandtftc.org/laws-policies/guide-to-the-fair-trading-act/.

D. *Education and Capacity Building*

38. The TTFTC's staff have and continue to benefit from a range of capacity-building and technical training programs (both in-person and virtual) provided by esteemed international and regional organizations. These include the ICN, the United Nations Conference on Trade and Development (UNCTAD), the OECD, as well as regional and international competition authorities. Additionally, the Latin American and Caribbean Competition Forum, the IDB, and the Regional Competition Center/INDECOPI have collectively contributed to enhancing the skills and knowledge of the TTFTC staff. These programs focus on various aspects of competition policy and enforcement, ensuring that TTFTC personnel are well equipped to address the challenges of a dynamic and evolving market environment.

IX. Regional and International Cooperation

39. The TTFTC recognizes the crucial role that regional and international cooperation plays in strengthening the enforcement of competition laws and promoting effective market regulation. As part of its ongoing commitment to fostering a competitive environment in Trinidad and Tobago, the TTFTC is actively engaged in several regional and global initiatives, despite not yet having established formal memoranda of understanding (MoUs) with other competition authorities.

A. *Regional Organizations*

40. The TTFTC is an active participant in regional organizations such as CARICOM, which plays a vital role in the economic integration and policy alignment of Caribbean nations. As a member of CARICOM, the TTFTC works collaboratively with other competition authorities in the region to harmonize competition laws and promote fair trade practices. The CARICOM Competition Commission, established under the CARICOM Single Market and Economy framework, serves as a platform where member states share best practices, discuss regional issues, and coordinate efforts to address anti-competitive practices that may transcend national borders.

B. *Bilateral Cooperation with Other Competition Authorities*

41. While the TTFTC does not currently have any formal MoUs with other competition authorities, it remains committed to enhancing cooperation with international regulatory bodies and authorities as the need arises. In the absence of formal agreements, the TTFTC continues to engage with international counterparts on an informal basis through networks such as the ICN and regional forums.

C. *Participation in Global Networks*

42. The TTFTC actively participates in global competition networks that support cooperation, knowledge sharing, and capacity building. Through the ICN, the TTFTC collaborates with peer authorities on cartel enforcement, merger review, and abuse of dominance matters, benefiting from best practices and contributing to international policy

development. The TTFTC also works with UNCTAD, engaging in its expert group to exchange experiences and strengthen competition frameworks in developing economies. Additionally, the Commission draws on OECD research and recommendations to inform its approach to market regulation and enforcement.

X. Challenges and Country-Specific Features

A. *Small Market Size and High Sectoral Concentration*

43. As a small island economy, Trinidad and Tobago faces inherent structural challenges that affect market dynamics and competition enforcement. Many sectors are highly concentrated, with only a few significant players, and face substantial barriers to entry, including geographical constraints, economies of scale, and a high dependence on imports. These features make markets more susceptible to dominance and reduce the likelihood of spontaneous competitive rivalry, complicating enforcement and limiting remedial options.

B. *Prominent Role of State-Owned Enterprises*

44. State-owned enterprises continue to play a central role, particularly in strategic sectors such as energy, utilities, and transport. The presence of public entities in commercial markets can blur the lines between regulation, industrial policy, and competition objectives, raising concerns about neutrality, market distortions, and the consistency of state actions with competitive principles. This intersection is a recurring theme in the TTFTC's advocacy efforts, including its 2025 meeting with Key Sector Regulators in Trinidad and Tobago, which was held under the theme "Competition Policy and Sector-Specific Regulation: Complementary or Irreconcilable?"

C. *External Dependence and Foreign Ownership*

45. Trinidad and Tobago is highly integrated into global markets. A significant share of goods, services, and industrial inputs are imported, and foreign-owned firms hold substantial market positions in several key sectors. While this openness brings benefits in terms of consumer choice and investment, it also creates enforcement challenges such as jurisdictional limits, difficulty in applying remedies to foreign entities, and constraints on shaping competitive outcomes that are determined by global supply chains.

D. *Institutional Capacity Constraints*

46. As a relatively young competition authority operating within a small jurisdiction, the TTFTC faces notable capacity constraints. Limited financial and human resources, restricted access to market data, and a lack of domestic and regional precedent all affect the pace and depth of enforcement. In addition, the TTFTC often contends with low response rates to surveys and limited stakeholder awareness, which hampers investigation efforts and market studies.

E. *Balancing Competition Enforcement with Development Objectives*

47. There is an ongoing tension between strict competition enforcement and broader socio-economic policy goals such as safeguarding employment, supporting local manufacturing, and promoting national champions in strategic sectors. This dynamic often requires the TTFTC to navigate trade-offs between competition principles and development imperatives, reinforcing the need for coherent policymaking.

F. *Underdeveloped Enforcement Record*

48. As of the date of submission of this paper, the TTFTC had yet to initiate formal enforcement actions under its mandate, a reflection of the structural and institutional challenges noted above. Translating legislative frameworks into practical enforcement outcomes requires stronger evidence-gathering tools, more reliable data, and greater legal certainty. To address these constraints, the TTFTC has been actively pursuing improvements, including strengthening inter-agency data-sharing agreements, advocating for increased funding and technical capacity, updating regulatory guidance to support timely merger notifications, and enhancing public awareness to foster compliance and voluntary cooperation.

G. *Gaps in the Informal and Customary Sectors*

49. Despite its relatively high level of industrialization, parts of Trinidad and Tobago's economy – particularly agriculture, artisanal services, and informal retail – operate outside the formal regulatory reach of competition law. These segments often lack structured market mechanisms, thereby making the detection and correction of anti-competitive practices more difficult. Extending the reach and relevance of competition policy into these areas remains an ongoing challenge for the TTFTC.

H. *Strategic Use of Advocacy and International Collaboration*

50. In the face of enforcement limitations, advocacy has emerged as a central pillar of the TTFTC's strategy. By engaging with public and private stakeholders, the Commission has been instrumental in fostering a culture of competition and guiding policy reform. Notable examples include its collaboration with the IDB and the European Commission (EC), which has led to impactful initiatives such as:

- Training programs for the Judiciary of the Republic of Trinidad and Tobago;
- Development of a Guide to the Fair Trading Act; and
- Publication of a Legislative Brief for Merger Regulations.

51. These efforts have helped to build institutional credibility, influence regulatory reform, and lay the groundwork for more robust enforcement in the future.

XI. Author's Perspective

52. Trinidad and Tobago stands at a pivotal juncture in the evolution of its competition regime. While the legislative and institutional framework is solid, the real challenge now lies in transitioning from a rules-based system to one characterized by a culture

of compliance, effective enforcement, and broad public understanding. True progress will not be measured by having laws on the books, but by the extent to which these laws are respected, trusted, and woven into the fabric of both businesses and consumers alike.

53. In small economies like Trinidad and Tobago, where markets tend to be highly concentrated and dominated by a few major players, competition law must strike a careful balance. It must prevent abuse of market power without stifling legitimate scale and growth, and it must promote market entry without destabilizing the economy. Achieving this balance requires more than technical enforcement; it demands strategic prioritization, contextual sensitivity, and consistent public engagement.

54. As the TTFTC moves forward, several opportunities present themselves for strengthening the competition regime:

- Strategic enforcement: Targeted, high-impact enforcement actions, even if limited in number, could send powerful signals about the TTFTC's intent and credibility. Clear, impactful cases would help establish key legal precedents and demonstrate that the law is not merely symbolic.
- Sector-specific compliance programs: Tailored outreach and compliance initiatives in sectors with high competitive risks (such as distribution, construction, and professional services) can drive behavioral change and promote proactive adherence to competition principles before market distortions occur.
- Data-driven market studies: In-depth inquiries into sectors where structural issues, rather than intentional anti-competitive conduct, may be hindering competition would provide valuable evidence to guide policy adjustments, sector-specific exemptions, or targeted enforcement.
- Capacity building through regional cooperation: Given the challenges posed by a small national market, deepening regional cooperation within CARICOM and international networks like the ICN and UNCTAD remains vital and can help build expertise, share investigative resources, and create economies of scale and collective strength in enforcement.

55. The TTFTC has already laid a strong foundation for competition law in Trinidad and Tobago. However, the true measure of its success will be in active enforcement, public education and the establishment of legal precedents. The TTFTC's work thus far has made it clear that advocacy plays a central role in building a culture of compliance. The TTFTC has and continues to engage with trade associations, professional bodies, and other stakeholders to ensure that businesses understand that fair competition is not only a legal obligation but also a pathway to innovation, consumer welfare, and resilience.

XII. References and Resources

A. *Law and Regulations*

- Fair Trading Act 2006 (Ch. 81:13), https://www.tandtftc.org/laws-policies/fair-trading-act/

B. *Public Reports*

TTFTC, Draft Merger Guidelines (2020) , https://www.tandtftc.org/laws-policies/merger-guidelines/TTFTC, Guide to the Fair Trade Act (2020), https://www.tandtftc.org/laws-policies/guide-to-the-fair-trading-act/

TTFTC, Laws & Policies, https://www.tandtftc.org

World Bank Group, Trinidad and Tobago – Country Overview, https://data.worldbank.org/country/trinidad-and-tobago

56. To learn more about the TTFTC:

Email Contact: Mr. Bevan Narinesingh, Executive Director, Fair Trading Commission
Tel: 623-2931 ext. 2202/2209/2212
Email: tandtftc@gmail.com
Website: www.tandtftc.org
Facebook: Trinidad and Tobago Fair Trading Commission

Wallis and Futuna

Odeya de La Mure, Jérôme Schall and Anne-Laure Vendrolini
French Competition Authority's Case Handlers

Supervised by Gwenaëlle Nouët
General Rapporteur at the French Competition Authority

I. Overview

1. The Territory of Wallis and Futuna is located in the South Pacific, with the nearest countries being Fiji to the southwest and Samoa to the east. It has a total surface area of approximately 142 square kilometers. Politically, Wallis and Futuna is a French overseas collectivity, governed under Article 74 of the French Constitution[4]. The islands transitioned from a protectorate to an overseas territory in 1961 and have been classified as an overseas collectivity since 2003. The official language of Wallis and Futuna is French.

II. Demographics and Economy

2. Wallis and Futuna had a population of approximately 11,151 inhabitants in 2024, corresponding to a population density of about 78 inhabitants per square kilometer. The nominal gross domestic product (GDP) of the territory was estimated at approximately EUR 189 million in 2019. The islands maintain a structural trade deficit, reflecting a heavy dependence on imports while exports remain virtually nonexistent. The economy of Wallis and Futuna is predominantly non-market-based.

3. Public administrations are the main source of wealth creation, contributing approximately 55 percent of total value added, followed by businesses at 28 percent. The public sector serves as the main pillar of the economy, driving construction activity and supporting consumption, particularly through the salaries it pays as the archipelago's largest employer.

III. Legal Framework for Competition

4. Article 4 of Law No. 61-814 of July 29, 1961, granting Wallis and Futuna the status of overseas territory, stipulates that "[t]he territory of Wallis and Futuna shall henceforth be governed: a) By the laws of the Republic and by decrees applicable, by virtue of their purpose, to the entire national territory and, upon their promulgation in the territory, by laws, decrees, and ministerial orders expressly declared applicable to overseas territories or to the territory of Wallis and Futuna."[5] Accordingly, the Commercial Code, and therefore French competition law, is automatically applicable there (see art. L. 950-1, 4°) (see arts. L. 954-1 to L. 954-15 and R. 954-1 to R. 954-3 for any applicable adjustments).

   (For further details, please refer to the "Guadeloupe" chapter.)

IV. Institutional Structure

5. The Autorité de la concurrence (hereafter the "French Competition Authority" or "FCA") was established in 2008 as a successor to the Conseil de la concurrence (French Competition Council).

---

4 It has an ad hoc status defined by organic law, and its own normative power in certain areas covered by law or regulations (French laws and regulations are not automatically applicable under the same conditions as in mainland France).

5 Our translation.

(For details regarding the supervising body, organizational structure, additional regulatory mandates, budget, resources, and enforcement powers, please refer to the "Guadeloupe" chapter.)

V. Enforcement and Sanctions

6. Since 2009, only a few decisions have been issued regarding Wallis and Futuna. For instance:
   - Decision 26-D-02 of March 10, 2026, regarding practices implemented in the quarry materials sector in the Wallis and Futuna Islands (see below);
   - Decision 18-D-21 of October 8, 2018, regarding practices implemented in the consumer goods sector in the Wallis and Futuna Islands (see below);
   - Decision 16-D-15 of July 6, 2016, relating to practices implemented in the distribution sector for consumer goods in overseas territories: The FCA fined Henkel and several of its importers for implementing unlawful exclusive import agreements between 2013 and 2016 in several French overseas territories – namely, La Réunion, the French Caribbean (Guadeloupe and Martinique), French Guiana, and Wallis and Futuna – in breach of article L. 420-2-1 of the French Commercial Code.

(For information on fines, sanctions, and private enforcement, please refer to the "Guadeloupe" chapter.)

VI. Noteworthy Cases

A. *Decision 26-D-02 of March 10, 2026, regarding practices implemented in the quarry materials sector in the Wallis and Futuna Islands*

7. *Facts.* Following a referral by the Prefect of the Territory of Wallis and Futuna, the FCA sanctioned the company BTP Sud for abusing its dominant position in the market for the supply of aggregates between 21 June 2021 and 30 September 2023.

8. The FCA found in particular that BTP Sud, which held a dominant position in this market, had refused to sell to the Territory's senior administration in the context of public procurement contracts and had imposed significant and unjustified price increases.

9. These behaviours constitute an abuse of a dominant position through the imposition of unfair trading conditions, contrary to Article L.420-2 of the Commercial Code. They are all the more unacceptable given that they were committed by a company that deliberately exploited its dominant position to evade its contractual obligations towards the administration and to compel the latter, outside the legal channels available to it, to grant it certain advantages to which it considered itself entitled.

10. *Legal Issue.* The FCA has imposed a fine of EUR 148,094 (17,672,351 CFP) on BTP Sud.

11. *Outcome.* N/A

12. *Impact or precedent set.* N/A

B. *Decision 18-D-21 of October 8, 2018, regarding practices implemented in the consumer goods sector in the Wallis and Futuna Islands*

13. *Facts.* Following the enactment of the Lurel Law, and until 2015, General Import held exclusive import rights for consumer goods in Wallis and Futuna. The suppliers and products concerned were Sun Rice (rice), Heinz (Pacific Corned Beef canned goods and Golden Circle products: beverages, sodas, fruit juices, and canned fruit), Campbell Arnott's (biscuits), Chelsea (sugar), and Anchor (powdered milk).

14. These agreements could not benefit from the exemption provided for in paragraph III of article L. 420-4 of the French Commercial Code because the companies involved failed to provide proof that consumers could derive a fair share of the profit resulting from such an exclusive import agreement. These practices have hindered the development of competing importers and wholesalers and reduced the competition among wholesalers that retailers had a right to expect for their supplies. They have had the effect of increasing costs for retailers and, consequently, the prices of basic food products needed by consumers in Wallis and Futuna, whose purchasing power is much lower than in mainland France.

15. *Legal issue.* The FCA has imposed a fine of EUR 250,000 on General Import and its parent company, ADLP Holding. It has also ordered them to inform each supplier affected by the prohibited exclusivity agreements of today's decision by letter.

16. *Outcome.* On February 20, 2020, the Paris Court of Appeal partially overturned the decision by reducing the amount of the penalty imposed to EUR 200,000.

17. *Impact or precedent set.* This is the fifth decision issued by the FCA concerning exclusive import practices in overseas territories.

VII. Merger Control

18. As with antitrust law, French merger control applies in Wallis and Futuna. However, the French Commercial Code lays down specific rules for mergers concerning overseas territories in article L. 430-2, III.

(For information on notification thresholds and review timeframes, please refer to the "Guadeloupe" chapter.)

VIII. Advocacy and Policy Initiatives

(See the "Guadeloupe" chapter)

IX. Regional and International Cooperation

19. Wallis and Futuna is represented through the FCA in the Pacific Island Network of Competition Consumer and Economic Regulators (PINCCER).

(For information on bilateral MoUs and participation in global networks, please refer to the "Guadeloupe" chapter.)

X. Challenges and Country-Specific Features

A. *Small Market Size and High Concentration*

20. According to IEOM's annual report for 2024, the territory is characterized by the existence of numerous monopolies in different sectors (aviation, food, etc.).

B. *Dependence on Imports/Foreign Investment*

21. According to IEOM's annual report for 2024, the Territory's foreign trade is characterized by a significant imbalance between increasing imports and the near absence of exports. In this context, the import coverage ratio is almost zero. The local productive economy is based on a traditional subsistence and domestic economy where agriculture, livestock farming, and artisanal fishing provide a significant portion of household food self-sufficiency and meet customary needs. Businesses operate in the primary and secondary sectors: chicken farming and egg production for domestic consumption, sawmills, aluminum joinery, and construction and public works. Public transfers from mainland France remain crucial for the Territory.

C. *Lack of Resources or Expertise*

22. According to information gathered by the state, the economy of Wallis and Futuna is essentially administered. The weak economy has resulted in significant emigration. In 1996, there were approximately in New Caledonia 18,000 inhabitants of Wallis and Futuna. Their number is now estimated at over 25,000.

D. *Interplay with Traditional or Customary Economies*

23. According to IEOM's annual report for 2024, Futuna's economic activity remains very traditional, focused on small scale fishing and agriculture geared towards poultry and pig farming (in line with customary practices) as well as food crops. Local crafts are based on the manufacture of various items, including tapas. Eighty-four percent of households in Futuna and nearly 75% in Wallis engage in pig farming. However, only 1% of pig production is sold commercially, with the rest being used for traditional purposes.

XI. References and Resources

A. *Laws and Regulations*

- Book IV of the legislative part of the French Commercial Code: On Freedom of Prices and Competition (arts. L. 410-1 to L. 490-14) (in French)
- Book IV of the regulatory part of the French Commercial Code. On Freedom of Price and Competition (arts. R. 410-1 to R. 490-10) (in French)

B. *Case Law*

- FCA, Decision 26-D-02 of March 10, 2026, regarding practices implemented in the quarry materials sector in the Wallis and Futuna Islands (in French)

- FCA, Decision 18-D-21 of Oct. 8, 2018, regarding practices implemented in the consumer goods sector in the Wallis and Futuna Islands (in French)
- FCA, Decision 16-D-15 of July 6, 2016, relating to practices implemented in the distribution sector for consumer goods in overseas territories (in French)
- CA Paris [Paris Court of Appeal], Feb. 20, 2020, No.18/24178 (in French)

C. *Public Reports*

- IEOM, Annual Economic Report of Wallis and Futuna 2024 (July 2025) (in French), https://www.ieom.fr/Rapport-annuel-economique-de-Wallis-et-Futuna-2024-6611
- FCA, Opinion 26-A-01 of Feb. 10, 2026, concerning the margins of wholesale importers and distributors of essential food products in Martinique (in French)
- FCA, Opinion 19-A-12 of July 4, 2019, concerning the functioning of competition in the French overseas territories (in French)
- FCA, Opinion 09-A-45 of Sept. 8, 2009, concerning the mechanisms for importing and distributing consumer goods in the overseas departments (in French)

24. To learn more about the French Competition Authority (FCA):
    - Website: https://www.autoritedelaconcurrence.fr/
    - Contact: communication@autoritedelaconcurrence.fr

Report for the ICC Task Force on Small and Insular Economies

**When Competition Cannot Be Perfect:
Adapting Antitrust to Small and Insular Economies**

Johanne Peyre
Chair of the ISLE's Executive Committee

John Oxenham
Advisor to the board of the ISLE Research Institute

1. The report on small and insular economies, from which this summary is drawn, was prepared as part of a public-private initiative of the International Chamber of Commerce (ICC) Task Force.[1] Its purpose is to enhance understanding of the particular challenges faced by competition authorities operating in small and geographically isolated jurisdictions and to formulate practical recommendations aimed at improving the effectiveness of competition policy in these contexts.

2. Competition policy is often discussed within the context of larger jurisdictions and integrated economies. However, small and insular economies operate under a set of structural conditions that differ fundamentally from those prevailing in large markets. Geographic remoteness, narrow domestic demand, dependence on imports, high transportation costs and limited economies of scale significantly affect market dynamics. These factors reinforce concentration tendencies, increase barriers to entry and narrow the scope within which competitive pressures can emerge organically.

3. As a result, markets in such jurisdictions frequently exhibit persistent oligopolistic structures. These outcomes do not necessarily reflect failures of competition law enforcement but rather the economic realities of small market size. In many sectors, a limited number of firms is not an anomaly but a condition for market viability. Competition authorities therefore face the challenge of distinguishing between anticompetitive conduct and structural features inherent to the economy.

4. The report finds that competition authorities in small and insular economies must operate within a uniquely complex environment shaped not only by market structure but also by developmental priorities and institutional constraints. Limited resources, high levels of market concentration, vertically integrated supply chains and the presence of diversified conglomerates all influence enforcement strategies. In practice, authorities frequently prioritize conduct affecting the largest share of consumers and sectors essential to daily life, rather than pursuing broad or highly technical enforcement agendas.

5. These authorities must also balance competition enforcement with broader socio-economic considerations, including employment, industrial development and access to essential goods and services. Strict application of competition rules may, in certain circumstances, risk undermining economic sustainability where markets cannot support a large number of operators. Consequently, enforcement often focuses less on market structure itself and more on preventing abuses of market power, exclusionary practices and coordinated behavior.

6. Small and insular economies also face heightened risks of regulatory capture and political pressure due to close economic and social relationships between market participants and public authorities. While most competition agencies are established as independent statutory bodies with transparent procedures and judicial oversight, safeguarding independence remains a continuous institutional challenge.

---

[1] This report was compiled based on the competition authorities' responses to a questionnaire in the participating jurisdictions. The authors of this report are grateful for the support received from these jurisdictions and the willingness of the respective authorities to participate in a project of this nature. The participating authorities included: the Cayman Islands, Eswatini, the Faroe Islands, French Polynesia, Guyana, Mauritius, New Caledonia, the Seychelles, and Trinidad and Tobago.

7. The report further highlights that competition authorities in these jurisdictions frequently perform functions that extend beyond traditional antitrust enforcement. Through market studies, advocacy initiatives, cooperation with sector regulators and advisory opinions to governments, they contribute to broader economic governance. In effect, competition authorities often act as key institutions for maintaining fair market functioning in economies where structural competition cannot be fully relied upon.

8. International and regional cooperation emerges as essential. Participation in regional networks provides technical expertise, training, investigative support and coordinated enforcement, allowing small authorities to overcome resource limitations and address cross-border conduct, particularly involving multinational firms.

9. Based on the responses received and analyzed, the Task Force concludes that competition policy in small and insular economies cannot simply replicate models developed for large jurisdictions. Instead, a contextualized approach is required – one that promotes competitive behavior, preserves market contestability, and prevents abuses of dominance while recognizing the structural constraints inherent to small markets.

10. Accordingly, the report recommends strengthening advocacy and market studies, prioritizing high-impact enforcement actions, enhancing cooperation agreements, and integrating into regional competition frameworks. These measures aim to ensure that competition law contributes to both consumer welfare and sustainable economic development.

11. Ultimately, the experience of small and insular economies demonstrates that the objective of competition policy is not always to maximize the number of competitors but to ensure that market power, where unavoidable, is exercised responsibly and transparently, and is subject to effective oversight.

I. The Economics of Small and Insular Markets

A. *Structural Characteristics of Small and Insular Economies*

12. Competition policy is often analyzed within the context of larger and more integrated jurisdictions. However, small and insular economies operate within structural conditions that differ significantly from those prevailing in large markets. These jurisdictions are characterized by geographic isolation, relatively modest population size, limited trade flows and dependence on a narrow range of industries. Economies of scale and scope that are achievable in larger economies frequently cannot be attained in these environments.

13. Remoteness and isolation have direct economic consequences. Transport and logistics costs are higher, supply chains are longer and less diversified, and reliance on imported goods is substantial. These factors contribute to elevated consumer prices and restrict the range of available products and services. At the same time, the limited size of the domestic market constrains demand and reduces the number of viable market participants.

14. As a result, many sectors naturally support only a small number of operators. In certain circumstances, a market may only sustain one or two efficient firms. These outcomes are not necessarily the result of anticompetitive conduct but arise from the economic realities of scale, infrastructure costs and market size. The small number of competitors narrows

the scope within which competitive pressures can emerge organically and increases the likelihood of persistent concentration.

15. Structural features are further reinforced by barriers to entry. New entrants face high fixed investment requirements, logistical constraints, limited access to finance, and uncertain revenue prospects. Geographic distance from major commercial centers also discourages potential entry, particularly where transportation delays or perishable goods are involved. Consequently, concentration often reflects structural constraints rather than enforcement deficiencies.

16. These economic conditions also interact with social and policy considerations. Small and insular economies frequently face higher levels of inequality and vulnerability to external shocks. Public authorities may therefore adopt policies intended to protect employment, ensure continuity of supply, or stabilize essential sectors. Such measures may include exclusive arrangements, sectoral protections or regulatory restrictions that further shape market structure.

17. Accordingly, competition authorities must assess market outcomes within the broader economic context. Market concentration, vertical integration and limited entry cannot automatically be interpreted as indicators of anticompetitive behavior. Instead, authorities must distinguish between conduct that harms competition and structures that are inherent to the functioning of a small economy.

B. *Structural Sources of Limited Competition*

18. The structural characteristics described above explain why competitive dynamics in small and insular economies differ from those in larger jurisdictions. Limited domestic demand reduces the number of firms that can profitably operate within a given sector. High fixed costs – particularly in infrastructure-intensive industries such as telecommunications, transport, utilities and fuel distribution – further restrict entry.

19. In such environments, oligopolistic market structures frequently emerge. A limited number of suppliers may provide essential goods and services to the entire population. The presence of few competitors does not necessarily indicate a failure of competition law enforcement but reflects the underlying economics of the market. In some cases, a certain degree of concentration is required for firms to remain viable and to ensure continuity of supply.

20. These conditions may also encourage vertical integration. Firms often control multiple stages of the supply chain in order to secure access to inputs, reduce logistics risks and ensure distribution reliability. In geographically isolated economies, integration from importation to retail distribution may represent an efficiency response to logistical uncertainty rather than an attempt to foreclose competition.

21. Similarly, diversified conglomerates frequently arise. A single economic group may operate across multiple sectors, spreading risk and compensating for limited opportunities in individual markets. While such structures can raise competition concerns, they may also contribute to economic stability and investment capacity within the jurisdiction.

22. Consequently, competition authorities must balance the promotion of rivalry with the preservation of economically sustainable firms. Excessive fragmentation of already small

markets may lead to firm exit, reduced investment and diminished service availability. Authorities therefore often focus enforcement on exclusionary conduct, coordinated behavior and abuse of dominance rather than on concentration alone.

C. *Essential Facilities and Natural Monopolies*

23. Certain sectors in small and insular economies present characteristics of natural monopoly. Infrastructure such as ports, maritime freight, energy distribution networks and telecommunications systems requires substantial capital investment but serves a limited consumer base. Duplicating these facilities is frequently economically inefficient.

24. Because access to these facilities is indispensable for market participation, they play a central role in competitive dynamics. Limited access, discriminatory conditions or restrictive arrangements may significantly affect downstream competition. At the same time, the operator of such infrastructure must maintain financial viability in a small market with limited demand.

25. Competition authorities therefore increasingly emphasize conduct-based oversight. Rather than challenging the existence of monopoly infrastructure, enforcement focuses on preventing exclusionary practices, discriminatory access or abusive pricing. This approach seeks to preserve contestability while recognizing the structural necessity of certain monopolistic arrangements.

26. These considerations illustrate a broader point: in small and insular economies, the objective of competition policy is not always to eliminate concentration but to ensure that unavoidable market power is exercised in a manner consistent with fair competition and consumer welfare.

II. Consequences for Competition Law Enforcement

A. *Enforcement Priorities in a Concentrated Market Environment*

27. In small and insular economies, competition authorities operate within a uniquely complex landscape. Their decisions are not made in isolation but are shaped by limited resources, market concentration and broader economic realities. Rather than adopting rigid or highly sector-specific approaches, many authorities favor holistic enforcement strategies intended to address issues affecting the largest portion of the population.

28. Responding authorities commonly indicated that enforcement priorities are guided by practical considerations. With small teams and modest budgets, it is often not feasible to pursue every complaint or to undertake extensive investigations across all sectors. Authorities therefore tend to focus on conduct with significant impact on consumers, particularly in essential goods and services.

29. This often leads agencies to prioritize clear anticompetitive practices such as price fixing, market allocation and exclusionary conduct. Highly complex or resource-intensive cases may be approached more cautiously, especially where evidentiary burdens are significant and the expected consumer impact is limited. In contrast, matters involving everyday consumer markets receive greater attention because they affect a substantial share of the population.

30. Market studies and economic monitoring are also widely used tools. Authorities rely on data collection, complaints and sectoral observations to identify competition concerns and guide enforcement. These mechanisms allow agencies to monitor behavior within concentrated markets and detect patterns of coordination or abuse even in the absence of formal complaints.

31. At the same time, enforcement approaches frequently incorporate developmental considerations. Authorities reported balancing competition objectives with employment protection, access to essential goods and economic stability. This does not imply a departure from competition principles but reflects the practical need to evaluate cases within the broader economic environment.

B. *Oligopolies and Coordinated Behavior*

32. Oligopolistic structures are a recurring feature of small and insular economies. The telecommunications, fuel distribution, retail grocery, construction, and transport sectors commonly exhibit high concentration. These industries typically require substantial investment and serve limited consumer bases, naturally restricting the number of viable operators.

33. In such markets, competition concerns often arise not from explicit cartel agreements but from coordinated behavior and parallel conduct. A small number of market participants, repeated interactions, and high price transparency can facilitate the alignment of commercial strategies even without direct communication. This makes detection and enforcement particularly challenging.

34. Authorities therefore face the difficulty of distinguishing between normal market behavior and tacit coordination. The absence of formal agreements complicates investigations, while legal standards may require a level of proof that is difficult to obtain in small markets. At the same time, market participants may be reluctant to file complaints due to commercial interdependence or fear of retaliation.

35. To mitigate these risks, agencies engage in advocacy and outreach. Educational programs, stakeholder meetings and open communication channels are used to encourage compliance and increase awareness of competition rules. Public communication of decisions also serves a deterrent function by signaling that anticompetitive conduct will be addressed.

36. Consequently, enforcement in oligopolistic environments often combines investigation with prevention. Rather than relying exclusively on sanctions, authorities seek to influence behavior and maintain competitive pressure within structurally concentrated markets.

C. *Vertical Integration and Conglomerate Structures*

37. Vertical integration is widespread in small and insular economies. Firms frequently operate across multiple stages of the supply chain, from importation to distribution and retail. This structure often emerges as a response to logistical uncertainty, supply security concerns and the need to reduce operational risks.

38. While vertical integration may raise concerns regarding foreclosure or discrimination, it can also generate efficiencies. Integrated firms may achieve cost savings, improve coordination and ensure continuity of supply in environments where transport delays and

limited suppliers are common. As a result, authorities typically do not treat integration as inherently problematic but instead evaluate specific conduct.

39. Merger review and market monitoring therefore focus on whether a firm has the ability and incentive to restrict access to inputs or customers. Behavioral remedies and commitments are frequently used to preserve market access and prevent exclusionary practices while allowing efficiency gains to materialize.

40. Diversified conglomerates represent a related phenomenon. In many small economies, a single corporate group may operate across multiple sectors. Such diversification can stabilize economic activity by spreading risk and supporting investment. However, it may also increase barriers to entry and reduce opportunities for smaller firms.

41. Authorities therefore assess transactions for potential leveraging, bundling or cross-subsidization effects. The objective is not to prevent firms from achieving scale but to ensure that market power in one sector is not used to distort competition in another.

D. *The Balance Between Competition and Economic Sustainability*

42. A recurring theme across jurisdictions is the need to balance competitive rivalry with economic sustainability. Markets in small economies may not support numerous operators. Excessive fragmentation can lead to firm exit, reduced investment and instability in essential services.

43. Accordingly, authorities often focus less on market structure and more on conduct. Dominance alone is not treated as unlawful; enforcement concentrates on abusive practices such as exclusionary behavior, discriminatory supply conditions and excessive restrictions on entry.

44. This approach reflects the understanding that competition policy must operate within the constraints of economic reality. The objective is not to maximize the number of competitors but to maintain contestability and prevent harm to consumers. In some circumstances, conditional approvals or behavioral remedies may achieve better outcomes than structural intervention.

45. Through this approach, competition authorities aim to preserve both fair competition and reliable market functioning. The challenge is therefore not simply to promote rivalry but to ensure that concentrated markets remain open, transparent and subject to effective oversight.

III. Institutional and Regulatory Implications

A. *Political Economy and Risks of Regulatory Capture*

46. Maintaining operational independence is a cornerstone of effective competition enforcement. In small and insular economies, however, this objective presents particular challenges. Close social and economic relationships between businesses, political authorities and regulators are more common in small jurisdictions, increasing the potential for perceived or actual influence on regulatory decisions.

47 Most competition authorities are established as independent statutory bodies with clearly defined mandates. Appointment procedures, fixed terms of office and the possibility of judicial review are intended to safeguard impartial decision-making. Authorities also

rely on transparency measures – including publication of decisions, annual reporting and public consultations – to reinforce accountability and public confidence.

48. Nevertheless, the small size of markets and communities can heighten exposure to political pressure. Decisions affecting major employers, essential industries or key economic actors may have broader economic implications. Authorities therefore operate in an environment where legal considerations must be applied alongside awareness of economic sensitivity.

49. In response, agencies emphasize adherence to formal procedures and evidence-based analysis. Collective decision-making by boards or commissions, disclosure of interests and recusal mechanisms are commonly used safeguards. The possibility of appeal to independent courts also serves as an important external check.

50. These institutional arrangements demonstrate that independence in small and insular economies is not a static condition but an ongoing process requiring transparency, clear governance rules and consistent application of competition law principles.

B. *Institutional Capacity and Resource Constraints*

51. Resource limitations represent one of the most consistent challenges reported by competition authorities. Many agencies operate with small teams and modest financial resources. Staffing shortages, limited access to specialized economic expertise and high staff turnover can affect the capacity to conduct complex investigations or comprehensive market studies.

52. As a consequence, authorities must prioritize their activities. Enforcement often focuses on cases with the greatest expected impact on consumers and the economy. Highly technical or resource-intensive matters may require cooperation with external experts or regional partners.

53. Limited resources also influence the tools used by agencies. Advocacy initiatives, compliance programs and guidance documents are frequently employed as cost-effective mechanisms to promote voluntary compliance and prevent anticompetitive conduct. Market monitoring and screening activities may substitute for extensive litigation in certain circumstances.

54. Training and capacity-building therefore become critical components of institutional effectiveness. Engaging in workshops, secondments, and knowledge exchanges helps offset internal resource constraints and strengthens investigative capabilities.

55. These realities illustrate that institutional design for small competition authorities must recognize practical limits. Effectiveness depends not only on formal powers but also on realistic prioritization, efficient use of available resources and the development of cooperative networks.

C. *The Expanding Role of Competition Authorities*

56. The experience of participating jurisdictions indicates that competition authorities frequently perform functions extending beyond traditional antitrust enforcement. Through advisory opinions, market studies and interaction with public authorities, agencies contribute to broader economic governance.

57. Authorities often provide guidance on legislation, regulatory frameworks and sectoral policies. They may recommend reforms to remove barriers to entry, improve market transparency or address structural distortions. In this way, competition policy becomes closely linked with public policy and economic development strategies.

58. Cooperation with sector regulators is also common. Memoranda of understanding and joint consultations allow agencies to address issues in regulated industries such as telecommunications, energy or transport. Such collaboration helps ensure that regulatory measures support, rather than undermine, competitive market functioning.

59. This broader role reflects the reality that, in small and insular economies, competition authorities may serve as central institutions for promoting fair market conditions. Because structural competition cannot always be relied upon, authorities contribute to maintaining contestability through oversight, advocacy and policy advice.

D. *Regional and International Cooperation*

60. International and regional cooperation plays a particularly important role for small competition authorities. Participation in regional networks provides access to expertise, training opportunities and information-sharing mechanisms that would otherwise be unavailable.

61. Cooperation allows agencies to coordinate investigations, especially where conduct involves multinational firms or cross-border transactions. It also facilitates the convergence of practices, the adoption of best practices, and the development of guidelines adapted to local circumstances.

62. Regional organizations and international forums provide technical assistance, joint training and opportunities for staff exchanges. These initiatives strengthen institutional capacity and help overcome resource limitations. Shared databases and collaborative enforcement mechanisms also enhance the ability to address complex cases.

63. While differences in legal frameworks and economic structures may create challenges, the benefits of cooperation are widely recognized. Collective action enables small jurisdictions to address competition issues more effectively than isolated national enforcement.

64. Accordingly, integration into regional and international networks emerges as a key component of effective competition policy in small and insular economies.

IV. Toward a Contextualized Competition Policy for Small Economies

A. *Rethinking Enforcement Objectives*

65. The responses gathered in this report indicate that competition policy in small and insular economies cannot be implemented in the same manner as in large jurisdictions. Structural market characteristics – limited size, geographic isolation and persistent concentration – require an adapted enforcement approach.

66. Competition authorities therefore increasingly emphasize the preservation of competitive behavior rather than the multiplication of competitors. In concentrated markets,

dominance alone is not necessarily problematic; the primary concern is the exercise of market power through exclusionary or abusive practices.

67. Enforcement priorities consequently focus on conduct that produces direct harm to consumers. Practices such as price fixing, market allocation, discriminatory supply conditions and exclusionary agreements typically receive the greatest attention. By contrast, purely structural concentration may require monitoring rather than intervention.

68. This approach recognizes that competition law must operate within economic realities. The objective becomes maintaining contestability and preventing harm, while allowing firms to achieve sufficient scale to remain viable and ensure continuity of supply.

B. *Advocacy and Market Studies as Core Tools*

69. Advocacy initiatives play a central role in this context. Because enforcement resources are limited and markets are concentrated, prevention is often more effective than *ex post* sanctions. Authorities therefore place emphasis on education, awareness and communication with businesses and consumers.

70. Public communication of cases, guidance documents and stakeholder outreach contribute to building a culture of compliance. Media engagement and educational programs help market participants understand the implications of competition rules and the consequences of anticompetitive behavior.

71. Market studies represent another essential tool. Unlike investigations focused on a single firm, market studies allow authorities to analyze entire value chains, identify structural barriers to entry and propose policy reforms. These studies facilitate dialogue with government institutions and private stakeholders and can prevent distortions before they result in formal infringements.

72. Civil society organizations and professional associations may also assist in disseminating competition principles. Their involvement can strengthen credibility, improve outreach and encourage voluntary compliance across sectors.

C. *Prioritization and Efficient Resource Allocation*

73. Given capacity constraints, competition authorities must prioritize their interventions. It is generally impractical to investigate every complaint or suspicion of anticompetitive conduct. Agencies therefore focus enforcement on sectors most widely used by consumers and on practices with significant economic impact.

74. In many cases, enforcement concentrates on hardcore cartel behavior and clear horizontal restraints. More complex matters – such as certain vertical arrangements or highly technical market structures – may require a selective approach depending on available resources and expected consumer benefit.

75. This prioritization enables authorities to maximize the effectiveness of limited institutional capacity while maintaining credibility and deterrence. Balanced allocation of resources between enforcement, advocacy and monitoring activities allows agencies to achieve practical results despite operational constraints.

D. *Cooperation and Regional Integration*

76. Even with prioritization and advocacy, national authorities may face limits in addressing complex or cross-border competition issues. Cooperation agreements and integration into regional frameworks therefore become essential.

77. Multilateral cooperation enables the sharing of information, experience and investigative support. Participation in regional organizations allows small authorities to access expertise, training and coordinated enforcement mechanisms. These arrangements can also facilitate review of mergers involving multinational firms and help address cross-border anticompetitive conduct.

78. Technical assistance from more established competition authorities – through training programs, internships, secondments and joint investigations – further strengthens institutional capacity. Such cooperation improves both substantive analysis and procedural effectiveness.

79. Regional integration also contributes to legal convergence and predictability for businesses. Shared standards and coordinated actions enhance credibility and allow small jurisdictions to exercise influence disproportionate to their individual size.

E. *Toward International Recognition of Contextualized Competition Policy*

80. The experience documented in this report suggests that small and insular economies should not simply replicate models developed for large markets. Instead, competition policy must be adapted to local economic conditions while maintaining core principles of fairness and consumer protection.

81. A contextualized approach does not weaken competition law. Rather, it recognizes that structural constraints may limit the number of competitors and require authorities to focus on market behavior, access conditions and transparency. The aim is to ensure that unavoidable market power is exercised responsibly and subject to effective oversight.

82. International organizations, regional networks and development institutions can support this approach by recognizing the specific challenges faced by small economies and by promoting tailored guidance, capacity-building and cooperation mechanisms.

83. Ultimately, competition policy in small and insular economies is not solely about increasing the number of firms in a market. It is about safeguarding fair market functioning, protecting consumers and supporting sustainable economic development within the structural realities of these jurisdictions.

V. Policy Recommendations

1. Adopt a contextualized approach to competition enforcement

84. Competition authorities in small and insular economies should interpret and apply competition law in light of structural market constraints, recognizing that high concentration may result from economic necessity rather than anticompetitive conduct.

2. Prioritize conduct over structure

85. Enforcement should focus primarily on exclusionary behavior, collusion and abuse of dominance rather than on concentration levels alone.

3. Use market studies and advocacy as core enforcement tools

86. Authorities should regularly conduct market studies and develop advocacy initiatives to address structural barriers to entry and promote compliance, particularly in essential consumer sectors.

4. Implement targeted enforcement prioritization

87. Given limited resources, agencies should prioritize sectors with the greatest impact on consumers and essential goods and services, and focus on clear anticompetitive practices such as cartels and market allocation.

5. Strengthen cooperation with sector regulators

88. Competition authorities should establish structured cooperation mechanisms with sectoral regulators to address issues arising in regulated or infrastructure-dependent markets.

6. Promote regional and international cooperation

89. Small jurisdictions should actively participate in regional competition networks and multilateral cooperation agreements to share expertise, coordinate investigations and address cross-border conduct.

7. Support capacity-building and technical assistance

90. International organizations and established competition authorities should provide training, secondment and technical assistance adapted to the needs of small competition agencies.

VI. Conclusion

91. This report has examined the experience of competition authorities operating in small and insular economies and the specific challenges they encounter in applying competition law. The evidence collected from participating jurisdictions shows that these challenges do not primarily arise from deficiencies in legal frameworks or enforcement efforts, but from structural economic conditions inherent to small and geographically isolated markets.

92. Limited demand, high transportation costs, dependence on imports and the need to achieve minimum efficient scale frequently result in concentrated market structures. In such environments, the presence of a small number of firms is often unavoidable. Competition authorities must therefore distinguish carefully between anticompetitive conduct and outcomes that reflect the economic realities of the market.

93. The analysis demonstrates that the effective application of competition law in these jurisdictions depends less on replicating enforcement models developed for large economies and more on adapting tools and priorities to local conditions. Authorities tend to focus on preventing abuses of market power, preserving access to markets and ensuring transparency rather than attempting to restructure markets that cannot sustain numerous competitors.

94. Institutional considerations reinforce this approach. Limited resources, exposure to economic sensitivities and the importance of essential sectors require pragmatic prioritization, reliance on advocacy and cooperation with other regulators. Regional and international cooperation also emerges as a central element of effective enforcement, allowing small authorities to access expertise, share information and address cross-border conduct.

95. The experience of small and insular economies thus highlights a broader lesson. Competition policy cannot always be applied as a uniform model. While its core principles remain constant, its implementation must account for the economic context in which markets operate.

96. Ensuring fair competition in small markets does not necessarily mean increasing the number of competitors. It means ensuring that market power – where it cannot be avoided – is exercised in a manner that is transparent, accountable and consistent with consumer welfare and sustainable economic development.

TABLE OF CONTENTS

Concurrences
Competition Laws Review

Concurrences Review

Concurrences is a print and online quarterly peer reviewed journal dedicated to EU and national competitions laws. It has been launched in 2004 as the flagship of the Institute of Competition Law in order to provide a forum for academics, practitioners and enforcers. Concurrences' influence and expertise has garnered contributions or interviews with such figures as Christine Lagarde, Bill Kovacic, Emmanuel Macron, Antonin Scalia and Magrethe Vestager.

Contents

More than 15,000 articles, print and/or online. Quarterly issues provide current coverage with contributions from the EU or national or foreign countries thanks to more than 2,500 authors in Europe and abroad.

Format

In order to balance academic contributions with opinions or legal practice notes, Concurrences provides its insight and analysis in a number of formats:

- Forewords: Opinions by leading academics or enforcers
- Interviews: Interviews of antitrust experts
- On-Topics: 4 to 6 short papers on hot issues
- Law & Economics: Short papers written by economists for a legal audience
- Articles: Long academic papers
- Case Summaries: Case commentary on EU and French case law
- Legal Practice: Short papers for in-house counsels
- International: Medium size papers on international policies
- Books Review: Summaries of recent antitrust books
- Articles Review: Summaries of leading articles published in 45 antitrust journals

Boards

The Scientific Committee is headed by Laurence Idot, Professor at Panthéon Assas University. The International Committee is headed by Frederic Jenny, OECD Competition Comitteee Chairman. Boards members include Douglas Ginsburg, Benoît Cœuré, Howard Shelanski, Richard Whish, Wouter Wils, etc.

Online version

Concurrences website provides all articles published since its inception, in addition to selected articles published online only in the electronic supplement.

Write for Concurrences

Concurrences welcome spontaneous contributions. Except in rare circumstances, the journal accepts only unpublished articles, whatever the form and nature of the contribution. The Editorial Board checks the form of the proposals, and then submits these to the Scientific Committee. Selection of the papers is conditional to a peer review by at least two members of the Committee. Within a month, the Committee assesses whether the draft article can be published and notifies the author.

www.ingramcontent.com/pod-product-compliance
Lightning Source LLC
LaVergne TN
LVHW052221200926
848481LV00001B/174
* 9 7 9 1 0 9 4 2 0 1 4 4 2 *